Texts of the Passion

Texts of the Passion

Latin Devotional Literature and Medieval Society

Thomas H. Bestul

PENN

University of Pennsylvania Press

Philadelphia

Copyright © 1996 by the University of Pennsylvania Press
Printed in the United States of America
Library of Congress Cataloging-in-Publication Data

Bestul, Thomas H. (Thomas Howard), 1942–
    Texts of the passion : Latin devotional literature and medieval society /
Thomas H. Bestul.
        p.   cm. — (University of Pennsylvania Press Middle Ages series)
Includes bibliographical references and index.
ISBN 0-8122-3376-X (alk. paper)
1. Christian literature, Latin (Medieval and modern)—History and criticism.
2. Devotional literature, Latin (Medieval and modern)—History and criticism.   3. Jesus
Christ—Passion—History of doctrines—Middle Ages, 600–1500.   4. Literature and
society—Europe—History.   5. Civilization, Medieval, in literature.   I. Title.   II. Series:
Middle Ages series.
PA8030.C47B47   1996
232.96′094′0902—dc20   96-26705
                                                                                            CIP

Contents

Acknowledgments

Like many books written by academics, this one has taken shape, or been put into shape, over a period of several years. It reflects my longstanding interest in medieval devotional literature and also reveals my efforts to understand medieval texts in new ways. Now I am pleased to express my gratitude for the help I have received in writing this book. I must begin by acknowledging a debt of very long standing: to the late A. O. Lee, my first teacher of Latin, who taught me not only to parse, but to love, the language of Cicero and Virgil.

I began this book at the University of Nebraska-Lincoln, while a faculty member in the department of English, and from that true community I received much support, for which I am deeply grateful. I want especially to thank the members of the Medieval and Renaissance Studies group, who listened to early versions of some of the chapters and offered valuable suggestions. Professors Robert Haller and Paul Olson should be singled out, as well as my former student Stephen Hayes. Professor Moira Ferguson deserves special thanks for helping me clarify some issues in critical theory and for other kinds of advice. The late John W. Robinson was my mentor in ways that extended far beyond the intellectual. My new colleagues at the University of Illinois at Chicago have offered generous support and encouragement in a period that was not without its difficulties. Professors James Schulz (now at UCLA) and Thomas Hall deserve my special thanks.

I want to thank the readers of the University of Pennsylvania Press, who gave me the benefit of their attentive and constructive engagement with the manuscript. Denise Despres had earlier read one of the chapters, and had offered me encouragement when the project was barely underway. Her invaluable suggestions have made this book much better than it otherwise might have been. Needless to say, neither she nor the other people I have mentioned above should be charged with the faults and infelicities of this book, which are entirely my own.

I am happy to express my gratitude for the help I have received from librarians of the University of Nebraska-Lincoln, the University of Illinois at Chicago, the Newberry Library, Chicago, the British Library, London, and the Senate House Library of London University. I am grateful to the British Library for permission to publish the text from MS. Cotton Vespasian E.i that appears in Appendix 1.

I am thankful for the material support of various kinds I received in the course of writing this book, specifically from the National Endowment for the Humanities, the American Philosophical Society, and the Research Council of the University of Nebraska-Lincoln. The award of a Faculty Research Fellowship from the latter institution gave me the leisure to advance the project beyond the talking and planning stages.

Finally, I want to thank my children, Mark and Nicholas, and my wife, Ellen T. Baird, for everything that matters most to me.

I

Introduction:
Methodology and Theoretical
Orientations

THE PASSION OF CHRIST has an unquestioned importance in the dominant Christian culture of the European Middle Ages. The great medieval engagement with the Passion expressed itself in many ways, in art, literature, theology, as well as in religious practice and the forms of everyday life. One of the most important modes of expression is the great number of tellings and retellings of the Passion story found in devotional works written in Latin from about 1100 to 1500. It is these narratives that are the subject of this study. The Latin Passion narratives, even though they are among the most popular, widely read, and influential of medieval texts, have received relatively little attention, at least in comparison with the literature of the Passion written in the vernacular languages, a topic I shall return to shortly. The Latin devotional narratives have not been sufficiently recognized for the prominent role they played in medieval religion and culture generally. When they have been the object of study, they have often been narrowly examined from a spiritual or theological point of view, and little effort has been expended to situate them within their specific cultural and historical contexts. To work toward accomplishing a cultural contextualization for them is a principal goal of this book, taken up primarily in the later chapters.

The Passion of Christ is treated in many kinds of texts: in noncanonical gospels, in the liturgy, in homilies and sermons, in poems and hymns, in meditations and private prayers, and, especially in later centuries, in a considerable body of visionary literature. These varied texts are always to be regarded as in continual and dynamic interrelationship throughout the centuries; moreover, it is important to recognize that they are in a reciprocal relationship with the representation of the Passion in the visual arts as well. A project such as mine, which examines a single mode of expression in isolation from others, perforce affords a view that is somewhat contrived, if not deceptive. In confining myself largely to a discussion of prose treatises in Latin intended for the uses of private devotion, I am aware of that limitation, and I am conscious that generic boundaries, especially those drawn between sermons and meditations, are often indistinct. Collections of sermons must often have served as devotional texts, and there is evidence that in the twelfth century texts that style themselves as meditations appear to have been punctuated with the requirements of oral reading in mind.[1] Visionary literature too, among its multiple social and religious functions, must often have served devotional ends. Yet the procedure I am about to follow, in which I will refer only incidentally to sermons, visions, and historical works, has the advantage of offering a manageable overview of one important portion of a body of writing that is daunting in its dimensions.

In dealing with the Passion texts that are the subject of my inquiry, I proceed at first chronologically. In this arrangement my work fulfills some of the purposes of a traditional literary history, in that a number of works are selected, grouped together, categorized, compared with each other, and disposed into a linear chronological sequence. Although the limitations of such diachronic procedures have been well described by post-modern literary and cultural theorists (a matter I shall take up later in this chapter), there remain some rather self-evident advantages in sequential arrangements. In the real world, things do happen one after the other and differences can be noticed that occur over time. Perceptible changes from decade to decade or century to century in institutions, literary discourse, and representational techniques have been and remain a profitable arena for scholarly inquiry. For western audiences at least, linear arrangements have a practical value as a way of organizing complex bodies of data and materials, even as one recognizes that the value set on such arrangements and their seeming "rightness" are best regarded as culturally determined rather than absolute. The second chapter of this study will present such a chronologically organized survey of Latin Passion narratives from the eleventh through the fifteenth centuries, in order to orient the reader to their enormous range and variety and to demonstrate their pervasive presence in late medieval culture. This synoptic survey will be followed by chapters on specific topics in the Passion narratives, all of them having to do with problems and techniques of representation and less concerned with chronological development than with social, cultural, and historical contexts. These chapters deal with the representation of the Jews, the representation of women, and the representation of the tortured body of Christ. Before proceeding to them, I wish to continue with further discussion of the rationale for my project, the methodology I will follow in pursuing it, and the theoretical assumptions that underlie it.

Among the most celebrated Middle English lyrics is a hauntingly beautiful poem on the Passion of Christ beginning with the words "In a valey of this restles mynde," which includes as a refrain the Latin phrase from the Song of Songs (2:5), "Quia amore langueo." The poem is found in two manuscripts of the fifteenth century (London, Lambeth Palace MS 853; and Cambridge, University Library MS Hh.4.12), and was printed for the first time in a collection of texts edited by F. J. Furnivall for the Early English Text Society in 1866.[2] Since its appearance, this poem of 128 lines has been often anthologized and has been the subject of frequent critical attention, as scholars have actively sought to identify its sources, determine its meaning, and explain its literary relations.[3] Whatever interpretational differences have arisen over the decades, there is general agreement that the poem incorporates a number of motifs, topics, and themes that are conspicuous in the Latin devotional literature of the later Middle Ages, including the idea of Christ as lover-knight and mankind as his spouse, the notion of Christ as mother, and a complaint spoken by Christ from the cross inviting mankind to regard his wounded body.

Although most of the critics have steadfastly affirmed the importance of Latin writing on the Passion in connection with this poem, they have typically thought of it either as simple "background" or, in more sophisticated terms, as "literary context." In either case the Latin works are considered as illustrative, cited to explain or interpret or occasionally to fix the meaning of the vernacular text, which always remains planted steadily in the foreground of attention, and which is always the primary subject requiring elucidation. Critics have rarely sought to engage the meaning of those Latin texts they cite, nor have they often granted them the same complexity and status as the vernacular work they are held to explain. These interpretive strategies and analytic procedures are not just characteristic of the twentieth-century criticism of this particular poem, but illustrate tendencies that define modern criticism of much medieval religious literature in the vernacular, indeed, much medieval vernacular literature of all kinds.[4] Latin literature is frequently cited as important to the understanding of vernacular texts, but in most cases always as a more or less unproblematic background that is rarely brought into the foreground for examination in its own right.

At the same time there is an inclination to regard the Latin literary traditions as determining the form and meaning of the vernacular text under examination. The assumption is that Latin culture is prior to and perhaps superior to the vernacular. The Latin literature of the Middle Ages is an immense pool of themes, topics, forms, and techniques that flow from high to low. There is good reason to question this interpretive model, particularly in the case of religious literature, as I shall argue later in the chapter, but the result of this critical position has been the paradox, which holds true especially in the case of medieval religious literature, that while the importance of the Latin background is everywhere proclaimed in modern criticism, the texts that constitute that background—the meditations, laments, dialogues, hymns, sermons, and prayers—are themselves radically underexamined.

It is important to remember that the terms "foreground" and "background" are always relative, demanding scrutiny and examination rather than uncritical acceptance. I would also argue that when they are applied to the analysis of culture and the interpretation of literary texts they are always historically contingent. It seems to me that the lack of attention to the Latin texts has as much to do with the organization of the humanities in the English-speaking world, namely the decline of Latin as an academic discipline and the enormous growth of departments of English, as with esthetic value or cultural significance in any absolute sense. If we speak confidently and uncritically of the Latin background or the Latin literary context, we have already decided on what kinds of texts shall receive priority in our discussion, and have adopted a fixed position in reference to which such terms as text and context, foreground and background, make sense at all.

In general terms my project of bringing to the foreground medieval Latin texts of a kind that have traditionally been thought of as constituting the background arises from a conviction, widely shared by medievalists, of the need for broader cultural contextualization, an undertaking which depends on a more inclusive understanding of the kinds of texts that are worth paying attention to, and which is compelled by an urgent sense that those texts should be placed more exactly within historical and social contexts. This project is, of course, very powerfully invigorated by the current debate about the literary canon, even though that debate has largely been conducted outside the boundaries of medieval studies, and it is further energized by modern theory, which has taught us to interrogate such notions as foreground and background, text and context, notions which in the old critical vocabulary were assumed to be fixed propositions.[5]

The Latin works on the Passion I will discuss are neither obscure or arcane, but among the most popular writings of the late Middle Ages. The fact of their wide success is one very good reason for subjecting them to greater scrutiny than they have yet received. They are cultural documents of primary importance that not only contribute to an understanding of late medieval religious culture, but, indeed, extend their influence upon the western European culture of the Renaissance, maintaining their popularity into the nineteenth and twentieth centuries, a fact that has not been sufficiently appreciated.

In Turin, Italy, in 1929, a volume of Latin devotions was published entitled *D. Aurelii Augustini Meditationes, Soliloquia, et Manuale; accedunt Meditationes B. Anselmi, D. Bernardi, et Idiotae Contemplationes*, which we can see as the likely endpoint of a remarkable cultural development. The book includes the *Meditationes*, *Soliloquia*, and *Manuale* of the pseudo-Augustine, the *Meditationes* of Anselm, and the *Meditationes* of the pseudo-Bernard. The *Meditationes* of Augustine includes one of the most popular medieval descriptions of the body of the crucified Christ, a description we will take up later. The Turin edition is ultimately, through a long line of editions, founded on an almost identical volume published by Henry Sommalius at Lyon in 1610, which is itself based on the content and arrangement of earlier printed books, which, in their turn, replicate fifteenth-century manuscript anthologies.[6] These anthologies were produced in response to the enormous demand of the time for devotional books, as Giles Constable has effectively demonstrated.[7] With the advent of printing, Latin devotional works were among the earliest and most frequently published, as Roger Chartier has shown, using the printing history of the Book of Hours as an especially compelling illustration of his point.[8] Narrative devotional works enjoyed a similar popularity. For example, the *Meditationes* of Augustine was first printed at Milan about 1480, and received at least ten further editions before 1500. The *Orationes sive meditationes* of Anselm appeared in print at least by 1491. The pseudo-Bernardine lament, "Quis dabit capiti meo," appeared in print about 1470.[9]

The Turin volume of 1929 would appear to be the last member of a remarkably prolific, widely disseminated, and persistently popular family of editions reaching back in a direct line to the edition of Sommalius. The Sommalius edition of 1610 was enormously successful, and its success endured for decades, even centuries: it was reprinted at Douay in 1613; at Lyon in 1616, 1620, 1646, 1674, and 1777; at Parma in 1616; at Cologne in 1621, 1631, 1649, 1681, 1702, and 1844; at Amsterdam in 1628; at Paris in 1634, 1656, 1824, and 1874; at Venice in 1718, 1755, 1760, 1772, and 1774; and so on. The edition was reprinted all over Catholic Europe from 1610 right into the twentieth century, retaining its popularity and finding an audience, it appears, through the vicissitudes of the age of enlightenment, the romantic era, and even twentieth-century Europe in the decade after the First World War.

The items included in the printed Latin devotional anthologies also appeared in numerous vernacular translations. For example, a Spanish translation of the *Meditationes* of Augustine was published in 1515; a Dutch version in 1548; an English version in 1558; an Italian version in 1568; a Polish version in 1629; a French version in 1662; and a Swedish version in 1708. English translations of the *Meditationes* are especially numerous, and the popularity of medieval Latin devotional works in English translation continued unabated even throughout the Protestant, rationalist, eighteenth century, an age when, according to the conventional interpretations of the period, one would hardly expect to find distinctly medieval forms of piety to be widely appreciated. At London in 1701 appeared a translation by George Stanhope, D. D., Dean of Canterbury, entitled *Pious Breathings: Being the Meditations of St. Augustine, his Treatise of the Love of God, Soliloquies and Manual: To Which Are Added Select Contemplations from St. Anselm and St. Bernard*. This is essentially an English version, with minor expurgations for the sake of Protestant sensibilities, of the long-lived Sommalius collection mentioned above. Stanhope's book went through eight further editions in the eighteenth century and one in the nineteenth, being reprinted in 1704, 1708, 1714, 1720, 1728, 1745, 1751, 1795; the final edition appeared in 1818.[10]

I have tried to demonstrate by the citations above that Latin devotional writing, including some of the key texts dealing with the Passion of Christ, enjoyed a continuous popularity, both in Latin and in the vernaculars, from the early Middle Ages until at least the nineteenth century. Despite this, I do not want to make universalizing claims, asserting that these texts had an appeal that transcended time and historical circumstance, speaking to a common humanity or universal religious sensibility. I do not claim that the audiences were uniform or that their uses of these texts were always identical. It would be a fascinating exercise to differentiate the readership, expectations, and social function of these texts: how they were received in Georgian London of the 1740s, for example, or in Fascist Italy of the 1920s (was the audience of this Latin book exclusively priests and male seminarians?).[11] Nor do I want to construct an argument, a retrospective argument, that popularity in the age of print proves that these texts were popular in the manuscript culture of the later Middle Ages. What I do want to assert is that devotional writings, especially those that originate in the medieval Latin tradition, are an important element of western European culture that have not been examined in proportion to their great popularity and influence. And I would also argue that the post-medieval popularity of these works cannot be completely sealed off from our historical understanding of them within a medieval context. That post-medieval popularity ought, in fact, to have something to do with the task of interpreting, reading, and understanding these works within their medieval setting, and must inevitably condition our interpretive procedures in dealing with them.

When we state that a medieval work was popular, we often base our claim on the number of surviving manuscripts known to us, and draw conclusions from what we can tell of their distribution, dissemination, and likelihood of survival. We also depend on information gleaned from library catalogues, inventories, wills, and letters, and take into account such ancillary evidence as translations, adaptations, versifications, borrowings, and the like. The *Meditationes* of Augustine, for example, had an extensive manuscript tradition from the end of the eleventh century right to the close of the Middle Ages. Studies of the surviving manuscripts and medieval library catalogues show that the work was known throughout western Europe and must have been a standard item in most monastic or ecclesiastical libraries.[12] The work was popular enough to have influenced vernacular poetry: in English, for example, there are several verse versions of the passage beginning "Candet nudatum pectus" ("His naked breast gleamed white"), including one found in John Grimestone's Commonplace Book, which also has the Latin original.[13] The treatise of Ogier of Locedio attributed to Bernard beginning "Quis dabit capiti meo" was perhaps even more popular. In addition to an extensive western European manuscript tradition that extends from the thirteenth through the fifteenth centuries, there are several distinct English versions of the fourteenth and fifteenth centuries, as well as Anglo-Norman, French, Netherlandish, Italian, and Provençal versions. Similarly, an enormous manuscript tradition exists for the *Meditationes vitae Christi*, as well as numerous vernacular adaptations of part or all of it, the best-known English version being Nicholas Love's

Mirror of the Blessed Life of Jesus Christ, a fifteenth-century work that acquired ample popularity in its own right.[14] All this suggests that these works dealing with the Passion of Christ were widely read throughout most of the later Middle Ages. This universal popularity, however, can be subjected to closer examination, an examination that will help to avoid unhistoricized overgeneralization and will lead to a more exact sense of what is meant when we state that a work is popular, especially if our aim is to place that work in opposition to a learned or an elite tradition. I wish now briefly to examine the popularity of these Latin works from three related perspectives: the first is the matter of audience, including the important questions of Latinity and vernacularity; the second is the matter of authorship; and the third is the matter of the condition of the texts themselves.

In discussions of devotional works, it is often assumed that the audiences for whom they were written were fixed and unvarying over the centuries, responding to the work uniformly and even predictably. It is much more reasonable to suppose, however, that the audiences that read devotional texts, or listened to them being read, were historically variable, not constituted in exactly the same way in the eleventh as in the fifteenth century. Over time, changes in audience composition are likely to have occurred that were governed by changes in social, economic, and political conditions. It is also seems reasonable to assume, although much harder to demonstrate, that audiences differed from place to place, from region to region, from city to city. When we speak of such a thing as a thirteenth-century European audience, we are, it must be recognized, employing a very coarse generalization, one that resists refinement because our knowledge is necessarily limited and, like all forms of historical knowledge, could never be complete, no matter how many documents we had at our disposal.[15]

Even within these limitations, however, it is still useful to formulate broad generalizations about the audiences of devotional texts. It is safe to conclude that the primary, but not exclusive, audience of Latin devotional writing in the eleventh and twelfth centuries was ecclesiastical, male, and monastic. There are many instances of devotional works written by monks addressed explicitly to other monks, as shown by the evidence of countless prefaces and prologues. At the same time, from very early on, there were works of spiritual guidance addressed to women religious that often included elements of devotion and meditation. The *De institutione inclusarum* ("Rule of Life for a Recluse"), which Aelred of Rievaulx addressed to his sister, and which concludes with a lengthy threefold meditation, is a notable example; Bonaventure's *De perfectione vitae ad sorores* ("On the Perfection of Life, for Sisters") is another. It is also the case that from early days the audiences of devotional literature were not exclusively clerical. The clerical authors of devotional texts sometimes recommended them to the laity, at first addressing them chiefly to aristocratic women, as Anselm of Canterbury did with his *Orationes sive meditationes*.[16] André Vauchez has pointed out that by the year 1200 the laity imitated clerical forms of spiritual life, including, for example, the recitation of monastic hours.[17]

Since in these centuries devotional texts all over western Europe are written exclusively in Latin, one assumes that the primary audience for them must have been those who knew how to read and write in Latin. At the same time, as Franz Bäuml has shown, in forming conceptions of audience, it is best not to base definitions on strict and overly rigid distinctions of literacy, but to allow for the possibility of an audience that might include persons who were illiterate or only partially literate in Latin.[18] This point seems especially applicable to Latin devotional texts. Although it is true that by the eleventh and twelfth centuries, as Bäuml observes, "Latin literary production was determined by a public with restricted, primarily liturgical, learned, administrative concerns," devotional texts seem always to have been relatively free of the authoritative or magisterial associations of their Latinity, intended for plainer purposes and the widest possible audience.[19] Anselm's invitation to start and stop reading his prayers and meditations at will, and to read only as much of them as the individual reader feels necessary, seems a conscious effort to offer an alternative to systematic, scholastic reading. Devotional texts were designed to be read in private, as we know from Anselm's Prologue to his *Orationes sive meditationes* and other sources, but there is ample evidence that Latin devotional texts were read aloud in public, most often, it seems, in the communal gatherings of monks required by their rules.[20] In circumstances such as these, it is quite likely that the partially or imperfectly literate in Latin might have formed part of the audience. And it is quite possible that the aristocratic female recipients of the Latin devotional texts addressed to them might have read them aloud or translated them orally and *ex tempore* into the vernacular for members of their circles whose command of Latin was less assured. While none of this can be demonstrated conclusively, I would like to argue for a much less monolithically conceived audience for Latin devotional texts than has been the case in the past.

An enlarged and expanded audience was brought about in part by religious reforms that occurred in the late eleventh and early twelfth centuries, when the newer contemplative orders allowed more occasions for private prayer and meditation than had been permitted in traditional Benedictine monasticism. At the same time, changing economic conditions created a laity that increasingly had the leisure required for private reading, including devotional reading. At first, as we have noted, the lay audience was almost exclusively aristocratic, but certainly by the fourteenth century in many parts of Europe, especially in England, Northern France, the Low Countries, and the Rhineland, that lay audience came increasingly to include members of the merchant middle class, both men and women. The fifteenth century saw an enormous increase in this audience for devotional texts. Most of the studies that have been made of the reading tastes of the mercantile class have stressed the great popularity enjoyed by religious works, including devotional treatises of all kinds.[21] Some of the works on the Passion we will be concerned with must have appealed very broadly to all kinds of audiences, male and female, clerical and lay, aristocratic and middle class.

Beginning in the thirteenth century, devotional texts were written in the vernacular as well as in Latin. There is a rich supply from most of the countries of western Europe. One can cite the Katherine Group and the *Ancrene Riwle* in English, the "Quis dabit" lament in Provençal, and the Anglo-Norman *Speculum ecclesie*. In the course of the thirteenth, fourteenth, and fifteenth centuries, Latin and the vernacular increasingly come to be on equal footing in the production of devotional texts. It is often assumed that this new vernacularity was conditioned both by the increasing demand of lay audiences for devotional works and by that of women religious who were denied the opportunity to develop their Latinity and for whom vernacular texts were therefore a convenience if not a necessity.[22] There is undoubtedly a measure of accuracy in this analysis, which in any case underscores the importance of taking into account vernacularity in any discussion of Latin devotional writing that seeks to understand the full complexity of the circumstances of its use and production.

Although the major focus of my study is on Latin devotional texts, I do not wish to adopt, or seem to be adopting, an interpretive model in which Latin culture is assumed to be primary and vernacular developments are seen as derivative reflexes of it.[23] Bäuml reminds us of the complex relationships between Latin and the vernacular languages, and this complexity is particularly acute in the realm of devotional writing. Some of the early Latin narratives on the Passion, I shall later claim, are properly regarded as foundation texts for subsequent developments, but at the same time, I also wish to avoid the undue privileging of Latin literary culture. Indeed, once the appearance of vernacular texts begins, it seems misguided to consider Latin and vernacular developments as isolated from each other, distributing them into separate traditions with impermeable boundaries. It seems especially fallacious in the case of Latin devotional texts of such wide distribution to consider the Latin tradition as representing the "official culture" and the vernacular as representing "popular culture." Aron Gurevich is rightly skeptical of the privileged position of the "Latin Middle Ages," but he errs, I think, in postulating an overly large separation between Latin literary culture and popular culture. At the same time, Gurevich recognizes the appeal of many types of writing for all classes of people, learned and ordinary, an appeal which certainly applies to many devotional texts as well as the types of writing he is concerned with.[24]

In considering the relation of Latin to the vernacular, I would like to move away from the transmitter-receptor model, and from hierarchical assumptions about the primacy of Latin culture in relation to the vernacular. I have in mind a much more fluid, dynamic, fragmented model, one which recognizes the competition of Latin and the vernacular in the marketplaces brought into being by the demands and requirements of audiences that were not monolithic, but varied, historically and economically individuated, and likely to have been at least partially determined by gender as well. This model sees the relation of Latin and vernacular in terms not of transmission from high to low, but in terms of mutual reciprocity and interpenetrability. This proposed model owes much to Foucault's questioning of the smooth continuities and orderly patterns of influence found by the positivist historians of the nineteenth century,[25] and relies on Roger Chartier's analysis of the popular literature of early modern France. Chartier's conclusions, while they are subject to qualification and adjustment, offer the basis for an explanation of the relation between Latin and vernacular cultures that is richly suggestive for an understanding of the popular devotional literature of the last centuries of the Middle Ages, especially the notions of popularity and audience and the relationship of Latinity and vernacularity. Chartier argues convincingly against some of the classic presuppositions in the common conception of popular culture:

first, that it is possible to establish exclusive relationships between specific cultural forms and particular social groups; second, that the various cultures existing in a given society are sufficiently pure, homogeneous, and distinct to permit them to be characterized uniformly and unequivocally; and third, that the category of "the people" or "the popular" has sufficient coherence and stability to define a distinct social identity that can be used to organize cultural differences in past ages according to the simple opposition of *populaire* versus *savant*.[26]

Elsewhere, Chartier argues that:

it no longer seems tenable to try to establish strict correspondences between cultural cleavages and social hierarchies, creating simplistic relationships between particular cultural objects or forms and specific social groups. On the contrary, it is necessary to recognize the fluid circulation and shared practices that cross social boundaries . . . Finally, the macroscopic opposition between "popular" and "high" culture has lost its pertinence. An inventory of the multiple divisions that fragment the social body is preferable to this massive partition, which often defines the common people by default as the collection of those outside elite society.[27]

Chartier's formulations are particularly applicable to the devotional literature of the later Middle Ages. They help us to grasp a social situation in which devotional texts could simultaneously appeal to many different groups in society, who might very well respond to them in different ways.[28] They suggest a more complex understanding of vernacularity and Latinity, laying the groundwork for a more sophisticated understanding of that relationship than the reductive model which postulates, in Chartier's words, "a simple process of diffusion, one generally thought to descend along the social ladder."[29]

In understanding the relationship between vernacularity and Latinity in the Middle Ages, devotional texts are especially valuable; from a very early date they exhibit several kinds of complexity not found elsewhere within medieval culture until much later. For example, devotional works are among the very first to be turned into Latin from an original in the vernacular, instead of vice versa. The Latin translations of the *Cloud of Unknowing* are well-known examples of this, and there are others.[30] The Latin *Vita Christi* of Ludolphus of Saxony seems to have borrowed from the German Passion tract of Heinrich of St. Gall, which in turn borrowed from earlier Latin treatises.[31] Some of the special perplexities in dealing with these matters are well illustrated by the *Speculum ecclesie* of Edmund Rich (d. 1240), a work that exists in distinct Latin, Middle English, and Anglo-Norman versions. Scholarly opinion is divided about whether the Latin or the Anglo-Norman was written first, that is, which of these is the "primary" version.[32] Instances such as these show the virtue of a dynamic interpretive model that understands vernacularity and Latinity in terms of the possibilities of reciprocity and interchange, even as it acknowledges the dominant Latinity of medieval culture in general. This model is applicable in the thirteenth century, at least in parts of Europe such as England, and it is essential for comprehending the culture of the fourteenth and fifteenth centuries, a period when the exclusive monopoly of Latin in authoritative discourse was steadily being eroded by the vernaculars in all areas of European life and culture. Tim Machan has spoken of the "unstable integrity" of Latin and English domains in late medieval England, and this seems particularly true in the realm of devotional texts, where it is sometimes difficult to see that Latinity is itself a necessary sign of authoritative discourse, or vernacularity a necessary sign of "popularity."[33]

Matters of authorship and text are especially important in defining the characteristics of the Latin devotional prose I will be considering, and they suggest ways of distinguishing the discourse of popular Latin devotional treatises from the authoritative Latinity of the learned elite. The conception of authorship in popular devotional texts is an extremely fluid notion. Works constantly were falsely assigned to the Latin fathers or to contemporary authors of high prestige. This is a characteristic of Latin devotional writing from the earliest moment. In the eighth- or ninth-century *Book of Cerne*, for example, one of the oldest surviving collections of Latin private prayers, prayers are erroneously attributed to Gregory, Jerome, and Ephraim the Syrian.[34] False attributions abound in much of the literature of the Middle Ages, of course, but it seems that both in degree and in wide variability this trait is especially conspicuous in popular Latin devotional writing. The treatise of Ekbert of Schönau, the *Stimulus amoris*, traveled under various names and was attributed in the manuscripts usually to Bernard, but also to Anselm, Ambrose, and Bonaventure. The Marian lament of Ogier of Locedio (d. 1214), beginning "Quis dabit capiti meo," was attributed to Bernard, Anselm, and Augustine. The *Meditationes vitae Christi* of unknown authorship and the *Stimulus amoris* of James of Milan were both attributed to Bonaventure from a very early date. By the fourteenth century, the body of devotional works circulating under the names of Anselm, Bernard, Bonaventure, and Augustine had grown immense, and very little of it was authentically theirs.

There is similarly an exceptionally wide variability in the textual traditions of popular Latin devotional works. It is typical for them to circulate in distinct recensions or in variable, unstable texts. This too is a quality that may be noted about Latin devotional writing from an early date. The text of the popular Carolingian prayer "Domine deus dominator omnipotens" is found in the manuscripts in numerous versions that differ considerably one from another.[35] More than in the case of authoritative discourse, these texts seem to have been available for ready modification, in some cases, we know, better to suit them to the special needs of their audiences. We can cite many examples from the later Middle Ages of such textual variability. Anselm circulated his Prayer to the Virgin in two distinct recensions; the *Speculum ecclesie* of Edmund Rich, noted above, is found in two distinct Latin versions, each with a different title, as well as in Anglo-Norman and Middle English translations;[36] there is enormous textual variation in the numerous manuscripts of the "Quis dabit" lament; the *Meditationes vitae Christi* frequently circulated in various excerpted forms; and the textual history of the *Stimulus amoris* of James of Milan is a complex matter of incorporation, amalgamation, and rearrangement.[37] In the vernacular, to cite one noteworthy example, the *Revelations of Divine Love* of Julian of Norwich (d. 1443) exists in two Middle English versions.[38]

The false attributions that accompany many medieval texts have often been taken to be merely naive, random, and unsystematic. When the question is looked at more closely, the usual explanation is that the false attributions are made to elevate the authority of the text, to increase its audience and claims to authenticity by attaching to it the name of a prestigious author.[39] In the case of devotional texts, those authors were often the great Latin fathers. The false attributions provided a fertile field for the operations of the positivist historians of the nineteenth and early twentieth centuries, whose task it was to set things right by ferreting out accretions and misattributions and establishing the authentic canon of a given author. These methods have been applied to Latin devotional writers, often with spectacular results. André Wilmart, for example, took up the canon of Anselm's *Orationes sive meditationes* in the 1920s, and when he had completed his work, of the 75 prayers and 21 meditations printed as Anselm's in the Patrologia Latina edition, which more or less accurately represented the late medieval textual tradition, only nineteen prayers and three meditations remained that Wilmart allowed as authentically Anselm's.[40] The devotional works of Bernard have been subject to a similar pruning in our own time. In the late nineteenth century, for example, the author of the *Stimulus amoris* was identified as Ekbert of Schönau rather than the Bernard of most of the manuscripts.[41]

Such enterprises, however gratifying to the scientific sensibilities of modern scholarship, actively distort the medieval situation. In order to understand such figures as Bernard and Anselm as devotional writers as they would have been known in the Middle Ages, much of positivistic scholarship needs to be set aside in order to recapture a more inclusive view of Bernard, Anselm, or Augustine. The collection of nineteen prayers and three meditations that Wilmart ascribed to Anselm, which forms the basis of the standard modern edition by F. S. Schmitt, is found complete in that form in only five of the earliest manuscripts, and many of these dispose the collection in different orders with non-Anselmian interpolations.[42] In the hundreds of manuscripts from the thirteenth, fourteenth, and fifteenth centuries, widely varied versions of the enlarged canon are presented. It may well be asked if it makes sense to speak of Wilmart's Anselm as the "real" Anselm, in place of the Anselm of the medieval manuscript tradition. Similarly, the understanding of Bernard as a medieval devotional writer cannot derive only from his authentic *Sermons on the Song of Songs*, but must be completed by taking into account the enormous number of devotional treatises that circulated under his name. Put in another way, the modern effort to establish on scientific principles the canon of Bernard has succeeded in unduly restricting the meaning of Bernard as signifier within the realm of medieval culture and society.

While there is much truth in the conventional explanation of the false authorial ascriptions, such an explanation seems incomplete. Other ways of viewing the matter may lead to a better understanding of the relationship of these texts to learned, elite, scholastic culture. We can see the attributions as a creative act of literary criticism that opposes the ideals of strict canon formation. Those ideals existed in some form throughout the Middle Ages and are especially locatable in the elite culture of scholasticism. Anselm's advanced treatises on logic, grammar, and theology are rarely anonymous and never misattributed in the manuscripts, nor is there any accretion of *spuria* corresponding to the vast apocrypha attached to his prayers and meditations. Similarly, their textual tradition is sound and comparatively free of variation. It is important to recognize that the variable attributions of authorship and the textual instability of devotional works are not simply inevitable consequences revealing the limitations of medieval manuscript culture, but are better explained as socially and culturally determined. When stability of the text and fixed determination of authorship were sought as goals, the technology of the codex and the scribal environment to which it belonged were quite adequate to sustain them, as shown most notably by the transmission of the text of the Bible.

The false attributions offer a way of looking at authorship that contrasts with the prevailing positivist ideals of our own time, and perhaps the prevailing ideals of the Middle Ages as well. We can see that one effect of the variable attributions is to remove the texts from their historical context and obscure their historical contingency. They contribute to the implicit intentions and explicit ideals of devotional texts to be timeless and transcendent. Within the discourse of popular devotion, the attributions suggest that this is what Anselm or Bernard might have written. An attribution to Bernard, for example, is a signal to the audience that the text that follows will be in his manner or thought worthy of him. If this is accepted, the misattributions may be seen as far from careless, and they resonate with much deeper implication than mere strategies of elevation and prestige. These are acts of appropriation that become a way of developing, maintaining, and extending a textual community united by veneration for Bernard as a spiritual guide. Considered in this way, it is understandable if we find the same text attributed to Bernard, Augustine, or Ambrose in manuscripts that may be nearly contemporary with each other and written within the same geographical area.

The modern argument about canon formation is relevant to my project. The issue, then as now, is what is qualified to be included in the canon. The current debate has taught us that stringent principles of canon formation can be repressive, inhibiting change and suppressing desire and aspiration.[43] A rigid canon is frozen in time and encodes value, depriving the culture of its dynamism, its energy, as it closes off the possibilities of self-renewal and redefinition. The expanding medieval canon of Bernard and Anselm, as well as of other devotional writers, can best be taken as a sign of creativity and vitality present in the culture, as a force that countervails the very notion of canon itself. These tendencies that oppose the idea of a fixed canon, I suggest, may be taken as a characteristic of popular culture.

It is important to notice that in the thirteenth and fourteenth centuries, at the same time that fluid notions of authorship were forming in the realm of popular Latin devotional writing, the text of the Bible within the high scholastic tradition was subject to treatment on an increasingly scientific and rationalist basis. The *Sententiae* of Peter Lombard (d. 1160) at the beginning of the period and the *Postillae* of Nicholas of Lyra (d. 1349) at its end are two notable examples.[44] At the same time that those fluid and unstable texts of the devotional tradition were put into wide circulation, the goal of biblical interpretation increasingly was to stabilize the text and to fix its meaning. I don't think it is necessary to view the variable authorship and instability of devotional texts as a reaction against such rationalism, but it is important to see that they represent two contesting impulses within late medieval culture.

This contest is especially apparent when it is remembered that the texts of the devotional works themselves are based on the Bible. The issue now becomes one of canon not in terms of modern theory, but in the specific medieval understanding of that word as having to do with the authentic text of Scripture. Foucault's epigram on modern developments in the understanding of canon, "The Bible has become a bookstore," applies with literal force to the late medieval situation.[45] In their innovative renarrations of the incidents of the life of Christ and their lively invention of non-biblical details, the Passion narratives present a rewritten, reformulated, highly variable, and decidedly non-canonical biblical text, which was self-consciously made and occasionally theoretically defended. The author of the *Meditationes vitae Christi* asserts a revised and more flexible understanding of the gospel, one which touches upon and examines the privileged position of literacy within medieval high culture:

Non autem credas, quod omnia quae ipsum dixisse, vel fecisse constat, meditari possimus, vel quod omnia scripta sint: ego vero ad majorem impressionem, ea sic, ac si ita fuissent, narrabo, prout contingere vel contigisse credi possunt, secundum quasdam imaginarias repraesentationes, quas animus diversimode percepit. Nam et circa divinam Scripturam meditari, exponere et intelligere multifarie, prout expedire credimus, possumus, dummodo non sit contra veritatem vitae, justitiae et doctrinae, et non sit contra fidem et contra bonos mores. Cum autem me narrantem invenies: "Ita dixit vel fecit Dominus Jesus," seu alia, quae introducuntur; si illud per Scripturam probari non possit, non aliter accipias, quam devota meditatio exigit.[46]

[However, you must not believe that all things said and done by Him on which we may meditate are known to us in writing. For the sake of greater impressiveness I shall tell them to you as they occurred or as they might have occurred according to the devout belief of the imagination and the varying interpretation of the mind. It is possible to contemplate, explain, and understand the Holy Scriptures in as many ways as we consider necessary, in such a manner as not to contradict the truth of life and justice and not to oppose faith and morality. Thus when you find it said here, "This was said and done by the Lord Jesus," and by others of whom we read, if it cannot be demonstrated by the Scriptures, you must consider it only as a requirement of devout contemplation.]

Although its author scrupulously strives to remain within the bounds of orthodoxy, nevertheless a small assault is found here on the textuality of scholastic Christianity, and certainly an alternative is presented to the

view that the biblical text was fixed and immutable. This implicit challenge
to scholastic hegemony concerning the manner of how the Bible is to be
used and read is contemporaneous with, and perhaps parallel to, the more
overt challenge to institutional and hierarchical authority presented by the
Wycliffite view of biblical interpretation.[47] Formulations of the kind found
in the Preface to the *Meditationes vitae Christi* and the gospel renarrations
that resulted from them seemed to have been deeply disturbing in some
quarters, a provocation for attacks on contemplatives whose spirituality
was based upon and guided by such texts. Two notable examples of such
criticism are found in the *Cloud of Unknowing* (which returns to Dionysian
spirituality as interpreted by the twelfth-century Victorines for a theory of
contemplation) and in Jean Gerson's *De mystica theologica*, where there are
warnings against those who use concrete natural analogies in describing
spiritual union.[48]

The popular Latin devotional works challenge the hegemony of the
scholastic method and its official monopoly on biblical interpretation by
presenting alternative and hypothetical reworkings of the gospel story
which do not depend upon a canonical text.[49] The canonical text is destabilized, the meaning unfixed and put into play, the Scripture is understood, in the words of the *Meditationes vitae Christi*, "in as many ways as
we consider necessary," so long as the truths of faith are not denied. In
reference to late-medieval mysticism, Steven Ozment has argued that the
mystical enterprise is at base a "dissent ideology," that it "bears a potential anti-intellectual and anti-institutional stance, which can be adopted for
the critical purposes of dissent, reform, and even revolution."[50] The popular Latin devotional works dealing with the Passion of Christ may likewise
be validly regarded from this perspective, with some qualification. It may
seem paradoxical, but these texts, in contradistinction to their free textuality, like much popular literature, most often encode, rather than subvert,
prevailing social and cultural norms, as I shall claim in later chapters. But
the possibility of a more broadly conceived opposition is always latent.

Although the framework of much of my study is diachronic, linear,
and sequential, at the same time I seek to avoid the pitfalls that modern
criticism has taught us to recognize in such ways of ordering the past.[51]
Most previous studies of these texts have followed evolutionary or teleo-
logical approaches in which every text is considered as the fulfillment of a
previous tradition or the foreshadowing of what is yet to come. The result
of these efforts has been a series of autonomous and self-contained histories

of spirituality or of devotional practice, in which the texts are largely considered as the products of a closed off and internally generated dynamic, apart from their relationship to the social, cultural, and historical world of which they are a part. I am persuaded that such evolutionary approaches are limited, offering partial, often distorted, and frequently reductive views of these texts, finally depriving them of their full significance as cultural documents. The interpretive paradigm built on these approaches can be seen as dependent on the evolutionary and organic thinking of the nineteenth century, as many critics have noticed. Hans Robert Jauss quotes Droysen on the "false doctrine of the so-called organic development of history" and warns us of the consequences of "The epic fictions of the completed process, of the first beginning and the definitive end, and of the self-presenting past."[52] Of the many post-modern critics who have perceived the limitations of that paradigm, Michel Foucault has offered us the most trenchant critique of the principles on which it is based, forcing us to recognize its limitations and simplifications, its overwhelming need to find continuity and progress in the face of what is complex, different, fragmented, and contradictory.[53] Foucault reminds us to question "the themes of convergence and culmination," to focus instead on "differentiated autonomies and dependences," and always to doubt those "ready-made syntheses" of development, evolution, tradition, and influence.[54]

Foucault's searching analysis is one of the many assaults on the premises and unexamined assumptions of the historiography of the nineteenth century that have altered our present conception of the historical undertaking. Paul Zumthor asserts that "the historical development of cultures (inasmuch as it is apparent) rarely proceeds by linear sequences, formalizable in a closed discourse, but generally by a multidimensional expansion."[55] We have become deeply suspicious of the idea of progress and, as Jean-François Lyotard has observed, "The grand narrative has lost its credibility, regardless of what mode of unification it uses, regardless of whether it is a speculative narrative or a narrative of emancipation."[56]

In my own study, I wish to adopt other perspectives, perspectives which are not so much concerned with the linear, evolutionary continuity that has been the principle focus of most previous studies, but which have as their aim the location of texts within their historical contexts. In an essay on Renaissance literary studies, Louis Montrose, speaking of the "Cultural Poetics" of Stephen Greenblatt, notes that a project of such a kind in effect "reorients the axis of inter-textuality, substituting for the diachronic text of an autonomous literary history the synchronic text of a cultural system."[57] The contextual approach I seek to follow will be, I hope, such a reorientation. It is an approach much indebted to theoretical propositions advanced by Mikhail M. Bakhtin and Raymond Williams. Both Bakhtin and Williams seek to offer alternatives to the conventional understanding of the text in relationship to its historical context that tends to regard it as either merely reflecting an objective historical reality or transparently communicating the intention of an author. Bakhtin offers the metaphor of "refraction" to describe the relationship between authorial intention and the text, insisting that text is not a mere neutral medium transmitting data, but is determined by its social and generic context as it shapes and contributes to the formation of the "reality" it represents.[58] Williams also insists that texts must be perceived as conditioned by specific historical circumstances, offering an insightful explanation of how texts are related to their cultural contexts. He argues that texts do not just neutrally reflect a culture and its values; nor is it sufficient to state only that they are determined by the culture: rather, the texts themselves play an active part in the constitution of a culture, in a complex reciprocal process of interrelationship and interdependence.[59] Following Williams's principles, I want to avoid an oversimplified reflectionist model of interpretation; instead I will urge that the religious texts we will be dealing with are not only determined by their cultural context but actively contribute to the formation of values, attitudes, and beliefs. The texts are not passive, but powerful agents; they do not stand outside history or exist separated or separable from a cultural "background." They should be seen as not only expressing but actively shaping, ratifying, and perpetuating an ideology, in an active process of mutual reciprocation that lies at the very heart of cultural formation.[60] This is the "text that functions in the heart of a cluster of social determinations," in the phrase of Paul Zumthor.[61]

It is a fundamental premise of this study that the devotional texts I will be dealing with are, as I hope to demonstrate, no different from any other category of texts; they are products of social processes, and at the same time have the capacity both to articulate and transform social attitudes and religious values. I urge this point in the face of the often explicit ideals of transcendence embodied in the texts, their proclaimed intention to remove the reader from the temporal, the historical, the particular, and above all the material. Despite these claims, I argue, these texts do not stand outside history, but, on the contrary, are saturated with ideology and actively contribute to its formation. In fact it may be said that it is precisely those claims of transcendence and a-historicity that render these narratives such powerful instruments of ideology.

In dealing with medieval religious and devotional texts, it is common for scholars to speak in terms of tradition, as in the "Franciscan devotional tradition" or the "tradition of affective piety." It is convenient to adopt this terminology, and I do so here. I mean as much as possible to use tradition as a neutral or objective word, meaning merely, in the root sense of the word "what is handed down." At the same time, I recognize that tradition can never be neutral and value free; as Williams observes, tradition "is always more than an inert historicized segment; indeed it is the most powerful practical means of incorporation. What we have to see is not just 'a tradition' but a selective tradition: an intentionally selective version of a shaping past and a pre-shaped present, which is then powerfully operative in the process of social and cultural definition and identification."[62] Williams is dealing with tradition as a general element constituting culture, and therefore in a much broader sense than I use the term in describing the transmission of texts, ideas, motifs, and influences from decade to decade or century to century. However, his analysis is a stimulating reminder that even in this more restricted sense of the word as it is used by literary critics and historians, the objectivity and neutrality of what is referred to as "the tradition" should not be merely assumed or left unexamined. Important for our purposes is Williams's observation that "any tradition can be shown, by analysis, to be a selection and reselection of those significant received and recovered elements of the past which represent not a necessary but a *desired* continuity."[63] When we speak of the "Franciscan devotional tradition," it is important to note that a selection and an arrangement have already been made, an act of interpretation has taken place, and a unity has been imposed which guides our perceptions and informs our understanding.

Any enterprise that has as its principal aim the situating of texts in their social, historical, and cultural contexts must be concerned with avoiding overly simple and unproblematized distinctions between text and context. Williams's assault on reflectionism offers a way of understanding the complex reciprocity of text and context, which is richly illuminating. At the same time, post-structuralist and deconstructionist critics have offered an analysis of text and context that shifts the emphasis away from the cultural materialism that underwrites Williams's formulations and turns it toward the textuality of history itself, arguing that it is an error to make too sharp a distinction between text and context, between representation and an external "reality." There is lively critical disagreement about these matters, but as Gerald Graff has noted, "there is considerable agreement on at least one point: that meaning is not an autonomous essence within the words of a text but something dependent for its comprehension on prior texts and situations."[64] Deconstructionist critics perform a useful function in reminding us of what Louis Montrose has called "the textuality of history, the historicity of texts."[65] As Dominick LaCapra notes, "the past arrives in the form of texts and textualized remainders—memoirs, reports, published writings, archives, monuments, and so forth."[66] Or as Jonathan Culler puts the issue, "context is not fundamentally different from what it contextualizes; context is not given, but produced; what belongs to a context is determined by interpretive strategies; contexts are just as much in need of elucidation as events; and the meaning of a context is determined by events."[67] These are salutary reminders of the complexity of the historical undertaking, reminders which are based in large measure in the work of Jacques Derrida, and summarized in his aphorism, "il n'y a pas de hors texte."[68] LaCapra trenchantly questions the pointed dichotomy between text and context, arguing that "The context itself is a text of sorts; it calls not for stereotypical, ideological 'descriptions' but for interpretation and informed criticism."[69]

The difficulties of reconciling such understandings with the analysis of culture and history proposed by Williams are many, and have been well described by Hayden White and Stanley Fish.[70] One response is, as Fish puts it, to "simply reject the post-structuralist textualization of history and insist on a material reality in relation to which texts are secondary."[71] This is a position I do not wish to adopt. I find it useful to recognize the textuality of history, to grant that context as much as text requires interpretation and analysis for its understanding, and that it is often productive to adopt, in dealing with each, similar interpretive strategies. At the same time, I think it is possible to insist on an external material reality, which we cannot, it is true, know transparently, certainly, and unmediated by textuality, but a reality to which texts belong, a reality by which texts are constituted and to the constitution of which they contribute.

The interpretations of texts I offer in this study, I would want to urge, are best seen as partial and incomplete, even though I have done my best to render them cogent and convincing. I seek to advance no totalizing thesis, but instead prefer to recognize the partiality and limitations of any interpretive act. Bakhtin has taught us that texts must always be seen from a variety of perspectives, that they embody competing voices, that texts and their contexts are in constant and continually evolving dialogue which resists reduction to a simple, monologic meaning.[72] The narratives of the Passion, their meaning and significance, their relation to their social and historical contexts, are best examined from different points of view, with different interpretive strategies and analytical methods: no single study can ever hope to be totally exhaustive and totally comprehensive, much less totally definitive, in the traditional way that "definitive" has been used to describe scholarly books and articles. I recognize that in conceiving of, organizing, and arranging my study I have already performed an act of interpretation; I have imposed a kind of artificial unity and coherence on what is in fact fragmentary, uncertain, complex, and finally too enormous, too challenging, for one study or one person ever to comprehend. In selecting these works for study and examination, I have inevitably excluded others from my attention. I have categorized, arranged, ordered, and selected according to my understanding of what is important, significant, and worthy of comment. It is well to remember Georges Duby's reminder that we "know" the past "virtually without exception from monuments that power has caused to be erected."[73] Moreover, my exposition inevitably reflects the limitations of my own reading and scholarly competencies, and is best regarded more as a heuristic than as having a compelling claim to objective certainty.

There is always a danger, in a study as broadly based as this one, to find too much unity, too much coherence, and to surrender to the blandishments of overgeneralization.[74] David Aers has offered the salutary reminder that the devotional tradition examined in this book, with its emphasis on the suffering Christ, while it may have been overwhelmingly predominant, was not the only way Christian piety was expressed, particularly in the later Middle Ages.[75] The propensity to seek out unity seems inevitably to accompany cultural and historical studies, and is best understood not merely as a literary convention of academic history writing, but also as deeply grounded in western philosophy and metaphysics. Foucault is among those who have reminded us that an unexamined assumption at the base of the historical enterprise traditionally has been the desire for unitary explanations; in the face of discontinuity, contradiction, and irregularity, "it regards it as its duty to find, at a deeper level, a principal of cohesion that organizes the discourse and restores to it its hidden unity."[76] Even as I advance my own interpretations and offer what I hope are modest and reasonable generalizations based on them, I do so with a consciousness that such acts have the potential to be distorting as well as clarifying, smoothing over genuine difference and deciding what is finally undecidable. To follow the insight and adopt the terminology of Macherey and Althusser, we can find in these religious texts, as in any other, "the gaps and fissures, the points of stress and incoherence," the contradictions, and conflicts of a cultural system whose complexity must always be recognized and taken into account.[77] The cultural "background" or context does not itself always readily offer itself up to unitary and harmonious explanation. As the anthropologist Roger Keesing has said, "Cultures are webs of mystification as well as signification."[78] We are better off to resist the universalizing claims of positivist historiography, better off to acknowledge what Lloyd Kramer calls "the inescapable perspectivism of historical research."[79]

The principal method followed in my study is to examine the way the story of the Passion of Christ is narrated and renarrated in Latin devotional treatises of the eleventh through the fifteenth centuries. I pay especially close attention to the modifications and enlargements of the narrative of the Passion as it is presented in the canonical gospels, because it is those alterations and expansions, made in different times and places, that reveal, I maintain, the inevitable impress of history upon the text. I do not attribute these alterations to naive error or a callow religious sensibility,[80] but see them as an indication of intellectual, spiritual, and imaginative fecundity, which presents us with a way of understanding an important aspect of the complex religious culture of the late Middle Ages. The story of Christ's Passion, of course, has high and continuous significance for the Christian society of the Middle Ages. It is a "master narrative" in the theological and religious sense, in that for Christians, it describes the central act of human history, the redemption of mankind, in relation to which every other event in history is referred and acquires meaning. The Passion story is also a "master narrative" as that phrase is used by the French historians of the Annales school, in that it is a narrative that organizes perceptions and gives meaning to a society over an extended period of time.[81]

Within the medieval renarrations of the Passion, the focus of attention is on the body of Christ. The physical body is described as twisted, torn, spat upon, struck, pierced, flagellated, and finally broken, pallid, and drained of blood. The medieval narratives are especially productive in vastly enlarging the gospel record to describe the tortured body of Christ in a continually expanding and enormously inventive series of elaborations of the gospel events. This concern with the body in the Passion meditations can be seen as an important and indeed foundational element of the general late medieval concern with the body that many recent critics have identified as a notable characteristic of the period.[82] As modern critics have also come to understand, the body is an especially important domain in seeking to comprehend the values, attitudes, and beliefs of a culture and society. Mary Douglas writes that "most symbolic behaviour must work through the human body," and she continues: "The social body constrains the way the physical body is perceived. The physical experience of the body, always modified by the social categories though which it is known, sustains a particular view of society."[83] If culture can be seen as a "realized signifying system," in the words of Raymond Williams,[84] then the body is among the most communicative of its signs. In the Christian society of the Middle Ages, the body of Christ in the Passion narratives becomes at once the locus of cultural transformation and the highly expressive site where values, attitudes, beliefs, desires, conflicts, contradictions, and ideologies are articulated. These matters will be taken up mainly in chapters 3–5.

The following chapter is a chronologically organized survey of Latin Passion narratives from about 1100 to 1500, with some notice of the Passion in Latin devotional poetry and in the vernacular languages of Western Europe. Readers familiar with the tradition or who have less interest in synoptic overviews may wish to consult it selectively or move directly to chapters 3, 4, and 5, which are chiefly concerned with matters of representation and the historical contextualization of the Passion narratives.

2

Medieval Narratives of the
Passion of Christ

THE LATIN NARRATIVES OF THE PASSION belonging to the devotional
literature of the later Middle Ages, partly because of their great popularity,
are central documents in the formation of the medieval consciousness of
the significance of the Passion. They contribute importantly to the emergence of the story of Christ's suffering and death as a cultural symbol of
increasingly potent force and of multivalent meaning. These narratives develop, in the first place, from a very long tradition of written texts in which
the Passion of Christ figures as the central act of human history. The fundamental texts on the Passion are the gospels themselves, but hardly less
important are the apocryphal gospels, the liturgy, and certain historical
and exegetical works. These are the foundations on which the Latin prose
narratives are built.

The Passion in the Gospels, Liturgy,
and Biblical Commentary

All medieval devotional writing on the Passion derives from the narratives
of the Passion found in each of the four gospels. Some Passion treatises follow the gospels closely, rarely departing from the sequence of events, and
seldom offering commentary or explanation, much less suggesting hypothetical additions or elaborations of the data as set out in the Bible. In many
cases, these treatises are mere centos of biblical passages or paraphrases that
attempt to harmonize the variations in the different gospel accounts into a
single coherent narrative. In the later Middle Ages, however, it is increasingly common to find narratives that go far beyond the gospel record by
including details that have no warrant in the biblical text. From the point

of view of the later Middle Ages, the gospels were meager in the specifics of Christ's sufferings and death. For example, John's description of the arrest in the garden states only that the band of soldiers with the tribune and the leaders of the Jews took Jesus and bound him: "comprehenderunt Jesum et ligaverunt eum" (Jn 18:12). In some of the late medieval treatises on the Passion, this description is elaborated with the additional detail that Christ's hands were tied so tightly that blood burst from his fingernails.[1] Similarly, the Bible gives few specifics about how Christ was actually crucified. The Gospel of Luke, for example, reports only that they came to the place called Calvary and there they crucified him (Lc 23:33). This lack of detail was remedied in many of the most popular late medieval treatises, where we find particularized descriptions of Christ's body stretched out on the cross prior to being fastened with nails, and descriptions of how the cross was raised from the ground and fitted into a mortise.

The gospel accounts of the Passion, although they seemed to the Middle Ages to be insufficiently particularized, yet contain in rudimentary form what proves to be a very productive method for embellishing the Passion story in a way that for them carried the highest theological sanction. All the gospel narratives on the Passion seek to demonstrate that Christ in his suffering and death fulfilled the messianic prophecies of the Hebrew Bible. Thus in the Gospels of Matthew and Mark Christ applies to himself the verse from Zachariah, "percutiam pastorem et dispergentur oves gregis" ("I will strike the shepherd and the sheep of the flock shall be dispersed," Mt 26:31, Mc 14:27; see Zach 13:7).

Such interpretations form the basis, in Christian hermeneutics, for the typological exegesis of the Hebrew Bible. F. P. Pickering has described the extension of the method in the later Middle Ages by which the words of Christ himself as recorded in Luke 24:44, "quoniam necesse est impleri omnia quae scripta sunt in lege Mosi et prophetis et psalmis de me" ("that all things must needs be fulfilled, which are written in the law of Moses, and in the prophets, and in the psalms, concerning me"), were taken as a justification for applying almost any verse of the Hebrew Bible to the events of Christ's life, especially those of the Passion.[2] In this way, the Hebrew Bible offered what was taken to be a divinely authorized way of filling out details of Christ's life where the gospels were silent.

In many cases, passages of the Hebrew Bible were not merely cited as being fulfilled by the events of the Passion but especially in the later Middle Ages, taken to be literal descriptions of the physical torments of Christ. For example, verses from Psalm 21 were applied to the Passion in a very specific sense. One of the most widely known of these applications is the phrase, "dinumeraverunt omnia ossa mea" ("they have numbered all my bones," Ps 21:18), which lay behind a host of narrative descriptions of Christ being stretched so tightly on the cross that all his bones were clearly visible and therefore numerable.

The liturgy for Holy Week develops in greater detail the notion that Christ's suffering fulfills Hebrew prophecies. Psalm 21, the prime source of many of the most striking images in medieval Passion narratives, is at the heart of the liturgy for Palm Sunday, Holy Thursday, and Good Friday. The lessons for Wednesday in Holy Week are the great messianic passages from the book of Isaiah, which are alluded to in the gospels (see Mt 26:63, for example) and elsewhere in the New Testament (see, for example, Rom 4:25, I Pt 2:24). Two passages from Isaiah from the lessons for Wednesday in Holy Week have an especially powerful influence on representations of the Passion in art and literature, offering a view of Christ both as suffering servant and as triumphant champion. The first of these was thought to describe the suffering Christ, meek before his accusers:

> Non est species ei, neque decor, et vidimus eum, et non erat aspectus, et deside-ravimus eum; despectum, et novissimum virorum, virum dolorum, et scientem infirmitatem; et quasi absconditus vultus ejus et despectus, unde nec reputavimus eum. Vere languores nostros ipse tulit, et dolores nostros ipse portavit; et nos putavimus eum quasi leprosum, et percussum a Deo, et humiliatum. Ipse autem vulneratus est propter iniquitates nostras, attritus est propter scelera nostra; disci-plina pacis nostrae super eum, et livore ejus sanati sumus. . . . Oblatus est quia ipse voluit, et non aperuit os suum; sicut ovis ad occisionem ducetur, et quasi agnus coram tondente se obmutescet, et non aperiet os suum. (Is 53:2–5, 7)

[There is no beauty in him, no comeliness: and we have seen him, and there was no sightliness, that we should be desirous of him: despised, and the most abject of men, a man of sorrows, and acquainted with infirmity: and his look was as it were hidden and despised, wherefore we esteemed him not. Surely he hath borne our infirmities and carried our sorrows; and we have thought him as it were a leper, and as one struck by God and afflicted. But he was wounded for our iniquities, he was bruised for our sins. The chastisement of our peace was upon him, and by his bruises we are healed. . . . He was offered because it was his own will, and he opened not his mouth. He shall be led as a sheep to the slaughter, and shall be dumb as a lamb before his shearer, and he shall not open his mouth.]

These lines from Isaiah are the foundation for many elaborate descriptions in the Passion narratives of the ugliness and deformity of Christ's body caused by the tortures inflicted on him.

The other prophetic passage from Isaiah prominent in the Holy Week liturgy emphasizes Christ's heroic action in the redemption of the human race:

Quis est iste, qui venit de Edom, tinctis vestibus de Bosra? iste formosus in stola sua, gradiens in multitudine fortitudinis suae. Ego qui loquor justitiam, et propugnator sum ad salvandum. Quare ergo rubrum est indumentum tuum, et vestimenta tua sicut calcantium in torculari? Torcular calcavi solus, et de gentibus non est vir mecum; calcavi eos in furore meo, et conculcavi eos in ira mea; et aspersus est sanguis eorum super vestimenta mea, et omnia indumenta mea inquinavi. (Is 63:1–3)[3]

[Who is this that cometh from Edom, with dyed garments from Bosra, this beautiful one in his robe, walking in the greatness of his strength? I, that speak justice, and am a defender to save. Why then is thy apparel red, and thy garments like theirs that tread in the winepress? I have trodden the winepress alone, and of the Gentiles there is not a man with me: I have trampled on them in my indignation, and have trodden them down in my wrath, and their blood is sprinkled upon my garments, and I have stained all my apparel.]

The man with red garments was taken as a type of Christ, fresh from the torments of the Passion. The man from Edom in the winepress was taken as an anticipation of Christ's sufferings on the cross from at least the patristic age. As James Marrow has shown, this passage from Isaiah, together with the exegesis surrounding it, was the source of an extremely common motif in late medieval art: the figure of Christ in the wine press oppressed by the weight of its beam.[4]

Another part of the Holy Week liturgy that had great influence on the Passion narratives of the later Middle Ages is the *improperia*, or reproaches, of the Good Friday service.[5] In reference to his Passion, Christ addresses the people who are the cause of his suffering and death. Especially common in the Passion narratives is the reproach: "Quid ultra debui facere tibi, et non feci?" ("What more should I have done for thee that I have not done?"). Other reproaches emphasize the contrast between Christ's royal power and the humility of his suffering: "Ego te exaltavi magna virtute: et tu me suspendisti in patibulo crucis" ("I raised thee up with mighty power: and thou didst hang me upon the gibbet of the cross"). This pattern of balanced antithesis, contrasting Christ's former beauty, glory, and regal power with his present deformity, abjection, and helplessness is a common rhetorical strategy of the Passion treatises.

In addition to the liturgy, the apocryphal gospels, particularly the

Gospel of Nicodemus, were a direct or indirect source for many medieval Passion meditations, although the contribution of the apocrypha is not nearly so significant as that of the liturgy and the Bible itself. The apocrypha fulfilled a need by providing details missing in the canonical gospels, for example, the names of the thieves crucified with Christ, Dismas and Gestas, and the name of the soldier who pierced Christ's side with a lance, Longinus; but since there is no elaboration or added detail about the actual sufferings undergone by Christ, they offer relatively little to the Passion treatises, which continually seek to heighten the emotionality of the Passion through vivid descriptions of Christ's torments. The Gospel of Nicodemus is important in the Passion narratives for its elaboration of the events occurring from the moment of Christ's death on the cross to his burial. The role of Joseph of Arimathea is much enlarged, the deposition of Christ's body from the cross is given in full detail, and Mary's lamentations expressing her reluctance to be separated from her son are especially influential.[6]

The long tradition of biblical exegesis and commentary is another source for the Passion meditations. The most influential commentaries were Augustine's *Tractatus in Iohannem*, Jerome's commentary on Matthew, Gregory's *Homilia in Evangelia*, and Bede's commentaries on Mark and Luke. Much of this commentary is summarized and codified in the *Glossa ordinaria*, compiled in the twelfth century. The *Glossa* was widely circulated, becoming a standard repository of biblical interpretation and the means by which much of the exegesis of the patristic age was transmitted to the later Middle Ages. Authors of devotional tracts might well have been versed in the commentaries themselves, but it is more likely that they owed their knowledge to such compendia as the *Glossa*. In keeping with the traditions of patristic exegesis, it contains relatively little in the way of concrete detail that could be used to heighten the emotional appeal of the events of the Passion. One detail with affective potential which is frequently used in later narratives is the claim that the column to which Christ was bound in the flagellation retains traces of his blood that can be seen at the present day.[7]

Many of the commonplaces of the Passion narratives probably originate in the *Glossa*. Christ's sorrow in the Garden was not from fear of his approaching Passion, but because of the loss of the wicked.[8] The fact that first Christ and then Simon the Cyrene carried the cross signifies that Christ suffered for us so that we should follow in his footsteps.[9] We are told that Calvary is incorrectly thought to be named for the baldness (*calvitia*) of

Adam.[10] Since Christ was buried in linen, Pope Sylvester decreed that the Eucharist was to be celebrated on a linen cloth.[11] The shape and measurements of Christ's tomb are given on the authority of Bede.[12] The rending of the veil of the temple signifies that the veil is removed from the hearts of believers, a veil which to this day remains in place for the Jews.[13]

Besides the sources we have mentioned, two very important works of wide popularity have great influence on the medieval Passion narratives. These are the *Historia scholastica* of Peter Comestor (d. 1179) and the *Legenda aurea* of Jacobus de Voragine (d. 1298). For the later Middle Ages the *Historia scholastica* is the standard historical account of the Passion of Christ; the *Legenda aurea* contains the standard hagiographical treatment.

The *Historia scholastica* is a retelling, with glosses, of the whole Bible; the sections on the Passion of Christ harmonize the gospel accounts and include some of the same authorities used in the *Glossa ordinaria*, for example, Jerome's commentary on Matthew and Bede's exposition of Mark and Luke.[14] Here again there is little elaboration of the incidents described in the biblical record, but one can find that inclination to literalize the Old Testament prophetic passages which is so much a trait of the later medieval Passion treatises. The best example in the *Historia scholastica* is the account of the imposition of the crown of thorns. Comestor tells his readers that it is credible to believe that the thorns drew gore from his head; there was already gore on his back as a result of the scourging; and the bloody sweat from the Garden touched the other parts of his body; so that not only his back, hands, feet, and sides but also his clothing, were covered with blood. In this way it can truly be said that Christ is the man from Edom with red-dyed garments of the messianic prophecy of Isaiah: "Quis est iste qui venit de Edom tinctis vestibus de Bosra? . . . rubrum est indumentum" ("Who is this that cometh from Edom, with dyed garments from Bosra? . . . thy apparel is red," Is 63:1, 2).[15] The association of this passage from Isaiah with the bloody body of Christ is found again and again in the Passion narratives.

Comestor further tells us that the crown was made up of sea-rushes ("juncos marinos"), the thorns of which are no less piercing than other kinds of thorns,[16] and he gives the reader information from the *Glossa* that the column of the scourging still shows signs of Christ's gore.[17] He tells us that the soldiers who guarded the crucified gave them vinegar and gall to make them die more quickly, so that they could go off duty sooner.[18] The cross on which Christ was crucified is thought to have been fifteen feet high, and the tablet that surmounted it one and a half feet high.[19] All these details are encountered again in the Passion treatises, and probably derive directly or indirectly from the *Historia scholastica*. Comestor, apparently following the *Glossa*, explains Pope Sylvester's edict about celebrating mass on a linen cloth, on the authority of Jerome denies that Adam is buried on Calvary, and cites Bede's commentary on Mark as the source of his information on the appearance and dimensions of Christ's tomb.[20]

The *Legenda aurea* of the Dominican friar Jacobus de Voragine (about 1270) is a large and extremely popular collection of saints' lives that includes a section on the Passion of Christ that influenced countless medieval treatments of the subject. J. A. W. Bennett has described the importance of this work as a source of non-biblical details, referring to it as the "chief quarry of all such materials."[21] The section on the Passion is influenced by the *Historia scholastica*, but it is important to note that it also borrows from medieval devotional writing on the Passion, notably the *Stimulus amoris* of Ekbert of Schönau, which in the *Legenda* is attributed to Bernard. The *Legenda* well illustrates the complex intertextuality of the various types of medieval writing on the Passion. Because of its enormous popularity, the *Legenda* became the means by which passages that may have originated in private devotional writing were widely disseminated, assumed the status of commonplaces, and were in turn borrowed and reborrowed by writers of meditations or treatises on the Passion. The *Legenda*, the *Historia scholastica*, and the *Glossa ordinaria* were the means by which a complex vocabulary of motifs, details, and commonplaces was diffused throughout later medieval society. Over the centuries these works and the works derived from and inspired by them, by developing and employing a highly stylized and conventional idiom, created an audience with a shared horizon of expectations (to use Jauss's term) for narratives with the topic of the Passion of Christ.[22]

There is little in the *Legenda* about the actual suffering of Christ. Following the Gospel of Nicodemus, the names of the thieves are given. Much of the section on the Passion is devoted not to the Passion itself but to the fate of Pilate, an account based largely on the *Historia scholastica*. The most affective part of the Passion story is the enumeration of the five causes of the pain of Christ. The catalogue of causes is common in Passion treatises; related to it is another frequently found enumeration, the five sheddings of Christ's blood, which is present in some manuscripts of the *Historia scholastica* and elsewhere.[23]

One of the five pains of the *Legenda* incorporates and heightens the emotion-charged language of the Good Friday reproaches.[24] Another of the causes of Christ's pain was that his body was exceedingly tender, an idea that is frequently found in the Passion narratives.[25] Another source of his pain is that he suffered in all of his senses, including touch, because he was wounded in every part of his body, in fulfillment of the words of Isaiah that from the sole of his foot to the top of his head there was no soundness in him but wounds, and bruises, and teeming sores ("A planta pedis usque ad verticem, non est in eo sanitas; vulnus, et livor, et plaga tumens," Is 1:6).[26] This passage from Isaiah is one of the most frequently cited texts in the Passion narratives, used as the biblical support for often extremely graphic descriptions of the wounds inflicted everywhere on his body in the course of the torments.[27]

The two passages in the *Legenda* taken from the Passion treatise of Ekbert of Schönau (discussed below) also refer to the torments of Christ before the crucifixion. These passages again associate a biblical text with a particular torment, and these associations become commonplace in the Passion narratives, diffused by the great popularity of the *Legenda* and of Ekbert's treatise itself. The first passage contrasts the beauty of Christ's countenance, now befouled by spitting, in the language of Psalm 44: 3, "speciosus forma prae filiis hominum" ("beautiful above the sons of men"): "facies pulchra prae filiis hominum sputis Judaeorum deturpatur" ("the face that was fairer than all the sons of men was fouled with spittle by the Jews").[28] The second passage also emphasizes the beauty of Christ's countenance and the indignities suffered at the hands of the tormentors (the biblical allusion is to I Peter 1:12, "in quem desiderant angeli prospicere" ["on which the angels desire to look"]): "vultum tuum, bone Jesu, desiderabilem, in quem desiderant angeli prospicere, sputis inquinaverunt, manibus percusserunt, velo pro delusione operuerunt, nec amaris vulneribus pepercerunt" ("Your lovely face, good Jesus, on which the angels desire to gaze, they have defiled with spittle, struck with their hands, covered with a veil in mockery, nor did they refrain from bitter wounds").[29]

In this way the *Legenda* disseminates certain descriptions of the torments of Christ that are frequently found in devotional treatises and meditations on the Passion. The account of the Passion in the *Legenda* itself is a rather unassimilated mixture of the emotionality of a Passion meditation and the objectivity of an historical account, especially at the conclusion where the merits of various sources are assessed and an effort is made to reconcile conflicts among them.

Devotional Writing in the Early Middle Ages

In turning to the earliest forms of devotional writing, much of the relatively little that survives from the period before 1100 is found in prayerbooks that seem to have been designed for private use, many of which are products of the Carolingian age. The Psalter was also commonly used for devotional as well as liturgical purposes, and Psalter manuscripts are frequently concluded by small collections of private prayers following the text of the Psalms.[30] The prayerbooks and Psalter collections often include prayers to the cross, and there is considerable evidence for devotional interest in the Passion of Christ. Although the crucifixion is a rare subject of the visual art of the early Middle Ages, as many scholars have noted, it is treated in poetry in such works as the *Carmen Paschale* of Sedulius and the Old English "Dream of the Rood." That interest in the crucifixion, however, as Barbara Raw has pointed out, is quite different in its outlook from the later medieval understanding of the importance of the Passion. The great eleventh- and twelfth-century theological reinterpretation of the meaning of the incarnation and the nature of Christ's redemption led to a sharper focus on Christ's humanity, and consequently, on his suffering, than can be found in the early Middle Ages. As Raw has put it, "Meditation on the Passion was not primarily a matter of recalling past events." In the conception of Gregory the Great, "the significance of Christ's Passion was that it was a point of transition from the seen to the unseen."[31] The written texts of the early Middle Ages dealing with the Passion, accordingly, do not emphasize the personal involvement of the reader with the figure of the suffering Christ, and there are no graphic details of the torments to stimulate an emotional response. At the same time, as Raw has shown, there are provocative suggestions that in Anglo-Saxon England certain liturgical practices and artistic representations were intended to encourage in the viewer or worshipper a sense of participating in the events of the Passion, a characteristic of so many of the Passion meditations of the high Middle Ages.[32]

Perhaps the most substantial devotional text on the Passion from the early Middle Ages is found in the *Book of Nunnaminster*, a late eighth- or early ninth-century collection of private prayers in Latin from Anglo-Saxon England, which begins with extracts from the Passion gospels and includes a series of prayers on the events of the Passion.[33] In keeping with the early medieval outlook, the theme is Christ's power as protector against enemies with little lingering on his suffering and little interest in his humanity.[34]

The profound changes in western theology and spirituality that are memorably expressed in the writings of Anselm of Canterbury in the late eleventh century have often been described, perhaps by no one more influentially than by R. W. Southern, who defines an "Anselmian transformation" in both theological outlook and devotional practice. The nature of the so-called transformation was a fresh interpretation of the Incarnation that led to a new understanding of the importance of Christ's propitiatory sacrifice of himself as a human on behalf of the whole human race. This in turn led to a heightened emphasis on Christ's suffering humanity, and an intense interest in all aspects of Christ's life in human flesh, an interest which, by extension, included the Virgin Mary as his mother.

Accompanying these changes was a new emphasis on individual spiritual growth, a greatly increased appreciation of the value of private meditation and contemplation as a means of effecting such spiritual growth, and an acknowledgment that love of God was the dynamic force that made it possible. The result was a form of spirituality that is often termed affective piety, where the emotions, especially love directed toward the divinity, are not regarded as deleterious but are esteemed as a means of opening the way toward spiritual perfection. The affective piety of the twelfth century is defined by an ardent love for Christ in his human form, compassion for the sufferings of Christ, and intense longing for union with God.[35]

These spiritual innovations originated in the traditional Benedictine monasticism of the eleventh century, as Southern has shown, but they acquire force and dynamism in the new orders of the twelfth century, particularly among the Cistercians, whose reforms responded to the pressures of the age for opportunities for solitude, meditation, and cultivation of individual spiritual growth. The full flowering of the movement is attained in the Franciscan spirituality of the thirteenth and fourteenth centuries, a spirituality defined by ardent devotion focused on the crucified and suffering Christ. The new forms of devotion were at first largely restricted to the members of religious orders, but as early as the late eleventh century changed social, political, and economic conditions led to increased leisure time for the aristocratic laity. Many of them, especially women, took advantage of opportunities to cultivate a spiritual life through the practice of private devotion based upon monastic example.

The spirituality of the eleventh and twelfth centuries led to a great demand for devotional texts that would reflect these new understandings, including manuals of practical instruction on the conduct of the contemplative life, theoretical treatises on contemplation, meditations, hymns, and prayers. The vast tide of medieval devotional literature can really be said to flow in earnest with the advent of the new spirituality of the eleventh and twelfth centuries. At the same time, these writings not only responded to the impulses of the time, they stimulated devotion, as they were often explicitly intended by their authors to do, and their diffusion spread the new devotional ideas among audiences who had access to them.

In this literary environment, the Passion of Christ is a prominent theme. In the eleventh and twelfth centuries the writings on the Passion by the Benedictines Anselm of Canterbury and John of Fécamp and by the Cistercians Bernard of Clairvaux and Aelred of Rievaulx are essential in formulating and expressing this new anthropology of Christ, which in turn lies behind the great Franciscan tradition of the thirteenth century.

Anselm of Canterbury and John of Fécamp

Anselm of Canterbury (d. 1109) composed nineteen prayers and three meditations, none of which is devoted exclusively to the Passion. Anselm's devotional writing remained continuously popular throughout the Middle Ages, and its influence can be traced in numerous later treatments of the Passion. The Passion is dealt with most thoroughly in Anselm's prayer to Christ.[36] From the point of view of later Passion meditations, Anselm's prayer is most important for its strongly affective language, expressed through rhetorical techniques and strategies (such as a series of questions addressed to the self) that later writers were quick to adopt.[37] The pathos of Christ's suffering is emphasized to a degree unprecedented in its time, but relatively restrained in comparison with later developments. Anselm does not elaborate upon the biblical account of the Passion nor does he use typological or prophetic passages from the Old Testament as a means of amplifying the descriptions of Christ's torments, even though his style is laden with biblical allusion. His imaginative reconstructions are reserved for attempts to convey the experience of Mary at the time of the Passion.

Of utmost importance in Anselm's prayer is his lively regret for not having lived to experience directly the Passion of Christ, coupled with a strong desire now to be an active participant in it: "Cur, o anima mea, te praesentem non transfixit gladius doloris acutissimi, cum ferre non posses vulnerari lancea latus tui salvatoris?" ("Why, O my soul, did not the sword of sharpest sorrow pierce you when you were there, since you could not bear that the side of your savior was wounded with a lance?").[38] It is only through memory and recollection that this is possible. In connection with these ideas, the role of Mary is especially crucial: she, in actually witnessing the events, suffered greatly, and Anselm finds in her emotional reaction to the Passion an ideal model of how one who contemplates these same events in meditation should be moved by them.[39]

We may find in the prayer the rudiments of a technique of meditation that was highly developed in later Passion narratives, that is, the imaginative reconstruction through vivid mental pictures of the events of the Passion. This technique, which was later to be known as "composition of place," is especially important in Franciscan spirituality, and has a very long history in later devotional literature.[40] The theme often closely associated with it, as in Anselm, is the compassion of the Virgin. Later meditations were increasingly to emphasize her role as a participant in the Passion, a fellow-sufferer with Christ, and to concentrate on her vicarious suffering as a representative of all humanity.[41]

Another exceptionally influential treatment of the Passion dating from about the same time as Anselm's *Orationes sive meditationes* is found in a series of meditations from the end of the eleventh century, usually attributed to Augustine in the manuscripts, but probably by the Norman monk, John of Fécamp (d. 1078). These meditations, like those of Anselm of Canterbury, enjoyed undiminished popularity throughout the later Middle Ages. The meditation on the Son incorporates a treatment of the Passion, which, although relatively brief, struck the imagination of later generations and inspired many later versions. As with Anselm, the pseudo-Augustine furnished an excellent model for the highly affective style of the later Passion meditations.

The meditation on the Son is notable for its orientation to the visual. God the father, for example, is boldly exhorted to gaze on the body of his tortured son, to consider systematically every torment. This close attention to the physical details of the suffering is often imitated in later Passion narratives. Nowhere else in the early Passion treatises can we find such graphic depictions of the suffering body, depictions which are designed to stimulate an emotional response to the Passion. To the later Middle Ages, the most memorable of these descriptions plays upon color, building upon the contrast between the gleaming whiteness of Christ's majestic naked body and the redness of the blood which disfigures it:

Candet nudatum pectus, rubet cruentum latus, tensa arent uiscera, decora languent lumina, regia pallent ora, procera rigent brachia, crura pendent marmorea, rigat terebratos pedes beati sanguinis unda.[42]

[His naked breast gleamed white, his bloody side grew red, his stretched out innards grew dry, the light of his eyes grew faint, his long arms grew stiff, his marble
legs hung down, a stream of holy blood moistened his pierced feet.]

This image of the spectacularized body of the suffering Christ was
especially appealing to later medieval taste; it was, for example, especially
popular in England. There are two Middle English verse adaptations of
these lines, and they are modified and incorporated into two of Richard
Rolle's poems on the Passion.[43]

Bernard of Clairvaux and Aelred of Rievaulx

The importance of Bernard of Clairvaux (d. 1153) in promoting devotion
to the Passion of Christ has long been recognized. Bernard left no independent treatise on the Passion, but he deals with the topic in his sermons,
most memorably in the *Sermons on the Song of Songs*, which must have been
used for devotional purposes. Bernard's great contribution is his unremit-
ting zeal for affective meditation on the Passion of Christ as a way toward
spiritual perfection. The foundation texts are in Sermons 20 and 43. In
Sermon 20, Bernard stresses that the Passion of Christ was an act of love
for humankind. When this is recognized, contemplation of the Passion inspires intense love for Christ. The love of God, according to Bernard, has
its starting place in love for Christ and devotion to his humanity. Sermon
43 contains the famous expression of Bernard's devotion to the crucified
Christ: "This is my philosophy, one more refined and interior, to know
Jesus and him crucified."[44]

Bernard's other influential treatment of the Passion is in his Sermon
for Holy Thursday (*Sermo in feria IV hebdomadae sanctae*). The sermon uses
a conventional catalogue of torments,[45] but more interesting in terms of
later developments is the use of certain biblical verses conventionally associated with the Passion. Among these is the phrase from Psalm 44, "speciosus forma prae filiis hominum" ("beautiful above the sons of men," Ps
44:3), used to draw the contrast between Christ's physical beauty and his
ugliness under the torments of the Passion, as foretold in Isaiah and Psalm
21.[46] The use of Psalm 44:3 to describe Christ's beauty, often in conjunc-
tion with the phrases from Isaiah on his ugliness, became, as noted above,
a commonplace of the Passion narratives. It is found, for example, in the
Legenda aurea and the *Stimulus amoris* of Ekbert of Schönau; variations are
present in Bonaventure, the *Meditationes vitae Christi*, and elsewhere.[47]

One of Bernard's early followers was Aelred of Rievaulx (d. 1167), whose works well illustrate the kind of affective devotional writing inspired by Bernard's example which were produced by the Cistercian community to satisfy the need for texts which would assist in the cultivation of the interior life. Aelred's *De institutis inclusarum* ("Rule of Life for a Recluse") is a general guide to the contemplative life addressed to his sister in religious orders; it ends with a meditation on the events of Christ's life, including the Passion.[48] The Passion section is relatively brief in comparison with later narratives, but it is highly emotional in tone and intensely subjective in approach. The technique of participatory meditation found in the pseudo-Augustine is advanced still further by Aelred. His meditation is full of exhortations to his readers to imagine themselves to be present at the episodes of the Passion, not merely as detached observers but strongly moved by the events they witness. They are not only to visualize the events in spirit but to participate in them by means of the imagination.[49]

In language richly textured with biblical imagery, Aelred invites the reader to dwell on Christ's physical body, bleeding and lacerated with wounds. What is encouraged is far more than a remote gaze, but a very active and tactile involvement with the body itself:

Festina, ne tardaueris, comede fauum cum melle tuo, bibe uinum tuum cum lacte tuo. Sanguis tibi in uinum uertitur ut inebrieris, in lac aqua mutatur ut nutriaris. Facta sunt tibi in petra flumina, in membris eius uulnera, et in maceria corporis eius cauerna, in quibus instar columbae latitans et deosculans singula ex sanguine eius fiant sicut uitta coccinea labia tua, et eloquium dulce.[50]

[Hasten, linger not, eat the honeycomb with your honey, drink your wine with your milk. The blood is changed into wine to gladden you, the water into milk to nourish you. From the rock streams have flowed for you, wounds have been made in his limbs, holes in the wall of his body, in which, like a dove, you may hide while you kiss them one by one. Your lips, stained with his blood, will become like a scarlet ribbon and your word sweet.]

A convention of patristic exegesis held that the blood and water flowing from Christ's side stood for the sacraments of baptism and the eucharist, but here we have a kind of sensualized version of a eucharistic meal informed by the language of the Song of Songs, which anticipates later eucharistic devotion to the *corpus Christi*. The sensuality of the passage is apparent. The meditator enters into the bleeding wounds of the body of Christ, kisses them, and stains her lips with his blood. Highly physical and affective devotion to the wounds of Christ characterizes much of the piety of the later Middle Ages, but the elements of this devotion can be found as early as the middle of the twelfth century, as this example from Aelred shows.[51]

For the most part, Aelred adheres closely to the gospel accounts for details of the Passion. Perhaps reflecting the influence of the Gospel of Nicodemus, most of his elaborations are reserved for the actions of Mary, Joseph of Arimathea, and Nicodemus after the death of Christ. Aelred reports that it was Joseph's task to draw out the nails and free the hands and feet of Christ, a detail found in later narratives, and that Nicodemus rubbed ointment on Christ's limbs.[52] The pathos of the scene is heightened by Aelred's call for the meditator to clasp in spirit the corpse of Christ, suggesting actions of a kind that later authors will not hesitate to assign to Mary herself.[53]

The *De institutis inclusarum* is an important document in the history of the medieval Passion narrative. Its pathetic style, its affective use of biblical allusion, and its rich store of concrete, visual representations make it an outstanding example of twelfth-century literary craft, and a model that was often emulated. The meditative parts circulated independently and are sometimes found in manuscript collections of Anselm's *Orationes sive meditationes*; the whole treatise was often attributed to Augustine or Bernard. Bonaventure quotes from the meditative part in his *Lignum vitae*.[54] There is some evidence that the *De institutis inclusarum* was widely read in fourteenth-century England when it was translated into Middle English.[55]

Ekbert of Schönau, Stephen of Sawley, Edmund of Abingdon

Among the works of the twelfth century that had profound and far-reaching influence on the Passion narratives of the following century was a text written not by a Cistercian but by a traditional Benedictine monk, Ekbert of Schönau (d. 1184). Ekbert was the brother of the more widely known Elizabeth of Schönau, whose visions he recorded.[56] His *Stimulus amoris* is a rich repository of themes relating to the Passion that was drawn on by many later writers. It seems to have been a great favorite of the Franciscans in particular. As we shall see shortly, Bonaventure adapts extracts from it in his *Lignum vitae*, and it is used extensively in the *Meditationes vitae Christi* of the pseudo-Bonaventure. In the manuscripts the work is variously entitled *Stimulus dilectionis* (in the earliest manuscripts), *Stimu-*

lus amoris, *Stimulus caritatis*, or *Meditaciones de passione Christi*, and from at least as early as the middle of the thirteenth century it was assigned to Anselm or Bernard, acquiring wide circulation and exerting vast influence under the borrowed prestige of their names.[57]

Ekbert's *Stimulus* is a complete meditative life of Christ, beginning with the incarnation and ending with the resurrection, which is small in scale in comparison to the examples of the late thirteenth and fourteenth centuries, but still a considerable expansion beyond most previous devotional accounts. His highly affective style is dense with biblical allusion and reminiscent of Anselm in its reliance upon apostrophe, direct exhortation to the reader, and interior dialogue, often in carefully balanced rhymed periods, all of which are devices designed to create a mood of intimacy with the reader and to heighten the emotional effect.

Ekbert does not rely as heavily as Aelred on highly concrete visual representations. In the important chapter on arousing the soul to devotion through memory of Christ's torments however, Ekbert calls upon his soul to contemplate the man of sorrows, to gaze on him whom the language of the gospel brings before us as though he were present before us.[58] His particularized enumeration of the torments is punctuated by repeated exhortations to gaze on the mangled body, a body which, as Ekbert says, was exceptionally beautiful, but is now exceptionally deformed:[59] "Iste formosus prae filiis hominum, quam deformis prae filiis hominum factus est!" ("He who was fair beyond the sons of men, how deformed has he been made beyond the sons of men!").[60] Christ is the leper of Isaiah ("quasi vir leprosus"), the abortion cast from the womb of his mother ("Et tanquam abortivum, quod projicitur a vulva, sic projectus est ab utero matris suae infelicis synagogae" ["And as an abortion cast from the womb, so was he cast from the womb of his mother the unfortunate synagogue"]).[61]

Ekbert's treatise includes an allegorical crucifixion based principally on the four cardinal virtues that suggests the stigmata of Francis and the seemingly more literal conformity to the Passion espoused by the later Franciscans: "Confige illi manus meas, et pedes meos, et totam formam passionis tuae servo tuo indue" ("Fix my hands and feet to it, and clothe your servant with the whole form of your passion").[62] Ekbert's allegory looks forward to more elaborate later examples, such as those found in Bonaventure's *Lignum vitae* and *Vitis mystica*. Ekbert also anticipates the late medieval interest in the instruments of the Passion, the *Arma Christi*, the subject of a widely popular devotion especially in the late fourteenth and fifteenth centuries.[63]

Although in the thirteenth century the Franciscan contribution is paramount, two treatments of the Passion important for their use of affective language and pictorial meditative technique are found in the works of the Cistercian Stephen of Sawley (d. 1252), an English follower of Aelred of Rievaulx, and in an influential treatise by Edmund of Abingdon, Archbishop of Canterbury (d. 1240).[64]

Stephen of Sawley follows Aelred in evoking vivid mental images of scenes from the gospels, urging meditation on them as though one were actually present at the scene ("quasi te praesentem interfuisse senseris").[65] Stephen's fullest account of the Passion is in his treatise on the recitation of the Divine Office, *De informatione mentis circa Psalmodiam diei et noctis*, which includes a brief meditation on the life and Passion of Christ organized around the canonical hours. This will be a pattern of meditation found in other Passion meditations, as we shall see. As he does in the *Speculum novitii*, Stephen exploits the techniques of pictorial representation to heighten immediacy and stimulate an emotional response, exhorting his readers to visualize the actual events in their own meditations.[66] Stephen incorporates many commonplace images and biblical allusions that by the middle of the thirteenth century are already part of the standard vocabulary of the Latin Passion narrative. For example, in describing the cruelty with which Christ was dragged from Annas to Caiphas with no word of human consolation, Stephen is reminded of Isaiah, observing that in this instance Christ truly trod the wine press alone.[67]

The *Speculum ecclesie* of Edmund of Abingdon reveals a number of traits that are common in the Passion narratives of the thirteenth century. The *Speculum*, a general treatise on attaining spiritual perfection within the religious life, has a complex textual history. It was probably written first in Latin, then translated into Anglo-Norman French, and then retranslated into Latin, possibly in the fourteenth century. This latter recension is known as the *Speculum ecclesie* to distinguish it from the earlier *Speculum religiosorum*. Both Latin versions include a substantial section on contemplating God, first in his humanity, and then in his deity. The chapters on contemplation of God in his humanity are organized around the canonical hours, as in the treatise of Stephen of Sawley on Psalmody. The editor of the *Speculum* points out that Edmund's tender devotion to the humanity of Christ seems indebted to the Cistercian tradition.[68]

Following the Cistercian example, Edmund uses visual images to evoke the pathos of the events of the Passion. His account of the Passion itself is made more graphic by reference to Old Testament verses which are seen to be literally fulfilled in Christ's sufferings. In describing the scourging he observes, in the words of Isaiah, that Christ was so cruelly beaten that from the top of his head to the sole of his foot there was no soundness in him.[69] The compassion of Mary is a principal theme. There is a sympathetic attempt to imagine what her sorrows might have been, using the affective language of the Song of Songs. To convey the depth of Mary's suffering, Edmund quotes a quatrain in English, a use of the vernacular that is unusual within the context of the Latin devotional tradition.[70] Edmund's treatise, like Aelred's *De institutis inclusarum*, acquired renewed popularity in the fourteenth and fifteenth centuries, in part, no doubt, because its affectivity was appealing to the taste of the period.

Bonaventure, the Franciscans, and the Thirteenth Century

In the thirteenth century, Franciscan spirituality carried devotion to the suffering humanity of Christ to new heights. The chief literary products of this devotion were written by Bonaventure (d. 1274), whose work had a profound and lasting influence, not just on Franciscans but on all later medieval authors who wrote on the Passion.[71] His two great treatises on the Passion are the *Lignum vitae*, a meditation on the life, death, and resurrection of Christ, and the *Vitis mystica*, or "tractatus de passione domini." Both of these works are organized around detailed allegories. The *Lignum vitae* uses the metaphor of the tree to refer to the events of the life of Christ, dividing the meditation into twelve fruits in groups of three. In the *Vitis mystica*, Bonaventure takes Christ's words from the Gospel of John, "I am the true vine" (Jn 15:1) and constructs a symbolic allegory of Christ as vine by relating episodes of the Passion to the cultivation, pruning, and tying up of the vine, showing Christ's likeness to the leaves and the flowers of the vine.

The meditation of the *Lignum vitae* is a well-stocked storehouse of earlier commonplaces on the Passion, with notable borrowings from Bernard and Ekbert of Schönau. The three parts of the book are on the mysteries of the Origin of Christ, the Passion, and the glorification. Taken together, they are a meditation on the whole life of Christ, from his incarnation and birth through the Passion, resurrection, ascension, and second coming. The prologue begins with the words of Paul, "Christo confixus sum cruci" ("With Christ I am nailed to the Cross," Gal 2:19), and expounds the characteristically Franciscan ideal of perfectly conforming one-self to the suffering savior.

The affective purpose of the meditation is also spelled out: the *Lig-num* was written to enkindle love for the crucified Christ.[72] To stimulate the emotions, Bonaventure relies on the techniques of "vivid representa-tion" he commended to his readers as a meditative strategy. The work has many concrete, visual evocations of the events of the Passion, employing an intimate, affective, apostrophic style, marked by familiar addresses to Christ himself not unlike the passage on the spitting and the apostrophe to Christ borrowed from Ekbert.[73]

In his account of the crucifixion, Bonaventure extends the gospel in a direction carried further in many later treatments of the Passion. The nail-ing to the cross is described in detail: Christ is hurled to the ground, and pushed, pulled, and stretched by his tormentors, "as though they would stretch a hide."[74] We have already noted some earlier uses of the stretching idea in connection with the verse of Psalm 21, "They have numbered all my bones," which is not, however, quoted here. A more active portrayal of the stretching of Christ's body becomes commonplace, and in later treat-ments, for example in the *Meditationes vitae Christi*, Christ's body is pulled in order to fit nail holes made too far apart.

Bonaventure gazes upon the tortured body of Christ, which is de-scribed in familiar biblical phrases. Christ suffers "from the sole of his foot to the top of his head," in the words of Isaiah (Is 1:6), and the bruised and wounded flesh of his naked body make him look like a leper covered with open sores, appearing thus literally to fulfill Isaiah's prophecy that Christ would be thought of as a leper, "quasi leprosum" (Is 53:4). The literaliza-tion of this phrase, "quasi leprosus," usually applied to Christ's appearance after the scourging, as here, becomes a commonplace in later medieval Passion treatises, and as James Marrow has shown, it provides the textual underpinning for a standard iconographic commonplace of the visual arts as well.[75]

Bonaventure's treatment of the Passion is notable for its attention to the physical details of Christ's suffering, bleeding body, deformed by pain and injury, an attention verging upon obsession. Bonaventure follows Ekbert in using the phrase from Psalm 44:3, "speciosus forma prae filiis hominum," to contrast the beauty of Christ with his present ugliness and deformity as he hangs on the cross moments before death.[76] The wounds of Christ also receive special notice. The outpouring of blood and water from the wound in Christ's side is given the conventional interpretation as a symbolic representation of Christ's institution of the sacraments of Baptism and the Eucharist, but the hole in the side is also compared to the dove-house of the Song of Songs, as in Aelred, and we are encouraged to apply our mouths to it to "draw waters with joy out of the Savior's fountains," as Isaiah has it.[77] Jesus is described as covered with blood from his sufferings, "cruentatus enim Christus Dominus sanguine proprio,"[78] and the four sheddings of Christ's blood are specified: the bloody sweat in the garden, the scourging and crowning with thorns, the nails, and the spear. Enumerations similar to this one are often found in other Passion narratives, usually with the addition of the circumcision, and form the basis of popular devotional exercises on the wounds of Christ.

In the *Lignum vitae*, just as Christ's bruised and lacerated body was shown literally to appear as a leper's in realization of Isaiah, so does Christ's naked body covered with blood make his "apparel" truly red, objectifying Isaiah's prophecy of the man in the wine-press and the story of Joseph's bloody tunic: "vestem pontificalem habuit rubricatam, quatenus vere rubrum appareret indumentum ipsius, et vestimenta eius quasi calcantium in torculari. Et sic, vero Ioseph in veterem dimisso cisternam, tunica ipsius intincta sanguine hoedi" ("He wore a priestly robe of scarlet; his apparel was truly red, and his garments were like theirs that tread in the wine press. Like that of a true Joseph thrown into an abandoned cistern, his tunic was steeped as in the blood of a goat").[79] In the last section of the *Lignum*, on the mystery of the glorification, Bonaventure's careful effort to portray the deformed and bloody body in the early part of the treatise is built upon to make a sharpened contrast with that body and the glorified body of the resurrected Christ, now restored in beauty.[80]

In describing Christ's sufferings, the role of Mary as a co-sufferer is an important theme, as it is in many later Passion meditations. Bonaventure is among the earliest writers to express Mary's mental anguish as she responds to the physical punishments and sees into the depths of Christ's tormented soul with the eyes of the mind.[81] The idea that Mary's feeling for the pain of Christ was unique is important in the Passion treatises, representing one of the means by which she mediates between man and God. Her interior suffering, both as an observer of the Passion and as a person granted a special insight into Christ's inner agonies, is held by Bonaventure to be far more severe than if she had suffered in her own body.[82] Other writers will develop this theme in such a way that emphasizes the special quality of Mary's experience.[83]

The *Vitis mystica* is a treatise on the Passion similarly organized around a controlling allegory, that of Christ as the true vine (Jn 15:1). Included are meditations on the seven words of Christ on the cross, which are associated with the leaves of the vine, and on the sheddings of Christ blood, which are counted as seven.[84] In the *Vitis mystica* there is greater emphasis on forming mental pictures of the Passion events, on seeing Christ vividly with the eyes of the mind.[85] The style is vigorously affective, personal, and intimate in the manner of Anselm; the imagery is densely biblical, and the fundamental allegorical conceit is worked out in painstaking detail, especially at the beginning of the treatise. Just as a fruit-bearing vine is pruned, for example, so did Jesus suffer circumcision; the gnarled trunk of the vine is Christ's body twisted and deformed by the suffering of the Passion, and so on. As does Ekbert, Bonaventure reminds us that Christ suffered not just on the day of his death but throughout his whole life.[86]

The first chapters elaborate on many of the Old Testament verses traditionally held to foreshadow the Passion. Christ is that most abject of men of Isaiah, as well as the man who has trodden the wine press alone.[87] He is "fairer in beauty than the sons of men," in the familiar phrase of Psalm 44, but, as to the outward man, in the words of Isaiah, "there is no beauty in him" because of his sufferings in the Passion.[88] He is the brave giant running his course mentioned in the Psalms.[89] In his great suffering, the words of Jeremiah are fulfilled, as traditional exegesis held, and as the Passion narratives repeat: "O all ye that pass by the way, attend, and see if there be any sorrow like to my sorrow!"[90]

Bonaventure stresses the desirability of conforming to the Passion of Christ, participating in his suffering so that we may regain the image of his divinity.[91] He forces our attention again and again on the deformed body of Christ, which is repeatedly seen as torn, disfigured, ravaged, covered with gore, and made ugly through pain.[92] That body, however, is not meant to be contemplated at a distance; instead we are invited to embrace it, in language which is physical, intense, and reciprocal: "amplectamur vulneratum nostrum, cuius impii agricolae foderunt manus et pedes, latus et cor; oremusque, ut cor nostrum adhuc durum et impoenitens amoris sui vinculo constringere et iaculo vulnerare dignetur" ("let us embrace our wounded Christ whose hands and feet and side and heart were pierced by the wicked vine-tenders; let us pray that he may deign to tie our hearts, now so wild and impenitent, with the bond of love, and wound them with love's spear").[93]

Bonaventure's descriptions of the scourging, the imposition of the crown of thorns, the buffeting, and the crucifixion itself are marked by intense pathos with many elaborations of the gospel narrative.[94] For example, Christ not only wears a scarlet cloak, as in the gospels, but his whole body is turned scarlet by the bloody sweat, the scourging, and the crucifixion.[95] As in the prophecy of Isaiah, there is no beauty or comeliness in him, and he is thought of as a leper.[96] We are asked to consider the causes of his bodily disfigurement.[97] We see no beauty in his face and there is no trace of beauty in his martyred body; in fact, according to Bonaventure's novel interpretation, Christ is stripped of his clothes, not merely to humiliate him, but so that the meditator may see the ravages done to his body.[98] Placed on the cross, his whole body is shattered, nearly drained of blood, and marked by the many wounds of the scourges and the nails.[99]

Christ's crucified body is described as lifted up and stretched out as a vine on a trellis.[100] Here Bonaventure speaks of the deformation of the body as a fulfillment of Psalm 21, as Bernard had done in his Holy Thursday sermon:

Cancellantur ligna crucis, elevatur in illam, distenditur brachiis et toto corpore vitis nostra, bonus Iesus. In tantum enim in cruce distentus fuit, ut numerari possent omnia membra eius; ita siquidem dixit per Prophetam: 'Foderunt manus meas et pedes meos, dinumeraverunt omnia ossa mea'; quasi diceret: tantum distentus sum dextrorsum, sinistrorsum et a summo usque ad deorsum, ut corpore meo in modum pellis tympani distento, facile possent dinumerari omnia ossa mea.[101]

[The beams of the gibbet are crossed; our vine, the good Jesus, is lifted up on it; his arms and his whole body are forcibly stretched out—with such distorting violence have they been extended that all the joints of his frame have been counted. For the prophet says, "They have dug my hands and feet, they have numbered all my bones"; as if saying: They have stretched me so much to the right and to the left and up and down that my body is as taut as the skin of a drum, and that all my bones could be easily counted.]

In the Passion narratives the stretching of Christ's body generated a number of comparisons that became conventional, as Pickering has shown, including, as here, the taut body as a drum-head, and the image of the harp, which Bonaventure uses in the following chapter: the wood of the cross is the frame of the harp and the body of Christ extended upon it represents the tightened strings.[102]

The final section of the *Vitis mystica* is in many ways the most metaphoric and that which seems most to anticipate the devotional practices of the later Middle Ages in its intense and systematic concentration on the blood and wounds of Christ and the heart of Jesus. We are exhorted to contemplate the wounds of Christ, at last entering the wound in his side and attaining his heart.[103]

Bonaventure's treatises represent a high point in the medieval literature of the Passion. Writers of later generations found in Bonaventure's mysticism, his vivid descriptions, and his fervent expression of love for Christ, much that they sought to imitate in their own writing. Perhaps the greatest, and certainly the most popular, of the works on the Passion belonging to the Bonaventuran and Franciscan tradition is the *Meditationes vitae Christi*, a work doubtfully attributed to the Italian friar John de Caulibus, which quite certainly arose from the Franciscan milieu of Northern Italy at the end of thirteenth century or the very beginning of the fourteenth.[104] In the Middle Ages, the work was almost always attributed to Bonaventure himself, and one modern scholar has proposed that the chapters on the Passion are his genuine work.[105] The *Meditationes vitae Christi* was intended in the first place for a Franciscan nun, or community of nuns, as the Prologue makes plain, and it follows in a tradition of treatises of spiritual guidance for women written by men that deal principally or incidentally with devotion to the Passion.

The *Meditationes vitae Christi* is much larger and more comprehensive than any previous narrative of the Passion or of the whole life of Christ, most of which are relatively brief (the *Vitis mystica* of Bonaventure, for example, takes up about sixty pages in a modern octavo edition). The extended scope of the *Meditationes* reflects the general late medieval taste for compendious treatises, which in the case of the life of Christ culminates in the monumentally proportioned *Vita Christi* of Ludolphus of Saxony. The Passion of Christ takes up some eleven of the one hundred chapters of the *Meditationes*.[106] From the early fourteenth century these chapters circulated separately as a self-contained treatise on the Passion, and it is to them that I will chiefly refer in the following discussion.

The chapters of the *Meditationes* on the Passion are organized according to the canonical hours, in a pattern which by this time had become conventional. There are frequent exhortations to visualize the scene in the mind's eye as if one were actually present at the events.[107] There is a free supply of additional dialogue, non-biblical speeches most often placed in the mouth of Mary. The style is more historical, less affective and apostrophic than that of Ekbert or Bonaventure. The author abandons the carefully wrought allegorical frameworks of Bonaventure in favor of a cogent, historical narrative sequence. Nevertheless, there is no lack of emotional appeal and direct address to the reader; like Bonaventure and Ekbert, the author relies on vivid concrete description often grounded in familiar typological imagery from the Bible to convey a sense of pathos surrounding the events.

Much of the treatment of the Passion draws on the earlier tradition. Christ's thirst on the cross, for example, was for the salvation of mankind;[108] the column to which he was bound at the flagellation still shows traces of his blood;[109] the dimensions of the cross and of the tomb are given from Bede by way of the *Historia scholastica*;[110] his body suffers in all its members in accordance with the verse from Isaiah that "From the top of his head to the sole of his foot there was no soundness in him."[111] After the scourging, the prophecy of Isaiah is fulfilled that he was thought of as a leper and there was no beauty in his form.[112]

Some of the most emotionally charged descriptions in the meditations are of the events preceding the crucifixion, where the author freely borrows from Bonaventure and Ekbert and pushes their heightened style to new limits, as in the account of the scourging:

Spoliatur ergo dominus, et ad columnam ligatur, et diversimode flagellatur. Stat nudus coram omnibus juvenis elegans et verecundus, speciosus forma prae filiis hominum, suscipit spurcissimorum flagella dura et dolorosa, caro illa innocentissima, et tenerissima, mundissima, et pulcherrima. Flos omnis carnis, et totius humanae naturae, repletur livoribus et fracturis. Fluit undique regius sanguis de omnibus partibus corporis, superadditur, reiteratur, et spissatur livor super livorem, et fractura super fracturam, quousque tam tortoribus, quam inspectoribus fatigatis, solvi jubetur.[113]

[The lord is therefore stripped and bound to a column and scourged in various ways. He stands naked before them all, in youthful grace and shamefacedness, beautiful in form above the sons of men, and sustains the harsh and grievous scourges on his innocent, tender, pure, and lovely flesh The flower of all flesh and of all human nature is covered with bruises and cuts. The royal blood flows all about, from all parts of his body. Again and again, repeatedly, closer and closer, it is done, bruise upon bruise, and cut upon cut, until not only the torturers but also the spectators are tired; then he is ordered untied.]

The meditations articulate an important rationale for use of graphic descriptions of this kind. These descriptions may indeed offend our sensibilities, but they are justified, even necessary, in order for us to recognize the depth of suffering Christ undertook for us: "non enim debet nos taedere ista cogitare, quae ipsum dominum non taeduit tolerare" ("We must not be repelled by those things that our lord Jesus did not hesitate to bear").[114]

Among the most influential chapters of the *Meditationes* are those describing the crucifixion, where two alternative means of fixing Christ to the cross are given. In the first version, Christ is forced to ascend the cross by means of a ladder, whereupon his arms are stretched as far as possible and his hands nailed to the cross. In the alternate version, Christ is stretched and fixed to the cross while it is on the ground.[115] In both accounts, the extreme stretching of the body is emphasized, and we are given a conventional comparison of the Passion meditations, that Christ's body is so taut that all its bones can be numbered, as foretold by the prophecy of the Psalms (Ps 21:18). The added nuance that only his head could be moved is occasionally found in later treatments of the Passion.[116] One of the most memorable details concerns the final stripping of Christ before the crucifixion itself. When his garments are pulled off, the wounds of the flagellation are reopened because the clothing has adhered to the flesh.[117] In Richard Rolle and other writers who were intrigued by this detail, the clothing stuck to Christ's body is pulled off so cruelly that gobbets of flesh are torn away with it.[118]

The *Meditationes* include a narrative of the events near and shortly after the death of Christ that enlarges upon the gospel account and greatly heightens its pathos. The emphasis is on the psychology of the suffering Mary, whose inner thoughts and emotions are put before us in detail, and whose speeches, monologues, and soliloquies are reported at length, with careful attempts to delineate the nuances of suffering.[119] The deposition is described in pictorial, almost clinical detail. For example, we are told that Joseph has difficulty in extracting the long heavy nail from Christ's hand because it is fixed so firmly in the wood, and he fears pressing on the hand of Christ.[120] As in the Marian lament beginning "Quis dabit," which we shall consider shortly, Mary is reluctant for her son to be buried, expressing the wish to be buried along with him.[121] Finally there is a long and emotional lament directed at his dead and disfigured body.[122] The augmented role of Mary in the events after the death of Christ rewrites the gospel to give priority to the mother-son relationship, creating a climate that allows for the extravagant display of intimate affection.

The *Meditationes vitae Christi* brings us to the very end of the thirteenth century, if not beyond it. Three briefer treatises, of uncertain authorship and problematic origin, achieve wide circulation in this century and are responsible for disseminating a greatly expanded, emotionally heightened role of Mary in the Passion.

The three Latin treatises are known by various medieval titles, confusingly and mistakenly attributed to Bernard, Anselm, Augustine, or Bonaventure. The treatises are the *Planctus beatae Mariae* (beginning "Quis dabit capiti meo aquam"), thought to be by Ogier of Locedio (1136–1214); the *Dialogus beatae Mariae et Anselmi de Passione domini* (beginning "Dic mihi carissima domina"), included among Anselm's work in the Patrologia Latina; and the *Meditatio de passione Christi per septem diei horas* (beginning "Septies in die laudem dixi tibi"), printed among the spurious works of Bede in the Patrologia.[123] If the attribution proposed for the "Quis dabit" lament holds true, then that work ante-dates Bonaventure and belongs to the end of the twelfth or the beginning of the thirteenth century. The meditation of the pseudo-Bede may be as late as the early fourteenth century, or as early as the twelfth.[124] The three works, especially the "Quis dabit" lament, have very complex textual histories with a number of widely different recensions surviving from different periods. They seem, however, to have acquired the form in which they became popular and influential during the course of the thirteenth century. Given the textual conditions, questions of borrowing and influence become very complex. For example, the *Meditationes vitae Christi* has some striking similarities to the lament "Quis dabit" down to nearly identical speeches spoken by Mary after the death of Christ. Yet it is possible that the *Meditationes* influenced a later recension of the lament, rather than borrowed from an earlier work. The editor of the chapters on the Passion has also claimed to find the influence of the treatises of the pseudo-Anselm and the pseudo-Bede upon them.[125] It is also worth remembering, given the large number of commonplaces associated with the Passion and their wide diffusion, that two works might well draw from common sources. The *Legenda aurea*, for example, seems to have been responsible for mediating many of the conventional associations and comparisons, just as Bonaventure transmitted much of what later writers borrowed from Ekbert of Schönau.

In light of these circumstances, it seems most useful to conceive of these Latin treatises on the Passion as the products of a productive and complex textual community built upon mutual relationship and interdependence in which many works reveal the textual traces of many other works, and in which the texts themselves are not static, but, attributed to various authors, subject to revision, recension, and modification, as noted in the previous chapter.[126] That textual environment can be described as clerical, and more specifically as religious, sustained by the ideals of Franciscan and Cistercian spirituality. In time, the period of creativity extends from about 1225 to about 1350, and in space from Northern Italy, through France and the Rhineland, possibly to include England and the

Low Countries. Most of the work seems to have been done in the second half of the thirteenth century, or perhaps a few decades into the fourteenth. A good boundary mark is furnished by the *Vita Christi* of Ludolphus of Saxony, written some time between 1348 and 1377, a work that codifies the previous traditions for the fifteenth century, when most creative impulses were channeled into the vernaculars and an enormous effort is made, by way of translation and later through printing, to transmit the Latin tradition to an audience that included an increasing number of lay people, both men and women.

The first of the three works belonging to the literary milieu I have described is the lamentation on the Passion of pseudo-Bernard ("Quis dabit"). Henri Barré has suggested that its genuine author was the north Italian Cistercian Ogier of Locedio (1136–1214). This may be true, but in some ways it hardly matters. The popularity of the work dates from about the middle of the thirteenth century, to judge from the manuscript evidence. The surviving manuscripts are from most parts of western Europe, and the treatise seems to have been especially popular in France and England. The lament, indeed, was among the most popular religious works of the entire later Middle Ages, as shown by the large number of manuscripts that survive dating from the thirteenth century onwards, citations in medieval library catalogues, and the like. In popularity it matches or exceeds the *Meditationes vitae Christi*, a work with which it was often associated in the manuscripts. The work lacks a fixed text and is found in several recensions. Partly because of its wide diffusion, it has a complicated textual history, and there has been, until recently, no satisfactory edition of such an important work.[127]

The "Quis dabit" is a fictional *planctus* placed in the mouth of the Virgin Mary. It is an outstanding representative of a Marian lament, of which there are many examples in medieval prose and poetry in both Latin and the vernacular.[128] The common theme of these laments is the compassion of the Virgin for the suffering of Christ, a theme which, as we have seen, is developed to varying degrees in other Passion narratives. The lament differs from the other works discussed so far in that it is an imaginary dialogue between the meditator and the Virgin. She responds to the meditator's questions about the Passion by explaining the torments from her point of view.[129] The canonical gospels provide the narrative framework, but there is no reluctance to supplement the biblical account. The elaborations are not often justified as the fulfillment of Old Testament prophecies, but assert their claim on authenticity because they are reported by an eye-witness, so to speak, in the person of Mary. This is the kind of authentication that supports such visionary accounts of the Passion as those of Bridget of Sweden, Angela of Foligno, or Julian of Norwich.

The work depends heavily upon emotional appeals, with a dynamic interplay between Mary and the meditator, as each of them responds to the suffering of Christ; the meditator is moved, in turn, by the suffering of Mary on account of the suffering of Christ. The style is affective to the point of being overwrought, with exuberant use of apostrophes (*exclamatio*) and rhetorical questions. Nearly half the work is devoted to Mary's conduct after the death of Christ. The Gospel of Nicodemus lies behind this part of the treatise, but these scenes are freshly described and realized in such a way as to carry the pathos to the highest level possible. The chief purpose of the work is to move the reader to an emotional response to the human suffering of Christ, but perhaps more importantly to stimulate feelings of compassion for the predicament of Mary as a witness to the torture of her own son. The narrative is not so much a sequenced arrangement of historical event as it is a series of personal laments in response to a selective number of incidents of the Passion. It is worth noting that the work appears to be, like the *Meditationes vitae Christi*, directed to a nun or to a community of nuns.

The work known as the *Dialogus beatae Mariae et Anselmi de Passione domini* is in the same tradition of Marian lament as the "Quis dabit." It was likewise a work that acquired considerable influence, although the surviving manuscript evidence suggests that it was not nearly so popular as the "Quis dabit" lament.[130] The oldest manuscript seems to have been written in the German Rhineland at the end of the thirteenth century or the beginning of the fourteenth. Most of the manuscripts are fourteenth century and later, and it is unlikely that the treatise is much older than the last quarter of the thirteenth century.

The *Dialogus* partially depends on "Quis dabit," which may have been its immediate formal model. There are a few identical phrases, and certain biblical phrases are used in identical contexts.[131] Mary's behavior after the death of Christ is similarly depicted in both treatises. The *Dialogus* also reveals the direct or indirect influence of other Passion treatises, particularly the *Stimulus amoris* of Ekbert .[132]

Despite these similarities, the two treatises are very different, in tone, style, outlook, and organization. The *Dialogus* speaks at the beginning of sighs, but the general tone is much more restrained and the style much less emotional than the "Quis dabit" lament. "Anselm" is a very passive interlocutor. The *Dialogus* is more historical and objective in emphasis. Long extracts are taken verbatim from the gospel accounts, and several details come from the *Historia scholastica* and other historical sources.[133] Much information is given about the manner of the crucifixion itself, to supply a lack in the gospels, as Mary explains to Anselm.[134] Many of the details are found in other treatments of the Passion, particularly the stretching of Christ to fit the cross and the associations with Psalm 21.[135] The deposition from the cross is also described at length, following the example of the "Quis dabit" lament. As in the "Quis dabit," Mary holds tightly to the body, begging to be buried with it.[136]

The treatise printed in the Patrologia Latina edition of Bede as the *De meditatione passione Christi per septem diei horas libellus* was a popular work in the later Middle Ages, surviving in many manuscripts, the oldest of which are no earlier than the fourteenth century. The evidence of the manuscripts suggests that the *Libellus* was more widely disseminated than the *Dialogus*, but not nearly so popular as the "Quis dabit" lament. The work is often attributed to Bernard, less commonly to Augustine or Bonaventure, and despite its inclusion among the *spuria* of Bede in the Patrologia does not appear to have been attributed to him in the manuscripts of the fourteenth and early fifteenth centuries.[137]

André Wilmart thought that the work was Cistercian in origin; compared with the exuberance of some of the Franciscan treatises, it has a certain sobriety that may have led Wilmart to his conclusion.[138] It is a systematic, schematically organized manual showing how to participate spiritually in the Passion of Christ. More attention is paid to the art of contemplation than in the many treatises devoted principally to recounting or augmenting the gospel events. It shares some of the same concerns for the theory of contemplation and the practice of meditation that are found in the beginning sections of the *Meditationes vitae Christi*. As is clear from the prefatory material and other internal evidence, its primary audience was the cloistered religious: whether male or female, or both, cannot be determined. Following the pattern of many earlier Passion narratives, it is organized around the canonical hours, with certain events of the Passion allocated for meditation during each of the seven hours. The *Libellus* makes clear that participation in the Passion of Christ is in spirit not in the flesh, thus differing in outlook from some contemporary treatises where participation in the spirit and in the flesh are fused, or the distinction is not always clearly made. Even in this treatise, however, the possibility is held out that on some occasions, participation in the Passion may be literal as well as spiritual through the voluntary infliction of pain with the aim of eventually being conformed to Christ in glory.[139] Following what by this time are well established Cistercian and Franciscan pathways, the practice of visual meditation is espoused.[140]

The use of imaginary dialogue and hypothetical speeches produces an atmosphere of immediacy. Sometimes the conversation is between the meditator and Christ, at other times between Christ and the witnesses to the Passion. The author constantly exhorts the meditator to be moved by the events, suggesting what he or she might or ought to say inwardly in response to them. These speeches are usually highly emotional, amply furnished with rhetorical question, apostrophe, and *exclamatio*, directed both to the meditator and to Christ.[141]

The author is fairly scrupulous about calling attention to the hypothetical nature of his embellishments of the gospel narrative, which, as is typical, are used to heighten the pathos of the suffering. We are told that in addition to the spitting and buffeting of the gospel, some tormentors pulled on Christ's beard and others dragged him by the hair and trampled him on the ground.[142] These details are found frequently in other late medieval Passion meditations.[143] Christ's feet were broken to pieces when he was rushed back and forth to Pilate because, we are told, neither he nor the disciples wore shoes.[144] We are also given the detail, found in other Passion treatises, of the pain caused to Christ when his clothing, which had stuck to his body because of the blood from the scourging, was ripped off.[145] The crucifixion is described in graphic detail. The nails are thick and dull and immediately cause profuse bleeding. Mary covers his nakedness with her veil, as in many accounts, and much emphasis is placed on the cruelty with which Christ was lifted, drawn, and stretched on the cross, although there is no specific allusion to the verse of the Passion psalm on the numbering of bones (Ps 21:18) that validated these actions in so many narratives.[146]

The theme of participation in the events of the Passion is taken up in the report of the buffeting and scourging, and continues throughout the treatise.[147] When Christ is left alone at night the meditator is encouraged to kiss his hands and feet as well as the chains that bound him, and to ask that Christ rest his head on his shoulder.[148] The most striking example is the literalization of the injunction of Christ to take up one's cross and follow him (Mc 8:34), which is seen in Mary's pathetic attempts to carry the cross for her son.[149] The treatise ends with the deposition from the cross and the burial of the body of Christ.[150] Compared to several other accounts of these scenes, notably those of the *Meditationes vitae Christi* and the "Quis dabit" lament, the descriptions of the *Libellus* seem exceptionally brief, even perfunctory.

The Fourteenth Century

The treatises we have been discussing are the foundation texts of a tradition of Passion narrative that takes shape in the course of the thirteenth century. In the next century Franciscan attention to the Passion continues in the *Stimulus amoris*, and there is growing interest in compendious *vitae Christi* (lives of Christ) which naturally include substantial sections on the Passion.

The *Stimulus amoris*, attributed to the Franciscan James of Milan, is one of those devotional works with a typically complicated textual history. The original core of the work was probably written by James at the end of the thirteenth century. In the fourteenth century, the work was considerably augmented by the addition of new material, including a series of meditations on the Passion of Christ.[151] The *Stimulus* in its enlarged version was one of the most successful devotional works of the later Middle Ages, found throughout western Europe. Its popularity was only slightly less than that of the "Quis dabit" lament and the *Meditationes vitae Christi*, works with which it is often combined in late medieval devotional anthologies. The meditations on the Passion in the *Stimulus* are notable for their affective quality. They are inspired no doubt by the stylistic example of Bonaventure, although they display none of his fondness for allegorical organization, nor do they dwell on particulars of Passion events. There is little amplification of the narrative with extra-biblical detail, but, as in other Franciscan meditations, we are invited to join the sufferings of Christ by exercising the faculty of the imagination.[152] The great Franciscan theme of conforming to Christ's Passion is given concrete expression in the *Stimulus* by the constant call to the reader to enter into the wounds of Christ and dwell in them, a recurring motif of the meditations that is worked out here to a greater extent than in any other widely known devotional work of the later Middle Ages.[153]

Another important Franciscan work of the fourteenth century is the massive *Arbor vitae crucifixae Jesu* of Ubertino da Casale, a work completed in 1305. Unlike the *Stimulus*, the *Arbor vitae* was not a popular work, although it achieved a moderate circulation in the fifteenth century. Like the *Meditationes vitae Christi*, which may have inspired it, it is a comprehensive meditative life of Christ of which book 4 is devoted to the passion, resurrection, and ascension. The work is an idiosyncratic blend of Franciscan apologetics and affective meditation. The sections on the Passion draw on the previous tradition and make ample use of extra-biblical detail and the biblical commonplaces associated with the Passion in other narratives. Christ, for example, is said to suffer in all parts of his body, in accordance with Is 1:6;[154] Bernard is cited as an authority for the belief that Christ's hair and beard were torn out at the arrest;[155] the familiar passage from Ekbert associating the spitting with I Pt 1:12 is adapted and modified without acknowledgment;[156] Christ is stretched cruelly on the cross in fulfillment of Ps 21:18, "Dinumeraverunt omnia ossa mea," and so on.[157] In keeping with the late medieval taste for spectacle and display, there is great emphasis on Christ's public suffering and on his bloody and disfigured body. On the cross he is described rather theatrically as a tri-colored banner, his white skin blackened by the blows of the flagellation and reddened by the outpouring of blood.[158] The description of the dead body on the cross is particularly graphic, and in it two popular late medieval devotions are anticipated; the instruments of the Passion are enumerated and apostrophized[159] and there is an injunction to join Mary and enter into the heart of Jesus through the wound made by the lance.[160] An important theme is the compassion of Mary, which is held to be unique, just as Christ's sorrow is unique.[161]

Perhaps the greatest devotional achievement of the fourteenth century is the *Vita Christi* of Ludolphus of Saxony (d. 1377), which can be seen as the fullest expression of efforts begun in the late thirteenth century to produce comprehensive narratives on the whole life of Christ. Examples are the *Meditationes vitae Christi*, the *Arbor vitae crucifixae Jesu* of Ubertino, and the *De gestis domini salvatoris* of Simone Fidati da Cascia (d. 1348).[162] In its scope, monumentality, and thoroughness, the *Vita Christi* far exceeded any previous medieval biography of Christ.

The *Vita* of Ludolphus is intended as a meditative work, written to encourage devotion to the humanity of Christ. It is, as Bodenstedt has pointed out, not a simple biography, but a harmonization of the gospel accounts incorporating much patristic and scholastic biblical commentary.[163] In this it is by far the most learned medieval treatment of the life of Christ. The work is at once both scholastic and affective in tone. A typical chapter includes lengthy extracts from patristic biblical commentators, allegorical interpretations and moral applications drawn from the biblical text, and impassioned language designed to incite the reader to fervent devotion.

The record of the Passion in the *Vita* is exhaustive and obviously intended to be comprehensive. The Passion takes up a substantial portion of part II, dealing with the public ministry of Christ. Ludolphus in effect recapitulates the entire previous tradition of Passion meditation, sometimes referring explicitly to previous sources, at other times taking whole extracts from earlier works without acknowledgment. He relies heavily on the *Meditationes vitae Christi* and the *Stimulus amoris* of Ekbert, which he attributes to Anselm. Ludolphus also uses Bonaventure's *Lignum vitae*, the two Passion treatises discussed above attributed, respectively, to Bede ("Septies in die") and Bernard ("Quis dabit"), the long version of the *Stimulus amoris*, and many of the standard sources that informed other Passion narratives, namely the *Glossa ordinaria*, the *Historia scholastica* of Peter Comestor, and the *Legenda aurea* of Jacobus de Voragine.[164] More esoteric are possible borrowings from the visions of Elizabeth of Schönau, and Ludolphus's apparent and unexpected familiarity with the revelations of Bridget of Sweden and the popular legends that grew up around them (Bridget had died in 1373, just four years before Ludolphus). The extent of his learning and the range of his allusion are thus very wide. The *Vita Christi* was among the most popular religious works of the fifteenth century. There are numerous vernacular translations and many early printed editions. Its size and its learnedness, however, undoubtedly restricted its audience somewhat, and, for all its undoubted appeal, it does not appear to have attracted an audience as large as those of more accessible works such as the *Meditationes vitae Christi* and the "Quis dabit" lament.[165] It is likely that the work was appreciated mainly in monastic circles, where it was a staple item of monastic libraries and remained so well into the sixteenth and seventeenth centuries.

Ludolphus follows the preface to the *Meditationes vitae Christi* in recommending "imaginativas repraesentationes" as an aid to meditation, illustrating the technique by giving a highly particularized, but wholly apocryphal, account of the physical appearance of Christ.[166] The chapters dealing with the Passion itself are organized according to the canonical hours, following the model of the *Meditationes vitae Christi* and the treatise of the pseudo-Bede, which are the principal unacknowledged sources for Ludolphus's treatment of the Passion. The late medieval fascination with the physical particularities of the suffering of Christ is everywhere apparent, perhaps nowhere more prominently than in the section on the exact number of wounds received by Christ in his Passion, said to be 5,490, according to a revelation of a pious woman recluse. Devotion to the wounds of Christ, accompanied by concerns to know their exact number, is common in fifteenth-century piety.[167] As in the *Meditationes vitae Christi*, there is much elaboration of the torments suffered by Christ from the moment of his arrest until his crucifixion.[168]

The description of the crucifixion itself is dependent on the *Meditationes vitae Christi*, with additional details from other sources. The account of Mary's behavior after the death of her son is based principally on the "Quis dabit" lament of the pseudo-Bernard, although its emotionalism is considerably moderated. As in the *Meditationes vitae Christi*, Christ's inner garment is stuck to his flesh from the blood of the flagellation, and his wounds are opened when the garment is torn cruelly from his body in preparation for the crucifixion.[169] There is much detail about stretching Christ's body to fit the cross laid upon the ground. The body is violently pulled by ropes to fit nail holes bored too far apart. Neither the ropes nor the nail holes are mentioned in the *Meditationes vitae Christi*, although ropes are found in the *Dialogus* of the pseudo-Anselm.[170] As in the *Dialogus* of the pseudo-Anselm, when the cross is raised the weight of the body pulls open the nail wounds so that the blood flows copiously.[171] The theme of the compassion of Mary is treated fully, and the meditator is encouraged to imagine the great sorrows of Mary and to have compassion on her as she suffers with her son.[172] Considerable attention is paid to the appearance of the dead body of Christ, in a section that is based closely on the Passion meditation in the *De perfectione vitae ad sorores* of Bonaventure.[173] Ludolphus adopts the conventional imagery of the Song of Songs found in Bernard, Aelred, the *Stimulus amoris*, and elsewhere, comparing Christ's body pierced by wounds to a dove house where Christians can take refuge in the holes, even building nests in those openings.[174]

The *Horologium sapientiae* of Henry Suso (d. 1366) is one of the most popular devotional works of the later Middle Ages. Suso's treatment of the Passion draws on many of the texts we have discussed, particularly the "Quis dabit" lament, and includes many of the commonplace elaborations of the gospel record.[175] Likewise, the *De spiritualibus ascensionibus* of Gerard Zerbolt of Zutphen (d. 1398) was also widely read and has a long section on meditating on the Passion that is fully indebted to the previous tradition.[176]

Other fourteenth-century texts of more limited circulation, such as the *Meditationes* of John Whiterig, an English Benedictine monk of Farne (d. 1371), and the *Meditationes vitae Christi* of the Augustinian Jordan of Quedlinburg (d. 1380), carry on the tradition of meditative writing centered on the Passion of Christ. A work such as the *De gestis domini salvatoris* of the Augustinian Simone Fidati da Cascia, on the other hand, is a lengthy compendium on the whole life of Christ in the tradition of the *Meditationes vitae Christi*, the *Arbor vitae crucifixae Jesu* of Ubertino, and the *Vita Christi* of Ludolphus.

The *Meditationes* of the monk of Farne, which survive in a single manuscript, includes a lengthy *meditatio ad crucifixum*. The meditation uses several biblical commonplaces conventional to the Passion narratives and borrows the familiar passage from Ekbert on the spitting, probably by way of the *Legenda aurea*.[177] Nevertheless, there is relatively little graphic description of the details of Christ's suffering, even though the tone of the meditations is affective and occasionally reminiscent of the fervid devotional style of Anselm.[178]

The fourteenth-century *Meditationes de passione Christi* of Jordan of Quedlinburg has left little manuscript evidence, but the work was printed at least six times before 1500 and thus seems to have been popular into the fifteenth century.[179] The meditations, comparatively restrained in emotional fervor, begin with a discussion of the twelve fruits of meditation on the Passion, and continue with a series of prayers organized around the sixty-five articles of the Passion. These draw on the full range of conventions and commonplaces associated with the earlier tradition. Article 46, for example, describes Christ stretched so cruelly on the cross that all his limbs and veins are broken and his bones can be numbered in fulfillment of the Passion psalm (Ps 21:18).

The *De gestis domini salvatoris* of the Augustinian hermit Simone Fidati da Cascia is also a harmony of the gospel accounts of Christ's life, but it is intended as a moral guide rather than a devotional biography.[180] The work was begun in 1338, and rivals Ludolphus and Ubertino in its monumentality and thoroughness; its vast expanse fills two folio volumes in the last printed edition.[181] Of the fifteen books of the treatise, one is devoted to the Passion.[182] There are few details about the physical circumstances of Christ's suffering, and little elaboration of the gospel account. For example, the binding of Christ at his arrest is the occasion for an allegorical interpretation (he is bound with the ropes of our sins), rather than an excuse for gory detail about his tightly squeezed flesh.[183]

The Fifteenth Century

The fifteenth century is in many respects the great age of Western European devotional writing, and the Passion of Christ was at the center of it.

Most of the works we have discussed continued to be read widely in the fifteenth century. Some of the great demand for devotional writing was met by recycling works of the twelfth, thirteenth, and fourteenth centuries, which were often expanded or modified to suit the needs of increasingly diverse social and religious communities, and much of it was naturally supplied by new works.

Meditations or treatises on the Passion in the fifteenth century are written by authors from a wide range of backgrounds. Good examples are the *Expositio in dominicam passionem* of Jean Gerson (d. 1429), the *Orationes et meditationes de vita Christi* of Thomas à Kempis (d. 1471), and the *Passio domini Christi* of the celebrated religious reformer and heretic Jan Hus (d. 1415), who apparently completed his treatise in the same year in which he was put to the stake at the Council of Constance. The writing of devotions on Passion, of course, persists beyond the Middle Ages among persons of all shades of religious commitment and belief. Noteworthy examples are the unexpected *La Passione di Giesu* of Pietro Aretino, published in Venice in 1545, and the *History of the Life and Death of the ever-Blessed Jesus Christ* of the Anglican bishop Jeremy Taylor (d. 1667).[184]

The treatise of Jan Hus is an interesting mixture of biblical exegesis and devotional exercise, combining a commentary on the Gospel of Matthew drawn from Bede and Jerome, largely by way of the *Glossa ordinaria*, with a full scale treatment of the Passion of Christ as it is found in the devotional tradition of the thirteenth and fourteenth centuries.[185] All of the standard sources are used, and Bonaventure and Ludolphus seem to have influenced the work especially. Several of the usual passages from Ekbert are present, including the passage on the spitting.[186] Hus also makes use of the commonly cited passage from the meditations of the pseudo-Augustine ("Quid comisisti, dilectissime puer, ut sic iudiceris"), which he attributes to Bernard,[187] as well as the "Quis dabit" lament, which he attributes to Augustine;[188] finally, he refers to the much more recent *Revelations* of Bridget of Sweden.[189]

Jean Gerson wrote an exposition of the Passion in French, which was later translated into Latin. Although the work may well have been used for the purposes of private devotion, it is homiletic in structure and penitential in intent. A verse from the gospel is given, followed by the exposition, and concluded with a prayer. There are frequent apostrophes and exclamations, as well as graphic extra-biblical details of the Passion drawn from the previous tradition. Christ's clothing, for example, sticks to his body when it is cruelly torn off, with so much flesh adhering to it that Christ appears,

in a comparison apparently original to Gerson, as though he had been ex-
coriated.[190] All the details of the crucifixion are given as in Ludolphus and
the *Meditationes vitae Christi*. He is stretched out on the cross so that his
joints are separated from the sinews, and so tautly that all his bones can be
counted, as in the Passion Psalm.[191]

Thomas à Kempis left a series of meditations on the whole life of
Christ, following in the tradition established in the thirteenth and fourteenth centuries. Those parts on the Passion are extensive and highly emotional, employing many of the earlier commonplaces. In a section apparently borrowed from Ludolphus of Saxony, for example, Christ's flesh is
said to be extraordinarily tender, so that his suffering at the flagellation was
especially acute.[192] The crucifixion is graphically described. Christ's body is
stretched so violently to fit the cross that his veins suddenly burst open, and
his skin is stretched as tight as a drumhead. All his joints are broken, and his
bones can be counted.[193] As in the words of Isaiah 1:6, from the sole of his
foot to the top of his head there is no soundness in him, but he is covered
with blood which flows from all parts of his body.[194] The section on the
Passion concludes with an exhortation to enter the wounds of Christ, as in
the *Stimulus amoris* and many other late medieval Passion narratives.[195]

Latin Devotional Poetry

As I noted at the beginning of this chapter, to restrict discussion of Passion
narratives to devotional works written in Latin is a somewhat artificial, if
expedient, procedure. The Latin prose tradition, I believe, is the principal
tradition, but concurrent with it, the Passion was treated in many other
types of literature. I will here mention briefly a few important Latin verse
narratives of a devotional character.

The *Vita beate virginis Marie et salvatoris rhythmica* is a 6000 line narrative poem probably from the first half of the thirteenth century. Probably
written in southern Germany or Austria, to judge from the manuscript tradition, it is a comprehensive biography of the Virgin and Christ employing a considerable amount of legendary material. The story of the Passion
is an extensive paraphrase of the gospels, containing many extra-biblical
details, including a minutely particularized description of the means by
which Christ was affixed to the cross. The poem includes several lengthy
laments of the Virgin in response to the suffering of her son, which seem
to be based closely upon the "Quis dabit" lament.[196]

The *Philomena* of John of Pecham (d. 1292), the Franciscan Archbishop of Canterbury, was an extremely popular devotional poem often mistakenly attributed to Bonaventure. The *Philomena* is not so much a narrative of the Passion events, but a poetic meditation based upon the stages of the life of Christ and organized, as are so many Latin prose treatises, around the hours of the day, which are here slightly modified from the traditional canonical hours. The nightingale, which stands for the virtuous soul, sings of the sufferings of Christ in his Passion at the sixth hour and of the death of Christ at the ninth hour. The details of the suffering and death are not given in detail, although the poem clearly reflects the tradition of the prose narratives, as can be seen, for example, in the summarized version of Christ's torments, which concludes with the observation that every part of Christ's body was covered with gore as a result of them.[197]

The *Philomena* of the English poet John of Hoveden (d. 1275), which has sometimes been confused with the *Philomena* of Pecham, is accurately described in one of the early manuscript rubrics as "a meditation on the nativity, Passion, and resurrection of the lord."[198] It is a long poem (1131 four-line strophes), which takes up the Passion of Christ in great detail. The *Philomena* is much more than a versified paraphrase of the gospel account, but a recasting of the events of the Passion into artful and highly wrought poetic language. Several of the commonplaces of the prose tradition are transformed in this way; for example, the detail that when Christ was arrested his hands were so tightly bound that blood bursts from his fingernails becomes:

> Ligaturis caro comprimitur,
> Et sub ungue cruor congeritur;
> Cum rubore livor adducitur,
> Quibus unguis totus contexitur.[199]

[His flesh is pressed with fetters, and the blood collected under his nails; the bruising led to redness, with which his nails were completely covered.]

The theme of Mary's compassion with the suffering of Christ is fully developed; there are several laments and emotional apostrophes directed to Mary and Christ. The poem is clearly meant to enkindle an affective response in the reader.[200]

The *Speculum humanae salvationis* is a fourteenth-century Latin poem of unknown authorship with some affinities to the devotional tradition. It deals with the whole of Christ's life and is chiefly concerned with pointing out parallels between the Old and New Testaments. The *Speculum* was an extremely popular work of wide-ranging influence that was translated into many of the vernacular languages of western Europe, including English, in the course of the fifteenth century.[201] A section of the *Speculum* entitled "De septem stationibus passionis" is arranged according to the seven canonical hours, and is built upon commonplaces of the Passion narratives. The description of the torments after the arrest includes an adaptation of the passage from Ekbert based on I Peter 1:12: "faciem tuam delectabilem, in quam desiderant angeli prospicere, / Non sunt veriti maculare suo nefando sputamine" ("your pleasant face, on which angels long to gaze they did not fear to stain with their abominable spittle").[202] After the flagellation, Christ is described as "adspectu horribilis" as if he were a leper.[203] Finally, we are told that Christ is stretched with ropes in order to fit on the cross.[204]

The Passion in the Vernacular

As the Middle Ages progressed, the vernacular became increasingly favored as a means of expression. Many of the works written first in Latin are adapted or modified in vernacular translations, a procedure which begins in the fourteenth century and reaches a peak in the fifteenth century. In French, one can cite the 2500-line verse compilation, *Li livre de la Passion*, a work composed in the fourteenth century based on such Latin sources as the *Legenda aurea*, the "Quis dabit" lament, and the *Meditationes vitae Christi*.[205] Also notable is the *Heures de contemplacion sur la Passion de nostre Seigneur* of Christine de Pisan (d. 1429?), a text written in French that remains unedited.[206]

In German, two vernacular prose tracts of the fourteenth century are especially important and influential. These are the treatises known as *Christi Leiden in Einer Vision Geschaut*, probably written in the Rhineland, and the Passion tract of Heinrich of St. Gall.[207] Both of these are based upon the standard Latin sources, including Ekbert of Schönau and the treatise of the pseudo-Bede, and make full use of the commonplaces of the Latin tradition. The two German treatises are notable for their extremely graphic descriptions of the sufferings of Christ; they often surpass in detail the Latin works on which they are built. These treatises are the forerunners of a large group of similarly graphic vernacular Passion treatises (known collectively as *De heimlike passie*, or "the secret Passion") that were written and circulated in the Rhineland and the Low Countries in the fifteenth century, and have been productively studied by James Marrow.[208] There are also late fourteenth- and fifteenth-century Netherlandish and German translations of the Passion treatises of Bonaventure, namely the *Lignum vitae* and the *Vitis mystica*.[209] Several translations of the enlarged version of the *Stimulus amoris* exist, including one made by Johann of Neumarkt about 1380, and numerous treatises in German or Netherlandish are adapted from the chapters on the Passion of the *Meditationes vitae Christi*; an especially popular treatise was made up of extracts from both Ludolphus and the *Meditationes*.[210] The treatise of Ekbert was translated into German in the fourteenth century.[211]

In Italian, we have the great fourteenth-century ottava rima poem on the Passion by Niccolò Cicerchia,[212] and, perhaps somewhat peripherally, the *Laude* of the Franciscan Jacopone da Todi (d. 1306), poems nearly contemporary with the great devotional achievements of Bonaventure, several of which deal in high emotion with Passion themes.[213] In the fourteenth century, the "Quis dabit" lament was translated into Italian.[214]

In English, the many lyrics on the Passion from the thirteenth through the fifteenth centuries have been the subject of excellent studies by Rosemary Woolf, Douglas Gray, and J. A. W. Bennett, all of whom consider the Latin background from which these lyrics are thought to emerge.[215] We have already mentioned the *Meditationes* of the pseudo-Augustine as the direct source of several of these poems. The vast fourteenth-century compendious historical poem known as the *Cursor mundi* has a section on the life of Christ that includes a lament of the Virgin on the Passion modeled very closely on the "Quis dabit" dialogue.[216] The *Southern Passion* is the name given by scholars to a late thirteenth-century versified English narrative of the Passion events found in manuscripts of the popular *South English Legendary*. The *Southern Passion* is a fairly exact paraphrase of the gospel texts (there are no laments of the Virgin, for example), but where it diverges from the Vulgate, it seems to reveal the influence of the *Meditationes vitae Christi* as well as one of its principal sources, the *Historia scholastica* of Peter Comestor.[217] The *Northern Passion* is a Middle English narrative poem of the fourteenth century, based on a French source, which exists in a shorter and an expanded version. The latter especially makes use of many of the commonplaces of the Latin Passion tradition, including the extra-biblical details on the hanging of Judas, the sticking of Christ's clothing to his body, and a particularly vivid description of Christ's body being cruelly stretched to fit holes drilled into the cross at least a foot too far apart.[218] The other major Middle English verse treatment of the Passion is in the *Stanzaic Life of Christ*, an account which closely follows the *Legenda aurea*, down to the citing of the same sources.[219] William of Nassington's fourteenth-century poem on the Trinity includes a section on the Passion which uses several of the extra-biblical commonplaces from the Latin tradition to describe the suffering of Christ.[220] In the fifteenth century, the Scots poets John Dunbar and Walter Kennedy both wrote narrative poems on the Passion of Christ that conform to the Latin tradition (the much longer poem of Kennedy explicitly names Ludolphus as one of its sources).[221]

The early Middle English devotional prose treatise *The Wohunge of Ure Lauerd* has an address to the crucified Christ that incorporates several of the commonplaces of the tradition, including the idea that the body of Christ was so stretched out that all his bones could be numbered.[222] In addition to an English verse meditation on the Passion incorporated in his treatise *Ego dormio*, Richard Rolle (d. 1349) wrote two *Meditations on the Passion* in Middle English prose, both of which are very fully indebted to the Latin tradition.[223] Several other English prose meditations on the Passion of the fourteenth and fifteenth centuries are collected in Horstman's anthology, *Yorkshire Writers*.[224] The fourteenth-century devotional prose treatise, *A Talking of the Love of God*, contains a concentrated and highly affective version of the Passion which depends heavily upon the extra-biblical commonplaces of the Latin tradition for its emotional effect. The stretching of Christ's body at the crucifixion, with his limbs pulled out of joint and his wounds torn open, is given in compelling detail.[225] A prose *Complaint of Our Lady*, probably of the late fourteenth century, follows in the tradition of the Latin Marian lament on the Passion.[226] At the very end of the Middle Ages, *The Tretyse of Love*, translated from French to English in 1493, has a section on the Passion adapted from the "Quis dabit."[227]

Late medieval England is particularly rich in vernacular adaptations or translations of Latin devotional works having to do with the Passion of Christ. There is an early fourteenth-century Middle English verse version of sections on the Passion of the *Meditationes vitae Christi* by Robert Mannyng of Brunne known as *The Meditations on the Supper of our Lord*, and a set of fourteenth-century English meditations in verse based on the *Philomena* of John of Hoveden.[228] The great works of the Franciscan tradition are well represented in Middle English versions. Several brief prose meditations on the Passion are based on the *Meditationes vitae Christi*, and the period is notable for Nicholas Love's very popular translation of the *Meditationes vitae Christi* known as the *Mirror of the Blessed Life of Jesus*

Christ, completed by about 1410.[229] The *Stimulus amoris* of James of Milan is turned into English, possibly by Walter Hilton.[230] The "Quis dabit" lament inspired a number of Middle English adaptations, including the fourteenth-century metrical version in Horstman's *Yorkshire Writers* and another found in the Vernon manuscript.[231] There is a Middle English version of Suso's *Horologium sapientiae*.[232] Among the Middle English translations of earlier Latin works are versions of the *Orationes sive meditationes* of Anselm of Canterbury,[233] the *De institutione inclusarum* of Aelred of Rievaulx,[234] and the *Speculum ecclesie* of Edmund Rich.[235]

This considerable activity in the vernacular languages alerts us to a number of things. In the first place, it should be seen in the general context of the steady rise in the prestige of these languages and the increasing use of them for literary purposes. In a somewhat narrower context, the vernacular writings on the Passion are part of a literary project whose aim was to supply vernacular spiritual and religious writings of all kinds for an enlarged reading public that included a significant number of pious laity. This is a European phenomenon, but it seems especially concentrated in the Rhineland, the Low Countries, and England.

The assumption that the increased number of vernacular religious texts is evidence of the growth in lay piety among an increasingly literate and leisured middle class, with especially sharp gains among the women of this class, seems generally reliable. Susan Bell has provided particularly convincing evidence for the active part of literate women in the development of lay piety in the later Middle Ages.[236] One should note, as Bell does, that vernacular religious texts were by no means used exclusively or even primarily by laity, male or female, as manuscript and other evidence makes plain. In England the Carthusian order played an especially important part in the creation and dissemination of vernacular spiritual texts, which were presumably designed in the first place to edify members of the order, whose Latinity may have been such that vernacular versions were welcome.[237] It is quite likely that the place of Latin in the general culture may have declined in the late fourteenth and fifteenth centuries among all classes and genders. On the other hand, as I noted in chapter 1, one should be wary of assuming that lay persons, whether male or female, were necessarily illiterate in Latin (Bridget of Sweden, for example, surely knew Latin), even though it is undoubtedly true that women both lay and cloistered were more often than not poorly instructed in Latin.[238] While the growth in lay reading public is certainly real in the fourteenth and fifteenth centuries, especially among women, it appears that the audience for the Passion trea-

tises remained predominantly clerical and predominantly male, with Latin
the principal language for them up to the end of the fifteenth century and
perhaps beyond. With few exceptions, such as Love's version of the *Meditationes vitae Christi*, most of the vernacular works are found in relatively
few manuscripts in comparison with their Latin counterparts. There are,
for example, only two surviving manuscripts of the Middle English version
of the *Stimulus amoris* of James of Milan, but some fifteen fourteenth- and
fifteenth-century Latin manuscripts of English provenance. Even making
allowances for accidents of survival—for example, the greater likelihood of
the preservation of a Latin manuscript thought to have more prestige than
one in English or for the conservatism and heightened preservationist in-
clinations of the religious houses that were presumably the chief repositories of the Latin texts—the imbalance is still notable and signifies that demand for good Latin texts on the Passion of Christ continued to be strong
in the fifteenth century. This is an assumption that is borne out by the history of printing in the latter part of the century, when the Latin texts we
have been discussing were among the first and most frequently committed
to the new medium.

Seen from this perspective, the growth in the number of vernacular
Passion treatises can be regarded as a sign of the continued vitality of the
Latin tradition, rather than as a token of its ossification or a forecast of
its impending demise. The vernacular works demonstrate its resiliency in
adapting to new cultural and social conditions and are the evidence of a
powerful means by which it became more broadly diffused in a society in
which women in particular were more actively involved in the religious life
as readers and consumers of texts than they had been before. That having
been said, it seems useful to speak of a single, integrated tradition, which,
certainly by the end of the Middle Ages, comprised both Latin and the vernacular, and which was capable of appealing to diverse audiences. It seems
especially misleading to speak of the Latin and the vernacular in bipolar
terms in the context of devotional writing, where, as I argued in the previous chapter, it would be very difficult consistently to associate meaningful
categories of class, social standing, or gender with the exclusive or even
primary use of either Latin or the vernacular.

3

The Representation of the Jews
in Medieval Passion Narratives

ANY MODERN READER OF MEDIEVAL Passion narratives is soon struck
by the anti-Judaism that overshadows so many of them. The anti-Judaism
is sometimes strident and openly contentious; at other times more muted
and subtle; but its presence, however it is felt, has often been difficult for
modern audiences to come to terms with. Perhaps for this reason, the anti-
Judaism of the treatises has been largely ignored by the scholars who have
examined them, many of whom were the great Catholic historians of spirituality of the twentieth century, who, no doubt, found the anti-Judaism an
embarrassment when viewed against the backdrop of modern liberal ideals
of religious toleration.[1] At the same time, historians of anti-Semitism, or
those who have dealt with the position of the Jews in the Middle Ages, have
concentrated on public acts and analyzed texts that were overtly polemical, rarely extending their attention to writings that were intended for the
use of private devotion.[2] To understand the Passion narratives, however,
particularly in relation to their specific audiences and their social contexts,
requires a careful examination of the treatment of the Jews in these treatises. But there is much more than this at stake. The treatment of the Jews
in the Passion narratives is much more than incidentally interesting; rather
it is rather crucially important in comprehending the purposes these texts
served in medieval culture and society. It will be my contention that the
formation of attitudes that led to growing hostility toward Jews in the
later Middle Ages was not merely reflected in, but actively supported by,
the way Jews were treated in narratives on the Passion of Christ.

From about the middle of the twelfth century, the role played by the
Jews in the Passion of Christ is greatly enlarged. The fact that Christ's tor-

mentors were Jews is repeatedly stressed and they are increasingly seen as the mockers, the torturers, and finally the murderers of Christ. Bernhard Blumenkranz has argued that after the adoption of Christianity as the state religion of Rome, the project of Christian exegesis over time was to minimize the responsibility of the Romans for the acts surrounding Christ's condemnation and death and to shift that responsibility to the Jews.[3] The attention to the specifically Jewish role in the Passion is thus best regarded as a rapid intensification of a process that had been under way for some centuries, an intensification fully noticeable in certain texts dating from about the third quarter of the twelfth century. In texts by many writers of the immediately preceding generations, there is scarcely any attention at all devoted to identifying the tormentors of Christ specifically as Jews, or to calling attention to or elaborating upon their part in the Passion. To the contrary, such writers as Anselm, Aelred, and the author of the pseudo-Augustinian *Meditationes*, maintain the much earlier tradition by stressing that it is the wickedness of all mankind that is the cause of Christ's sufferings and death.

The Jewish tormentors of Christ stand as representatives of all humanity or as symbols of man's sinful nature. The Prayer to Christ of Anselm of Canterbury, which dates from the end of the eleventh century, notes without further specification that Mary saw the flesh of her flesh "cruelly butchered by wicked men."[4] The Gospel of Nicodemus contains no special emphasis on the Jewishness of the tormentors of Christ, although it does offer the elaboration of the gospel story that the Jews were responsible for the immurement of Joseph of Arimathea and that they bribed the guards at the tomb to put out the story that Christ's disciples had stolen his body on the day of the resurrection.[5] Likewise, neither of those standard storehouses of patristic commonplace, the *Historia scholastica* of Peter Comestor (d. 1179) nor the *Glossa ordinaria*, places any special emphasis on the fact that the tormentors of Christ were Jews.[6]

The elaboration of the Jewish role in the sufferings of Christ resulted in part from a two-fold division of the events of the Passion current in the twelfth century in which Christ was tormented first by the Jews, then by the gentiles when the sentence of crucifixion was pronounced. Christ was crucified, according to Alexander of Ashby, who wrote in about the year 1200, first by the tongues of the Jews and then by the hands of the gentiles ("primo linguis Iudeorum, et postea manibus gentilium"); or, as in the opening words of the Passion treatise of Ekbert of Schönau, "Iesum Nazarenum innocentem, a Iudeis nequiter condempnatum, a gentibus crudeliter crucifixum" ("Innocent Jesus of Nazareth, wickedly condemned by the Jews, cruelly crucified by the gentiles").[7] The treatises of the late twelfth and early thirteenth centuries extend this "Jewish" part of the Passion, from the betrayal of Judas through the release of Barabbas, by expanding the gospel account through fuller and more detailed descriptions of these events and by throwing emphasis on the fact of Jewish participation in them, an extension fully reflected in the visual arts of the time, as Blumenkranz has shown.[8] In the course of the thirteenth and fourteenth centuries, the Jewish role in the Passion is extended to include the events surrounding the crucifixion itself, and much less is made in many of the later treatises of the joint responsibility of Jews and gentiles for the death of Christ.

These developments can partially be explained within a narrowly defined domain of religious sensibility and the writing that resulted from it, a sensibility given shape by the growth of a Christo-centric piety with increased emphasis on the humanity of Christ. As we have noted, the new interest in Christ's humanity led to an intense hunger to know the details of his earthly life, including his childhood, but especially his suffering and death. Just as increased devotion to Mary and John can be seen as one result of this new piety, so too, conversely, can the increased attention paid to those who were perceived to be Christ's enemies during his life on earth, namely the Jews. The heightened devotion to the Passion with its greater attention to the physical sufferings of Christ, had as its by-product an inevitable attention to the perpetrators of the torments, showing them to be exceptionally cruel or depraved as a means of increasing the emotional response of readers to their reality.

Observed in this way, the role of the Jews in the Passion narratives seems to conform entirely to the explicit ideals or stated intentions of devotional literature in the Middle Ages, which, broadly speaking, can be defined as the arousal in the reader of the emotions of either love or fear directed toward the deity. Love for Christ may be stimulated by making us feel, through concrete visual representation and various other devices, the intensity of the suffering that he endured at the hands of the Jews on our behalf. The magnified role of the Jews in the Passion treatises and the increasingly aggressive expressions of animosity toward them thus can, and often have been, subsumed into an internal history of western spirituality, propelled by its own dynamic and evolutionary in its perspective. Our attention is directed to the origins of affective piety in the eleventh century as an anticipation of its highest stage of development, the fermented emotionalism of fifteenth-century religiosity.[9]

The representation of the Jews in the Passion treatises can also be interpreted in esthetic terms as an instance of the developing pictorial realism which many critics have found characteristic of the affective devotional
literature of the twelfth and thirteenth centuries.[10] Devotional theories
which encouraged meditation aided by formation of vivid mental pictures
yielded texts which paid close attention to the specific details surrounding
the life of Christ. The torments of Christ are described ever more graphically, and the Jews themselves as the perpetrators are described in realistic,
although highly exaggerated terms, as the physical embodiments of malice,
instead of abstract symbols of human sinfulness. From the point of view of
a stylistic development, the culmination of these tendencies is in the works
inspired by the techniques of visual meditation advocated by the Franciscans of the thirteenth century, notably by Bonaventure. The expanded role
of the Jews, in other words, is a symptom of the growth of Franciscan
realism in the thirteenth century, part of a larger hypothesis about the development of medieval realism in general.[11]

Yet such approaches to the Passion texts in general, and particularly
to the anti-Judaism that we perceive in them, are finally unsatisfying. We
are left with views of these texts that are both narrowed and foreshortened,
with every text owing its interest chiefly to other texts which preceded it
or followed it. While I would not wish to underestimate the value of diachronic approaches and the synthetic overviews that are possible because
of them, we are nevertheless limited to partial explanations that leave many
questions unaddressed and ignore the many cultural and esthetic assumptions that lie behind these texts. If we move somewhat beyond the confines
of textuality and into the social and historical realm in which these texts
existed, the texts acquire new dimensions. We can see, for example, that
eleventh- and twelfth-century devotional interest in Christ's humanity has
some relationship to contemporaneous developments such as the crusad-
ing movement to recover the physical sites where Christ's earthly life was
acted out, Anselm's reformulation of a theology of redemption emphasizing the satisfaction Christ made for us in human form, and the doctrine of
transubstantiation which insisted on the reality of Christ's bodily presence
in the Eucharist.[12]

Yet it is possible to go much further than this. I am persuaded by the
arguments of many recent critics that the meanings of texts are not limited by intentionality, nor confined by the explicit ideals of the texts, nor
circumscribed by the canonical purposes of the genre. Devotional texts,
I would argue, are no different from other forms of written discourse,

in that they are self-evidently located within social and cultural matrices which endow them with meaning and significance. They are products of historical communities, connected to dense networks of relationships and processes.[13] As I argued in chapter 1, it seems to me that it is important to recognize the power of texts to articulate an ideology, to form social perceptions and contribute to social formations.

Many readers will be deeply skeptical of my claim that devotional texts are historically contingent; their professed purpose is to lead the reader away from the material world to contemplate what is timeless and transcendent, as opposed to what is local and immediate. The meditative techniques that lie behind the devotional tradition encourage a process by which the historical—for example, the events of Christ's suffering and death in Palestine in the time of Tiberius—is transmuted into the ahistorical, or rather, into the transhistorical: a timeless contemplative present. This transmutation is accomplished through continual reconstruction in the imagination and by the dynamic and ongoing invention of hypothetical detail. The ultimate aim is to transcend even these atemporalized perceptions to arrive at the unchanging and the immutable, that which is not dependent upon the material world. These texts seem to offer an escape from history, and I do not deny that for some audiences and some readers they served their intended devotional function. But that air of timelessness, that implicit claim of exemption from historical contingency—not to mention, especially in the case of the Passion treatises, an intimate association with the verities of the biblical text—renders them especially effective in maintaining and advancing the dominant ideology.

There may be some devotional texts that succeed in transcending their own historicity, or, to state the matter more accurately, are more successful in concealing their historical contingency, in blocking out the traces of the social contest. The Passion meditations that treat the Jews, however, because those representations are constructed of such readily identifiable alterations, modifications, and refashionings of the biblical narrative, provide us with an especially promising group of texts against which to test the validity of these hypotheses.

In order to contextualize the Jewish part in the Passion narratives, we need to have some sense of the historical position of Jews in western European society in the years from about 1150 to 1350, the period in which most of the popular and influential Passion narratives were written. In general, medieval society in these centuries was very far from the serene, well-ordered, homogeneous organism bound together by bonds of fidelity, mutual trust, and universally agreed upon social and religious values, that historians and literary scholars once asserted it to have been. On the contrary, these centuries seem to have been particularly turbulent and contentious. One can cite the weakening of the feudal order, the development of an economy based on markets and exchange, the emergence of an urban merchant class that vied for power and privilege with the traditional land holding seigneurial class, and, toward the end of the period, a revitalized peasantry with a slowly evolving consciousness of its economic power. To these may be added the social dislocations caused by the crusades, the prosecution of heresy, and, in the fourteenth century, the horrifying mortality of the black death. Society in this period was riven by contradictions and ambivalences, marked by competing claims for power and authority in both church and state, and notable for social diversity as much as for uniformity.

More particularly, in connection with the Jews, one of the central tasks of the earlier part of the period was the creation by the dominant ecclesiastical culture of new, and more exact definitions of what it meant to belong to the social organism, specifically, the Christian community, perhaps as a defensive response to a new and disturbing social diversity. Qualifications of membership were established and enforced; a whole series of excluded categories were instituted that had the result of marginalizing large groups of people, or resulted, at least in theory, in excluding them altogether from the human community. R. I. Moore has compellingly traced the process through which categories of otherness were created and institutionalized in the period from 950 to 1250. The excluded groups were most notably the Jews and the heretics, but they also included lepers, homosexuals, and female prostitutes.[14]

The pronouncements of the Fourth Lateran Council of 1215 are of paramount importance as the official textual inscriptions of these social values, which, as Moore points out, had been evolving for some time. The Lateran Council imposed the requirements of communion during the Easter season and annual confession to a parish priest as criteria for membership in the Christian community. It also contained the sharpest condemnation yet made of heresy, reiterating and expanding the provisions for its identification, control, and elimination made by the Third Lateran Council of 1179 and the papal bull *Ad abolendam* issued by Lucius III in 1184.[15] It also contained a series of legislative acts directed against the Jews, forbidding them from the practice of usury; requiring them to wear distinctive clothing so they could be distinguished from Christians; forbidding them, on pain of punishment by secular authorities, to appear in public during the last three days of Holy Week and on Easter Sunday; reconfirming earlier prohibitions against Jews holding any public office; and forbidding converted Jews from returning to the practice of their old religion.[16] As Michael Camille observes, the Jews were to be controlled by being made into images, into "spectacles of alterity."[17] The Jews were increasingly alienated from the dominant Christian culture.[18]

Before examining the implications of these social processes for our understanding of the medieval Passion narrative, we need to examine more closely the status of Jews in the period preceding the momentous codifications of the Fourth Lateran Council of 1215. As many scholars in addition to Moore have affirmed, there was a general decline in the social and legal standing of Jews beginning in the second half of the eleventh century and continuing through the twelfth and thirteenth. Christian attitudes toward Jews and Judaism became more and more hostile and aggressive, and Jews were increasingly subjected to degradation, violence, and economic expropriation. There were settlements of Jews throughout western Europe, mainly in cities, with notable concentrations in the Rhine valley and in southwestern France.[19] The Jews in general seem to have shared in the increasing prosperity of medieval town life and were, it seems (although subject to restrictions peculiar to them that never permitted them to be on equal footing with Christians) begrudgingly tolerated and reasonably well integrated into the fabric of a predominantly Christian society, even taking into account the insurmountable barrier of religious difference. John Hine Mundy observes that "in numbers and cultural wealth, Western European Jewry reached its peak in the later twelfth century and early thirteenth."[20]

One of the most dramatic signs that that position of relative peace and stability had begun sharply to deteriorate was the series of massacres of the Jews at the hands of Christians in the in the wake of the First Crusade in 1095–96, the most thorough and bloody of which were in the cities of the Rhineland, where Jewish communities were large.[21] Hundreds of innocent Jews died in Speyer, Worms, Mainz, Cologne, Trier, Metz, Bamberg, Regensburg, and other places.[22] Subsequent crusades led to further attacks on the Jews. In connection with the Second Crusade of 1146, a pogrom was preached in Cologne, Mainz, Worms, Speyer, and Strasbourg, which led to violence and death, partly mitigated by Bernard's arguments that Jews should not be killed because "they are living tokens to us, constantly recalling our Lord's Passion."[23] At the time of the Third Crusade, Jews were attacked and killed in London, and in 1190 the Jewish population of York was systematically massacred.[24]

At the same time, stories of the ritual murder of Christian children by

Jews began to circulate throughout western Europe; the earliest of these is the tale of the alleged murder of the boy William at the hands of the Jews of Norwich in 1144.[25] These stories had horrible consequences in reality: as a result of accusations of ritual murder, 38 Jews were burned at Blois in 1171, and 100 died at Bray-sur-Seine in 1191.[26] Also from this time, Jews began frequently to be persecuted as profaners of the sacred host; one of the earliest of such incidents was said to have occurred at Cologne in 1150.[27] The child-murder charges, which often involved a story of a mock crucifixion, permitted Christians to substantiate in the present the view that the Jews had been, and continued to be, the enemies of Christians, the murderers of Christ.[28]

Literary texts of this time also match this growing hostility to Jews. Beginning in the second half of the eleventh century there is a whole body of controversial literature directed against Jews, often in the form of an imaginary debate or dialogue. While the earlier examples of the genre are marked by serenity and rationality, in the course of the twelfth century the tone grows increasingly strident and threatening.[29] The newly heightened hostility is well illustrated by the *Tractatus contra Judaeorum inveteratam duritiem* of Peter the Venerable (d. 1156), and the *Invectiva contra perfidiam Judaeorum* of Peter of Blois (d. 1212). The truculent language of these tracts, especially the clamor against the perfidy of the Jews, is adopted in papal bulls, in sermons, monastic chronicles, and many other texts, and in a somewhat moderated form, in the later Passion narratives, forming exceptionally dense intertextual networks. A common vocabulary of speaking about the Jews is developed in this period which is employed throughout the rest of the Middle Ages, just as the period creates a long-lasting stereotype of the Jew.

Peter the Venerable contributes to the degradation and marginalization of Jews in his *Tractatus adversus Judaeos* by placing them in the category of beasts, on the grounds that if they had the rational capacity of human beings, they would be persuaded by the logic of arguments for the incarnation of Christ. Since man is endowed with reason, and Jews fail to accept the rational arguments for the truths of Christianity, it follows that the Jews must not be human.[30] Even Bernard of Clairvaux (d. 1153), the contemporary of Peter the Venerable, who had argued against the murder of Jews at the time of the Second Crusade, expresses similar attitudes, attitudes which came to be part of a common anti-Jewish vocabulary underlying later developments in Passion narratives. In his Sermon 60 on the Song of Songs he affirms that the Jews are the murderers of Christ; he calls them "cow-like" in their understanding because they failed to recognize the divinity of Jesus, and defends himself from the charge of insulting Jews by stating that while he puts the Jews at the level of beasts, their own prophet Isaiah sets the Jew below beasts in the passage: "Cognovit bos possessorem suum, et asinus praesepe domini sui; Israel autem me non cognovit, et populus meus non intellexit" ("The ox knows its owner, and the ass its master's crib; but Israel does not know me, my people does not understand").[31] Such exclusions of the Jews from the category of the human were the justification for violence, degradation, and murder; in the Passion narratives and in the art that was inspired by them, these same attitudes lead to the literal association of the phrases of Psalm 21, "circumdederunt me vituli multi" ("many bullocks surround me," verse 13), and "circumdederunt me canes multi" ("many dogs surround me," verse 17), with Christ's Jewish tormentors, where it is made strikingly clear, especially in later medieval artistic representations of these scenes, that the beasts who surround Christ are Jews in subhuman form.[32]

In a remarkably violent and vitriolic letter written to King Louis of France by Peter the Venerable in 1146, we find expressed another attitude toward the Jews that was to have dire consequences. Peter, perhaps responding to the clamor for pogrom inspired by the Second Crusade, asserts that the Jews are not to be killed, in keeping with the verse of the Psalms, "Deus ostendet mihi super inimicos meos, ne occidas eos" ("God shall let me see over my enemies: slay them not," Ps 58:12); rather they are to be subjected to even greater torments and greater ignominy, punished in a manner that suits the crimes they have committed. Christians are justified in oppressing Jews and in stealing their property, because Jews received their money fraudulently, presumably through the practice of usury.[33] Moreover, the servile condition of the Jews in modern society is entirely justified, as punishment for the murder of Christ.[34]

The idea that Jews were the servants of Christians has a long and complicated history: Augustine's plain statement of the idea in the *De civitate dei* was the foundation of many later developments: "The Jew is the slave of the Christian."[35] But what to Augustine was clearly metaphorical was in this period increasingly and insistently taken in a literal sense, to justify present practices of oppression and cruelty. The authoritative statement of the idea is found in a letter of Pope Innocent III to the Count of Nevers written in 1208:

Thus the Jews, against whom the blood of Jesus Christ calls out, although they ought not to be killed, lest the people forget the Divine Law, yet as wanderers ought they to remain upon the earth, until their countenance be filled with shame and they seek the name of Jesus Christ, the Lord. That is why blasphemers of the

Christian name ought not to be aided by Christian princes to oppress the servants of the Lord, but ought rather to be forced into the servitude of which they made themselves deserving when they raised their sacrilegious hands against Him who had come to confer true liberty upon them, thus calling down His blood upon themselves and upon their children.[36]

It is ideas like these that not only served to justify oppression, but in a particular sense, led to the creation and maintenance of a political theory that the Jews were royal serfs, the property of the secular ruler, to be treated by him as though they were his chattels.[37]

All the textual developments we have described had consequences in the real world. When we examine the realms of the literary and the empirical we can recognize certain common elements that allow us to see the discursive practices and the behavior of empowered groups in terms of a relatively uniform and consistent system of cultural symbol formation. The common element seems to be a pervasive semiology in which the materiality of the sign is insisted upon. In politics, the Jew is literally the slave of the Christian; he is in reality an animal without reason; in theology, the bread and wine are indeed the physical body of Christ.[38] In economics, the same tendency toward the material may also be expressed in the growing use of money as the basis for social relationships. This semiology of the concrete certainly lies behind the technique we have found to be characteristic of so many Passion narratives of this period in which Old Testament passages become literalized when they are made to apply to historical events of the life of Christ as it is described in the gospels, a process in which the metaphorical or the symbolic is substantiated or reified. The same mentality that would find it possible to equate the dead body of Christ with the bundle of myrrh referred to in the Song of Songs would be disposed to regard the Jew as the slave of the Christian, or to put the Talmud on trial for heresy and to burn it at the stake,[39] or to establish a festival of Corpus Christi as an affirmation of the reality of the doctrine of transubstantiation, or be haunted by stories of re-enacted crucifixions and insults to the consecrated host.[40]

It has sometimes been suggested that the charge of host profanation allowed Christians to project onto Jews their doubts about the doctrine of transubstantiation, which was declared dogma only at the Fourth Lateran Council of 1215 and was never universally accepted.[41] There is no doubt much truth in this explanation, but the mentality we have just described would explain this and related phenomena not so much as a crisis of belief, but rather as the result of a deep longing to affirm and participate in sacramental realities. The new realism of the Passion narratives, with their intensified anti-Judaism, together with the sharpened social hostility to Jews, seem to reflect on the part of Christians a new yearning to belong to the body of Christ more intensely and more physically, a body which is conceived of at once as sacramental and material, a body which, at both levels, must be urgently defended against threats to its purity in order for that participation to be completely fulfilling.[42]

In general terms, it is easy to see that the augmented role of the Jews in the Passion narratives coincides with the evolving consciousness among Christians of the dominant classes that the Jew was the other, a threat to the well being and purity of the social order, who needed to be excluded from Christian society. When we come to the task of situating the Passion treatises within a narrower and more finely particularized historical context many problems arise, problems endemic to the study of medieval history. We are often lacking specific information of the most basic sort: for many of the Passion narratives we cannot be sure of their date, their authorship, or their origin. When we do know the author, the biographical information is usually sketchy; and our knowledge of the historical community in which that author worked is often limited to grand and momentous events, with hardly any sense to be gained of ordinary social relationships or of everyday life. But within these limitations, there are a few instances where we are fortunate to have enough specific information to situate a text in a context that it is possible to describe with some precision, even though there must be many details we would like to know that are beyond recovery.

As I have already said, the eleventh-century *Stimulus amoris* of Ekbert of Schönau is the earliest Passion treatise that we know of in which the role of the Jews is noticeably emphasized. It is a treatise of fundamental importance and wide influence, and seems uncannily precocious in its anticipation of later medieval developments. I do not think it is merely incidental that it had its origin in the urban culture of the Rhineland, the site of many large and prosperous Jewish communities, which were subject to persecution and harassment, as most dramatically evidenced by the massacres of 1096 and 1146. Moreover, as we shall see later, it seems a reasonable hypothesis to conclude, on the basis of what is, to be sure, limited evidence, that most of the influential medieval treatises dealing extensively with the Jewish part in the Passion arose from those regions of western Europe, largely urban, and largely economically advanced, where the presence of the Jews was keenly felt and where the struggle to marginalize them was undertaken with special fervor.

Ekbert of Schönau was born in the Rhineland about 1132. He was a member of a powerful patrician family, which, as was typical, had many connections with the local ecclesiastical hierarchy. Besides his authorship of the *Stimulus amoris* and his recording of his sister Elizabeth's visions, there are other aspects of his life and literary career of greater interest for our purposes.[43] His great uncle Ekbert (d. 1132), who became Bishop of Münster after serving as a deacon at Cologne cathedral and provost of St. Cassius in Bonn, was much involved in the events surrounding the conversion to Christianity of Judas Levi of Cologne. Ekbert the nephew began his ecclesiastical career as a canon of St. Cassius at Bonn, where the converted Judas (known as "Hermannus Judaeus") also resided. Anne Clark suggests that they must have known each other.[44] In 1155 Ekbert entered the Benedictine double monastery of Schönau near Trier, where his sister Elizabeth was already a nun. He became abbot in 1166 and died in 1184.[45] The Jewish communities of his homeland had been the object of horrible violence once within his own lifetime and once within recent memory.

We also know that in Ekbert's lifetime the Cathar heresy had spread to the Rhineland, and that the Cathars were especially numerous in the cities of the Rhine valley, where they had established a formal ecclesiastical structure by the middle decades of the twelfth century.[46] Like the Jews, the Cathars were subject to policies of exclusion, persecution, and physical attack. In Ekbert's youth, in 1143, large numbers of Cathars were burned at Cologne, apparently as the result of mob violence against them.

Ekbert may have been a devout contemplative and a Benedictine monk, but we know with a reasonable degree of certainty that throughout his life he was very much immersed in the world outside the cloister, and deeply implicated in this highly contested and culturally advanced social milieu. The urban Rhineland was composed of a complex society of Christians, Jews, and Cathars who lived at least at first in close proximity to each other, with all the ambivalences and anxieties that typically arise from the contradictory processes of assimilation and disengagement. In this competitive atmosphere, the central task of the Christian element of society, particularly the province of the ascendant class of which Ekbert was a member, was to engage in a struggle to assert and maintain its exclusive claims of dominion, not only in the spheres of religious practice and dogma, but also in the social and economic realm. It was especially important to assert this dominion in relation to the Jews, who were in this period, in the words of R. I. Moore, "culturally far superior to their Christian counterparts," and a credible threat to the economic hegemony of the Christian majority.[47]

Ekbert was particularly noted for his activities against the Cathars, as a preacher, a writer, and a kind of proto-inquisitor. On August 2, 1163, Ekbert was in Cologne at the summons of the Archbishop to examine and dispute with a group of Cathars. His superior arguments completely vanquished them, according to the chronicler, but still they refused to recant. Three days later the secular authorities burned alive eight men, two women, and one young girl, who escaped from those who were restraining her and cast herself into the flames.[48] Ekbert also examined Cathars at Coblenz, probably in 1167, with an unknown result, and at Mainz at an indeterminate date, when the result was the complete expulsion from the city of all the Cathars who were convicted of their errors, save one of their chief leaders, who recognized his error and reverted to Catholicism.[49]

Ekbert's most enduring activity against the Cathars, however, was the series of twelve sermons against the Cathars (*Sermones contra Catharos*), which he wrote in the period 1163–64 and dedicated to Rainauld, Archbishop of Cologne. Ekbert's achievement was to invent the category of Cathar as dangerous heretic and to define precisely the identifying traits of a Cathar. Ekbert is largely responsible for classifying Catharism as a re-emergent form of the Manichaeism which had been described and condemned by Augustine, thus laying the foundation for the myth of the medieval Manichee.[50] At the end of his life, Ekbert was using his pen in another project of exclusion, this time a treatise against the Jews, which he had completed except for the conclusion when he was interrupted by death.[51]

Ekbert's skill at identifying Cathars and detecting their errors, his biographer mentions, resulted from the fact that while he was a canon at Bonn he was familiar with many Cathars, who sought out his acquaintance in the hope of converting him to their sect: "Multa etenim de secta eorum noverat, quoniam, dum adhuc Bunne maneret, quidam de hac heresi familiares se ei fecerant, sperantes in sectam suam se eum abducere posse" ("For indeed he knew much of their sect, since, while he was still in Bonn, certain ones of this heresy made themselves familiar with him, hoping that they could lead him into their sect").[52] This is an intriguing statement, which we ought to be skeptical about taking at face value. After all, this is the only permissible construction to put on those events within the confines of the genre of sacred biography. We are given only a scrap of information, but it may throw some light on the likely complexities of the everyday social reality of the time: that is, the confrontation with the other is likely to have frequently been a complex dialectic of intimacy and distance, attraction and repulsion, along the road to forging an official system of classification and exclusion, which in part is what Michael Camille describes as the projection of the collective inability of individuals to deal with the other.[53]

In considering the meaning of Ekbert's career, before we turn to the *Stimulus amoris* itself, we must note the ideas of R. I Moore. Moore's thesis has nuances which my summary cannot do justice to, but his general point is that neither violence nor persecution should be envisaged as endemic to medieval society, nor were the agents of secular authority who engaged in those activities of necessity merely reflecting the values of the larger society around them.[54] Moore argues that mechanisms of persecution—that is, "deliberate and socially sanctioned violence . . . directed, through established governmental, judicial and social institutions, against groups of people defined by general characteristics such as race, religion, or way of life"[55]—may well have developed in the period in which Ekbert lived in part as the effort of an emerging literate and competitive clerical class. This class had many natural alliances with the seigneurial class whose interests it served and from which its members were largely drawn, and strove to maintain its own hegemony (and along with it, that of the dominant secular classes) against all rivals.[56] Ekbert was certainly a Benedictine monk, but his noble birth and his career show that his primary social identity, his outlook, and his sympathies, were those of the ascendant class. Ekbert used his learning, his command of history, his rhetorical and literary skill, not exclusively, but frequently, in the creation of the categories of otherness. He was a chief actor, in the root sense of the word, in that "great operation of exclusion" (as Le Goff terms it),[57] which Moore has so forcefully described; in fact, in chronological terms, he may have been in the vanguard of it. At the time of his death he was at work on a treatise *Contra Judaeos*. I suggest that as much as his polemical works, the *Stimulus amoris* fulfills some of the same purposes of classification and that its rhetorical strategies are designed to promote the sense of otherness. His *Stimulus amoris* is in its own way perhaps even more powerful in the service of ideology than any polemical tract could ever be.

We do not know the date of Ekbert's *Stimulus amoris*. Presumably it was written some time after 1155, when he entered the monastery of Schönau; it could have been written any time between then and the year of his death in 1184, when he was still active as a writer, as his biographer's description of his uncompleted treatise against the Jews suggests. Taken as a whole, with its asceticism and its general theme of spiritual growth and improvement—the conclusion speaks of how a Christian might be brought to life again through Christ and united with him forever—this treatise of modest length sits comfortably within the confines of a traditional Benedictine monastic milieu. Its attention to the humanity of Christ and particularly the Passion, as well as the goal of arousing love proclaimed in its title shows the influence of the newer forms of spirituality promulgated by Bernard and the Cistercians, which must have been current in the Rhineland by this time. It is reasonable to assume that the audience envisaged for the treatise was primarily a monastic one, albeit one whose immediate audience at least is almost certain to have included women, since Schönau sheltered nuns as well as monks. On the other hand, Ekbert's polemical works show that he was capable of writing for the secular clergy and it is possible that he had a wider audience in mind.

As noted above, the treatise begins by pointing out the Jewish role in the condemnation of Christ. Ekbert summarizes the events of Christ's childhood and youth, then speaks of Christ's ministry to the lost sheep of the house of Israel, vigorously condemning the Jews for rejecting his teaching, and thereby positioning his work within the discursive environment of the anti-Jewish polemical treatises of his time:

Sed obscuratum est insipiens cor eorum, domine, et projecerunt sermones tuos retrorsum; neque attenderunt ad omnia mirabilia, quae operatus es in eis, exceptis perpaucis nobilioribus athletis, quos inter infima et abjecta mundi elegisti, ut per ipsos alta et fortia magnifice expugnares. Nec solum ingrati gratuitis tuis beneficiis exstiterunt, sed et contumeliis affecerunt te, domine dominantium, et fecerunt in te quaecunque voluerunt. Te enim faciente opera dei, quae nemo alius fecit, quid dixerunt? "Non est hic homo a deo; in principe daemoniorum ejicit daemonia. Daemonium habet; seducit turbas; vorax est et potator vini; amicus publicanorum et peccatorum." Quid fles? Quid suspiras, O homo dei, dum sustines verborum injurias? Non audis quanta propter te in dominum deum tuum ceciderunt opprobria? Si patrem familias Beelzebub vocaverunt, quanto magis domesticos ejus? Et haec quidem et similia blasphemantes, et aliquoties lapidibus te impetentes, Jesu bone, patienter sustinuisti, et factus es coram eis quasi homo non audiens, et non habens in ore suo redargutiones.[58]

[But their foolish heart is darkened, lord, and they flung your speeches back, nor did they pay attention to all the wonders which you performed among them, except for very few, nobler athletes whom you chose among the weak and abject of the world that through them you might wonderfully vanquish the high and the mighty. Not only were they ungrateful for your freely given favors, but they afflicted you, the lord of lords with insults, and did to you whatever they wished. For as you were doing the work of God, which no one else had done, what did they say? "This is not a man of God. Through Beelzebub, prince of demons, he casts out demons; he has a demon. He misleads the multitudes, he is a glutton and a drinker of wine, a friend of sinners and publicans." Why do you weep? Why do you sigh,

O man of God, while you suffer the injuries of words? Do you not hear how many reproaches fall against the lord your God on account of you? If they have called the head of the household Beelzebub, how much more his servants? And indeed, you patiently endured them saying these and similar blasphemies, and sometimes attacking you with stones, good Jesus, and you became in their eyes as a man not hearing and having no retorts in his mouth.]

Against this background, Ekbert's treatment of the betrayal of Christ is especially significant. The meaning of Ekbert's transformations of the gospel story becomes decidedly more complete if we see them as determined by the historical context we have earlier described. The gospel account of the behavior of Judas, as given in Matthew, is as follows:

Qui autem tradidit eum, dedit illis signum, dicens: Quemcumque osculatus fuero, ipse est, tenete eum. Et confestim accedens ad Jesum, dixit: Ave rabbi. Et osculatus est eum. Dixitque illi Jesus: Amice, ad quid venisti? Tunc accesserunt, et manus injecerunt in Jesum, et tenuerunt eum.

[And he that betrayed him, gave them a sign, saying, Whomsoever I shall kiss, that is he, hold him fast. And forthwith coming to Jesus, he said: Hail, Rabbi. And he kissed him. And Jesus said to him, Friend, whereto art thou come? Then they came up, and laid hands on Jesus, and held him. Mt 26:48–50]

Ekbert conflates the version in Matthew with those of the other gospels in his version:

Quam promptus enim fuerit spiritus tuus, bone Jesu, ad passionem, evidenter ostendisti, quando venientibus una cum proditore tuo viris sanguinum, quaerentibus animam tuam cum laternis, facibus, et armis per noctem, ultro occuristi, et signo quod a duce flagitii acceperant teipsum manifestasti. Nam accedentem ad osculum oris tui cruentam bestiam aversatus non es, sed os, in quo dolus inventus non est, ori quod abundavit malitia, dulciter applicuisti. O innocens agne dei, quid tibi et lupo illi? Quae conventio Christi ad Belial? [59]

[How willing your spirit was for the Passion, good Jesus, you showed clearly when you met of your own accord those bloody men coming with your betrayer, seeking your soul in the night with lanterns and axes and arms, and you revealed yourself at a sign which they received from the leader of the shameful act. For you did not turn away from the bloodthirsty beast approaching for a kiss of your mouth, but the mouth in which no deceit was found, you applied sweetly to the mouth which abounded in malice. O innocent lamb of God, why you and that wolf? What linking of God to Belial?]

This is not merely an emotionally heightened and rhetorically elaborated description of the encounter between Jesus and Judas but also, I suggest, the dramatization of a confrontation between Christian and Jew which instantiates the special apprehensions of late twelfth-century Christian society in regard to Jews, acquiring its peculiar potency from the multivalent symbolism the kiss had acquired in medieval cultural life.

Ekbert's emotional disgust, of course, can be seen as general and undifferentiated moral outrage against a breach of faith, the violation of a bond of love and fidelity, but his indignation acquires special pointedness within the context of feudal attitudes and social values, which are here alarmingly inverted as a vassal has dared to betray his lord. M. D. Chenu has analyzed the weakening of the feudal system in the twelfth and the thirteenth centuries, observing a process of "desacralization" of the vertical vassal-lord relationship, and a substitution of "horizontal and fraternal agreement," the basis for which increasingly came to be, as it was for Judas, money.[60] The unease felt among the dominant class over these threatening transformations of the social order is a readily identifiable subtext in Ekbert's account of the betrayal.

But it is in the more specific context of the confrontation of Christian and Jew that these anxieties are even further sharpened. What is so vividly represented is, in the first place, not only an acutely transgressive inversion of a social hierarchy, but the horror of contamination by physical contact with a despised class, an increasing anxiety that was soon to be expressed in rigorous series of prohibitions and regulations about close social contact, even bodily contact, with Jews. Ekbert describes a Jew who dares apply his lips to a Christian. To heighten the horror of this, Ekbert refashions the biblical narrative, dehumanizing Judas in the same manner as his near contemporaries Bernard and Peter the Venerable dehumanized the Jews, by referring to him twice as a beast. The disgust at defilement is most vividly expressed in the description of the kiss, which is much elaborated beyond the account in the gospels, where it is, except in the Gospel of Luke (the kiss is not mentioned at all in John), treated incidentally merely as a signal. Observed within the context of medieval devotion and liturgical practice (including of course the Mass), the kiss of Judas can be seen as a perversion of the kiss of peace. As Aelred of Rievaulx explains the meaning of the kiss, commenting on the first verse of the Song of Songs: "Quid est osculum? O quid desiderabat? Certe osculum, et osculum oris sui. Osculum dilectionis et pacis est signum" ("What is the kiss? O what did he desire? Certainly a kiss, even a kiss of his mouth. A kiss is a sign of peace and love").[61]

The kiss, however, is as well known, is also a powerful symbol in medieval feudal society, and it seems to me that it is those latter associations that are paramount here.[62] Jacques Le Goff has studied the kiss in the context of medieval feudalism, and his observations are pertinent to Ekbert's account. In the first place, Ekbert, unlike the gospels, makes it clear that this is a kiss mouth to mouth, an essential requirement of the feudal kiss between vassal and lord.[63] Also, unlike the gospel account, but part of the feudal ritual and clearly present in Ekbert, the kiss had to be mutual, mouth applied to mouth, the kiss given and the kiss received.[64] The kiss was a symbolic gesture of fidelity between vassal and lord. It is related to the symbolism of the *immixtio manuum* (mingling of hands), with one important difference: where within the hierarchical values of the feudal system, the *immixtio manuum* symbolized that part of the relationship involving inequality and subordination of the vassal to the lord, the kiss was a sign of the mutual fidelity and the equality of the relationship: "Like the *immixtio manuum*, the mouth-to-mouth kiss places the two participants in a hierarchical relationship, in the one case on a footing of inequality, on the other of equality."[65]

It is these symbolic associations that makes the kiss of Judas and Jesus as Ekbert represents it so horrifying and, indeed threatening, expressing as it does not only close physical contact of Jew and Christian but the psychologically and politically unacceptable idea that Jews could be on any kind of equal social footing with Christians. This was a horror that Ekbert's treatise effectively promotes and which would strike especially deeply the social classes to which Ekbert belonged, for whom, as Le Goff points out, the "kiss of equality" was not freely accepted from all one's fellow-Christians, let alone from Jews: commoners and villeins were excluded from it. A passage from Guillaume de Lorris's part of the *Roman de la Rose*, quoted by Le Goff, well expresses aristocratic revulsion at the thought of physical contact with the socially unworthy that gives special force to Ekbert's renarration of the gospel narrative:

> Je veuil pour ton avantage
> Qu'orendroit me fasses hommages
> Et me baises emmi la bouche
> A qui nus villains home ne touche
> A moi touchier ne laisse mie
> Nul home où il ayt villenie
> Je n'i laisse mie touchier
> Chascun vilain, chascun porchier;
> Mais estre doit courtois et frans
> Celui duquel homage prens.

[For your sake from this day / From my person I shall turn away / Any man low-born or uncouth / Who would do me homage or kiss my mouth. / No man who is base / May have leave to touch my face. / Neither swineherd nor villein / Will tomorrow my presence gain. / He to whose homage I agree / Must be one both courtly and free.][66]

It is worth noting that in later literature reflecting aristocratic values, Jews and peasants are frequently equated in subhuman categories requiring subjection and control.[67]

After the arrest, Ekbert elaborates on the gospel account of the torments Jesus suffered at the hands of the Jews, using the same strategies of emotional heightening:

Amantissime domine Jesu, quanta illic indigna a propria gente pertulisti? Vultum tuum honorabilem, in quem desiderant angeli prospicere, qui omnes coelos adimplet laetitia, quem deprecantur omnes divites plebis, polluti labii sputis inquinaverunt, sacrilegis manibus ceciderunt, velo operuerunt in derisionem, et te, dominum universae creaturae, tanquam servum contemptibilem, colaphizaverunt. . . . In omnibus his non est perfidorum Judaeorum satiata impietas.[68]

[Most beloved lord, how great were the indignities you bore there at the hands of your own people! Your honorable face, on which the angels long to gaze, which fills all the heavens with joy, which all the wealthy of the people entreat, they befouled with the spittle of defiled lips, struck it with impious hands, covered it with a veil in derision, and they beat you, the lord of all creatures, as though you were a contemptible servant. . . . In all these things, the impiety of the wicked Jews was not sated.]

Once again the horror of Christian defilement by contact with Jews is powerfully expressed by imaginative exaggerations of the gospel account which throw emphasis on the inversion of a hierarchical relationship and create a powerful sensation that social boundaries have been transgressed. The spittle is from "pollutis labiis"; Christ is struck with "sacrilegis manibus," a phrase Bernard had used in his anti-Jewish polemic in an identical sense: "Out of this blindness no less monstrous than miserable they rushed into that horrifying and incredibly crude crime of laying sacrilegious hands on the majestic lord,"[69] and which was to find its way regularly into the rhetoric of papal bulls directed against the Jews, as in the letter of Innocent III written to the Count of Nevers in 1208, quoted above (Innocent's phrase is "manus injecere sacrilegas").[70]

Christ is beaten, as in the gospels, but Ekbert contributes the detail, "tanquam servum contemptibilem," a detail which is pointed enough within the context of medieval feudal values, but especially so within the discursive realm of the freshly intensified contemporary project of the ecclesiastical and secular ruling classes to insist on the servile status of Jews in relation to Christians, for which the bull of Innocent III just referred to provides altogether typical evidence. It was to the Jews, not of course to Christ, that the phrase "tanquam servi" was applied in the statute issued by Louis IX in 1230, which sought to define the legal status of Jews in contemporary France as serfs belonging to the king.[71] The insults to Christ are recast as the violations of feudal norms in many later Passion narratives. One of the most striking of these embellishments of the gospel account is in the Passion treatise of the pseudo-Bede, where Christ is dragged by the hair, trampled underfoot, and even, the author speculates, forced to sit on the ground before the leaders of the Jews as though he were a villein ("et eum sine honore sedere fecerunt forte in terra viliter coram ipsis").[72]

What is most striking about Ekbert's refiguring of the gospel is that the fear of Jewish contamination is expressed so physically, in terms revulsion over bodily contact. We see this first of all in the kiss of Judas mouth to mouth, but also in connection with the other torments, notably the spitting and the striking with hands. Such emphasis on defilement through physical contact is the characteristic way medieval Christians, or perhaps more accurately, those medieval Christians who belonged to the dominant classes, expressed their anxieties about mingling with Jews, or indeed, with any group perceived to be the other, as the quotation from the *Roman de la Rose* illustrates in relation to the peasantry. A twelfth-century bishop of Prague lamented on his death-bed that he had been too intimate with Jews, polluting himself through physical contact: "Vae mihi quia silui, quia apostatricem gentem non revocavi, nec in gladio anathematis pro Christo dimicavi; sed me ipsum et populum christianum passus sum per tactum manus cum gente non sancta pollui" ("Woe unto me that I have been silent, that I have not restrained the apostate race, nor have I brandished the sword with anathemas for Christ; but I allowed myself and the Christian people to be defiled by touching hands with an unholy race").[73]

Le Goff speaks of "the essential place occupied by the symbolism of the body in the cultural and mental systems of the Middle Ages," reminding us that "The body not only reveals the soul but is the symbolic site where man's fate—in all its forms—is fulfilled."[74] In such a cultural milieu we can readily see why the heightened emphases of Ekbert on the kiss, the spitting, and the buffeting are so forceful in expressing as well as promoting the fear of social contamination. On a more submerged and universal level, we can see that these same emphases are consistent with the findings of modern anthropologists who have studied defilement and the fear of pollution as part of cultural systems. In the analysis of Mary Douglas the filth which is held to be a dangerous threat to the symbolic order is made up of the "marginal stuff" which is jettisoned from the body: "Matter issuing from them [the orifices of the body] is marginal stuff of the most obvious kind. Spittle, blood, milk, urine, faeces or tears by simply issuing forth have traversed the boundary of the body. . . . The mistake is to treat bodily margins in isolation from all other margins."[75] Ekbert's treatise employs this powerful symbolism to express horror at Jewish transgression of those social margins that the Christian society of his own time was attempting to construct and maintain.

The spittle is the most egregious symbol of the kind Douglas describes, and it is not surprising that others appear in later Passion treatises, notably, the non-biblical detail that the Jews cast dung on Christ's head.[76] The kiss of Judas also takes on deeper significance when it is reexamined in the light of Douglas's formulations. Even the twelfth-century Aelred of Rievaulx has almost a modern anthropologist's understanding of the kiss mouth to mouth: "Qui se osculantur, utique sibi labia porrigunt et sic ora coniungunt. Ore spiritum emittimus et resumimus" ("Those who kiss each other at the least extend their lips to each other, and thus join their mouths. By the mouth do we send forth the spirit and take it in").[77] Lying behind such beliefs, according to Le Goff, is the connection of the kiss on the mouth with beliefs prescribing exchange of either breath or saliva, symbolic exchanges in initiation rites which rendered the participants equal.[78] There are many instances in medieval saints' lives in which holy persons are asked not only to kiss—but to spit into—the mouths of devotees.[79]

It is worth noting that this symbol system of contamination and defilement, which is so prominent in Ekbert and many of his successors, has, of course, no place in the gospels, which do not yet reflect the strong social differentiation between Christian and Jew. Early Christians, as a tiny subgroup within a much larger Jewish society, could not have felt that the Jews were a threat from beyond the margin of the social order. The danger of pollution by Jews, is, however, very much a part of the outlook of twelfth and thirteenth century medieval Christian culture, and continues to be expressed, as we shall see shortly, in terms of the body. The legends of Jewish desecration of the consecrated host that are found as early as the date of Ekbert's treatise and which circulate widely in the next century are essentially alternate versions or variations on this same theme. As in Ekbert, in the legends it is Christ's physical body, now in the transubstantiated form of the host, that is subjected to physical defilement by the Jews.[80]

It is hard to underestimate the importance of Ekbert's treatise as a cultural document. It recasts the gospel of Christ in feudal terms to express the increased anxiety of Christians about close social contact with Jews; in an age of sharpening social categorization, it expresses and contributes to a strongly articulated view of the Jew as dangerous and menacing other, a source of pollution and a threat to the purity of Christian society; it expresses as well as provokes the greatest fear of all: it relates a story in which the subordinate relationship of Jew to Christian is inverted, in which Jews have power and authority over a Christian, in which the social boundaries between Christian and Jew are violated, in which it is a Christian, and not a Jew who is subjected to degradation and stigmatization. The reality of those anxieties is attested in a different way in the constant complaints about Jewish insolence that appear in the papal bulls of the next century, and later, in Christians' fears of being poisoned by Jews in revenge for bad treatment.

Ekbert's greatest intellectual innovations may be found in his overtly polemical effort to marginalize the Cathars, but his transformation of the gospel is equally the powerful agency of what is at root the same ideological purpose. The rhetorical strategies and representational techniques of the *Stimulus* are different, of course, from those of the *Sermones contra Catharos*, and from those he presumably used, or would have used, in his treatise *Contra Judaeos*. None of those violent sentiments of the chroniclers directed against the Jews of their own day find their way into Ekbert's *Stimulus*.[81] The specific historical circumstances of the Jews in the Rhineland of the twelfth century, the massacres, the exploitation, the moneylending beneficial to both sides, and the struggles for domination, are of course completely blocked out. But within the generic confines of a devotional treatise, Ekbert creates a way of regarding Jews as a horrifying threat, thereby implicitly legitimating the need for strict policies to control them, to keep them in that state of servitude which, as the Popes beginning with Innocent III repeatedly proclaimed, they deserved because they were the murderers of Christ.

Ekbert's treatise very much spoke to the concerns of the thirteenth century, and it is no wonder that it was so extraordinarily popular and that its influence continued to be felt. The treatment of the Jews in the thirteenth century Passion narratives can be viewed largely as continuations and extensions of rhetorical strategies and methods definitively instituted in his *Stimulus amoris*.

The status of European Jews worsened steadily in the course of the

thirteenth century, as the policies of exclusion codified in the pronouncements of the Fourth Lateran Council were applied, and persecution increased in most parts of western Europe. The legal status of Jews deterio-
rated, as rulers attempted, with varying degrees of success, to assert their
control over them as royal serfs.[82] The logical outcome of such actions
was the official effort to remove Jews entirely from the societies of western Europe, an intermittent campaign again only partially successful, but
marked by the expulsion of the Jews from England in 1290, and later from
France.[83]

Of primary importance is the role of the new orders of Franciscans
and Dominicans in anti-Jewish persecution. As the orders charged especially with missionizing and Christianizing, they were entrusted by the
Pope with the detection of heresy through the inquisition, but they were
deeply involved with efforts to control the Jews and to reduce, if not eliminate, their part in Christian society. Jeremy Cohen has described the activities of the new orders in these powerful words:

From the establishment of these first and most important mendicant orders in the
Roman church early in the thirteenth century, until the end of the medieval period
and even beyond, Dominican and Franciscan friars directed and oversaw virtually
all the anti-Jewish activities of the Christian clergy in the West. As inquisitors, mis-
sionaries, disputants, polemicists, scholars, and itinerant preachers, mendicants engaged in a concerted effort to undermine the religious freedom and physical secu-
rity of the medieval Jewish community. It was they who developed and manned the
papal Inquisition, who intervened in the Maimonidean controversy, who directed
the burnings of the Talmud, who compelled the Jews to listen and respond to their
inflammatory sermons, and who actively promoted anti-Jewish hatred among the
laity of Western Christendom.[84]

The other notable contribution of the mendicant orders to thirteenth-
century cultural life was the development and promulgation of a spirituality grounded in intense devotion to the humanity of Christ. It clearly
would be mistaken to make crude connections between the anti-Judaism
of the Dominicans and Franciscans and their spirituality. We may observe that the friars were certainly among the most dynamic elements of
thirteenth-century society, and as such were in the vanguard of a broad
array of educational, religious, and political innovations, including the Inquisition and the development of universities. The anti-Judaizing activity
of the friars should, nevertheless, be recognized as a significant part of the
historical context in which their spiritual writings are implicated. It is the
case that many of the major thirteenth-century narratives of the Passion in

which the role of the Jews is given special attention were written by friars. Chief among these authors are Bonaventure (d. 1274) and John Pecham (d. 1292), who were Franciscans, and Jacobus de Voragine (d. 1298), who was a Dominican. In the fourteenth century, Ludolphus of Saxony (d. 1377), who ended his life as a Carthusian but seems likely to have spent a considerable portion of his career within the Dominican order, might be added to this group.

The most important mendicant spiritual writer of the thirteenth century was undoubtedly Bonaventure, who was born in Italy about 1217, rose to become the Minister General of the Franciscan Order in 1257, and died while attending the Second Council of Lyons in 1274. He came from a prosperous family, the son of a physician. He was, in short, a member of that emerging middle class which contributed most of the members of the mendicant orders. Bonaventure's works are numerous and varied: he wrote notable works of theology and biblical exegesis, as well as several series of sermons and two biographies of St. Francis. His ascetic and mystical works had an extraordinary influence on the development of later medieval theories of contemplation. Unlike the case of Ekbert of Schönau, there is no evidence in his life or writings that he was directly involved in polemical activities against Jews or heretics, except perhaps for his battle against Joachism.

In his position as a leader of the Franciscans, however, he can hardly have been unconcerned about or oblivious to the great project of his order to eradicate heresy and eliminate the Jewish presence in Christian society. Bonaventure lived in Paris from about 1234 to 1257, where he was a student and later a master of theology. He returned there in 1266–68, and it is in those years that it is thought that his ascetic works, including his two treatises on the Passion of Christ, may have been written.[85] The Paris of this period was the arena in which some of the greatest and most dramatic of the persecuting activities directed against Jews took place, and it hardly seems likely that anyone living in Paris at this time, least of all a Franciscan friar, could not have known of them or have been affected by them. Among these activities was the attack on Rabbinical literature, conducted throughout France under the auspices of the friars, but with its focal point in Paris.[86] In June 1240 a great public disputation took place in Paris between eminent Christians and Jews over the charges against the Talmud; the Queen Mother, Blanche of Castile, presided over the proceedings. A formal inquisition was also held before a panel of judges that included the Chancellor of the University of Paris. The Talmud was found guilty of teaching false doctrine and condemned to burning at the stake.[87] In 1242, after a period of delays caused by Jewish efforts to forestall the verdict, twenty-four wagon loads of Jewish books, probably amounting to ten to twelve thousand volumes in Cohen's estimate, were burned in Paris in the Place de Grève.[88] In 1248, in response to Jewish efforts to rehabilitate the Talmud, the verdict was re-examined by a commission headed by Albertus Magnus, which only repeated the earlier judgment.[89] This dramatic series of events directly inspired at least one literary response, the *Desputaison de la Sainte Eglise et de la Synagogue*, by the jongleur Clopin, which dates from the period of the controversy in Paris.[90]

I am by no means about to suggest that the spectacular events surrounding the trial and the burning of the Talmud provided the occasion for Bonaventure's Passion treatises, in any narrow sense, but only to position them within a Parisian "textual environment" that was also rich in symbolic action, to see them in association with what Paul Strohm has termed, in speaking of late fourteenth-century England, "a broad array of roughly contemporary statements and gestures."[91] The chapter on remembering the Passion of Christ in his treatise *De perfectione vitae*, addressed to nuns, contains a typical outburst against the Jews as the murderers of Christ: "Heu me, heu me, ecce libertas captivorum capitur, gloria angelorum illuditur, vita hominum occiditur. O Iudaei miseri, bene implevistis quod promisistis! Dixistis enim: Morte turpissima condemnemus eum" ("Alas, alas! The Liberator of Captives is caught; the Glory of Angels is derided; the Life of Men is put to death! O wretched Jews, how well you have fulfilled your intent!—for you had said: 'Let us condemn him to a shameful death'").[92] There is a similar emotionally charged condemnation in the *Vitis mystica*, which, in the now conventional rhetoric of anti-Jewish polemic, denies human status to the Jews by equating them with beasts. Bonaventure's reference is to the fate of Joseph in the Hebrew bible, a typological comparison he was not the first to make; but the sharpness of tone and the specific equation of the mad dog with the mass of Jewish people, the *plebs judaica*, is his own imaginative refiguring: "Ecce, fera pessima, rabies canina, plebs Iudaica devorat illum, pessima fera condemnat filium tuum, fratrem tuum, sponsum tuum. Quis hic non doleat? Quis lacrymas gemitusque contineat?" ("See, a wild beast, a rabid dog—the Judean mob—devours him; a wild beast condemns your Son, your Brother, your Spouse! Who would not be filled with sorrow at the sight? Who could keep back sobs and tears?")[93]

The use of the term *plebs* to describe the Jews in this passage and elsewhere in Bonaventure (see below, note 100) is significant in terms of contemporary discourse on social relations. Georges Duby has studied the evolving sense of the word *plebs* in the twelfth and thirteenth centuries, especially in northern France, where Bonaventure spent most of his life. Increasingly, *plebs* was a term with pejorative connotations, as it was used by those who described society from a position of privilege to refer to all those who were not members of the dominant class. A dualistic, oppositional structure was developed, with the seigneurial class on one side and the masses set apart and distant from it. By the thirteenth century *plebs* was undoubtedly a disparaging term, describing the unnoble and the subjected, a resonance that must be heard in Bonaventure's usage.[94]

In the *Vitis mystica*, Bonaventure, following a method perfected by Ekbert, focuses on the part of the Passion for which the Jews were responsible, expanding their role in it by constructing hypothetical incidents on the basis of Old Testament typology, incidents presented in highly emotional language:

Tertia sanguinis effusio erat in vellicatione genarum, cuius testimonium habemus in Propheta dicente ex persona amabilis Domini Iesu: Corpus meum dedi percutientibus, genas meas vellentibus; quod quidam exponunt de laceratione maxillarum facta cum unguibus impiorum Iudaeorum, quidam vero de extractione barbae Domini Iesu; quod sive utrumque sive alterum verum sit, non tamen sine effusione sanguinis factum est. Video ergo sacrilegas manus impiisimae gentis, non saturatas colaphis et alapis et conspuitione desiderabilis vultus optimi Iesu, sed etiam ad genarum ipsius vellicationem exarsisse et a vultu dulcissimo ad rubricationem rosae nostrae sanguinem elicuisse. Video, agni illius immaculati patientiam admirabilem et imitandam genas pudicissimas impudicissimorum unguibus lacerandas cum omni mansuetudine praebuisse.[95]

[The third shedding of blood occurred when they plucked his cheeks, as the prophet testifies speaking in the person of the lovable Lord Jesus: I have given my body to the strikers, and my cheeks to them that plucked them. Some interpret this to mean that the wicked Jews tore his face with their fingernails; others, that they plucked his beard. Neither could have been done without the shedding of blood. I see the sacrilegious hands of this most impious mob, who are not content with striking, slapping, and covering with spittle the adorable face of Jesus all-good, but now, in their burning rage, also pluck his cheeks and draw from the most sweet face the blood which reddens our rose. I see in this lamb without blemish a patience worthy of admiration and imitation, as He turns in all meekness his cheeks most pure to the harrowing of impure claws.]

The avowed aim of this stylistic virtuosity and of these affective rhetorical strategies is to increase the reader's sense of pity for the sufferings of Christ: but this is done by emphasizing in vivid detail the horrible deeds of the Jews; the result is a subtext with a strong, but much different meaning, a subtext that surely led to the arousal in the reader of emotions quite other than love of Christ. We may note the emphasis on bodily defilement and physical transgression, as in Ekbert, the "sacrilegious hands," and now the "impure claws." There is also the subtle effort to universalize the traits that may apply to this particular historical mob to the Jewish people in general, a strategy which de Vinck's English translation obscures, as in Bonaventure's phrase, "video ergo sacrilegas manus impiissimae gentis." [96]

Bonaventure's most extended treatment of the Jewish part in the Passion is in his allegorical treatise, the *Lignum vitae*. This treatise is particularly interesting because a major intertextual presence, although not explicitly acknowledged, is the *Stimulus amoris* of Ekbert of Schönau. Bonaventure's borrowings from Ekbert illustrate the continuing vitality of his treatise. They well illustrate the rich intertextuality of many devotional texts in general, and they can give us a good idea of the reception of the *Stimulus* in Franciscan literary circles in the middle years of the thirteenth century. Bonaventure probably turned to the treatise in part because of its great authority, believing like most of his contemporaries, that the *Stimulus* was the genuine work of Bernard, who by this time had already acquired enormous stature as a figure of the contemplative life. When we examine the specific borrowings Bonaventure took from Ekbert, we can gain an idea of what elements of Ekbert's *Stimulus amoris* were most striking to Franciscan sensibilities of this time. Moreover, we would probably not be unjustified in concluding that these elements were likely to have appealed to the general literary sensibility of the thirteenth century, inasmuch as Bonaventure's treatise was itself popular and influential, disseminating those passages from Ekbert to new audiences.

There are at least eight instances in Bonaventure's relatively brief treatise where he has quoted or adapted phrases from Ekbert, who, except for Bede, Anselm, and Boethius (each of whom is referred to only once or twice), is his only non-biblical authority. Of these eight borrowings, four of the longest and most extensive concern the Jewish role in the Passion. It is obvious that in Bonaventure's efforts to constitute the meaning of Ekbert's treatise, it was his innovative treatment of the Jews, which supplemented what must have been felt as a lack in the gospel account, that struck him as especially memorable and worthy of imitation. There is other evidence that Ekbert's treatise was similarly perceived by the thirteenth-century, at least by friars: the account of the Passion in the *Legenda aurea* of the Dominican Jacobus of Voragine, which dates from about 1270, has only two borrowings from Ekbert: the memorable passages on the defiling of the face of Christ with the spittle of Jews.[97]

Bonaventure's treatment of the kiss of Judas is from Ekbert, with its emphasis on the kiss mouth to mouth.[98] He also incorporates nearly verbatim Ekbert's description of the defilement of Christ by the Jews, found also in the *Legenda aurea*:

Nam vultus ille venerabilis senibus, desiderabilis angelis, qui et omnes caelos adimplet laetitia, polluti labii sputis inquinatur, ab impiis sacrilegis manibus caeditur, velo in derisionem obtegitur, et Dominus universae creaturae tanquam servus contemptibilis colaphizatur.[99]

[His face, worthy of the elders' reverence and the angels' desire, His face which fills the heavens with joy, was defiled by spittle from impure lips, struck by impious and sacrilegious hands, and covered in derision with a veil. The Lord of all creation suffered blows as if He were a lowly slave.]

Bonaventure also appropriated a passage from Ekbert describing Christ's reaction to his tormentors, who are called "accursed dogs." He borrows Ekbert's interpretation of the story of Joseph in Genesis as a prefiguring of Christ's Passion, making its application to the Jewish part in the Passion much more pointed, as his additions, which I have italicized, plainly reveal (especially to be noted is his addition of *plebis*, a term of which the significance has been indicated above):

Cognosce igitur, clementissime Pater, tunicam praedilecti filii tui Ioseph, *quem invidia fratrum secundum carnem tanquam fera pessima devoravit* et conculcavit in furore vestimentum ipsius et omnem decorem illius reliquiis cruoris inquinavit; nam et quinque scissuras lamentabiles in ea reliquit. Hoc enim est, Domine, vestimentum quod in manu meretricis Aegyptiae, *synagogae videlicet*, innocens puer tuus sponte dimisit, magis eligens, spoliatus a carnis pallio, in carcerem mortis descendere, quam adulterinae *plebis* acquiescendo voci temporaliter gloriari.[100]

[Recognize, therefore, O most merciful Father, the tunic of your beloved son Joseph *whom the hatred of his brothers in the flesh has devoured, like a wild beast*; whose garments it has trampled in rage, befouling the beautiful apparel with blood, leaving on it five ugly gashes. This indeed, O Lord, is the garment which your innocent son willingly abandoned into the hands of the evil woman of Egypt, *that is, the Synagogue*; for he preferred to be deprived of his clothing of flesh and to descend into the prison of death rather than seek a passing glory by yielding to the cries of an adulterous *mob*.]

Bonaventure's account of the delivery of Christ to Pilate has a few borrowings from Ekbert, but here the intensity of anti-Jewish feeling is chiefly his own, and the role of the gentile Pilate is minimized:

Horrenda prorsus Iudaeorum impietas, quae tantis iniuriis satiari non potuit, quin potius, ferali rabie fremens, impio iudici tanquam rabido cani animam iusti deglutiendam exposuit! . . . Verum, quamvis non ignoraret Pilatus, Iudaicam gentem adversus Iesum non iustitiae, sed invidiae zelo commotam.[101]

[Oh, horrible impiety of the Jewish mob [102] that, not content with inflicting upon him insults innumerable, went on convulsed with animal rage, to abandon the life of the Just One to a pagan judge, throwing him, as it were, to a mad dog's fangs . . . Pilate was fully aware that it was not for the sake of justice, but out of the depth of their hatred, that the Jews were thus frenzied against Jesus.]

We can see that Bonaventure's changes in the gospel story and his adaptations of Ekbert emphasize the collective guilt of the Jewish people in the death of Christ, whose tormentors are identified specifically as Jews (as in Ekbert) but also referred to in such universalizing phrases as the "plebs Iudeorum" or the "Iudaica gens." Bonaventure also, much more than his sources in either the gospels or Ekbert, describes the Jewish tormentors of Christ as a raging mob, unrestrained, out of control, and animal-like. What is expressed in these passages is that new aristocratic sense of the subjected as a hostile, undifferentiated, alien mass, as Duby has described it. These attitudes are likewise expressed in terms of the Passion story in the commentary of Stephen Langton (d. 1228) on Christ's entry into Jerusalem, which includes the chilling observation, "the Lord does not like the mob." [103] More specifically, Bonaventure's treatise seems to reveal an emerging fear in the consciousness of the dominant classes about the potential for mob action by those whom they dominated, a fear expressed powerfully in such later works as Gower's *Vox clamantis*, where the peasants are described as wild beasts: "This is a race without power of reason, like beasts, for it does not esteem mankind nor does it think God exists. I believe that in a short time the lords will submit to them, unless justice shall have been obtained by means of fear." [104] It is reasonable to suppose that passages on Jewish behavior like those in Bonaventure's *Lignum vitae*, together with the artistic productions they inspired, had a bearing on the fourteenth-century equation of peasant mobs with Judas and the Jews.[105]

Bonaventure's adaptations, rewritings, and extensions of the Jewish part in the Passion he found in Ekbert's treatise very powerfully reinscribe for the thirteenth century that continuing and increasingly intensified sense of the Jews as a threat to Christian society and a source of social contamination, as well as articulating a general fear of the *plebs*. It is not difficult to demonstrate that these are indeed some of the overriding concerns of thirteenth-century Christian culture; within such a social context we can see why it is that the texts we have described—whether by Ekbert under the guise of Bernard, by this "Bernard" as filtered through Bonaventure or Jacobus de Voragine, or by Bonaventure himself—are ideological agencies of durable power and influence.

The fear of impurity through sexual mingling of Christians and Jews is repeatedly expressed in the papal bulls of the thirteenth century and underlies the requirement for distinctive Jewish dress, lest such commingling occur inadvertently. Older prohibitions against Christians acting as servants in Jewish households were strongly reaffirmed because such relationships seemed to be troubling inversions of the subordinate position God had intended for Jews in relation to Christians. As the thirteenth century advanced, fears of bodily contamination were expressed with increasing thoroughness and rigor. Christians could not act as wet-nurses for Jewish children, nor as midwives for Jews, nor could Christians be treated by Jewish physicians (a prohibition widely ignored by the nobility and the papacy itself). Similarly grounded are the efforts to prevent Christians from buying food from Jews or from sharing meals with them.[106]

The Christian prohibitions against sexual impurity with Jews also were prosecuted with increasing rigor, in a generally repressive atmosphere in which what was perceived to be sexual misconduct of all kinds was harshly dealt with. Mundy notes that the Council of Arles of 1337 included cohabitation with Jews, Muslims, or beasts as sins that could not be absolved by a confessor without special permission from a bishop.[107] In late thirteenth-century England those who cohabited with Jews, or engaged in bestiality, or were sodomites were to be buried alive.[108] In thirteenth-century France, Michael Camille cites the instance of a Christian man convicted of cohabiting with a Jewess who was condemned to death by burning, along with the woman, on the grounds that sexual intercourse with a Jew was the same as copulating with a dog.[109]

It was a professed goal of thirteenth-century Christian culture to convert the Jews to Christianity, and some of them did so. More surprisingly, considering that conversion placed one at the risk of the most severe penalties, including death, there are a few recorded instances of Christians who converted to Judaism. In the second half of the thirteenth century, the English Dominican Robert of Reading embraced Judaism, married a Jewish wife, and held public disputes against the Christian religion.[110] Much more common must have been the deep personal conflicts and the social tensions that ensued when Jews who had converted to Christianity, perhaps under duress, reverted to their former religion, or when the children of converted Jews, born Christians, attempted to maintain some sort of connection with their Jewish heritage. A society that exhibited these kinds of complexities and conflicts was a continuing cause of anxiety to the established order in the latter half of the thirteenth century, as vividly illustrated by the papal bull *Turbato corde*, addressed to the friars of the Dominican and Franciscan orders by Clement IV in 1267, and reissued by his successors three times, in 1274, 1281, 1288, presumably because the problems of Christian apostasy and social intermingling which it had attempted to address were still felt to be real. In the bull, Clement laments that Christians have converted to Judaism and blasphemed the name of Christ. He empowers inquisitors to seek out the guilty, with the aid of secular authorities. Converted Christians are to be judged as heretics, and Jews who have promoted such apostasy are to be punished.[111]

The vigorous prohibitions and regulations that the thirteenth century had constructed to prevent social intimacy between Christians and Jews did not, of course, succeed in forestalling it entirely, and those feelings of fear and anxiety about such contact that are expressed in many of the Passion treatises belong to the conflicting and contradictory attitudes toward Jews that characterize thirteenth-century Christian society. On the most elementary level, the requirement of distinctive dress for Jews shows that they must not have been the distinctly other. They must have been fairly well integrated into the Christian community, at least at the beginning of the thirteenth century, before the stringent application of policies of exclusion.[112] Throughout the thirteenth century there were continuing complaints in the papal bulls about the dress requirements not being observed, with dangerous familiarity as a result. There was very occasionally a begrudging sense that the Jews provided valuable services to the Christian community; much more prevalent was the less enlightened view, held especially by rulers and magnates, that Jews could be a valuable source of profit.

Telling and poignant evidence of continuing intimacy between Christians and Jews is provided by the petition presented to Pope Nicholas IV in 1291 by Enfridus, an acolyte of Trier who had been born out of wedlock of a Jewish father and a Christian mother, asking for his birth to be legitimized.[113] And interesting in the light of the long-standing prohibition against social mingling is the story of a group of citizens of Hereford who attended a Jewish wedding in 1286 even when threatened with excommunication.[114] Something of the ambivalence and guilt that such forbidden associations caused in Christians of the ruling classes generally, particularly when money-dealings were involved, can be recognized in the large number of papal reassurances given to noble ladies whose consciences were troubled by profit won from dealings with Jews, through either extortion or usury. For example, in 1291 Pope Nicholas IV wrote to Queen Marguerite of France, allowing her to keep the money on condition that a third of it should be contributed to support the Holy Land.[115]

In a social setting of such complexity, the works of Ekbert and Bonaventure would resonate with particular force. They are devotional works with the stated object of promoting love for Christ and sympathy for his human suffering; they also very eloquently disclose dread of the Jew as a source of contamination, reinforcing the sense that the Jew is the other that must be controlled and excluded. In addition to expressing love and compassion, these texts also powerfully express the guilt, terror, and ambivalence that accompanied life in thirteenth-century society: anxieties that are remarkably articulated, in what seems to be a defining trait of late medieval culture, in terms of the body.

John Pecham was, like Bonaventure, a Franciscan who was deeply enmeshed in some of the leading controversies that marked the middle years of the thirteenth century. He also, like Bonaventure, was noted for his devotion to the humanity of Christ. Pecham's chief work on the Passion is the allegorical poem in Latin, the *Philomena*, a work that was extremely popular in the Middle Ages and was usually attributed, by later generations, to Bonaventure himself. Pecham was a student at Paris, perhaps as early as the 1240s, at a time when Bonaventure would have been there.[116] He became a Franciscan at Oxford some time between 1250 and 1259, and some time between 1257 and 1259 he revisited Paris to study theology, returning to England in 1271 or 1272. He became Archbishop of Canterbury in 1279 and died in 1292. In the contentious atmosphere of Paris in the 1260s he was an active participant in the Joachite controversy, the debate about poverty initiated by the spirituals, the Averroist controversy, and the dispute between the mendicant and secular masters. After his return to England, the existing record shows that he exhibited that sharp hostility to the Jews that characterized the mendicant orders. He was much troubled by the problem of relapsed Jews, as Douie explains: "Two years after his arrival in England Pecham had drawn the King's attention to their existence in large numbers in London and elsewhere, and, while condemning all forcible conversions, he was strongly in favour of compulsion being used to prevent baptized Jews from abandoning the Christian faith."[117] Pecham soon became involved in official dealings with Jews, first in 1275, at Oxford, as the royally commissioned judge in a case between Robert de Flemingvill and the Jewess Comitissa, the wife of Isaac Pulet.[118] After he became Archbishop, he again, in 1281, wrote to Edward I complaining about relapsed Jewish converts, urging Edward to use strong measures against them.[119] He also wrote sternly to queen Eleanor in 1283, rebuking her for borrowing money from Jews.[120]

The Jewish presence in a Christian society was perceived to be an urgent problem in the England of the years following Pecham's return from Paris. The decrees of the Fourth Lateran Council were enforced with new severity. From 1253 onward no new synagogues could be built, and in 1272 the London synagogue was confiscated and closed.[121] The Statute of Jewry of 1275 severely restricted Jewish commercial activities and attempted to prevent all social contact between Christian and Jew.[122] In 1279 it was decreed that Jews who blasphemed the Christian religion or relapsed after having converted were to be punished by death.[123] The Synod of Exeter in 1287 proclaimed again the perpetual servitude of the Jews and reaffirmed and extended the provisions for Jewish exclusion decreed by the Fourth Lateran Council.[124]

In the previous year, Pope Honorius IV had addressed a particularly venomous bull to Pecham complaining of the outrageous activities, in detriment to the Catholic faith, of the Jews in England. The abomination of the Talmud was censured; Jews were accused of attempting to convert Christians to their sect. The Pope had heard of Jews employing Christian servants in their homes, with sexual intermingling as a result, of Christians who worshipped at Jewish services, and of Christians and Jews who visited each others' homes and ate and drank with one another. Pecham was encouraged by any means possible, secular as well as spiritual, to put a stop to these grievous abuses, which were characterized as a dangerous disease.[125] A period of great social turmoil ensued, in which Pecham, by virtue of his position and interest in the problem of the Jews, must have taken a principal part. Newly rigorous policies against the Jews were defined and enforced, yet they were also resisted and evaded, frequently to the accompaniment of scandal. The final outcome was a royal edict that compelled all Jews to leave England by All Saints Day, 1290, or be subject to death; the King confiscated the property they left behind.[126]

The date of Pecham's poem on the Passion, the *Philomena*, is not known to us, although we do know that he wrote some of his poetry while at Paris.[127] It seems unlikely, but not impossible, that he could have written it after 1279 when he was occupied with his duties as Archbishop of Canterbury. In any case, it is certainly not possible to forge any chrono-

logical link between Pecham's poem on the Passion and his activities involving the Jews, which were, as far as the record reveals, confined to the
period after his return to England from Paris. I am not so much interested
in these activities for what they might tell us, or seem to tell us, about aspects of Pecham's mind, attitudes, and dispositions; rather, I am interested
in them as they broadly illuminate the social circumstances which surround
his poetry.

Pecham's poem is a religious allegory, but it does not therefore exist
in a historical vacuum, but lives within an environment of texts and events.
In the poem, the nightingale, representing the virtuous soul filled with
love, sings at various hours of the day in songs which mark the various
stages of salvation history: at dawn, she sings of the creation; at prime,
of the incarnation; at terce of Christ's infancy; at sext, of Christ's Passion;
and at none, when she dies, of Christ's burial. Writing a devotional poem,
Pecham adopts a literary form which appears to succeed almost entirely in
obliterating any sign of the turbulent social, political, and intellectual environment of which he was part. It is indeed mainly in the stanza of the
prologue, in which he summarizes the part of the poem that is to deal with
the Passion, that we can detect the intrusion of history and feel the weight
of thirteenth-century circumstance:

> Sextam, cum a perfidis
> voluit ligari,
> Flagellari, conspui,
> dire cruciari,
> A Iudaeis perfidis
> nequiter tractari,
> Crucifigi denique,
> clavis terebrari.[128]

[The sixth hour, when he wished to be bound, scourged, spit at, and cruelly tortured by the perfidious; to be wickedly treated by the perfidious Jews, finally to be
fixed to the cross, to be pierced with nails.]

In his emphasis on the Jews as the agents of the Passion, Pecham conforms to, and advances the prevailing thirteenth-century standard. It is his
double use of the adjective "perfidus" in connection with the Jews that is
particularly telling. No such association, of course, exists in the Bible, but
perfidus is the adjective regularly applied to the Jews in the liturgy, even in
early Christian times.[129] It is also, significantly, along with the noun form
perfidia, applied to Jews over and over again in contemporary polemical

and official texts dealing with Jews. Peter of Blois (d. 1212) wrote an *Invectiva contra perfidiam Judaeorum*, and Innocent III's bull of protection issued on behalf of the Jews in 1199 begins with the words, "Licet perfidia Judeorum."[130] The "Judeorum perfidia" is mentioned in the decree of the Fourth Lateran Council against usury; a letter of Innocent IV to Louis IX of France in 1244 laments the "impia Judeorum perfidia."[131] A bull issued by Clement IV to the King of Aragon in 1267 begins with the resounding phrase: "Damnabili perfidia Judaeorum propter ingratitudinis suae vitium."[132] The bull addressed by Honorius IV to Pecham himself in 1286 speaks of the "damnata perfidia" of the Jews; Pecham used the phrase "Judaica perfidia" to describe the false Jewish religion in his letter of warning to Edward I written in 1281.[133]

This is the environment within which the intertextuality of this stanza is best understood. We can recognize in this devotional poem, cast in the form of an allegory which seems to be exempt from history and local circumstances, not only characteristic mendicant animosity toward the Jews, especially the *relapsi*, but the traces of the mendicant project to diminish and punish the Jews of thirteenth-century Christian society. This project was aided, along with many other things, by a ready and universal identification of Jews with perfidy.[134] Pecham's widely-read poem, seen in this light, is a textual utterance of great significance within a larger discursive and symbolic environment.

In the fourteenth century the position of European Jews continued to worsen. The period was marked by organized campaigns of violence against them, and new policies of degradation and restriction were devised. Much of the violence was concentrated in France and Germany. In Röttingen in Franconia in 1298 Jews were charged with the profanation of the host and marauding bands systematically slaughtered all Jews who refused to convert in most cities of Franconia and Bavaria.[135] In France, Philip the Fair expelled the Jews in 1306; they were recalled by Louis X in 1315, to be expelled again in 1321, and recalled once more in 1361.[136] In 1320 a group of northern French peasants, driven by conditions of famine, formed what became known as the "Shepherd's Crusade," and set off on a campaign of pillaging in which Jews were singled out as victims and killed.[137] In 1321 a rumor spread through Aquitaine of a conspiracy by lepers and Jews to kill all Christians by poisoning their wells. In 1336 Jews were massacred in Alsace and Swabia. As Poliakov notes of this period, for the first time all Jews were held responsible for a crime allegedly committed by one or a few.[138]

It is within this historical context that we must understand the representation of the Jews in the account of the Passion in the *Vita Christi*, the great devotional compendium of Ludolphus of Saxony. Ludolphus was a Carthusian, and it might be expected that a member of this most austere and reclusive contemplative order would be very far removed from the pressures of contemporary events. Ludolphus's Carthusian-ness has indeed tended to obscure the relation of his work to history. Ludolphus, however, was a Carthusian in the Rhineland, where, in a period of expanding growth and influence, Charterhouses had been founded not in remote and rural situations, but in the large commercial cities—Mainz in 1320, Coblenz and Trier in 1331, Cologne in 1334, and Strasbourg in 1335. David Knowles remarks of this period in general that: "The Carthusians made themselves more familiar to the world in this century by accepting, perhaps even desiring, urban rather than desert sites, and the presence of such men at the very heart of cities such as Paris, Cologne, London, and others made them a cynosure and a center of spiritual direction."[139]

Ludolphus entered the Carthusian order at Strasbourg in 1340, and served as Prior of the Charterhouse of Coblenz from 1343 to 1348. He then moved to the Charterhouse of Mainz and finally returned to Strasbourg where he died in 1377.[140] We have no reliable evidence from his life or writings that Ludolphus was involved in secular or controversial affairs. A tradition that he began his religious life as a Dominican seems reasonably sound.[141] Although the details of the life of Ludolphus are meager, we can note with certainty that he was present in the cities of the Rhineland which had large Jewish communities that were increasingly subjected to severe legal and social restrictions and policies of degradation of an even more intense kind than those earlier applied in France, England, and elsewhere. Poliakov notes that the fourteenth century was a particularly difficult time for the Jews of Germany, speaking of the "background of permanent anarchy then prevalent there."[142]

More precisely, in the years 1347–48 there occurred a dramatic series of events that could hardly have failed to touch deeply Ludolphus and every other urban dweller of the Rhineland. In 1347, an epidemic of the Black Death broke out in Western Europe. It was one of the most deadly and virulent in history, from which the German cities were by no means exempt. In the search for causes of this calamity, suspicion fell, quite irrationally but not surprisingly, on the Jews, who for so long and so intently had been categorized as enemies of Christians and a threat to Christian society. Rumors that a conspiracy of Jews had caused the plague by

poisoning wells arose in Savoy, where certain Jews confessed under torture to having committed the crime. From Savoy, the accusations spread
to Switzerland, where trials were conducted and Jews executed in Bern,
Zurich, and in the area of Lake Constance. From there, the legend quickly
spread to the Rhineland. Pope Clement VI attempted to protect the Jews
by issuing a bull in 1348 pointing out that Jews as well as Christians died
of the plague, and that the plague occurred in places where there were
no Jews. These and other official efforts had little effect, and a series of
great massacres occurred in many German cities, especially those of the
Rhineland. Looting and slaughter took place in Cologne, Colmar, Worms,
Oppenheim, Frankfurt, Hanover, and Erfurt, among other places. In Strasbourg the struggle over the Jews was particularly prolonged and intense.
An investigation conducted by city officials concluded that the Jews were
not guilty. This municipal government was then overthrown and the new
one that replaced it proceeded against the Jews, first by imprisoning every
Jew in the city, then by burning them to death in the Jewish cemetery on
February 14, 1349, confiscating their property and distributing it to the
Christian citizens. In all, some two thousand Jews were murdered. "Such
was the poison that caused the Jews to perish," was the laconic judgment
of the chronicler.[143]

The accusation that the Jews had caused the plague by poisoning
wells and other acts of defilement should be seen in connection with the
intensified charges of host desecration and ritual child murder that also accompanied the plague. All three charges can be seen as expressions of fears
of Jewish attack on the body of Christ, whether conceived of as Christian
society as a whole, or its most vulnerable individual members, or the physical body itself (the host).[144]

When the black death broke out, Ludolphus was at Coblenz, where
he was Prior until 1348 before moving on to the Charterhouse of Mainz.
There is one tradition, probably unreliable, that placed him at Strasbourg
at the time of the black death, when he is alleged to have taken an active
role in the political life of the city.[145] We do not know what Ludolphus
made of the momentous events occurring up and down the Rhineland in
the wake of the black death, but it is after that time, during the years at
Mainz, when he is most likely to have turned his attention to the composition of his great devotional masterpiece, the *Vita Christi*.[146]

The *Vita* includes a chapter harshly denouncing the infidelity of the
Jews, which, while it cannot be characterized as specifically mendicant
in tone, is certainly consistent with an outlook on the Jews that Ludol-

phus might have acquired if he had been a member of the Dominican order. Rather chilling in light of the political events of his era, when peasant uprisings occurred as well as massacres of Jews, is his endorsement of mass punishment as an appropriate way of dealing with the hopelessly recalcitrant—lumped together with the Jews: "Istis Judaeis similes sunt multi, qui nec flagellis, nec beneficiis, a malo revocari, vel ad bonum provocari possunt, et ideo cum superbis et perversis Judaeis, in fasciculis simul colligati, poenas merito sustinebunt" ("Many are like those Jews, who cannot be called from evil or roused to good, neither with whips nor with favors; and therefore, gathered together in groups, they, with the proud and perverse Jews, deservedly bear punishment").[147] Such a statement seems indeed to display mendicant truculence more than Carthusian serenity. But however it is construed, within the confines of a devotional treatise it reveals an awareness of the ways of the world and an allegiance to the values of the dominant feudal order.

Ludolphus incorporates the entire previous tradition established by Ekbert and Bonaventure in his treatment of the role of the Jews in the Passion of Christ, at the same time that he contributes several significant innovations apparently of his own invention. Among the many borrowings from Ekbert in the section on the Passion, which include most of the passages on the Jews, is the emotion-charged passage from Ekbert on the kiss of Judas (attributed by Ludolphus to Anselm). This passage must have been especially striking in the age of the great plague, when fear of contamination by contact with Jews was never more intense.[148] Following Ekbert and Bonaventure, Ludolphus adopts the rhetoric of inversion to heighten sympathy for the suffering of Christ. The Jews, who are slaves, treat Christ, the Lord, as though he were a villain: "alii manu reversa dulcissimum et mellifluum os ejus percutiebant, . . . alii sanctissimam barbam ejus evellebant, alii per suos venerabiles capillos ipsum trahebant, et viliter inter pedes conculcabant, ac sine reverentia et pietate aliqua Dominum angelorum male tractabant" ("Some struck his sweet and mellifluous mouth; . . . others plucked his most holy beard; others dragged him by his venerable hair and trampled him wickedly under foot, and badly treated the lord of angels without any piety or reverence").[149] The passage from Ekbert that Bonaventure had borrowed is adopted again by Ludolphus to describe Christ's face stained with the spittle of impure lips, struck with sacrilegious hands, covered with a veil in derision, and the lord of all creation beaten as though a contemptible servant.[150]

But the most striking example of the technique of inversion is found in the description of the spitting; Christ is spat upon as though he were a vile and pestiferous man, worthy of death: "tanquam hominem vilem et pestiferum, et morte dignum."[151] The adjective *pestiferus* had not before this time, as far as I know, ever been associated with Christ. Its meaning here seems not merely figurative, but quite literal, "as one who bears the plague." The comparison may be intended only to evoke the revulsion and fear felt toward anyone who was infected by disease, but it was the Jews, of course, who were of vile status and were especially stigmatized as bearers of the plague in the society inhabited by Ludolphus. As in the case of similar passages, these lines intensify the horror provoked by the degradation Christ suffered at the hands of the Jews by projecting onto him the position of Jews in contemporary Christian society. Ludolphus himself need not have been fully conscious of the process of ironic inversion. Such passages would be powerful rhetorically among contemporary audiences just because these implied comparisons were so apt in a society where Jews, along with lepers with whom they were often linked were indeed the most striking living exemplifications of the outcast and the vilified.[152]

Ludolphus pays considerable attention to the spitting, adding fresh detail to refashion the narrative he found in Ekbert and Bonaventure. His innovations describe the spitting with an intensity and a wealth of physically graphic language that had never been used in previous accounts. The spitting is repositioned and universalized by being tied to disgusting practices of Jews in general:

Proprium enim Judaeorum erat, in contemptum ac vituperium et despectum, spuere in faciem ejus quem abjiciebant; et tam horribiliter et incessanter in facies hominum spuebant, ut quandoque eos suffocarent. Quid turpius? Quid despectius? Quid ignominiosius et vituperiosius, quam in faciem exspuere, et maxime in illam faciem speciosissimam, in quam desiderant Angeli prospicere.

[Indeed it was the custom of the Jews, out of contempt, vituperation, and scorn to spit in the face of one they despised. And they spit so horribly and ceaselessly into the faces of men that sometimes they suffocated them. What is more shameful? What more despicable? What more shameful and contemptible than to spit in the face, and especially in that most beautiful face, on which angels long to gaze.]

Nor is this all. Ludolphus explains in detail that this is not ordinary saliva, but rather foul excretions:

O quam caeca aemulatio infelicium Judaeorum, qui non exhorruerunt turpissimis sputis suis maculare et deturpare faciem tam amabilem; et non tantum simplicibus salivae sputis, sed verisimiliter etiam excreationibus suis foetidissimis! Unde Matthaeus non dicit: spuerunt; sed exspuerunt, quasi excreando spuerunt. Marcus autem dicit, conspuerunt, quia non tantum unus sed plures simul hoc fecerunt. Et sic illa facies benedicta facta est ita abominabilis, quasi esset leprosa, ex sputis et verberibus, quae ei dederunt.[153]

[O how blind this malevolence of the unfortunate Jews, who did not shrink from staining and befouling with their most shameful spittle that face so lovely—and not merely with simple saliva, but truly with their most foul excretions! Hence Matthew does not say, "they spit," but "they spit forth," as if they spit by excreting. And Mark says, "they spit together," because not just one but many did this at the same time. And so that blessed face is made as abominable from the spitting and the blows which they gave it as if it were a leper's.]

The emotional force of the passage is unmistakable, as is the new level of disgust and horror at the prospect of physical defilement at the hands of the Jews. The basis for Ludolphus's description of the Jewish custom is the apocryphal story that Hur, the brother of Aaron, had been smothered with spittle, a legend reported in the *Historia scholastica* of Peter Comestor.[154] Yet it is interesting to observe that none of the standard pre-fourteenth-century exegetical authorities attach any typological significance to that episode in connection with the Passion of Christ.[155] The story of Hur's death by spittle is associated with the Passion in the *Speculum humanae salvationis*, a work almost exactly contemporary with the *Vita Christi* of Ludolphus. An account of the aggravated spitting very similar to that of Ludolphus is found in the Passion tract of Heinrich of St. Gall, written in German some time in the fourteenth century, perhaps under the influence of Ludolphus, although it is possible the influence went in the other direction.[156] The new detail seems to belong almost exclusively to the German speaking world, at least before the fifteenth century, when the influence of Ludolphus began to be extensive. It is found in several Netherlandish Passion treatises of the fifteenth century, for example.[157]

The graphic detail about Jewish excretions that could lead to death by asphyxiation vividly expresses, I think, some of the fears of contemporary Christians about being poisoned by the Jews, perhaps in revenge for the treatment they had received, but perhaps out of sheer malice toward Christians. It is this fear that lies behind the prohibitions against Christian treatment by Jewish physicians, and the regulations that began to appear in the third quarter of the thirteenth century forbidding Christians to buy food from Jews. The legislation of the Council of Vienna (1267) prohibiting such purchases makes the rationale perfectly plain. The Jews, "who regard Christians as their enemies, might perfidiously poison them."[158] As we have seen, those fears of being poisoned by Jews reached a fever pitch during the plague years of 1347–48, especially in those parts of Europe inhabited by Ludolphus and Heinrich of St. Gall, with a horrifying result in reality.

To better understand the pertinence of the connection I am attempting to establish between the spittle of the Jews in the Passion story and contemporary Christian fears of poisoning by Jews, it is useful to examine the physical form such a fear assumed. We are inclined to regard poisoning largely as a matter of chemical reaction, governed by impersonal and immutable physical laws. It was quite otherwise in the Middle Ages, when toxicity was most often thought of as something that inhered in the matter itself; where poisons were not chemical solutions but foul concoctions that often included the secretions or body parts of both men and animals, particularly the most loathsome and despised. One description of a compound with which the Jews were alleged to have poisoned the wells of Christians specified that it was made up of human blood and urine, three unknown herbs, and the ground-up consecrated host.[159] Another account describes a poison made up of frogs' legs, snakes' heads, and women's hair, mixed with a "very black and stinking" liquid horrible to look at as well as to smell. The description of Jewish spittle in Heinrich of St. Gall emphasizes its foul stench, which was so strong that it was said to have broken Christ's heart.[160] The medieval form of poison survives in the witches' brew in *Macbeth* (IV.i.1–38), whose first ingredients are "poisoned entrails" and "sweltered venom," and which includes, in addition to "eye of newt and toe of frog," "Liver of blaspheming Jew" and "Nose of Turk and Tartar's lips."

It is within this context that the new descriptions of the spittle of the Jews as more than saliva, but rather the "excreationibus foetidissimis" of the sort that had been fatal to Hur, must, I think, be understood. In any case, in his account of the spitting Ludolphus has succeeded in giving a powerfully expressive form to all those fears, anxieties, and feelings of revulsion which arose in Christians at the thought that their society (conceived of as the body of Christ) might be contaminated by a Jewish presence. At the same time, he articulates, under the guise of a story of lethal Jewish spittle, the quite specific fears among his audience that they might be poisoned at the hands of the Jews in time of plague.

Finally, we may observe that the description of the spitting of the Jews in Ludolphus is notable for its extreme physical verisimilitude, an absorption with the details of bodily function. To be invited to imagine someone smothered by spit, or to be asked to contemplate foul excretions of mucus and bile, transgresses modern boundaries of good taste. More importantly, such excesses seem to have been intended to be provocative to medieval audiences. Descriptions of this kind are a regular part of late medieval rhetorical strategies to arouse disgust toward the Jews: the little Clergeon of the Prioress's Tale is cast in a privy "Where as thise Jewes purgen hire entraille" (line 573), as Chaucer does not neglect to remind us, for example. These intrusive preoccupations with the physical are, in a way, strategies of degradation. They have their analogue in the increasingly physical and concrete forms of humiliation that are found in the regulations and law codes of the late thirteenth and fourteenth century, particularly in Germany—a fact especially interesting in connection with the work of Ludolphus and Heinrich of St. Gall.[161] The Schwabenspiegel decreed that a Jew had to take his oath standing on a pigskin. A Silesian law of 1422 required a Jew to take an oath standing on a three-legged stool and staring at the sun. This is also the period when the image of a sow giving suck to Jews appeared in many parts of Germany. Jews condemned to capital punishment were often hanged upside down, sometimes with a dog beside them.[162]

In all these developments, in literature, art, or the legal codes, we can recognize the formation, especially in Germany, of a crude physical semiology which reduced the Jew to the object of ridicule and repulsiveness.[163] Gavin Langmuir has eloquently reminded us of the dire consequences of all such systems which categorize human beings in these terms:

To think that material realities such as bread, wine, pork, cows, or flags are in reality what they evoke symbolically in non-rational thinking is dangerous enough; to treat human beings that way is deadly. Millions of human beings died because other human beings inhibited their rational empirical capacities to the point that they could no longer recognize in the defenseless victims they symbolized as "Jews" the readily perceptible human characteristics they shared.[164]

The Passion narratives participate in the formation of such a semiology, and we must consider that they may have contributed to the baleful outcomes described by Langmuir. If they did so, this is the terrible fulfillment of their function within medieval society. In this chapter I hope I have at least demonstrated that the way Jews were represented in the Passion narratives not only reflected, but actively contributed to, the anti-Judaism of the later Middle Ages. That is a blander and more academic conclusion, but it should not let us ignore its horrifying consequences for real human beings.

4

Gender
and the Representation of Women
in Medieval Passion Narratives

A NOTABLE DEVELOPMENT IN MEDIEVAL narratives of the Passion is a steadily increasing attention to the role played in that event by the women who are mentioned in the biblical account. Naturally most of this attention is focused on the Virgin Mary, but the parts of Mary Magdalene and the unnamed women are also often imagined in greater detail. The gospels themselves offer a very limited part in the Passion story for the Virgin Mary. Except for her role in giving birth to Jesus, Mary is hardly an actor at all in the drama of human salvation. Only the Gospel of John mentions her in connection with the Passion, where she is described as present at the foot of the cross with Mary Magdalene and Mary of Cleophas. Christ addresses her from the cross, "Woman, behold thy son," and commends her to John: "Behold, thy mother" (Jn 19:27). Mary herself speaks not a word, and the gospel tells us absolutely nothing about her feelings or emotional state. In all four of the gospels, on the other hand, Mary Magdalene is identified as present at the tomb of Christ on the morning of the third day. She receives a vision of the risen Christ, with whom she converses, and then announces his resurrection to the disciples.

These modest narrative elements are gradually elaborated upon in the course of the patristic period and the early Middle Ages. The full details of that process need not concern us here.[1] It is sufficient to note that a considerable body of legend grew up around both Mary Magdalene and the Virgin Mary. Mary Magdalene is described as the companion of Christ, and attained semi-apostolic status. She was thought to have been responsible for bringing the faith to southern Gaul, among other places.[2] Her special standing was the result of her being the first to learn of the resurrection; she was early esteemed as the "apostle to the apostles."[3] The legends and apocryphal gospels concerning the mother of Christ, on the other hand, tend to concern themselves with supplying the missing details of her early life (her espousal and marriage to Joseph, for example), instead of expanding upon her participation in the events of the Passion, although the fourth-century Greek apocryphal gospel known as the Acta Pilati B describes her as "fainting on the way to Golgotha" and weeping at the foot of the cross.[4] The earliest expositions of the passage from John locating her at the crucifixion proclaim her stoic behavior in response to the suffering of her son, a direct contrast with the later medieval emphasis on the display of her own suffering. Ambrose, for example, tells of a stalwart Virgin unmoved by the sight of her son's suffering, pointing out that the gospel says only that she was standing, not weeping.[5] This and similar patristic interpretations of the passage in John are rather obviously colored by a strong residue of the still potent cultural ideals of stoicism and impassivity formulated in republican and imperial Rome. With some modification these same values animated the heroic idealism of the early Middle Ages, so much so that the representation of Mary as inexpressive persists into the twelfth century before it is overwhelmed by the pictorial and narrative tradition of the weak and suffering mother. Traces of the older conception can be found in Richard of St. Victor (d. 1173), in Alan of Lille (d. 1202), and to a lesser extent in Stephen of Sawley (d. 1252).[6]

The representation of Mary as emotional and pathetic seems to originate in the eastern church as early as the fourth century, where Mary is the imagined speaker of a number of laments spoken at the foot of the cross. Ephraim the Syrian (d. 373) is the author of one of the most celebrated and intense of these laments, which gives full expression to the emotional extravagance and extreme agony suffered by the Virgin. The lament of Ephraim, as Sandro Sticca has described it, gives a detailed account of the suffering of Mary, emphasizing her tears, sighs, and sobbing. She asks to kiss the wounds of her son and to embrace his body, motifs that are later fully developed and constitute a commonplace in the high medieval versions of the Passion story.[7] Mary's desire for physical contact with her son's body, as we shall see, is placed at the foreground of many of the most important later Passion narratives, where it takes on enormous significance in expressing the dominant cultural attitudes about control of the body. The Marian lament is productive and influential as an independent subgenre in the Middle Ages. As a theme, the sorrow of Mary at the foot of the cross is common in medieval culture: throughout western Europe we can find versions in poetry and prose, in Latin and in the vernaculars, ranging from brief lyrics to fuller accounts embedded in lengthy prose meditations; and it is a frequent subject of the art and drama of the later Middle Ages.[8]

The new concern with Mary's role in the Passion of Christ occurs in the west at a relatively well defined historical moment, roughly the turn of the twelfth century. The attention to Mary in the Passion narratives in some ways may be regarded as the natural accompaniment of the greatly increased interest in the Passion of Christ that occurs at this time. This interest can be regarded in a general context as a part of the growing pre-occupation with all aspects of the humanity of Christ, especially the part played by his suffering in human form in the economy of human salvation. In the course of the twelfth century a theological doctrine began to form that stressed the idea of Mary's unique compassion, or co-suffering, with Christ, a doctrine that gradually created an exalted position for Mary as the co-redemptrix of the human race.[9]

These greatly expanded narrative emphases on women and the Passion, focused primarily but not exclusively on Mary, are striking enough to lead us to ponder their situation within a broader network of historical developments, social relationships, and cultural practices. We may ask why the emphasis on the passive and suffering Mary appears rather suddenly around the year 1100, and in seeking the answer to that question we are justified in searching beyond the realms of devotional practice and theological speculation to the broader social and historical matrix where devotion and theology are inescapably coordinated. In seeking to understand the representation of women in the Passion meditations, it is useful to leave for a moment questions of origin and patterns of influence to adopt a synchronic view that observes these phenomena in relationship to other phenomena in the culture at large.

In the first place, it is important to notice that the increased attention to Mary coincides with a new focus on female characters in secular narrative. In the poetry and romances of the twelfth century, as has often been observed, a new conception of woman is articulated that places her at the center of the action: women become, in what is known as the courtly tradition, the objects of love and devotion. While women themselves do not often have active parts in these narratives, they are often the chief motivators of male activity. Many have noted that the idealization of women which begins in the twelfth century has two complementary faces: that of the Virgin in religious literature and that of the aristocratic lady in literature reflecting the milieu of secular court life of the period. Moreover, critics have observed similarities in the representations of the Virgin and the lady of secular romance.[10] Both are idealized paragons of virtue, remote and aloof, yet largely governed and defined by their appearance, emotions, desires, and physicality. The lady of the secular romance is quite transparently portrayed as the object of male sexual desire, but the same current of sexuality and eroticism, while perhaps more subliminal, is by no means absent from the way the Virgin is perceived in the laments and Passion narratives.[11]

These parallel and related developments have sometimes been accounted for by changes in the material conditions in European society that occurred after the year 1000, particularly changes that affected the position of aristocratic women. The successful consolidation of land and power in the hands of a relatively small number of seigneurial families created the surplus wealth that allowed a male dominated aristocratic society to maintain women in ever more splendid leisure. Among the dominant classes, as feminine roles became more strongly differentiated from masculine ones, males grew fascinated by the increasingly remote and distant object that their economic acquisitiveness had created; they projected onto woman the ideals and values that their culture either aspired to or sought to maintain. The relationship between material conditions and the development of social ideals is, of course, a complex matter, but at a minimum it seems reasonable to connect the idealization of women in both sacred and secular art and literature with the expansion of the wealth and power of the seigneurial class.[12]

It was once conventional to view these developments benignly, even as a sign of general progress in the evolution of the human race. The liberal humanist interpretation of these changes in attitudes toward women tended to regard them as evidence of the smoothing out of the rough edges of a grim and warlike feudal society that began shortly after the year 1000. There arose in western Europe a greater comprehension and more profound respect for the dignity of human personhood than had ever been conceived in previous societies. The violent heroic aggressiveness of the masculine secular warrior of the early Middle Ages is mitigated by the newly valued emollients of love and pity; one finds general concern for the inner life of individuals in both secular and religious domains.[13]

In recent decades, however, other perspectives have emerged to challenge these optimistic and benevolent understandings of the new, and seemingly exalted, place of women. Cultural historians and feminist critics and have taught us the importance of gender issues in understanding medieval society and have identified a pervasive discourse of misogyny in medieval cultural practices. Caroline Bynum, for example, notes about the misogyny of the later Middle Ages:

Not merely a defensive reaction on the part of men who were in fact socially, economically and politically dominant, it was fully articulated in theological, philosophical and scientific theory that was centuries old. Male and female were contrasted and asymmetrically valued as intellect/body, active/passive, rational/irrational, reason/emotion, self-control/lust, judgment/mercy and order/disorder.[14]

Howard Bloch is among those critics who have argued provocatively that most medieval idealizations of women, secular or religious, are, in fact, as misogynous as the most bitter overtly anti-feminist polemic. He offers a unified explanation of the contradictory views of women in medieval Christianity that regarded them as either the "devil's gateway" or the "bride of Christ." Both are totalizing interpretations that offer no middle ground; by transforming woman into an immutable and ahistorical category the function and worth of real women in society is denied. The result is that, "women are pushed to the margins, excluded from the middle, in other words, isolated from history" and therefore more easily controlled by the male-dominated power structure.[15]

Similar arguments that seem immediately applicable to the representation of Mary in the Passion narratives have been advanced by Marina Warner in her study of the cult of the Virgin. The new idealizing texts of the twelfth century seem to offer a view of Mary that exalts and ennobles rather than degrades the status of women, providing a positive image to counter the negative one that prevailed in the anti-feminist tracts and other writings that deal with women's position. Mary is recognized as the co-redemptrix of the human race, placed above all women in her virtues, frequently depicted as the bride of Christ in nuptial imagery derived from the Song of Songs, and in her sorrow and tender compassion for her suffering son she is held to be a model of behavior for all to emulate. Yet this idealization of Mary carries with it, according to Warner, a distinctly misogynous current.

Warner argues that the tendency in doctrine, art, and literature was to set the Virgin apart from other women, to emphasize that she was not like other women. She had very little in common with the experience of the mass of women for whom she was putatively an ideal, from the way she was engendered, to her manner of conceiving and giving birth, to the circumstances of her death. Even the suffering she endured in her life, that part of her experience that might be thought most likely to form the basis of a common bond with her fellow humans and especially women, was treated by some late medieval commentators, notably Ubertino da Casale, as unique and fundamentally different in kind from the suffering undergone by the other members of the human race. All these various strategies of separation, Warner maintains, had a misogynous effect that was deliberate.[16] Her conclusion is that through the idealized passive Virgin the "myth of female inferiority and dependence could be and was perpetuated."[17]

According to Elizabeth Robertson, such misogyny is manifest in varieties of devotional prose of the time, especially those texts intended for women. Her study of the twelfth- and thirteenth-century English *Ancrene Wisse* and the Katherine Group is important for its emphasis on audience. Many of Robertson's conclusions seem capable of extension to the Passion narratives that were written in approximately the same period and in a similar cultural and social environment, many of which were likewise envisioned for female readers. Robertson argues that even works that appear on the surface to be gender-neutral in respect to audience (such as the *Ancrene Wisse*) embody values, ideals, and attitudes that are constructed from a male point of view to promote roles for women in which obedience, acceptance, suffering, silence, and repression of the sensual are essential.[18] In style, these works, much in the manner of the Passion narratives, often employ realistic, concrete imagery—largely, Robertson contends, because their male authors considered those literary strategies specifically appropriate for female readers, who in the prevailing discourse of misogyny were associated with the physical and the literal, thought to be less capable than men of understanding the spiritual, and as lacking in meditative powers.[19]

Still more recently, however, other vantage points have been adopted that regard the representation of women in male-authored devotional or religious texts and in women's mystical and visionary literature as much less uniformly misogynous than critics such as Bloch, Warner, or Robertson might allow. At first glance, these new interpretations might seem to revert to the generous optimism of the pre-feminist era, but on closer inspection, they recover that more positive outlook from entirely different critical and theoretical bases. These interpretations take into account reception theory and post-structuralist ideas about textuality and the complex cultural signification of signs by insisting on the multiple and even conflicting meanings that texts can have to differently constituted audiences (including, especially, differently gendered audiences). They by no means minimize the discourse of misogyny, but maintain that both misogyny and resistance to misogyny might coexist within a single text; that a single textual representation of female behavior might be understood as confining and normative, or emancipatory and transgressive. Karma Lochrie, for example, has examined women's mysticism taking into account medieval theories about the body and Julia Kristeva's ideas on abjection to show that the discourse of female mysticism has the potential to disrupt and subvert, not merely reinforce, the claims of the dominant patriarchy.[20] Theresa Coletti finds that the representation of Mary in certain mystery plays "may contest rather than simply reproduce traditional gender roles and meanings," an especially challenging idea in the face of the widely held view (described above) that the medieval cult of the Virgin served to perpetuate existing power arrangements by imagining woman as weak and subordinate.[21] Anne Clark Bartlett's study of devotional literature emphasizes the complexities of audience and the reading process and attempts to show that various "counterdiscourses," favorable to women, compete with the misogynous representations of woman in many religious texts.[22]

My own position is similar to this latter group of critics, with some qualifications I will explain later. I have argued earlier in this study that texts often reproduce prevailing power relationships and contribute to their formation and perpetuation. At the same time, a view that this is the only social function of texts is far too limiting, as Jauss, among others, has argued.[23] We must, I agree, allow for the possibility of emancipation, subversion, challenge, and revolution, even in texts that are produced from inside the dominant culture. We must also recognize the reality of spiritual or idealizing understandings of these texts, even as we realize that the supratemporal (whether considered as real or as an illusion) is created within history itself.[24]

Questions of audience and reception are obviously important in understanding these potentialities. Jauss has shown us that audiences take an active part in constituting whatever it is we might term the "meaning" of a text;[25] many modern theorists have urged that texts, signs, and images must be regarded as having multiple and often competing significances, the complexities of which can be understood by recognizing that audiences themselves were multiple and diverse, differentiated by gender, class, and education, and located within different social and cultural frameworks. Margaret Miles reflects these understandings in her description of the function of religious images in medieval culture as she argues that "no account of the role of images in the religious life of fourteenth-century communities that assumes that the perspective of only one group of persons within the culture can even begin to tell us about the complexity of the

images and their possible interpretations."[26] The notion of variously constituted audiences with multiple and even contradictory responses, some
organized along the lines of gender, is, I believe, necessary in understanding the social and literary function of the Passion narratives.

While affirming this position, I would like to argue for a somewhat
subtler, less universalizing, understanding of the notion of audience than
seems to be current (although not among the critics I named in preceding paragraphs). In reference to gender in particular, I think it is important to acknowledge that not just men but some women (or audiences of
women), whether considered "immasculated" or internalizing dominant
male-constructed values, may have read these texts in misogynous ways.[27]
Not just women but some men, "feminized" or themselves ambiguously
or alternatively gendered, may have found in the texts resistance and opposition to prevailing norms, including those having to do with gender relations. It is also quite likely that even within a single reader, male or female,
competing, indeed contradictory beliefs and value systems may have been
held in tension, struggled for supremacy, or peacefully coexisted. Thus at
the smallest unit of audience, the individual reader, the text's meaning may
have been understood in a conflicted, confusing manner, with different
understandings held simultaneously or sequentially—perhaps (and the suggestion is not altogether facetious) depending upon the day of the week, or
perhaps conditioned by how one was located at any given moment within
the immediate, social micro-environment. I refrain, however, from completely atomizing the notion of audience, and will not assert that because
no two persons read the text in exactly the same way the text could mean
anything and therefore nothing, making it futile to talk about reception
at all.[28]

I also believe that the current tendency to find oppositional readings
in texts that seem to reproduce the dominant ideology must be examined
cautiously, if not problematized. If we can now be said to find ourselves
firmly planted inside the post-modern age, then even from that necessarily
restricted outlook I think we can discern our special affinity for the subversion and resistance in narratives. We want to see not only how ideology
is reinforced but how it is undermined. This affinity has undeniably en-
riched our understanding of medieval texts, opening them up to interpre-
tative possibilities that a previous generation of readers and critics could
not conceive. In approaching medieval texts, however, we must be conscious that the extent of the opposition and subversion we find is likely to

be conditioned by our own historical positioning. The danger in this kind of reading is a crude and forced alliance of medieval and modern ideals, of the kind Derek Pearsall complained of in his anatomy of the ironizing tendency in modern Chaucer criticism: "By this means Chaucer can be recruited to worthy causes, and all need of effort at true understanding is removed."[29] Recent criticism of medieval religious texts having to do with women has been far more subtle than this. I only raise a cautionary note, and I will certainly not fall into a positivist blunder by claiming that a certain quotient of subversion is "really there" in the texts, awaiting discovery, and that some modern readers have miscalculated it. But I do think it is important to appreciate that the subversive elements of texts may seem more important to us than to medieval people, and that we may have exaggerated, or as post-modern people, be prone to exaggerating, their scope and significance within medieval culture. I will argue for a plural text in the readings that follow, but I will keep in mind the need to avoid "a naive fusing" of horizons of expectations, in Jauss's terminology, in our critical practice and discussions of reception.[30] Taking into account the terms of my own cautionary, in my reading of women's roles in the Passion narratives I will probably notice less opposition, less potential for subversion than many other readers would find.

One of the reasons this is so lies in my belief that it is a matter of consequence that males are the authors of most of the texts dealt with in this study. The perspective on women and women's roles formed in the Passion narratives is, it can be argued, a deeply masculine one, even in the many cases when their intended audience is female. That perspective tends to affirm the rightness of the subordinate position of woman in medieval society by constructing an image of the Virgin Mary that largely conforms to male expectations of female behavior and male understandings of female personality, psychology, and appropriate demeanor.

The enlarged role of the Virgin in the Passion narratives seems, in fact, to be a product of the male imagination. It may seem at first counterintuitive, but it is nevertheless generally true that when women wrote about the Passion of Christ the Virgin Mary was rarely at the center of the narrative the way she often was in narratives written by men. Angela of Foligno, Bridget of Sweden, Julian of Norwich, and Margery Kempe all give us detailed accounts of the Passion in which the Virgin Mary plays either no part at all or only a minor one. In describing the devotional practices of women in general in the later Middle Ages, Caroline Bynum observes

that "there is no evidence that women were especially attracted to devotion to the Virgin or to married women saints (indeed there is some evidence that they were less attracted than men)."[31] Bynum notes that women
(and Margery Kempe provides a good example of this) tend to emphasize
a handsome, young, human Christ, whereas males more frequently have
visions of the Virgin Mary.[32]

While this distinction along the lines of gender may be generally true,
I want to avoid universalizing statements about these texts at the level of
production (authorship), just as I argued above for multiple possibilities at
the level of consumption (audience and reception). I want to allow for the
possibility of variety and conflict in male-generated perspectives on gender issues within the predominant misogynous discourse. If males were
the authors, they were not all gendered alike, and this multiplicity, it is
logical, might find expression in the texts they wrote. In representing the
Virgin there might be multiple male vantage points within a community
of writers or even within a single male author.

When we turn to the texts themselves, despite their idealizing of the
Virgin, it is easy to see how they are aligned with the prevailing discourse
of misogyny; it is perhaps less easy to see how they express resistance or
opposition to hegemonic social norms.

Most readers of medieval Passion narratives in which Mary plays a
central role will immediately have been struck by the care the authors have
frequently taken to describe the subjective emotional state of the Virgin,
especially in her suffering and sorrow. Over and over again, these texts insistently invite us to imagine what it would have been like for Mary to
have seen her son tortured and to conform ourselves to her mental condition in order to grieve along with her; at the same time they recount the
full extent of Mary's suffering in vivid and concrete detail. The pains that
are taken to represent the interior life have both a general and a specific
significance. They may be seen, and have been seen, as among the many
indications of the twelfth-century "discovery of the individual," part of the
"search for the self" that is held to define the period.[33] We may note that
the intense interest in female psychology manifested so strikingly in certain of the Passion meditations is related to the general interest in the self
and subjectivity that intensified in twelfth-century Europe, and remained
a vital and persistent concern, as Lee Patterson has reminded us, from that
time forward into the Renaissance.[34]

It is important to remember that this new attention to female subjectivity is largely male constructed, and to affirm that it is a complex matter capable of multiple interpretations. When social and gender issues are carefully heeded these new literary efforts may be seen, for example, as something much less benign than part of a noble effort to understand common humanity and the varied face of human nature. Questions of appropriation and control come to the foreground.

Elaine Tuttle Hansen has argued in reference to Chaucer's Clerk's Tale and the *Legend of Good Women* that, despite the centrality of their female subjects, they are really poems about the masculine imagination.[35] Carolyn Dinshaw's study of Chaucer reminds us pointedly of the limitations of adopting a view of the masculine writer with an imagination so capacious and humane that he can project himself into the feelings of women as well as men.[36] What results when these assumptions are made is the obscuring of the strong differentiation in the valuing of genders in a patriarchal culture, and an overly simple idea of the "naturalness and ease of cross-gender or double-gender identification."[37]

These ideas are pertinent to a consideration of female subjectivity in the Passion narratives. As noted earlier, the Passion narratives that pay attention to Mary's suffering seem, as far as we can tell, to have been written by men. The representation of the sorrowing Mary can only be fully understood, I believe, if it is regarded from a gendered perspective, the product of the male imagination. It is a representation intended for both male and female audiences, but, as I shall suggest later, probably operating upon them quite differently and appealing to them on quite different levels.

From the first appearance in the eleventh century of the expanded accounts of the Passion, a certain curiosity about and fascination with the idea of female suffering permeates them; one senses that here is unknown terrain to be explored, understood, and consequently, perhaps, managed if not controlled. Anselm, for example, addresses Mary as follows in a prayer written by 1104:

Domina mea misericordissima, quos fontes dicam erupisse de pudicissimis oculis, cum attenderes unicum filium tuum innocentem coram te ligari, flagellari, mactari? Quos fluctus credam perfudisse piissimum vultum, cum suspiceres eundem filium et deum et dominum tuum in cruce sine culpa extendi et carnem de carne tua ab impiis crudeliter dissecari?[38]

[My most merciful Lady, what can I say about the fountains that flowed from your most pure eyes when you saw your only Son before you, bound, beaten and hurt?

What do I know of the flood that drenched your matchless face, when you beheld your Son, your Lord, and your God, stretched on the cross without guilt, when the flesh of your flesh was cruelly butchered by wicked men?]

Bonaventure, in the *Lignum vitae* of the mid-thirteenth century, asks: "Quae lingua dicere vel quis intellectus capere sufficit desolationum tuarum pondus, Virgo beata?" ("O Virgin blest, what tongue could utter, what mind could grasp, the heaviness of your sorrow!").[39]

These expressions may be understood, from a humane and generous perspective, as an effort to imagine what it would be like to experience the world from another's point of view. An imaginative attempt is made to construct female subjectivity as part of a liberating and inclusive project promoting a more finely nuanced understanding human nature. But there is also a sense, increasingly palpable in versions of the theme that appear in the thirteenth and fourteenth centuries, that the concern to know and understand Mary's suffering becomes, from a modern standpoint, nearly an obsession. Hans Belting has spoken of the "almost pathological description of Mary's emotions" found in late medieval accounts.[40] The *Meditationes vitae Christi* provide many examples of what Belting noticed, as the following passage illustrates:

Ipsa cum filio pendebat in cruce; et potius elegit mori cum ipso, quam amplius vivere. Undique sunt angustiae, et tormenta sentiri poterant, narrari vero nullatenus poterant. Stabat mater juxta crucem ejus, et inter crucem latronis, non avertebat oculos a filio, angustiabatur ut ipse.[41]

[She hung with her son on the cross and wished to die with him rather than live any longer. Everywhere are tortures and torments that can be sensed but in truth hardly described. The mother stood next to his cross, between the crosses of the thieves. She did not turn her eyes away from her son; she was in anguish like his.]

The desire to "know" the degree of her suffering and to imagine her torments can be interpreted as invasive, nearly voyeuristic. Julia Kristeva's analysis of female abjection is helpful in understanding the masculinist representation of Mary in these accounts of the Passion. Voyeurism, Kristeva notes, "accompanies the writing of abjection."[42] Kristeva analyzes the male desire to lay bare and expose the female innards through writing, noting that, "if that monologue spreads out the abject, it is not because there is a woman speaking. But because, *from afar*, the writer approaches the hysterical body so that it might speak, so that he might speak, using it as a springboard, of what eludes speech."[43] Leaving aside the challenging psychological subtleties of Kristeva's analysis, in broad terms I think it is applicable to the literary strategies employed by the male authors of the Passion meditations in their effort to come to terms with the suffering of Mary. There is much more that can be said on the subject of voyeurism in relation to the Passion meditations. Turning to the social and political implications of voyeurism, Georges Duby, for example, suggests that the lack of privacy, the laying open of the most intimate details of one's life for public view, has every thing to do with the enforcement of power relationships; a similar point is made by Foucault about the development of surveillance in the eighteenth and nineteenth centuries.[44]

When Mary's behavior is described in the Passion narratives, the emphasis is usually on her great physical weakness, immobility, and muteness. In the *Meditationes vitae Christi*, for example, she cannot approach Christ because of the crowds, and when she meets him carrying the cross we are told: "semimortua facta est prae angustia, nec verbum ei dicere potuit" ("she was half dead of anguish and could not say a word to him").[45] When she girds the naked Christ with her veil at the foot of the cross: "Eripitur enim filius suus de manibus ejus furibunde" ("Her Son was torn furiously from her hands").[46] She is "insensible" or "half dead" from her grief: "Tunc mater semimortua cecidit inter brachia Magdalenae" ("then the mother, half dead, fell into the arms of the Magdalene"), and so on.[47] Much is made in many of the meditations of her repeated fainting and the need for others to support her since she is unable to walk unassisted. This is, of course, the physical counterpart of the extravagant inner suffering we have spoken of above. It embodies the consistent working out of the story of a tortured and victimized woman as seen from the dominant male point of view. Mary, in her very public fainting, sobbing, sighing, collapsing, weeping, touching, and embracing, has her body on display; her inner feelings and emotions are also relentlessly anatomized and probed in many of these narratives.

What is expressed in many of the later Passion meditations, it seems, is male fascination with a woman tormented, passive, and frequently (as the earlier quoted passage from the *Meditationes vitae Christi* illustrates), literally immobilized by suffering. These texts irretrievably reduce, limit, and therefore confine the female role by defining it solely in terms of a single dimension or characteristic, the capacity to endure suffering. The foregrounding of the female psyche and its convincing representation in the person of Mary may be a tribute to the sympathetic imagination of male authors, but equally present are those voyeuristic and invasive strategies, which taken to their extreme can be humiliating and degrading. The extravagantly suffering Mary can be interpreted as an attempt to appropriate female subjectivity to serve male-defined ends having to do with the dissemination and perpetuation of established ideas about gender relationships.

These same texts, however, might have had been received quite differently by their female audiences, although I again would urge that such reception, whether by male or by female audiences, should not be monolithically imagined. The behavior of Mary is a complex sign capable of multiple signification within medieval society. It may be said that the very presence of woman in these narratives is itself significant, with the capacity to be empowering for women, even if, or perhaps because, the representation emphasized suffering, passivity, and extravagant display of emotion.[48] In ways that had never been imagined before, a woman is at center stage in the drama of human salvation, the chief act of human history. The worth of passive suffering and weakness, essential to "femininity" (as medieval society had constructed it) is not denied. In the Passion narratives, Mary is represented as a model of suffering and compassion, not just for women but for the entire human race, to promote emotional responses to the sufferings of Christ. The famous thirteenth-century Latin poem "Stabat Mater" is quite clear about the exemplary function of Mary: "Quis non posset contristari, / piam matrem contemplari / dolentem cum filio?" ("Who could not have compassion in contemplating the pious mother suffering with her son?").[49]

The kind of suffering undergone by Mary is understood to be mental and interior rather than physical. Bonaventure declares that Christ knew that her heart: "quam compassionis suae gladio amplius, quam si proprio patereris in corpore, vere sciebat transfixam" ("was more severely wounded by the sword of compassion for him than if you had suffered in your own body").[50] That specifically interior quality of female suffering, together with that projection onto the female of a special capacity for suffering noted in the discussion above, may be positively understood as the feminization of suffering, a project that should be associated with the feminized body of Christ in the later medieval devotional tradition. Such projects tended to bring about a blurring of rigid gender distinctions, or to suggest a different set of standards by which to value "masculine" or "feminine" behavior.[51] And the expressionistic emotional display in the Passion meditations, the extravagant gestures, the fainting, the weeping need not necessarily be read in modern terms as "pathological" or lurid, but as articulations of a late medieval cultural ideal that transcended sexual difference and may have been understood as doing so by both male and female audiences. Fainting and tears were not confined to women nor to the cloistered, as any reader of Malory (or any number of other seemingly male-directed works) soon discovers.

The valorization of the feminine in a highly charged way can sometimes be uncovered in the writings of male authors of the Passion narratives. Anselm's passionate declarations to the Virgin Mary quoted above (note 38) or those of the author of the *Meditationes vitae Christi* — "O qualis tunc erat anima matris, cum sic poenose videbat eum deficere, languere, lacrymari, et mori!" ("Oh, what was the soul of the mother like, then, when she saw him thus painfully weaken, faint, weep, and die!")[52] — express explicitly a desire to understand Mary. Those passages also, it seems to me, express implicitly a wistful and not very deeply submerged longing for feminization, particularly poignant in a society that insisted on rigidly maintained distinctions between genders. This is a masculine perspective that may coincide in these texts with the predominating misogyny and unsettle the certitude of hegemonic norms.

In the gospel record of the Passion, as we have noted, Mary's part is extremely small, and no speech or any other form of utterance is assigned to her. Many of the Passion meditations supply this want, but they often do so in ways that define and limit women's speech, keeping it in conformity with totalizing male-constructed understandings of the nature of women's discourse. Speech, of course, is a prerequisite to power and autonomy in individual persons, the necessary means by which one negotiates one's place in social relationships and asserts identity. The kind of speech the male authors of the Passion meditations create for Mary tells us much about the occulted ideals of these texts. Here the contrast between the Virgin Mary and Mary Magdalene reveals much about medieval attitudes and social values. In the gospels Magdalene is favored as the person to whom Christ first appeared after his resurrection, and she uses her facility of speech to announce the resurrection to the male disciples. For Magdalene, her speech act is highly valued and hence empowering and liberating. It is not peripheral but primary. Nor is it merely expressive; it is for Christians the vehicle of truth and meaning of the highest order: the fact of Christ's victory over death. The feminist possibilities inherent in this story were sometimes developed in a discourse that countered the passivity of the Virgin by offering an ideal that authorized women as users of language, as in the fifteenth-century *Book of the City of Ladies* of Christine de Pisan:

Similarly, God endowed women with the faculty of speech—may he be praised for it—for had he not done so, they would be speechless. But in refutation of what this proverb says, (which someone, I don't know whom, invented deliberately to attack them), if women's language had been so blameworthy and of such small authority, as some men argue, our Lord Jesus Christ would never have deigned to wish that so worthy a mystery as his most gracious resurrection be first announced by a woman, just as he commanded the blessed Magdalene, to whom he first appeared on Easter, to report and announce it to his apostles and to Peter. Blessed God, may you be praised, who, among the other infinite boons and favors which you have bestowed upon the feminine sex, desired that woman carry such lofty and worthy news.[53]

The language given to the Virgin in the Passion narratives, however, is conditioned by male evaluations of women's speech. The Virgin's speeches do not convey meaning (in the form of factual information) but serve merely to express emotion and to identify her as weak and powerless. The utterance given to her in the pseudo-Bede in response to the death of her son is typical:

O fili dulcissime, quid facit haec misera et moestissima, cui me miseram commen-datam relinquis, fili mi dulcissime? Memento mei et omnis familiae tuae, quam sic desolatam dimittis, memento omnium qui tibi serviunt, fili mi; in manus tuas et patris tui commendo me ipsam et totam familiam tuam. O pater sancte Deus, O pater, in manus tuas commendo filium meum, imo et dominum meum, in quan-tum possum, et non in quantum debeo, quia non possum, quia deficio et hoc desidero ante filium in conspectu tuo mori.[54]

[O sweetest son, what will your wretched and sorrowful one do, to whom have you commended me, miserable, my sweetest son? Remember me and all your family, which you have left so desolate, remember all those who serve you, my son; I com-mend myself and all your family into your hands and those of your father. O father, holy God, O father, I commend my son into your hands, indeed my lord, as much as I can, and not as much as I ought, for I cannot, because I grow weak and desire to die before the son in your sight.]

Among the Passion narratives which appear to challenge this concep-tion of women's speech is the *Dialogus beatae Mariae et Anselmi de passione domini*. Here the male, Anselm, is the passive interlocutor about the events of the Passion, and Mary is placed in the position of authoritative tutor, possessed of special knowledge by virtue of her being an eyewitness. Mary enjoys her status as teacher (*magister*) because she has been glorified and speaks to Anselm in a vision. In heaven, she explains, she is exempt from all the suffering, weeping, and extravagant emotions that defined her existence on earth. Significantly, she is given the detached, objective, "magisterial" voice associated with male written authority, at the same time as she speaks from within a vision, the most credible and prestigious mode of female discourse in medieval society from the time of Hildegard of Bingen onward. Mary, in her exalted position, speaks a few words of her own in her story of the Passion, but mostly she recites verbatim the relatively austere language of the gospels.[55] The Virgin therefore adopts the apostolic role of Mary Magdalene, reconceived and refigured in a greatly enlarged and expanded sense, by becoming, for a male audience, the vehicle of the gospel truths that explain the meaning of the Passion. The prestige and agency given to the Virgin is carried over even into her self-reporting of the non-gospel elaborations of her behavior after the death of her son, which were usually the place in the tradition where the passivity and subordination of the Virgin was most prominently represented. After the body of Christ is removed from the cross, Mary does not wish to be separated from her dead son; she wishes to be buried with him. She is persuaded otherwise by John, but, unlike many of the versions of the story, it is she who explicitly gives permission for her son to be buried: "Tandem invita, permisi ut sepeliretur" ("Finally, reluctantly, I allowed him to be buried").[56] We shall explore later the significance of other variations of this narrative detail.

Mary becomes an actor and acquires a voice in the Passion narratives, such as the *Dialogus*, that extend the gospel narrative by focusing on her behavior after the death of her son. These narratives, as noted in chapter 2, derive from the *planctus* tradition, and the voice of Mary is mediated through its generic and rhetorical conventions, which above all emphasized emotional expressiveness. The foundation text is the Passion treatise beginning, "Quis dabit capiti meo aquam," by Ogier of Locedio (d. 1214) but quickly attributed to Bernard. As noted in chapter 2, the lament was one of the most widely circulated devotional texts of the later Middle Ages. In its treatment of Mary's suffering it became a mastersource for countless other medieval narratives, many of which in turn were popular in their own right. Hans Belting has demonstrated its importance in the formation of affective devotional images in the later Middle Ages.[57] It is also worth noting that the work arose from the same northern Italian-southern French cultural milieu of the late twelfth century within which there seems to have been a special interest in women's feelings and the representation of women, as shown, for example, by the flourishing of courtly love poetry.[58] The "Quis dabit" appears to be addressed to women—"O vos filie Ierusalem, sponse dilecte dei, vna mecum lacrimas fundite donec nobis noster sponsus in sua speciositate benignus et suauis appareat vel occurrat"

("O you daughters of Jerusalem, beloved brides of God, pour out your tears together with me until our bridegroom appears to meet us, sweet and kind in his beauty") [59] — but judging by its vast manuscript tradition it certainly must have found very many male readers.

The tract is in the form of a first person lament, notable for its highly wrought emotional style, which its male author may have felt was especially appropriate for the female audience he envisaged (or the female audience he invented in his text). The narrative is formally complex, even confused and inconsistent at times. It proceeds, after the narrator's initial lament, in the form of a dialogue, with the narrator asking questions about details of the Passion events and Mary responding. The questioning narrator soon drops away, however, and Mary relates what purports to be her eyewitness account of the Passion. This in turn modulates into standard third person omniscient narration, as Mary's distinctive point of view is no longer maintained, and the fiction that it is she who is reporting the Passion events is lost sight of entirely. Although Mary has acquired a voice in this Passion treatise, it is significant that at some difficult to determine point it disappears, submerged into the voice of the general narrator — in contrast for example, to the continuously felt presence of Mary in the *Dialogus* of the pseudo-Anselm considered above.

Mary's male-constructed self-description emphasizes her passivity, her emotionality, her physical weakness and lack of power. She reports of herself, for example: "Quando hec audiui, gressu qualicumque potui, et vix potui, ad dominum meum, filium meum, veni plorans. Cumque eum fuissem intuita . . . commota sunt omnia uiscera mea, et defecit spiritus meus, et non erat michi sensus, neque vox, neque sonus" ("When I heard these things, I came weeping to my lord, my son, by whatever course I could, and I was scarcely able to do so. And when I looked at him . . . all my innards were stirred, my spirit failed, and there was in me neither sense, nor voice nor sound").[60] This passage, and others like it, contribute powerfully to the project of the dominant male culture to constitute suffering as a gendered activity, in which suffering of a certain kind belongs to women, and the physical forms used to give it outward expression are defined in terms of the prevailing subordinate conception of women.

Much of the fascination of the treatise, and perhaps one of the reasons for its wide appeal, resides in its almost uncanny success in uncoiling the dynamic tension between a Mary who is most often passive, restrained, even insensate, and at other times, a desperate Mary on the verge of lurching out of control. These tensions and contradictions are illustrated several times by Mary's behavior at the foot of the cross, where the body of Christ is the site of contention and conflict. The first instance is her effusive and repetitive outburst in which she begs to be taken up on the cross and crucified along with Christ, a speech that seems to reveal the author's attempt to represent the discourse of female suffering. Mary laments:

Quid faciam? Moritur filius meus. Cur secum non moritur, hec mestissima mater? Fili mi, fili mi! Amor vnice, fili dulcissime, noli me derelinquere post te! Trahe me ad teipsum, vt moriar tecum. Male solus moreris. Tecum moriatur ista tua genitrix. O mors misera, noli michi parcere: tu sola michi places pre cunctis. Exaggera vires: trucida matrem, matrem cum filio perime simul. Fili dulcor vnice, singulare gaudium, vita anime mee et omne solacium, fac vt ego ipsa nunc moriar, que te ad mortem genui. O fili, recognosce teneram et exaudi precem meam. Decet enim filium exaudire matrem desolatam. Exaudi me, obsecro! In tuo me suscipe patibulo, vt qui vna carne viuunt et vno amore se diligunt, vna morte pereant. . . . O fili care, o nate benigne, miserere matris, suscipe preces. Desine matri nunc esse durus, qui cunctis semper fuisti benignus. Suscipe matrem tecum in cruce, vt viuam tecum post mortem semper. . . . O vere dei nate, tu michi pater, tu michi mater, tu michi sponsus, tu michi filius, tu michi omnia eras. Nunc orbor patre, viduor sponso, desolor prole, omnia perdo.[61]

[What shall I do? My son is dying. Why cannot this most sorrowful mother not die with him? My son, my son! My only love, sweetest son, do not leave me behind! Take me to yourself, that I might die with you. It is wrong for you to die alone. Let your own mother die with you. O wretched death, do not spare me: you alone are pleasing to me above all things. Increase your strength: slaughter the mother, kill the mother together with the son. O son, sole delight, singular joy, life of my soul and my entire solace, make me die now, who bore you for death. O son, recognize that I am weak, and hear my prayer. It is fitting for a son to hear his desolate mother. Hear me, I beg you. Take me up onto your cross, that those who live as one flesh and love each other with one love might perish in one death. . . . O dear son, o kind child, have mercy on your mother; hear her prayers. Be no longer harsh to your mother, you who were always kind to everyone. Take up your mother with you on the cross, so I might live with you always after death. . . . O true child of God, you were my father, you were my mother, you were my bridegroom, you were my son, you were my everything. Now I am deprived of a father, bereft of a bridegroom, forsaken by a son, I lose everything.]

Here is female identity with the Savior commended in Bonaventure's *De perfectione vitae* taken to unsettling excess.[62] The reversal of roles implied in Mary's lament might be emancipatory for female readers, but at the same time deeply disquieting for male audiences. The whole speech has subversive inflections, notably illustrated by the last words of Mary on the

breaking down of gender roles and the dissolution of the hierarchy of patriarchal familial relationships: Jesus is her father, mother, bridegroom, son.
This is rhetoric that is used elsewhere in the devotional tradition, notably
by Anselm, but its intensity and unrelenting thoroughness are remarkable
here. Her wish is not just a death wish; her radical proposals, made *in ex-
tremis*, carry with them the suggestion of female assumption of the masculine role of agent of human redemption, or at the very least a more active
participation in that event. Mary here acts the part of the destabilized, off-
center woman, disturbing comfortable male certainties, described by Luce
Irigaray and other feminist critics; closer at hand, Mary's behavior may
have been modeled on the transgressive, unruly behavior reported in lives
of medieval women saints and mystics.[63] Yet in the "Quis dabit" lament it
is important to see that it is not merely her being out of control, but the
prospect of her being in control, that is worrisome.

In the text, however, Mary is out of control and allowed to play
against her conventional passivity for a limited time only. From a male
point of view, these tensions are resolved and anxieties over female usur-
pation and outrageous behavior are soon relieved. The resumption of
restraint and the imposition of control are careful, pointed, and deliberate. Observing his mother's behavior, Christ from the cross commends
his mother to John, telling her, in addition to the words of the gospel, "Interim Iohannes, qui est nepos meus, tibi reputabitur filius. Curam
habebit tui et solacium fidelissimum erit tibi" ("In the mean time, John,
my nephew, will be thought of as your son. He will take care of you, and
will be a most faithful comfort to you").[64] Thus is male dominion firmly
reinstated.

Another crisis is reached at the moment of Christ's death on the cross.
Mary has resumed her pattern of extravagant, passive, voiceless, insensate
suffering:

Non lingua loqui, non mens cogitare valebit, quanto dolore afficebantur pia viscera
Marie. . . . Iuxta Christi crucem stabat emortua mater. Et que sancto <spiritu>
conceperat, vox illi non erat. Dolor enim vires abstulit. . . . Ista stabat, hic pendebat.
Immo ista strata iacens pallebat anima viuens. Viuebat moriens, et viuens moriebatur. Nec potuit mori, que viuens mortua fuit.[65]

[The tongue cannot speak, nor the mind conceive, the extent of the sorrow that
affected the pious innards of Mary. . . .The dead mother stood near the cross of
Christ. And she who had conceived by the holy spirit had no voice. Sorrow truly
had carried off her strength. . . . She stood there; he hung on the cross. Rather, her

living soul grew pale as she lay prostrate. Dying she lived; and living, she died. Nor could she die, who was a living dead person.]

But Mary rouses herself from prostration, regains her voice, and once again makes an outrageous proposal with the potential for subversion: she asks for control of the body of her dead son, and her excessive behavior and speech suggest again the woman potentially out of control. She gazes on his body, presses against his feet, kisses the blood stains on the cross, and attempts to embrace the body while it is still on the cross; her attempt pointedly fails, reinforcing the gendered norms of female physical weakness and ineffectuality:

Volebat amplecti Christum in alto pendentem, sed manus in frustra tense, in se complexe redibant; se eleuat a terra tangere dilectum, vt sic saltem doloris sui aliquatenus demulceat aculeum. Et quia tangere nequibat, membra virginea ad terram collisa iaciuntur.[66]

[She wished to embrace Christ hanging on high on the cross, but her hands stretched out in vain and returned enfolding themselves. She raised herself from the ground to touch her beloved, so that she might in this way soften the sting of her sorrow, at least to some extent. And because she could not touch, the virgin limbs were thrown down to the ground and dashed together.]

Mary's final attempt to control the body of her son is the most excessive and outrageous, again carrying the theme of identity with the suffering Christ to its literal and subversive extreme: she wishes to be buried with her son. Her struggle against the stronger males who are in charge of the body is vividly expressed: "Nolite, queso, eum tam cito tradere sepulture. Date illum michi, vt michi saltem defunctus; aut si filium in sepulcro deponitis, matrem, iam non matrem, cum illo sepelite: vt quid viuam post illum?" ("Do not, I beg, commit him so quickly to the grave. Give him to me; to me even though he is dead; or if you wish to place the son in the grave, bury the mother, now not a mother, with him, for why should I live after him?").[67] An unseemly tussle ensues over control of the dead body, a struggle between one weak woman and several powerful men: "Illi tumulare volebant. Hec ad se trahebat, hec retinere studet; illi sepelire conantur. Sicque vertitur inter eos pia lis et miseranda contencio" ("They wished to bury him. She drew him to herself and sought to keep him; they attempted to bury him. and so a pious dispute and pitiful struggle broke out among them").[68] Even though the text tells us that all had compassion for the virgin's sorrow, there is no doubt of the outcome of the struggle in this nar-

rative thoroughly governed by male-constructed views of the power relationships between genders. The body is buried as the male members of the
company desire. Mary collapses, reassuming for good her safe and comfortable passivity in the most drastic terms yet expressed in the text; her
will and body are now completely in the control of others. Significantly,
Mary is raised from the ground by John. Tortured by sobbing, worn out
by pain, unable to stand on her own feet, she is then led toward Jerusalem
supported by other women. Once again the text raises male anxieties about
uncontrolled female behavior precipitated by emotionalism, and succeeds
in resolving those anxieties by definitively reinstating patriarchal values at
the end of the narrative. The woman who had engaged in a physical contest with John and Joseph of Arimathea for the body of Christ is reduced
to a tortured woman unable to walk or speak, led by other women into
the house of John, and reinserted into the enclosed domestic space of the
secular patriarchy.

In my reading of these Marian episodes, I have emphasized how they
work to reinforce established hierarchical values, relegating women to a
position of submissiveness and dependency. Even if we grant that this is
the primary function they serve, it is important to recognize other possibilities and other potentialities in this series of incidents. For example, it is
quite likely that some readers, particularly some female readers, might have
found in these examples of outrageously inverted female behavior the possibility that the existing order could be challenged or subverted. As Natalie
Zemon Davis reminds us in her analysis of the temporary inversions of expected behavioral patterns in times of festivity or carnival, such inversions,
even as they serve to reinforce existing hierarchies, at least offer the possibility of new ways of thinking about social arrangements, and a wider
range of conceivable options for ways of behaving: thus they can promote
resistance to existing norms.[69] If we follow Bakhtin's analysis of carnival,
such inversions always have the potential to be liberating.[70]

Thus, as I stated earlier about the Passion treatises in general, the
"Quis dabit" lament might have had quite different and even contradictory
meanings to different audiences; it is best regarded as a richly multivalent
text. Certain audiences of women might have seen the lament as an emancipatory or empowering narrative, with Mary's "outrageous" behavior a
literary representation suggesting that the emotionality of women might
be a source of strength, that a social system might be imagined that would
tolerate a wider range of behavior and opportunity for women.

These invented post-crucifixion episodes of extraordinary richness and complexity are capable of sustaining many levels of interpretation and serving multiple, conflicting social functions. Not only do they bring to the foreground the asymmetries in political, social, and domestic power relationships between men and women in medieval society, but they also reveal the sexual dynamic underlying those relationships and express the anxieties that such a dynamic might generate in a male audience thoroughly implicated in the enforcement of the prevailing norms of repression and control. At the same time, these episodes contain the seeds of subversion and challenge, and might have been read in those terms especially by female audiences.

As we have seen above, issues of control in this narrative are most often contested over the body. The importance of the body in matters of power and authority has been emphasized by recent critics. In the "Quis dabit" lament the union of Christ and Mary is often expressed in terms charged with sensuality and bodily intimacy.[71] Mary begs her son: "In tuo me suscipe patibulo, vt qui vna carne viuunt et vno amore se diligunt, vna morte pereant" ("Take me up onto your cross, that those who live as one flesh and love each other with one love might perish in one death").[72] She exclaims, "Nil vero dulcius est michi quam te amplexo in cruce tecum mori" ("Nothing indeed is sweeter to me than to embrace you and die with you on the cross").[73] Her suffering is an ecstasy of self-annihilation: "Mater senciebat, et sentit Christi dolores. Que virgo peperit, gladium est passa doloris, Christi morientis. Vulnera matris erant Christi dolores; seui fuere tortores in anima matris" ("The mother felt and feels the pains of Christ. The Virgin who gave birth suffered the sword of sorrow, the dying Christ. The pains of Christ were the wounds of the mother, they were cruel torturers in the soul of the mother").[74] Her handling of the body of Christ is marked by a whole cluster of erotic images. Christ is Mary's "dilectum" ("beloved"),[75] whose virgin limbs she repeatedly attempts to touch. When she finally has the dead body in her control, intimate physical contact with the beautiful male body is emphasized:

Namque manus, caput, brachia, supra triste pectus habebat vel trahebat, dumque eum tangere potuit parumper, in osculis et amplexibus ruens, quia suo dilecto saciari non potuit. Virgo compaciens pie considerat, et tanti candoris, tantive splendoris et pulcritudinis iam erat corpus Iesu, quod nec lingua fari nec litera sufficit ostendere.[76]

[For she held or drew over her sad breast his hands, head, and arms, and as long as she could touch him a little while, she fell down in kisses and embraces, for she could not be sated with her beloved. The suffering Virgin piously gazed, and the body of Christ was now of such brilliance, of such splendor and beauty, that neither speech nor writing sufficed to show it.]

The most spectacular image has Mary smeared with the gore of her son and drinking his blood: "O sanguens pectus virgineum! Liquefacta est anima, facies pallet rosea, sed precioso filii sui rubet cruore respersa. Cadentes guttas sanguinis ore sacro tangebat" ("O bloody virgin breast, your soul has dissolved, your rosy face grows pale, but grows red sprinkled with the precious gore of her son. She touches the falling drops of blood with her sacred mouth").[77]

This may be explained as eucharistic, sacramental imagery, but it also suggests the sexual dimensions of the struggle for control of the male body. What is expressed in these episodes where Mary, for a time at least, has power over a very passive male body, is not only male alarm over female political or domestic power, but, on a deeper psychological level, male anxiety over aggressive female sexual behavior and the surrender of sexual control to a woman.

The emphasis on the body in "Quis dabit" is usefully viewed in relation to social and religious practices that belonged especially to the thirteenth century, the time when the lament was disseminated throughout western Europe. The Passion narrative confronts us with a woman in intimate physical contract with the wounded and bleeding body of Christ. In the course of the thirteenth century this was an increasingly important motif in women's visionary and spiritual writing. Bonaventure encouraged his women readers to enter into the wounds of Christ, and women's visions record increasingly graphic and detailed accounts of their experiences with the body of Christ. These accounts often employ the same erotic imagery, borrowed from the Song of Songs, that is used in the "Quis dabit" lament. In Jacques de Vitry's life of Marie d'Oignies (d. 1213), for example, we are told that Marie receives visions in which she holds the body of Christ in the form of a child's body: "Sometimes it seemed to her that for three or more days she held him close to her so that he nestled between her breasts like a baby, and she hid him there lest he be seen by others. Sometimes she kissed him as though he were a little child and sometimes she held him on her lap as if he were a gentle lamb."[78] Likewise the visions of Hadewijch of Brabant (fl. 1240) describe, in highly tactile language, her experience of sacramental and physical union with Christ:

With that he came in the form and clothing of a man, as he was on the day when he gave us his body for the first time; looking like a human being and a man, wonderful, and beautiful, and with glorious face, he came to me as humbly as anyone who wholly belongs to another. Then he gave himself to me in the shape of the sacrament, in its outward form, as the custom is; and then he gave me to drink from the chalice, in form and taste, as the custom is. After that he came himself to me, took me entirely in his arms, and pressed me to him; and all my members felt his in full felicity, in accordance with the desire of my heart and my humanity. So I was outwardly satisfied and fully transported.[79]

The *Revelations* of Gertrude the Great (d. 1301/2) include a remarkable devotion to the five wounds of Christ in which Gertrude receives the stigmata and imagines herself in intimate relationship to his wounded body.[80] In an episode quite similar to "Quis dabit," Angela of Foligno (d. 1309) in her *Liber de vere fidelium experientia* reports a vision in which she finds herself commanded by Christ to drink from the wound in his side.[81] In the early fifteenth century, the *Book of Margery Kempe* describes Margery's intense devotion to the Passion of Christ, a devotion sustained by visions shaped by her knowledge of treatises on the Passion. Margery's visions carry the motif of female intimacy with the body of Christ to new levels:

& a-non sche saw wyth hir gostly eye owr Lordys body lying be-forn hir, & hys heuyd, as hir thowt, fast be hir wyth his blissyd face vpward, þe semeliest man þat euyr myth be seen er thowt. And þan cam on wyth a baselard-knyfe to hir syght & kytt þat precyows body al on long in þe brest. And a-non sche wept wondyr sor, hauyng more mynde, pite, & compassyon of þe Passyon of owr Lord Ihesu Crist þan sche had beforn. . . . An-oþer tyme, þe seyd creatur beying in a chapel of owr Lady sor wepyng in þe mynde of owr Lordys Passyon & swech oþer gracys & goodnes as owr Lord ministryd to hir mynde, & sodeynly, sche wist not how sone, sche was in a maner of slep. & a-non in þe syght of hir sowle sche sey owr Lord standyng ryght up ouyr hir so ner þat hir thowt sche toke hys toos in hir hand & felt hem, & to hir felyng it weryn as it had ben very flesch & bon.[82]

[And at once she saw, with her spiritual eye, our Lord's body lying before her, and his head, as she thought, close by her, with his blessed face turned upwards, the handsomest man that ever might be seen or imagined. And then, as she looked, there came someone with a dagger and cut that precious body all along the breast. And then she wept amazingly bitterly, having more thought, pity and compassion of the Passion of our Lord Jesus Christ than she had before. . . . Another time, the said creature being in a chapel of our Lady, weeping bitterly at the memory of our Lord's Passion, and such other graces and goodness as our Lord ministered to her mind, suddenly—she knew not how soon—she was in a kind of sleep. And at once, in the sight of her soul, she saw our Lord standing right up over her, so near that she thought she took his toes in her hand and felt them, and to her feeling it was as if they had been really flesh and bones.]

It is within this context of women's visionary literature that the "Quis dabit" should be read and interpreted. On some level, these visions of female religious experience must have been deeply unsettling to male audiences, even though they belong to the generally ungendered category of devotion to the body of Christ. In the female visions, the body of the male Christ is stripped of its power, majesty, and authority, although frequently, not of its beauty. This is accomplished either by infantilizing the body of Christ (as in the visions of Marie d'Oignies) or by reducing it by figuring it in the role of compliant lover, deprived of remoteness to the extent that it could be kissed, handled, manipulated, and controlled by a woman.[83] The "Quis dabit" lament, I suggest, might have functioned as a potent antidote to male apprehensions that were likely to have been raised by the literature of women's visionary experience. That is one reason why the lament would have been particularly useful in a male culture, with such male reception being the basis of its persistent popularity to the end of the Middle Ages. Female visionary literature shows women either in a position of control over a male body, often expressed in terms of an intimacy that may have seemed either embarrassing, or as potentially threatening to males. The "Quis dabit" lament presents a narrative of a woman who also in some measure achieves physical intimacy with, and domination over, the male body, but under strictly governed circumstances. Mary's intimacy with Christ's body is indulged for only a limited time before it is put in check by the males who, it is clear, are the ones who hold real power in that setting.

On a less psychological level, in the specific context of late medieval spirituality, the "Quis dabit" lament may have been particularly appealing as a profoundly reactionary document set over and against a burgeoning female spirituality in which intimacy with the body of Christ was an important part. This female spirituality was ambivalently regarded by the dominant male ecclesiastical establishment. On the one hand, it was valued and promoted, as attested to by the many male biographers and recorders of women's visions; on the other hand there were persistent fears of this female spirituality going to extremes, ranging out of control, and even veering into heresy—feelings and fears which led to repeated efforts to channel and institutionalize female religious movements, such as the Beguines. In a reassuring dramatization, the "Quis dabit" narrative shows a limited version of a popular but disturbing type of female devotion which flourishes only under strict terms of male supervision. The excessive female devotion to Christ's crucified body is illustrated, but carefully restrained and finally terminated.

Caroline Bynum has suggested that among the possible explanations for the efflorescence of thirteenth-century women's visionary literature, which often centered on devotion to the body of Christ and frequently took the form of eucharistic visions, was the loss of female privileges over the eucharist and a general diminishing of female roles as intermediaries of God's grace. Women religious had formerly enjoyed such privileges that were now denied to them by an increasingly professionalized male clergy jealous of its prerogatives. The eucharistic visions and the female visions of handling Christ's body were, in this view, a form of compensation or displacement, a "mystical alternative," which was a "complement to, not a contradiction of, the clerical role," giving women some measure of spiritual power and authority over the body of Christ.[84] In this thirteenth-century religious context, the "Quis dabit" narrative acquires a particular resonance. The struggle between Mary on the one side and Joseph of Arimathea and John on the other over control and disposition of Christ's torn and bloody body may be taken as symbolic of the clerical battle between male and female over control of the eucharist, a battle with a narrative outcome that sustains the prevailing arrangements ordained by the male clerisy.

There are other ways by which the "Quis dabit" lament can be historically contextualized. When the narrator of "Quis dabit" recounts the struggle between Mary and her male companions over the body of Christ, he uses the phrase, "pia lis" ("pious dispute") to describe it. The Latin word *lis* in its unrestricted form means strife, dispute, or quarrel. But the word also had a specialized meaning in the Middle Ages, namely, it was the usual term for lawsuit, a usage it retains in present day legal terminology. I suggest that this intrusion into the text of the discourse of law raises a complex of intertextual associations that implicates this text in the social realities of the late Middle Ages. It is exactly within the secular social and political milieu in which the "Quis dabit" lament resides that women increasingly participated in the system of control and disposition of real property as inheritors, testatrices, and land-owners in their own right.[85] Such new levels of involvement inevitably meant that women increasingly had recourse to the legal system to protect and maintain their property rights. The landed property of women, especially widows, was often subject to depredation and appropriation by powerful acquisitive males, and the medieval record is filled with instances of unmarried women who had to resort to litigation in constant struggles to protect their property and inheritances.

In the later Middle Ages, Christine de Pisan, widowed at the age of 25, examines this problem in her *Treasure of the City of Ladies*. She warns that after the death of her husband, a woman can expect that attempts will be made to cheat her out of her property, and that she must consequently be prepared to rely on litigation in order to obtain justice. Christine offers this counsel to widows: "If she has no children and anyone wishes to cheat her out of what belongs to her (as often happens to widowed ladies, be they great or little), she will summon good assistance and will use it to protect and defend her rights boldly by law and reason."[86] Later in the book she explains that one of the principal evils afflicting widows is "the various suits and many requests to do with debts or disputes over land or pensions."[87] In her own life, Christine at one time was engaged in four simultaneous lawsuits in order to protect her small inheritance.[88]

In this litigious atmosphere the episode in "Quis dabit" is especially poignant. The "pia lis" described by the narrator shows a weak and powerless woman who attempts to assert authority over what might most legitimately be thought to belong to her, the body of her own son. But this is a *lis* she cannot win: she is defeated by males who have the power of decision and take control of what is hers. The suggestion of legal terminology in the account of the struggle for control of the body enmeshes the episode in history, in part converting it into a powerful legitimization of contemporary social practices in which the legal system was exploited by males to the disadvantage of unprotected women, practices undoubtedly justified, as they are implicitly in this narrative, by being in the long-term best interest of the woman who is victimized. In this narrative, Mary is a victim who is overwhelmed by what the text presents as the good intentions of her male protectors, who determine the outcome in light of what they decide is her own good. In part through the strong emotional appeals exerted by the text, readers are made to become complicit in those strategies and invited to give assent to them. The text teaches that a woman, particularly a grieving, emotional woman, cannot exert control over what is hers, but must inevitably lose control over what she possesses to powerful male "protectors"; and this is presented as a benign and laudatory outcome. Besides being a male fantasy of control, the text powerfully reinforces a particularly male and seigneurial ideology of how the legal system ought ideally to work when women are litigants.

The account of the Passion in the "Quis dabit" lament is, I hope I have shown by now, contingent in manifold ways upon the historical context of which it is inescapably a part, expressing the values, attitudes, and anxieties of both secular and religious society. As noted above, the "Quis dabit" narrative became a foundational text, consistently popular in its own right throughout the thirteenth, fourteenth and fifteenth centuries and a source for other narratives. By the end of the fourteenth century, the web of inter-textual relationships had grown very complex indeed. There are extensive traces of "Quis dabit" in the *Dialogus* of the pseudo-Anselm, in the *Meditationes vitae Christi*, and in the *Vita Christi* of Ludolphus of Saxony (d. 1377). All these works were popular and all include the lengthy episodes concerning Mary's behavior after the death of her son.[89]

The influence of the "Quis dabit" was also pervasive in the vernacular. We have already mentioned an early Provençal version, and there were others in Italian, French, Anglo-Norman, and Dutch.[90] Early in the fifteenth century, Margery Kempe knew some version of these episodes: the Middle English of her Book in effect records what is in effect a truncated version of the "Quis dabit" narrative.[91] Margery must have known these gospel embellishments either directly (and I do not discount the possibility that she acquired knowledge of them through her own reading) or mediated through their appearance in other literary texts, either Latin or English. Margery's own additions to the episodes are significant for what they tell us about how such a strongly misogynous text might have been received by a female audience and how its episodes might be refigured to challenge existing norms. Margery reports a vision that is clearly based on the "pious dispute" over the burial of the body of Christ found in the "Quis dabit" lament:

And as-swythe sche saw Seynt Iohn þe Euangelist, Ioseph of Aramathye, & oþer frendys of owr Lord comyn & woldyn beryn owr Lordys body & preyide owr Lady þat sche wolde suffyr hem to berijn þat precyows body. Owr dolful Lady seyd to hem, "Serys, wolde ʒe takyn a-wey fro me my Sonys body? I myth neuyr lokyn vp-on hym j-now whil he leuyd; I pray ʒow, late me han hym now he is ded, & partith not my Sone & me asondyr. And, ʒyf ʒe welyn algatys beryin hym, I prey ʒow berith me wyth hym, for I may not leuyn wyth-owtyn hym."[92]

[And at once she saw St. John the Evangelist, Joseph of Arimathea, and other friends of our Lord, come and want to bury our Lord's body, and they asked our Lady that she would allow them to bury that precious body. Our sorrowful Lady said to them, "Sirs, would you take away from me my son's body? I might never look upon him enough while he lived. I pray you, let me have him now he is dead,

and do not part my son and me from each other. And if you will bury him in any
case, I pray you, bury me with him, for I may not live without him."]

But Margery offers an explanation for Mary's defeat that rehabilitates
her dignity, rationality, and capacity for agency, where none of this is to
be found in the "Quis dabit" lament itself or most of the textual traditions
that depend on it (my italics): "And þe creatur thowt þat þei preyid owr
Lady so fayr til at þe last owr Lady *leet hem* beryin hir der Sone wyth gret
worschep & wyth gret reuerens as longyth to hem to do" ("And then this
creature thought that they asked our Lady so beautifully, until at last our
Lady *let them* bury her dear son with great worship and great reverence, as
was fitting for them to do").[93] We can witness here a radical act of textual
appropriation and resistance. Margery has apparently chosen to follow the
feminist reading of the episode found in the pseudo-Anselmian *Dialogus*
discussed earlier: "Tandem invita, permisi ut sepeliretur." Thus she partici-
pates in the reorienting of the male-constructed tradition in a way that restores to Mary the authority over the disposition of her son's body that the
dominant literary tradition, exemplified by the "Quis dabit" lament, had
denied her. It is a poignant act, an act entirely consistent with Margery's
own indomitable efforts to exert her will in the face of male authority, a
prominent theme of her book.

The emotionality of "Quis dabit," I have said, is one of its most
predominant characteristics. There are other Passion narratives, however,
which are more restrained in style, and which, in particular, take pains to
represent women's speech not as exuberant, emotional, and uncontrolled
(as in "Quis dabit"), but as constrained, rational, and indeed, carefully
scripted. We have already remarked on the restraining of Mary's voice in
the *Dialogus* of the pseudo-Anselm, a work that essentially renarrates the
material of "Quis dabit," moderating its emotionality. Similar strategies are
in effect in other Passion narratives, particularly, it seems, in those arising
from male clerical communities of the late thirteenth and early fourteenth
centuries. These examples of restrained female language may be understood as a reaction against other kinds of women's speech, particularly
religious speech, which proved profoundly disturbing to the church and
threatened to undermine the established canons of patriarchal discourse.

The Passion treatise of the pseudo-Bede is a good illustration of the
modified affectivity of certain of the later narratives. At the moment of
Christ's death, Mary utters an emotional lament at the foot of the cross

very much in the manner of the "Quis dabit," a work that probably supplied its stylistic model.[94] The emphasis on Mary's weakness is a familiar one in the tradition; the narrator reports that she was unable to support herself and fell on her face onto the ground.[95] The significant point is that this is Mary's final speech in the treatise. The deposition from the cross is treated in a perfunctory manner, taking up barely a paragraph, and those invented episodes recounting the extravagant behavior of Mary, her subversive utterances and her emotional outpourings, are here all suppressed. Indeed the method of narration employed throughout the treatise emphasizes control. The narrator in the prologue promises to supply a method of contemplating the Passion according to the seven canonical hours, a familiar kind of devotion in the later Middle Ages, and one that emphasizes system and order. The narrator's presence is always felt, as he guides the meditative practices of his audience (which is not identified as specifically male or female): "de qua coena et de sacratissimo dono sui corporis et sanguine ibi tradito debes frequenter et devotissime cogitare" ("you ought to repeatedly and devoutly think about this supper and the most sacred gift he made there of this body and blood"); "Secundo hic cogitabis qualiter dixit dominus discipulis suis, Surgite, eamus hinc" ("In the second place, you will think how the lord said to his disciples: 'Arise and go hence'").[96] This is a narrative stance consistent with the restraint that is imposed on Mary's behavior and language. In place of the fully developed, richly detailed, and strikingly affective narrative that occupies the last lines of the "Quis dabit," the deposition and burial are reported in a final sentence or two, the narrator again directing the meditator to imitate in spirit the conduct of Mary:

Hora vespertina venies devotis gressibus et spiritualibus incessibus ad deponendum dominum de cruce, ad plangendum illum cum matre sua benedicta, et ad lavandum lacrymis corpus ejus sanctissimum, sanguine aspersum, et ad ungendum eum unguentis orationis, et ad portandum brachiis charitativae et humilis operationis, et ad sepeliendum cum bonis aromatibus, et bona conversatione et bonis doctrinis et exemplis et lamentis et planctibus, et cooperies sub pavimento conscientiae tuae amoris et devotionis, et sedebis ibi juxta eum ad monumentum ejusdem domini nostri Jesu Christi.[97]

[At the evening hour you will come with devout steps and spiritual approaching to take your lord down from the cross, to mourn for him with his blessed mother, and to wash with tears his most sacred body, spotted with blood, and to anoint it with the ointment of prayer, to carry it with the arms of charitable and humble deeds, to bury it with good spices of good conduct, good doctrine and examples,

and with wailing and laments, and you will cover it under the stones of your consciousness of love and devotion, and you will sit there near him at the monument
of our lord Jesus Christ.]

In addition to the highly summarized narrative and the drastic reduction in
concrete detail, the physical and emotional immediacy of the "Quis dabit"
is further mitigated by the turn to allegory.

A different strategy is followed in the *Vita Christi* of Ludolphus of
Saxony. In the narrative of the Passion the presence of the "Quis dabit" is
commanding, but its force is blunted by the technique of interlarding the
emotional episodes with long stretches of exegesis and moral application.
Mary's extravagant behavior and emotional lamenting are only reported;
she hardly appears as a character and the actual laments are not given in the
first person. Ludolphus affirms the extreme nature of Mary's language on
the death of Christ, but he is unique among the authors of Passion narratives in insisting that despite its extremity and emotionality, her language
does not exceed the bounds of rationality:

Et ideo quantas lamentationes, ululatus, planctus et fletus super idem corpus unici
filii sui tunc fecerit, verbis explicari non posset. Credendum tamen est, quod nullos
planctus irrationabiles fecerit, quia dolor ejus ad rationem superiorem non per-
tingebat.[98]

[And therefore it cannot be explained in words how many lamentations, wailings,
complaints, and weepings she made then over the body of her only son. Yet it must
be believed that she made no irrational complaints, for her sorrow did not extend
to the higher reason.]

These more sober versions of Mary's behavior and speech may be accounted for sufficiently, perhaps, on esthetic grounds as reflections of differing standards of taste in respect to emotionality in narrative, or as arising from different conceptions of the purposes of such narratives. Or they
may be explained as owing to the personality or character of a particular
religious order or community: we may recognize the difference between
Franciscan exuberance and Cistercian sobriety, for instance.

While such explanations may be partially true, it is important to
locate these representations of restrained, rational female speech in a cultural context which included other kinds of women's utterances that male-
dominated society found to be threatening, out of control, and often
dangerous and heretical. This kind of language frequently arose in the
thirteenth and fourteenth centuries from the Beguine movement, a form

of female spirituality that was always under surveillance and frequently suspect by ecclesiastical and lay authority. For example, the language of Marguerite Porete, as recorded in *The Mirror of Simple Souls*, in its lack of concrete specificity, its elusiveness, its extreme detachment from the world of the senses, and in its subversive content, could hardly be more antithetical to the kind of female discourse assigned to women by the male authors of the Passion treatises mentioned above. Marguerite's description of the fifth state of the pious soul is an outstanding example:

Now such a soul is nothing, for she sees with an abundance of divine knowledge her nothingness which makes her nothing and reduces her to nothingness. And she is all, for she sees with the profundity of the knowledge of her wickedness, which is so profound and so great that she finds there neither beginning, nor measure, nor end. Who cannot reach himself cannot find himself; and the more he sees himself with such a knowledge of his wickedness, the more he truly knows that he cannot know his wickedness, not even the least particle of it. Thus this Soul is an abyss of wickedness and a gulf of such lodging and garrison—as is the flood of what is sin—that she contains in herself all perdition.[99]

Marguerite's *Mirror of Simple Souls* was condemned as heretical, in part because of views on the soul such as those expressed in this passage, and Marguerite herself was burned alive as a heretic in the Place de Grève at Paris on June 1, 1310. Marguerite's case may be extreme, but her work illustrates a form of female speech that was undoubtedly disquieting to large numbers of the ecclesiastical establishment. Similar examples could be found in the work of Hadewijch of Brabant (fl. 1240), Mechthild of Magdeburg (d. ca. 1294), Gertrude the Great of Helfta (d. 1301/02), and others. This mystical, visionary language was a form of female speech that must often have seemed on the verge of escaping the bounds of rationality and about to transgress the boundaries of orthodoxy.[100]

In such a textual environment, the representation of female discourse in these selected later Passion narratives might serve as a powerful counterexample. These representations present a male-constructed idea of women's speech that does not cross over into irrationality even under duress of the most extreme kind, nor do these representations ever threaten to escape the concrete world of the senses or of the pictorial discourse conventionally assigned to women, evaporating into evanescence and transcendence. We have the essentialist assignment of affectivity to women, but it is comprehensible, narratively limited, and therefore subject to control and appropriation. These popular narratives, regarded in their historical context, might have supplied an assuaging alternative to the kind of female discourse that an audience, especially a male ecclesiastical audience, might often have found not exhilarating, but threatening and deeply unsettling. Women's utterance is emotional, but as Ludolphus reassures us through his sober recasting of the language of the "Quis dabit," it does not go beyond the boundaries of the rational. Thus the lamentations of Mary serve at once to warn of the dangers of women's speech and to articulate an ideology of its suppression, restraint, and control.

The Passion of Christ
and the Institution of Torture

In the fourteenth-century vernacular German Passion treatise known as *Christi Leiden in Einer Vision Geschaut* the crucifixion of Christ is described in horrifying terms. In this one instance, I depart from my stated practice of using Latin examples for two reasons. The first is that the passage, and the whole treatise in which it is embedded, are strongly related to the Latin tradition, if not directly derived from it. In the second place, the passage seems in its intensity to be a culmination of tendencies that had been developing side by side, or more accurately, simultaneously and interdependently, in both vernacular and Latin popular writings on the Passion. The following is an extract from a much longer account:

Alas, then the suffering began. They took the cross and threw it from his back and took the clothes off the God-man. And they took him by the hair and threw him on the cross—he could have broken apart completely. And they pulled his wounded and tender back over the knots of the cross, so that the stumps of the wood tore the wounds apart. They also jumped with wild ill-breeding with their impure feet on the mortally wounded body of Christ. They kneeled on his chest and stretched his arms apart as far as they were able. They took his right hand and pulled it to the hole in the arm of the cross and drove a nail through it. The nail was blunt and triangular and the edges were sharp as a knife, and they carried the skin of the hand and quite a lot of the flesh through the hole of the cross. They drove the nail so powerfully that the head of the nail stood in the palm of the hand, and filled the wound so full that not a drop of blood could come out of it. Then they took his other hand and pulled it over the arm of the cross. The hand was so far from the hole that they could not reach it. Then they took rope and put a line on his hand and pulled it so powerfully that the veins and the limbs pulled apart so that the hand reached the hole. And they drove a nail through so far that not a single drop of blood could come out of it. Then they went down to his feet and stretched his feet on the stem of the cross. Then it happened that his feet were not able to reach the hole by quite a few handspans.

Then they took rope and fastened a line to both of his feet and pulled it so strongly and stretched it so much that no string had ever been stretched on a board so much or so tight, until his feet reached the hole. And they stepped on his legs and placed one of his feet on top of the other. And before the lower foot was nailed through, the upper foot was split apart, and they hit the nail so hard, that the head stood covered in the foot. They thought that his suffering was not enough, and they took another nail, which was larger and longer than any of the others: they placed it on the arch of the foot, on the thick part near the bone, and struck the nail so furiously with all their strength, that the nail received 32 hammer blows, and the wounds became so enlarged by the nail that not a single drop of blood could come out of them. And then they raised the cross up and placed it in a stone that they had brought there. The stone reached very nearly as far above the ground as a man's belt.[1]

This report of the crucifixion is remarkable for its richly detailed, almost mechanical, description of the way the bodily torments suffered by Christ are put into practice, yet it is by no means unique to the fourteenth century in particular or the later Middle Ages in general. James Marrow's study of numerous Netherlandish Passion treatises shows that vivid, pictorial writing of this kind was widespread in northern Europe of the fourteenth and fifteenth centuries.[2] In England, there are similar, if not quite so grotesquely particularized, accounts of the Passion in the writings of Julian of Norwich, Margery Kempe, and in the Passion meditations of Richard Rolle. Rolle, for example, describes his vision of the crucifixion thus:

Now, swete Ihesu, me þinkiþ I se þi bodi on þe rode, al bled, and streyned þat þe ioyntis twinnen; þi woundis now openen, þe skyn al to-drawen recchiþ so brode þat merueile is it halt; þin heed crowned wiþ þornis, þi bodi al ful of woundis, nailis in þin hondis & feet so tendre, and in þi synewis, þere as is moost peinful fe-linge; þere is no leninge to þin heed, þi bodi is streyned as a parchemynskyn upon þe harowe; þi face is al bolned þat first was so fair; þi iointis vndoon; þou hongist and stondist on nailis; stremes of blood rennen doun bi þe rode; þe siȝt of þi mo-dir encresiþ þi peyne.[3]

In these narratives, not only are the torments of the canonical gospels portrayed in a much elaborated level of detail and exactitude, but numerous other torments never mentioned in the gospels become a part of these accounts. Christ's beard is pulled, he is dragged along the ground by his hair and forced to kneel on hot egg shells. His cloak is removed with such violence that pieces of bleeding flesh which have stuck to it from the scourging are ripped from his back. The thorns of the crown of thorns are so sharp and long that they pierce his brain-pan.

It is easy to see that these narrative elaborations reveal late medieval attitudes toward the Passion which moved the weight of representation toward Christ's suffering in human form. The texts that resulted from the heightened devotion to Christ's humanity often include descriptions of the Passion presented with a physicality and depth of detail not found before the twelfth century. As we have noted, many twelfth-century treatises encourage intense meditation on the Passion, recommending that the meditator place himself as though actually present at the events, forming detailed pictures through the faculty of the imagination. These developments belong to a form of devotion known as *imitatio Christi*, which emphasized participation in the events of Christ's life, especially the Passion. Such participation and imitation expressed itself increasingly in literal or material, physical ways, often straining the limits of what was humanly possible to attain.

Whether one thinks of the heightened spectacularism of the narratives of the Passion as a consequence of these newer devotional and ascetic practices, or in more general terms as the product of broader cultural understandings, by the end of the twelfth century Passion narratives are increasingly particularized and realistic as they describe the agonies of Christ. In their representational techniques they seem to be preoccupied with the problem Elaine Scarry has identified as the inexpressibility of another person's physical pain.[4] She points out that the pain of another is radically averse to us, that there is an "absolute split between one's sense of one's own reality and the reality of other persons."[5] Pain also, Scarry observes, is unsharable, in large measure "through its resistance to language."[6] There is no vocabulary, there are no linguistic strategies, which are adequate to the task of registering the pain of another. This resistance to language "is not simply one of its incidentally or accidental attributes, but essential to what it is."[7] Pain requires a "shattering of language."

The authors of the Passion narratives, now newly concerned with the expression of the pain of Christ, are confronted with an esthetic problem, the task of creating a language for pain, "to accommodate this area of experience normally so inaccessible to language."[8] Needless to say, the formidable esthetic and linguistic problems of the writers of the Passion narratives are mingled with moral and theological questions of equal complexity.

One solution seems to have been the adoption of a naturalistic representational style, a broad movement in the late Middle Ages that extends to characterization in the romance and pictorial realism in the visual arts. F. P. Pickering has placed this so-called naturalism in a more focused intellectual context, arguing that its techniques do not arise so much from absolute esthetic imperatives favoring realism in general, but rather are a radical, highly concretized, working out of an inventive system of biblical interpretation which foresaw events of the Passion, even those not fully described in the gospels, as prefigured in the prophecies of the Hebrew bible.[9] It is a system often associated with Franciscan exegesis, which was inclined to privilege the literal. Many examples of the technique identified by Pickering could be cited. For example, Bernard in his *Sermons on the Song of Songs* compares Christ to the bundle of myrrh of Cant 1:12; in later workings out of the image, the dead body of Christ on the cross is described as withered, shriveled, and deprived of beauty: it is, indeed, like a bundle of dried myrrh.[10] As noted earlier, a frequent commonplace of the Passion narratives is to include the non-gospel detail that on the cross Christ's body was so stretched that all his bones could be seen, a literalization of the lines of the Passion Psalm 21:18, "dinumeraverunt omnia ossa mea" ("they have numbered all my bones"). Pickering cites a late medieval narrative which tells us that on the way to Golgotha, Christ's tormentors broke out his teeth, a literal fulfillment of Lamentations 3:16, "Et fregit ad numerum dentes meos" ("And he hath broken my teeth one by one").[11]

This expressive, detailed, and often luxuriantly emotional representation of bodily pain has caused difficulties for modern sensibilities, even when it is regarded or explained, as Pickering and Marrow do, as the thorough working out of an exegetical technique. The problem is one of decorum and prior standards of good taste. Critics in the early part of this century were often either embarrassed by these late medieval descriptive techniques, if not openly hostile to them. G. R. Owst spoke of the "lurid imagination" and "morbid delight in detail" which to him characterized such descriptions.[12] And even the generally sympathetic J. A. W. Bennett usually judges such descriptions as "flamboyant," as displaying "extravagances," or as "bizarre."[13]

These modern critical attitudes, coupled with a disposition to regard the development narrowly, as swept up in a story having to do with the growth of formal realism, have tended to obscure the relationship of these representations to the historical contexts in which they reside. Recently critics have begun to see in the culture of the late Middle Ages a concern for the body that crosses boundaries of literary genre or artistic type. This is a concern expressed in ways that are manifold and highly diverse, including a heightened interest in attempts to bridge the unbridgeable barrier between the pain felt by one human being and the sense of one's own inner reality, in Scarry's terms.[14] These newer understandings of the importance of the body offer a better way of accounting for the increasing brutality and violence of the Passion narratives and their preoccupation with the mechanics of bodily suffering and the semiotics of pain.[15]

First of all, it is important to recognize that those extreme representations of brutality and violence do not suddenly appear fully formed, but rather develop over the course of time. Once this point is established, I will argue that the trajectory of increasing bodily violence in the narrative representations of the Passion is paralleled by and related to a significant historical occurrence, namely, the rise in the thirteenth century of the systematic use of judicial torture, a scheme under which the human body is also subject to excruciating pain.

Already in the eleventh century, in Anselm's description of the suffering of Christ, we can find a retelling of the Passion that surpasses in its range and affective immediacy any earlier medieval version;[16] but it is important to note that there is in Anselm's description no concrete, visual detail, nor an elaboration of the gospel, but rather an enumeration of the torments intended to arouse an emotional response in the reader. In the next generation of Passion writers, there is little physical detail in the accounts of the Benedictine Ekbert of Schönau (d. 1184), of the English bishop Edmund Rich (d. 1240), or of the English Cistercian Stephen of Sawley (d. 1252).

A noticeable shift in expression is found in the second half of the thirteenth century. It is not necessary to regard this as a "turning point," or a harmonious transition, or an evolutionary development. The works of Bonaventure (d. 1274) on the Passion are a good illustration of this shift in sensibility. What is found in Bonaventure is paralleled and pushed further in the late thirteenth- or early fourteenth-century *Meditationes vitae Christi*. I do not wish to argue that either Bonaventure or the author of the *Meditationes* is responsible for the shift, nor do I want to regard them as the founders of a new stylistic school. I take their writings only as typical of what I see as a remarkable heightening occurring in the second half of the thirteenth century in descriptions of the bodily suffering of Christ. Although a change can be observed, at the same time it seems plain that neither of the Passion accounts in Bonaventure and the *Meditationes vitae Christi* are thoroughly innovative, but are substantiated by a complex web of intertextual relationships. Nevertheless, I would argue that by the second half of the thirteenth century a transformation has occurred in the way the Passion of Christ is represented in narrative art, a stylistic development that continues in the fourteenth century, resulting in versions of the Passion similar to those quoted at the beginning of this chapter.

It is possible to see that lying behind both the practice of torture and the graphic representations of suffering is a general cultural attitude toward the body and a common understanding of what can fittingly be done by a human person to the body of another and what can be fittingly represented. We are speaking here of the interrelationship of cultural and social ideals and artistic decorum.

Before the thirteenth century, graphically detailed narrative representations of the tormented human body are found most notably in the stories of the Christian martyrs dating from the third and fourth centuries of the late classical period, the other "golden age" of lurid accounts of tormented flesh. Many examples could be cited from the hagiographical writings of this period, and many are transmitted to the later Middle Ages by the enormously popular *Legenda aurea* of Jacobus de Voragine (d. 1298). A famous repository of these accounts is the *History of the Church* of Eusebius (d. 339), written in Greek but soon translated into Latin and widely influential in the west. Eusebius describes the torments of the Christian martyrs in graphic detail, without reticence, without squeamishness, with no sense of propriety being violated, in a tone that is not unlike that of the thirteenth-century Passion narratives:

Sometimes they were torn with scourges to the innermost veins and arteries, so that even the secret hidden parts of the body, the entrails and internal organs, were laid bare; sometimes they were forced to lie on pointed seashells and sharp spikes. After going through every kind of punishment and torture, they were finally flung to the beasts as food.[17]

The period of Eusebius, too, was notable for the wide use and acceptance of the practice of judicial torture. In the twelfth and thirteenth centuries, just as the Roman legal system was revived with its acceptance of torture, so too are we presented with a coincident revival of a representational system in narrative which did not shrink from dwelling upon tormented flesh. The *Legenda aurea* itself may be seen as belonging to this revival, supplying the taste of the time with graphic portrayals of human suffering.[18] In his study of the body in early Christian society, Peter Brown notes that in the late classical period, the physical body became an object of "obsessive compassion" at exactly the same time as the cruelty and intensity of punishments inflicted upon the body increased.[19] To a great extent that observation applies to conditions in western Europe of the twelfth and the thirteenth centuries. Brown notes further that at the end of the classical period, especially in the East, the body was increasingly subjected to mutilation and public display as a form of punishment. It is also increasingly true of the late medieval Passion narratives (and certainly of the visual arts as well) that the public spectacle of Christ's sufferings is regularly emphasized.

At the same time, we must notice that there are significant differences in the attitudes toward the body and the representation of human suffering that ought not be overlooked. It is not at all clear, for example, that the stories of the spectacular sufferings of the early Christian martyrs had any direct influence on the later medieval Passion narratives. The attitude toward the suffering body is also in some ways fundamentally different. In the stories of the martyrs, what is repeatedly proclaimed is the inviolability of the body, even in the face of the most gruesome and violent assaults. Despite the invasions of the flesh, the degradation and humiliation, the twisting, wrenching, burning, and cutting, we are told again and again that the body, often miraculously, retains it integrity, even its luminosity and beauty. Caroline Bynum has remarked on the absence of physical suffering in the early martyrologies, where the emphasis is on impassibility as a warrant of impending blessedness.[20]

A most significant difference is that the late classical or early medieval narratives describe in detail only the suffering of mortals and never dwell on the suffering of Christ himself. As is well known, the crucifixion is an extremely rare subject of early medieval visual art, and it is also true that there is very little narrative description of the agonies endured by Christ in his human form. This is conditioned by early Christian views of the nature of Christ and the theology of the redemption, but it is probably strongly affected by general classical esthetic values and social norms of decorum and propriety, particularly when describing or depicting anyone of elevated status is concerned. We can notice, then, beginning in the late eleventh century, the slow disappearance of this attitude and a dissolution of the restraints that found it inappropriate to describe the deity in what might be taken as demeaning or undignified terms.

The older emphasis on the resplendence of Christ's suffering body is expressed in the famous phrase of the pseudo-Augustinian meditation of the late eleventh century: "Candet nudatum pectus,"[21] but by the thirteenth century, in the narratives of Bonaventure and others, the vision is much darker. Christ is beaten and covered with spittle so that he appears like a leper, almost without recognizable human form.[22] In fulfillment of the words of the Psalm, "Tunc formosus prae filiis hominum, caligantibus oculis et pallentibus genis, pro filiis hominum deformis apparuit" ("The one who is fairer in beauty than the sons of men, with his eyes clouding and

his cheeks growing pale, became ugly for the sake of the sons of men").[23]
In the *Vitis mystica* Bonaventure, speaking in the moving phrases of the
Psalter, is particularly eloquent in his description of the shattered body of
Christ:

Attendite vestrum manu fortem, quomodo contritus est; desiderabilem vestrum,
quam miserabiliter deformatus est; pacificum vestrum, quomodo in bello peremp-
tus est. Ubi est rubor roseus, ubi candor niveus, ubi in corpore tam contrito decorem invenies? Ecce defecerunt dies nostrae diei, benignissimi Iesu, qui est solus dies
sine tenebris; et ossa eius sicut cremium aruerunt, percussus est ut foenum, et aruit
cor eius, elevatus est, allisus est valde.[24]

[Behold how your strong one is broken, your desirable one disfigured; behold your
peaceful one dying in battle. Where are now the cheeks flushed with life, the skin
fair as snow? Where in this ravaged body will you find any beauty? Behold they
have passed away, the days of our day, of Jesus most kind, the only day without
darkness. His bones have been parched like firewood, his heart cut down and dried
like grass; he has been lifted up and cast down to the depths.]

Christ, of course, retains his inner beauty, as Bonaventure reminds us, and
at the resurrection the splendor of his physical form was completely restored, in accordance with the prevailing theology of bodily resurrection,
with its emphasis upon material integrity.[25] Nevertheless, we see in the narratives of this period a great tendency to dwell upon the details of a body
twisted by pain and disfigured by suffering.[26] Caroline Bynum notes that
"it is as though—at least visually—Christ, because he is God, takes on all
the culture's obsession with torture and partition, while the saints are guar-
anteed (by their participation in beatific vision and blessedness) to be free
of pain and fragmentation."[27] By the end of the thirteenth century, any reluctance or restraint seems entirely to have disappeared.

The extreme suffering so graphically described in the Passion narratives has been variously interpreted. It has been thought to have an ameliorating effect, as giving dignity and meaning to all forms of human suffering. As Christ is rejected and cast outside the boundaries of human society,
subject to the most horrible degradation and pain, so too those whose lot
it is to suffer, by accepting pain and suffering find meaning in their own suffering and participate in the work of Christ, and like Christ, look forward
to a glorified and restored human body. As Bonaventure declares, Christians conform themselves to the Passion so they may be reformed in glory
at the end of time.[28] Christ's suffering in mild patience is held to furnish a
model that humans can imitate. J. A. W. Bennett argues that devotion to

the suffering of Christ may have inspired acts of compassion.[29] At the end of his chapter on what he calls "the meditative moment" in medieval religious life, he observes that: "If in the Middle Ages the sufferings of men came to be concentrated on those of one Man, his suffering in turn came to give meaning to those of all mankind."[30]

But the most eloquent and convincing statement of this position is made by Caroline Bynum, whose subtle studies of the suffering of Christ as the special object of devotion of medieval women present us with a way of understanding not only the impulses behind the detailed representations of Christ's torments, but their function in society in general. In speaking of women's piety of the late Middle Ages, she notes:

> When women spoke of abstinence, of eucharistic ecstasy, of curing and healing through food, they called it *imitatio Christi*. "Imitation" meant union—fusion—with that ultimate body which is the body of Christ. The goal of religious women was thus to realize the *opportunity* of physicality. They strove not to eradicate body but to merge their own humiliating and painful flesh with that flesh whose agony, espoused by choice, was salvation. Luxuriating in Christ's physicality, they found there the lifting up—the redemption—of their own.[31]

The Passion narratives we have been describing can be regarded as both promoting and as a consequence of the kind of religious impulses Bynum describes.

There is, no doubt, much that is true in the interpretations of Bennett and Bynum, and much that contributes to an understanding of the cultural context of the Passion narratives that is sympathetic and generous. The narratives themselves, however, can be, and often are, seen in a light that is much less positive. Douglas Gray, for example, speaks of an "excessive attention to a multiplicity of details" that marks many popular religious images of the late Middle Ages, and notes that the same is true of certain of the Passion meditations, "where the rehearsal of grim, naturalistic details of physical suffering can sometimes produce nothing but a sense of unreality."[32] I would like to pursue another way of regarding these narratives, not so much arguing from esthetic norms, but by returning to the ways they are involved with history.

The steady growth of increasingly graphic descriptions of the torments undergone by Christ in Passion texts from the end of the eleventh to the end to the thirteenth century is paralleled very closely, almost exactly, as I pointed out, by an event occurring in the realm of history and politics, namely the revival and spread of the use of judicial torture. By the end of the thirteenth century it was common in most parts of western Europe, and by that time it had attained new extremes of brutality. It does not seem entirely coincidental that those texts arise in those parts of Europe, notably France, the Rhineland, and northern Italy, where the new legal system was erected and where the use of torture was promoted and extended to more and more social categories.

I suggest that the textual and the historical should be viewed together, although I wish to avoid oversimplified assertions postulating cause and effect. I argue that the parallelism is noteworthy, and my tentative suggestion is that these developments are linked together in a complex web of history and text. They are best seen as mutually reinforcing: the contemporary cultural practice of torture in some measure conditioning the textual representation of the Passion, and the narratives of the Passion in some measure legitimating the violence of unspeakable acts by developing an imaginative register about the pain and torture that came to be taken for granted as a natural and inevitable part of reality.

The rise of torture in the twelfth and thirteenth century was essentially a revival of a Roman juridical practice that with the fall of the empire had largely fallen into disuse in most parts of Europe, especially in the Germanic societies of the north and west. The revival has been well detailed by Edward Peters and John Langbein, among others. Langbein shows that the use of torture was a consequence of the general legal revolution that began at the end of the eleventh century and was largely accomplished during the course of the twelfth century. The revolution was founded upon the recovery of Roman jurisprudence, which permitted the use of torture in judicial proceedings in order to obtain confessions in instances where a probability of guilt existed. Langbein points out that the action of the Fourth Lateran Council of 1215 in abolishing the use of the older, non-rational, Germanic system of proof by ordeal, "destroyed an entire system of proof," which was then replaced by the newer Romano-canonical procedures requiring rational proofs dependent on confession or the testimony of two eye-witnesses. The adoption of such a rigorous system of proof opened the way for the use of torture in obtaining confessions, and indeed Langbein argues that such a development was not merely likely but inevitable, given society's need to see guilty parties receive punishment.[33]

Edward Peters points out the close connection between the rise of torture and the growth of the inquisitorial procedure and the prosecution of heresy. As in the case of the Roman law on which it was based, the newly revived system in theory reserved torture for known criminals and the lowest and vilest members of society, a concept known as legal infamy. The papal bull *Ad abolendam* issued by Lucius III in 1184 is highly significant, not because it mentions torture but because it reestablishes the Roman notion of legal infamy, applying it to heretics, thus considerably broadening the range of persons who might be subjected to torture.[34] In 1199 Innocent III declared that heretics were traitors to God and therefore liable to the severe procedures and punishments that applied in cases of treason.[35] The Fourth Lateran Council of 1215 corroborated the idea that heretics were legally infamous in both secular and canon law. Peters observes that the transformation in the legal system progressed gradually through the twelfth and thirteenth centuries, and that the theoretical foundations first became entrenched before the use of torture became widespread.[36] A turning point is marked by the bull *Ad extirpanda* of Innocent IV issued in 1252. Heretics are described as murderers of souls, and the use of torture is permitted in their examination in order to extract confessions. These procedures are confirmed and extended by Alexander IV in 1256. Peters notes that after the mid-thirteenth century "torture had a secure place in ecclesiastical inquisitorial procedure."[37] In 1254 Louis IX allowed the use of torture in secular proceedings.[38] By the end of the century a judicial procedure sanctioning torture in criminal and ecclesiastical cases was fully in place in most parts of Europe, England being a notable exception.[39]

Knowledge of contemporary methods of torture and experience of the spectacle of tortured victims may have conditioned the representation of the sufferings of Christ in the late thirteenth- and early fourteenth-century Passion narratives. To take one specific example, among the commonplaces found no earlier than in the Passion narratives of the thirteenth century is the non-biblical detail that when Christ was arrested, his hands were bound so tightly that blood burst from beneath the nails. Peters notes that one of the common forms of torture, "used in its less severe form chiefly for lesser offenses and on children and women," was "the tight tying of the hands; when the offense was greater, the cords would be tied extremely tightly, released, then tied again."[40] As we have seen, many thirteenth-century Passion meditations include highly detailed and innovative descriptions of the horrible stretching and pulling of Christ's limbs in order to fit him onto the cross; another, related commonplace is to describe Christ as squeezed in the winepress of Isaiah 63:3.[41] Stretching of the limbs, by means of the strappado or the rack or by other devices designed to distend the joints and muscles, was, according to Peters, the most commonly used form of torture in the Middle Ages.[42] Peters also mentions the use of sleep deprivation as a method of torture; in the *Meditationes vitae Christi* and elsewhere we are told that after his arrest Christ was kept awake for the whole night by his tormentors.[43]

If scenes of torture had been witnessed by the authors of these texts, they must have left a vivid impression on their imaginations that could have provided them with a store of concrete visual images to describe the suffering of Christ. The cries of the torture victims might have impressed on them the inadequacy of language to express such severe degrees of pain. But of course the situation is not quite so simple as that. We know that a rich array of textual commonplaces as much as lived experience contributed to the intertextuality of the Passion narratives; and it is also possible to see that these powerful narrative (and pictorial) depictions of Christ stretched and pulled, sustained or reinforced, if they did not inspire, the means of causing pain to a human body.

In the narratives Christ is not only horribly tortured, but he is subject to degradation and insult. He is, in fulfillment of the words of Isaiah 53:3, "despectum, et novissimum virorum" ("despised and rejected of men"). He is also, in the typological interpretation of the same chapter of Isaiah, described as though he were a leper: "quasi leprosum" (Is 53:4). In the course of the thirteenth century, what was a simple comparison in the biblical text is increasingly materialized or literalized. After Christ has been scourged, buffeted, and covered with spittle, he is said, by Bonaventure and many others, to look like a leper.[44] This narrative focus on Christ as leper coincides with a time in western Europe when the fear of leprosy, which was a prevalent disease from the end of the eleventh century, reached new heights. The Third Lateran Council of 1179 provided for the segregation of lepers and the deprivation of their legal and property rights.[45] As R. I. Moore has shown, the image of the leper that developed in this period was as a loathsome, dangerous creature, increasingly regarded as a spectacle of public humiliation.[46]

The growth of the image of Christ as "quasi leprosus" is a particular instance of the imaginative register describing his suffering, but it points to a way of understanding the general social function of the detailed descriptions of the torments inflicted on the body of Christ. It is possible to see the Passion narratives as a kind of textual institution for the promotion and maintenance of certain attitudes, toward lepers specifically, but also toward suffering inflicted by one human being upon another. In his history of punishment and torture, Michel Foucault has shown that in the medieval practice of torture the body of the victim was to be horribly broken, marked, and mutilated, placed on public view for all to see, in order to make indisputably clear to every observer the vast discrepancy between the impotence of the victim of torture and the power of the sovereign authority.[47] Leaving aside for a moment the question of power relationships and their applicability to the Passion narratives, it is not hard to see that the body of Christ becomes a public spectacle of degradation and intense suffering much in accordance with the victim of torture described by Foucault, and, I would argue, that such display inevitably serves an ideological purpose.

The Passion narratives arise from that same cultural environment which, in the eleventh, twelfth, and thirteenth centuries, constructed what R. I. Moore has called a persecuting society. The Passion narratives contain several of those more or less interchangeable images identified by Moore as representative of the despised, the outcast, the dangers to society, that are to be excluded and persecuted, namely lepers and Jews. The narratives contain as well graphic representations of one of the chief physical means, namely torture, used to control and persecute another outcast group, the heretics. I do not argue that the religious intents of the Passion narratives are subverted to become crude instruments of conscious propaganda, but I will argue that they promote values and beliefs about torture and punishment and encourage an outlook that certain ways of behaving are expected and legitimate.

First of all, the Passion meditations in their account of elaborate, prolonged, and detailed punishments of Christ well illustrate the workings out of a fully developed state mechanism for the prosecution of an undesirable and dangerous outcast. Even though Christ himself is certainly intended to be an object of our sympathy and compassion and not our revulsion, as is Foucault's victim of torture, the acute portrayal of the chilling effectiveness of the mechanism compels us to recognize the enormous disparity between the power of those in charge of such a mechanism of persecution and those who are the victims of it.

It is important to observe, in connection with the Passion narratives of which we have been speaking, that there is a genuine historical parallel between the biblical Palestine and the western Europe of the twelfth and thirteenth centuries. That is, Christ of the gospels was subjected to the kind of punishment provided for by the concept of legal infamy in Roman law: degradation and certain punishments—public humiliation and ridicule, being stripped naked, death by crucifixion—which were not punishments inflicted on citizens but reserved only for the outcast. The revival of Roman law and with it the notion of legal infamy in the twelfth and

thirteenth centuries gave legal sanction once again to such a range of punishments, which are reflected in the Passion narratives of the period.

In the Passion narratives, the victim of the tortures, of course, is
Christ. The emphasis of the texts is upon his otherness: he is deprived of
any human beauty, with a body gashed and deformed by pain; he is an
outcast beyond the margins of society, in appearance a leper, the most
horrifying image of marginality in the later Middle Ages. As I have said,
through Christ's exemplary patience and the degree of his pain, these narratives have been interpreted as creating sympathy for the suffering and the
marginalized, giving dignity to all forms of human existence. These narratives, some of which are of Franciscan origin, seem powerfully to articulate ideals which are consistent with the early Franciscan project of reform,
which, at least in its finest moments, sought to reincorporate within the
boundaries of the Christian community those marginalized human groups
that the official culture of the thirteenth century had been so busy excluding. Bynum has described ascetic practices centered on the care of lepers,
which included washing their lesions, and extended even to drinking the
liquid from their wounds. Moore has noted that the care of lepers was
"almost a fashionable religious exercise."[48]

Yet another view of these narratives asserts a claim on our attention, a
view which is less readily apparent on the surfaces of these texts, and if not
directly contradictory, at least in competition with the one just described.
In the narratives, Christ is the spectacularly tortured victim on public display, a figure now increasingly familiar in thirteenth-century society and
increasingly, it seems, belonging to lived experience. The Passion texts do
not merely reflect these new social conditions but reinforce and give shape
to the reality that surrounds them and of which they are a part. The Passion narratives, universalized and cloaked in semi-biblical authority, teach
the lesson by their imaginative vigor that such spectacles are part of human
experience—through repeated assaults on the human body they show us
that such behavior is not unthinkable.

The extremes of violence are directed at Christ. According to the
stated ideals of the Passion narratives, the graphic descriptions of violence
are intended to arouse compassion and sorrow for Christ as victim and
provoke our anger against those (the Jews) who perpetrated such ignomi-
nies against him. Yet the victimization of Christ serves another purpose
with a double aspect. The Passion narratives encourage us to think about
the sufferings of Christ in a way long established in the exegetical tradition, a way founded upon the Latin rhetorical comparison *quanto magis*:

how much the more. The Passion narratives show that if such bodily suffering and degradation could be visited on Christ, who was God, should they not, *quanto magis*, be also visited on the Jew, the heretic, the criminal, the outcast? Why should, in fact, this trouble or concern us very much if this is so? These were conditions endured by the savior of mankind, the innocent lamb: those who suffer in a similar way are non-persons who deserve to be persecuted and excluded from society. It might almost be said that in order for a Christian society to tolerate a widespread, public, and officially sanctioned use of torture, it is necessary that Christ himself be vividly imagined as a spectacularly suffering victim of it.

Looked at in another way, it might also be said that the construction of categories of persons excluded from society and subjected to persecution and violence is sanctioned and supported by the Passion narratives. These victims of violence are not Christ, but they can be seen as forming a context, even a necessary context, against which we are meant to measure the magnitude of Christ's suffering for us. That is, the suffering of Jews, heretics, and lepers provides a reference point in the contemporary material world that helps the Christian to reconstruct imaginatively, as much as it is humanly possible to do so, the immeasurably greater and finally inexpressible pain that Christ endured in the cause of human salvation.

In this sense, my understanding of the meaning of the medieval Passion narratives differs deeply from the analysis of the gospel account of the Passion of Christ offered by René Girard. Girard concludes that the gospels contain an account of a "persecution that has been abrogated, broken, and revoked," a rejection of persecution and a discrediting of the illusions of mythologies, dependent upon their insistence on the innocence of the sacrificial victim.[49] I would argue that, in the centuries between the gospels and the Passion narratives of the twelfth and thirteenth centuries, a profound transformation had occurred that irrevocably altered the significance of the Passion as it is presented in the narratives of the time. The Passion story is no longer a text that exposes and discredits persecution, but instead has become itself what Girard has called a "persecution text,"[50] a transformation that is a consequence of another observation made by Girard, who merely reaffirms what many others have noticed, particularly in the case of western Europe in the eleventh through the thirteenth centuries as demonstrated by R. I. Moore, that "Christianity suffered persecution while it was weak and became the persecutor as soon as it gained strength."[51]

I want to explore somewhat further another aspect of the violence of the Passion narratives, its effect on their audiences, and more generally, its broader impact upon society at large. Douglas Gray suggests that in describing the suffering of Christ the detail of the Passion narratives is so excessive as to produce an air of unreality. That is, the descriptive techniques may have the opposite effect from their intent by distancing us from the horror and desensitizing us to the suffering and violence of the narratives, and perhaps, through repeated representations, desensitizing society at large to suffering and violence in the material world. Morton Bloomfield has claimed that in the case of Chaucer's Man of Law's Tale we are distanced from the persecution and suffering undergone by Constance by the very rhetorical strategies that seem designed to involve us or to arouse our emotions.[52] In the Man of Law's Tale, the rhetorical strategy depends most heavily on the emotional apostrophes of the narrator; in the Passion narratives, the rhetorical strategy is the use of naturalistic pictorial description.

I have proposed that the Passion narratives can be seen as ideological documents legitimating the use of violence by agents of authority, in particular their use of torture. It is an important and related question to ask whether these narratives functioned also to inure medieval society to the ready acceptance of violence, along the lines suggested by Gray and Bloomfield, largely through excesses in both quality of representational techniques and the sheer quantity of representation itself. The question is, of course, a particularly poignant one in our own time, as we ponder the connections between what seem to be increasingly graphic representations of violence in film and television and the violent behavior of society. The paradox is that artistic or textual representations of extreme violence seem not to arouse society against it, but to harden it to an acceptance of it as routine. As in the case of our modern age, there is no easy way to demonstrate the social impact of represented violence in the Middle Ages. If we look at societies where the image of a spectacularly tortured Christ was or is especially popular—Flanders in the fifteenth century, Poland in the sixteenth century, many Latin countries today—it is hard to demonstrate that those societies have made an especially easy accommodation to violence, nor would it be possible, on the other hand, to show that devotion to the suffering Christ has had an ameliorating effect on social behavior or the use of violence in society. In respect to the Middle Ages, our view of this must remain inconclusive, although it seems to me, judging by what we know of how the Passion texts were received, that the effect was not to desensitize their audiences to violence or anesthetize them to brutality, but rather to instruct them that this was not an unthinkable way to treat the flesh of a fellow human being. The horror seems to have remained—the distancing and the unreality seem a product of modern esthetic sensibilities—and the result seems to have been acceptance of such practices as an inherent part of the social order.

I have thus far concentrated my attention on drawing the relationships between the graphic violence of the Passion narratives and the rise of torture, suggesting that both may be products of a new materiality that led to an increased attention paid to the body. Torture is socially sanctioned violence directed against an individual; there is also possibly a connection between the violence of the Passion narratives and socially sanctioned spectacular violence directed toward groups, as in massacres. Those massacred, as those tortured, are perceived as threats to the purity of the body of society, which, like the tortured body of Christ, is deconstructed to be triumphantly reconstructed.[53]

There are other important and related cultural developments of the period which are also fruitfully examined in relation to the Passion narratives. It is possible to see, for example, that the naturalistic and detailed descriptions of bodily suffering of the Passion narratives have something to do with the new twelfth-century concerns about the conscience and the cultivation of the interior life, concerns which were manifested in treatises analyzing the soul, in practical manuals devoted to the examination of the conscience, and in the requirement of the Lateran Council of 1215 of annual private confession for all Christians. Edward Peters notes that confessions also became central in the revived Roman legal system of this time, a fact which contributed directly to the rise of torture as a means of procuring them.[54] This cultural emphasis on verbal self-revealing—which can be seen also in the remarkable confessional prayers of Anselm and in the soliloquies spoken by the characters of the romances of Chrétien de Troyes and Gottfried von Strassburg—may have overcome by analogy the reluctance to expose in words the intimate details of the bodily sufferings of Christ. That level of intimacy achieved can be seen, for example, in Bernard's exegesis of the words of the Canticle, where Christ's afflicted body is the bundle of myrrh that lies between the breasts of the lover.[55]

This exposure of the self in language is most closely connected to the discourse of mysticism, to which the sermon cited from Bernard above certainly belongs. Michel de Certeau has in fact argued for a close connection between torture and mysticism, seeing them not as separate or opposing phenomena, but profoundly related, often flourishing side by side, bound together by what he calls "hidden alliances."[56] The same decades that saw the practice of torture becoming institutionalized and entrenched also saw one of the great ages of mysticism: in addition to Bernard, one would quickly name Hildegard of Bingen, Elizabeth of Schönau, Mechthild of Magdeburg, and Hadewijch of Brabant, as well as point to the enormous interest in the writings of the pseudo-Dionysius and the composition of numerous treatises and handbooks on contemplation. De Certeau argues that the destruction of human dignity that occurs in torture, accompanied by the "theatricalization of the body," is the beginning point for mystics, who must annihilate the body, and come to regard themselves in their human bodies as the victims of torture do, as refuse, as so much rottenness.

In terms of the techniques of representation, Elaine Scarry has noted that "to be intensely embodied is the equivalent of being unrepresented and (here as in many secular contexts) is almost always the condition of those without power."[57] Julia Kristeva's analysis of abjection is also pertinent here. Both the mystics and the victims of torture, including the Christ of the Passion narratives, become above all what is on the other side of the border, transformed into the corpse, what Kristeva describes as "the most sickening of wastes."[58] De Certeau's analysis is difficult to apply to the mystics of the Franciscan school who began with the material world and proceeded to more spiritual levels of contemplation, but it applies especially well to the fourteenth-century Rhineland mystics, among them Suso and Eckhart, whom de Certeau discusses. Their type of mysticism, profoundly shaped by the Dionysian "via negativa," emphasizes complete denial of the self and annihilation of the will, and did flourish, in fact, in a cultural milieu in which torture was prevalent and which also produced Passion narratives with extremely naturalistic representations of the agonies of Christ.[59] The chief "hidden alliance" I find, however, is that both the discourse of mysticism and the discourse of the Passion offer us intimacy, exposing what it had been usual to conceal, the one in reference to the soul, the other to the body, in both cases striving after a representational fullness that must forever remain elusive.

This is a point made in a somewhat different way in Elaine Scarry's analysis of the Passion of Christ. I have already suggested that the deep concern of these narratives with the body in general and with the details of bodily suffering can regarded as the product of a growing materialism that developed in the Christian culture of western Europe from the eleventh through the thirteenth centuries, and indeed continued to intensify up to the end of the Middle Ages. Scarry would trace a direct line of progression in western culture from this medieval Christian piety through

Protestantism to the Marxism of the nineteenth and twentieth centuries. Her wide-ranging study provides us with a sophisticated understanding of the relationships among torture, pain, materiality, Marxism, and, among many other things, how these are related to representations of the suffering Christ. In contrasting the differing manifestations of materiality between the Hebrew scripture and the radical Christian revision of it, particularly in respect to the prominence of embodiment in the gospels, Scarry observes the following:

If in the Hebraic scripture we repeatedly move from the human body to a more extreme materialization of that body in the exposure of the interior (whether benignly as in reproduction or not benignly as in scenes of hurt), so now in the Gospels we begin with the body of God and move relentlessly toward the more extreme materialization, the exposure of the interior of Jesus in the final wounds of the crucifixion. The relation between body and belief remains constant in the two scriptures: in each the interior of the body carries the force of confirmation. The difference resides in whose body it is that is required to confer the factualness of the material world on the immaterial realm: in the one it is the body of man that substantiates God; in the other, the body of God that substantiates God. The Artifact becomes for the first time self-substantiating.[60]

The medieval Passion narratives can be understood as a further progression toward extreme materialization, manifested in an "exposure of the interior of Jesus" that surpasses the gospel accounts by an enormous magnitude. They are an affirmation of the certainty of the body: the end-product, or the intermediate-product, of what Scarry describes as those "centuries of visual representations" (to this I would add narrative representations as well) that "have made Christ's embodiment more prominent, have made it their central content."[61]

The overwhelmingly detailed accounts of the suffering of Christ, which in the later narratives become almost mechanical in their descriptions of the wounding, invasion, and tearing of the flesh, have the effect of isolating the body of Christ for clinical attention, separating it in these narratives from a social context of which it had traditionally always been a part. René Girard notes the importance of the crowd in the biblical accounts of the Passion, and Julia Kristeva observes that in the main tradition of representation in the medieval visual arts Christ suffers and dies always in the presence of others.[62] Kristeva's critique of the visual representation of the body of Christ in the late medieval painting of Holbein well delineates the shift from Gothic expressionism to the chilling loneliness of Holbein's picture of the dead body of Christ. Kristeva observes that

Holbein's portrayal of the body moves beyond pathos toward banality, in consequence attaining the highest point of humanization, since all glory is removed from the image.[63] In the visual arts, the very late medieval portrayals of the man of sorrows overwhelmingly emphasize the solitude and loneliness that accompanied Christ's suffering.

In her analysis of Holbein, Kristeva seems to be describing the transition from a sacramental to a rationalistic, non-cultic, conception of the world. That transition, however, was completed well beyond the end of the Middle Ages, and the sacramental world view, with its attendant participatory sense of belonging to the body of Christ, was very much alive at the close of the medieval period and persisted beyond the Reformation, as Eamon Duffy has shown.[64] Yet Kristeva's recognition of the quality of banality and her rich description of its implications in late medieval depictions of the Passion are important insights, offering a fruitful alternative to the more usual opinion that finds in those same representations only a repetitive mechanicality that deadens sensitivity to suffering. Her observations about the "desacralized reality" of Holbein's representation of Christ are applicable also, with some qualification, to the narratives of the Passion of the late Middle Ages. The intimacy with which they lay bare the details of the suffering human body perhaps affirms the sacramental outlook through the marvel of restorability and wholeness, even for such bodies. At the same time, the intimacy of that suffering begins to express the inevitable isolation and loneliness of all forms of suffering, of all expressions of pain: a "desacralized reality" indeed which at once points to the loneliness that we feel belongs so poignantly to the modern condition. And yet, as Kristeva declares, that intimacy and desacralized reality form the foundation of a new understanding of human dignity.[65] Those late medieval images and narrative representations of the tortured body of Christ, robbed of all traces of the hieratic and deprived of any sign of classical idealism—the body exposed, invaded, and alienated from its surroundings—those representations, across the barriers of time and belief, pronounce to us the new condition of modernity.

Appendix 1:
Meditation by Bernard on the Lamentation of the Blessed Virgin

(Meditacio Bernardi de lamentacione beate virginis)

[London, British Library, MS. Cotton Vespasian E.i, s. xiv]

(fol. 196v) Quis dabit capiti meo et oculis meis imbrem lacrimarum,[1] vt possim flere per diem et noctem, donec seruo suo dominus appareat visu vel sompno consolans animam meam? O vos filie Ierusalem, sponse dilecte dei, vna mecum lacrimas fundite donec nobis noster sponsus in sua speciositate benignus et suauis appareat vel occurrat.

Recolite, (fol. 197r) recolite, sedula mente pensate, quam sit amarum ab ipso separari cui vos promisistis, cui vos in omni sanctitate vouistis. Vouistis uota: reddite ea. Vos ipsas ergo vouistis: vos ipsas ergo reddite. Currite filie, currite virgines sacre, currite matres Christo castitatem vouentes: omnes ad virginem currite que genuit ipsum. Ipsa enim portauit regem glorie, ipsum omnipotenti datura. Ipsa genuit eum, lactauit eum, et die octaua circumcidit eum. Quadragesima die presentauit eum in templo, duas turtures vel columbas pro eo offerens holocaustum. Fugiens ab Herode ipsum portauit in Egiptum. Lactans et nutriens eum, curam illius habens, loquens eum fere quocumque pergebat.

Credo firmiter quod illa fuit inter mulieres illas que Christum sequebantur ministrantes ei. Nullus inde debet admirari, si sequabatur eum, cum ipse eius esset totus dulcor, desideriumque solamen. Hanc arbitror fuisse etiam inter ipsas dolentes atque gementes, que lamentabantur flentes dominum. Poterat hec ecclesia esse inter illas feminas Ierusalem, ad quas Iesus non clarus imperio, sed plenus opprobrio, spinis coronatus, sputis illusus, flagellis afflictus, similiter in angaria mortis crucem baiulans, conuersus dixit: "Filie Ierusalem, nolite flere super me, sed super vosipsas flete, et super filios vestros."[2] Putasne, domina mundi, domina mea et mater dilecta eiusdem Christi, estne verum quod dico? Vnde obsecro vt dicas seruulo tuo decus paradisi et gaudium celi, veritatem scilicet huius rei.

Obliuiscere tamen doloris, rogo, quia tunc te passam fuisse non dubito. O vtinam dolor ille sic cotidie inheret visceribus meis, sicut inhesit tunc tuis. Vtinam die quo assumpta fuisti in celum, vt in eternum cum tuo gauderes filio, michi lacrimas tuas indicasses, quo per illas cognoscerem quantum tibi amaritudinis fuit, cum Iesum dilectum tibi—heu, heu, (fol. 197v) parum dilectum michi—clauis in ligno confixum, capite inclinato suum exalare spiritum uideres sanctissimum. Sed peto ne te moueant

---

1. Quis dabit capiti meo et oculis meis imbrem lacrimarum: cf Ier 9:1.
2. Filie Ierusalem . . . filios vestros: Lc 23:28.

Who will give a stream of tears to my head and eyes so I might weep night and day until the lord appears to his servant in a vision or a dream to comfort my soul? O you daughters of Jerusalem, beloved brides of God, pour out your tears together with me until our bridegroom appears to us or meets us, sweet and kind in his beauty.

Reflect, reflect, think with a diligent mind, how bitter it is to be separated from him to whom you have promised yourself, to whom you are pledged in all holiness. You have made vows: fulfill them. Therefore you have pledged yourselves: therefore yield yourselves. Run, daughters; run, holy virgins; run, you mothers pledged in chastity to Christ: everyone run to the Virgin who bore him. She indeed carried the king of glory, to give him to the omnipotent. She bore him, suckled him, and circumcised him on the eighth day. On the fortieth day she presented him in the temple, offering two turtle doves or pigeons for him as a burnt offering. Fleeing from Herod, she carried him into Egypt. Nursing and feeding him, caring for him, speaking with him, she went with him nearly everywhere.

I firmly believe that she was among those women who followed Christ, serving him. No one ought to marvel, therefore, if she followed him, since he was all her sweetness, her desire, and her solace. I think that she was present among those sorrowing and sighing ones who wept and made lament for the lord. The church could be among those women of Jerusalem, to whom Jesus, not glorious in majesty, but full of dishonor, crowned with thorns, mocked with spittle, struck with whips, also carrying his cross in the service of death, turned and said: "Daughters of Jerusalem, do not weep over me, but weep over yourselves and over your sons." Do you not think, mistress of the world, my lady and beloved mother of the same Christ, that it is true what I say? I beseech you, that you tell your servant of the splendor of paradise, the joy of heaven, and the truth of this matter.

Nevertheless, forget, I ask, the pain; for I do not doubt that you suffered then. O would that that sorrow might cleave to my innards every day as it clung to yours! Would that on the day in which you were taken up into heaven to rejoice forever with your son, you would show me your tears, so that through them I might know how much bitterness you had when you saw your beloved (alas, alas, too little my beloved!) fixed to the tree with nails, giving up his most holy spirit with his head bowed. But I ask that the words that I say might not move you, although even rocks ought to be sundered by them. Whoever, whether reigning above or wandering on earth below, could restrain his tears, when he heard or considered in

verba que dico, cum tamen saxa deberent scindi ad illa. Quis vncquam, regnans in celo sursum, vel peregrinans in terra deorsum, audiens uel mente pertractans, quomodo est factus obprobrium hominum,[3] ipse dominus angelorum—miser ego, quare non ploro?—et abiectio plebis[4] factus est filius dei patris, quis poterit lacrimas continere? Verumtamen tu gaude gaudio magno valde, ab ipso nunc glorificata in celis, que in mente clauis amarissime fuisti confixa piissime mortis. Michi tamen obsecro lacrimas illas infunde, quas ipsa habuisti in sua passione, et, vt id affluat largius, de passione filii tui dei et domini mei ad inuicem conferaramus. Narra michi, te flagito, seriem veritatis, que mater es et virgo tocius summe trinitatis.

Illa respondet: "Illud quod queris conpungitiuum est et magni doloris; sed quia iam glorificata sum, flere non possum. Tu tamen cum lacrimis scribe ea, que cum magnis doloribus ipsa perpensi."

Cui inquam: "Flere peropto, sed quia nichil aliud libet, sed miser ego: cor lapideum[5] habens, flere non possum. Regina celi, mater crucifixi, domina mea, da quod iubes et prebe quod cupio; quia audit seruus tuus,[6] dicat domina mea. Dic, mater angelorum, si in Ierusalem fuisti, quando captus fuit filius tuus et vinctus, et ad Annam tractus et ductus?"

Cui illa: "Fui vtique in Ierusalem. Quando hec audiui, gressu qualicumque potui, et vix potui, ad dominum meum, filium meum, veni plorans. Cumque eum fuissem intuita, pugnis percuti, alapis cedi, spinis coronari, conspui, et obprobrium hominum[7] fieri, commota sunt omnia uiscera mea,[8] et defecit spiritus meus,[9] et non erat michi sensus, neque vox, neque sonus. Erant mecum et mee sorores et alie femine multe plangentes eum, quasi vnigenitum. Inter quas erat Maria Magdalene, que super (fol. 198r) omnes, excepta me, plorabat, dum Christus deus, precone clamante, Pilato imperante, sibi baiulans crucem[10] ad supplicium traheretur. Factus est concursus populorum post ipsum: alii ridebant illudentes ei, alii proiciebant lutum et fimum et inmundiciam super caput eius.

---

3. obprobrium hominum: Ps 21:7.
4. abiectio plebis: Ps 21:7.
5. cor lapideum: Ez 11:19.
6. quia audit seruus tuus: I Rg 3:9, 10.
7. obprobrium hominum: Ps 21:7.
8. commota sunt omnia uiscera mea: cf Gn 43:30.
9. defecit spiritus meus: Ps 76:4.
10. baiulans crucem: Io 19:17.

his mind, how he was made the reproach of men, the very lord of angels (wretched me, why do I not weep?), and the son of God the father is made a thing despised by the people [Ps 23:6]? Nevertheless, may you rejoice greatly with great joy, now that you are glorified by him in heaven, who were fixed in your mind most bitterly by nails of a most holy death. Yet, I beseech you, pour out for me those tears which you had at his passion, and, so they might flow more copiously, let us exchange words with each other concerning the passion of your son, my lord and my God. Tell me, I beg, the true sequence of events, you who are virgin and mother of the highest trinity.

She responded: "What you seek inspires compunction and is very sorrowful; but because I have been glorified, I cannot weep. You, however, write with tears those things which I have pondered with great pain."

To whom I said: "I greatly wish to weep, for nothing would please me more; but I am a wretch with a stony heart, and I cannot weep. Queen of heaven, mother of the crucified, my lady, grant what you command and provide what I desire: let my lady speak, for your servant hears. Tell me, mother of the angels, if you were in Jerusalem when your son was captured and bound, then dragged and led to Annas?"

To which she responded: "I was indeed in Jerusalem. When I heard these things, I came weeping to my lord, my son, by whatever course I could, and I was scarcely able to do so. And when I looked at him, struck by fists, beaten with blows, crowned with thorns, spat upon and made the reproach of men, all my innards were stirred, my spirit failed, and there was in me neither sense, nor voice, nor sound. With me there were my sisters and many other women, weeping over him as though their only child. Among these was Mary Magdalene, who wept more than all the rest, except for me, when Christ our God was led to the place of torture carrying his cross as Pilate had commanded, with a herald crying out. A crowd of people came after him. Some laughed at him and mocked him. Others threw dirt, dung, and filth on his head.

Sequebar eum ego mestissima mater, cum mulieribus que secute eum fuerant a Ga<lilea>;[11] tenebar et sustentabar, quousque peruentum est ad locum passionis, vbi crucifixerunt eum ante me. Et ipse videns me fuit in cruce leuatus, et ligno durissimis clauis affixus. Ego videns eum et ipse uidens me, plus dolebat de me quam de se. Ipse vero tamquam agnus coram tondente se vocem non dabat, nec aperiebat os suum.[12] Aspiciebam ego infelix dominum meum et filium meum in cruce pendentem, et morte tur-pissima morientem. Tanto dolore et tristicia uexabar in morte, quantus non posset explicari sermone. Nec mirum: erat enim aspectu dulcis, colloquio suauis, et in omni conuersacione benignus. Discurrebat namque sanguis ex quatuor partibus rigantibus vndis, ligno manibus pedibusque confixis.

De vultu illius pulcritudo effluxerat omnis, et qui erat pre filiis homi-num forma speciosus[13] videbatur indecorus. Videbam quod complebatur illud propheticum in eo: "Vidimus eum et non erat ei species neque decor,"[14] quia vultum illius verberibus iniquorum fedauerat liuor. Iste erat dolor maximus, quia videbam me deseri ab ipso quem genueram; nec supererat alius, quia michi erat vnicus, et ideo non potuit in me capere dolor meus. Vox mea fere pertransierat omnis, sed dabam pro gemitibus suspiria doloris. Volebam loqui, sed dolor verba rumpebat, quia verbum iam mente conceptum, dum ad formacionem procederet oris: ad se imperfectum reuocabat dolor nimis cordis. Vox triste sonabat foris, vul-nus denuncians mentis. Verba dabat amor, sed rauca sonaba<n>t, quia lin-gua magistra uocis vsum loquendi perdiderat. Videbam morientem quem diligit anima mea,[15] et tota liquefierat[16] pre doloris angustia.

Aspiciebat et ipse vt et benignissimo vultu me matrem plorantem, et verbis (fol. 198v) paucis me voluit consolari, et nullo modo potuit. Flebam dicendo, et dicebam plorando: 'Fili mi! Ve michi, ve michi! Quis modo dabit vt ego moriar pro te?[17] Quid faciam? Moritur filius meus. Cur se-cum non moritur, hec mestissima mater? Fili mi, fili mi![18] Amor vnice, fili

---

11. Here and elsewhere, letters or words in pointed brackets have been supplied by the editor.

12. tamquam agnus . . . os suum: cf Is 53:7.

13. pre filiis hominum forma speciosus: cf Ps 44:3.

14. Vidimus eum et non erat ei species neque decor: Is 53:2.

15. quem diligit anima mea: Ct 1:6.

16. liquefierat: cf Ct 5:6.

17. Quis modo dabit vt ego moriar pro te: II Rg 18:33 (David on the death of Absolon).

18. Fili mi, fili mi: II Rg 18:33.

"I followed him, a most sorrowful mother, along with the women who had followed him from Galilee. I was held up and supported by them, until we arrived at the place of his passion, where they crucified him before me. As he looked at me, he was raised on the cross and fixed to the wood with hard nails. I looked at him, and he looked at me, and he grieved more for me than for himself. As a lamb before the shearer, he did not make a sound or open his mouth [Is 53:7]. I was miserable, looking at my lord and my son hanging on the cross and dying a most shameful death. I was tormented by such great sorrow and sadness in death that it could not be expressed in speech. No wonder: for he was sweet in appearance, pleasant in conversation, and kind in all his behavior. Blood ran down from four sides, flowing in streams, his hands and feet fastened to the wood.

"From his countenance all the beauty ebbed away, and he who was fair in form beyond the children of men [Ps 44:3] seemed unbecoming. I saw that the prophecy was fulfilled in him: 'We saw him, and there was no beauty in him, nor comeliness' [Is 53:2], for bruises from the blows of the wicked had disfigured his face. That was the greatest pain, for I saw myself forsaken by him whom I had borne; nor did anyone else remain, for he was my only child, and therefore my sorrow could not be kept within me. My voice had nearly gone, but I uttered sighs of sorrow and moans of grief. I wanted to speak, but sorrow broke off the words, for a word is first conceived in the mind, then proceeds to formation by the mouth. Too great sorrow of heart calls back the word imperfect. A sad voice sounds on the outside, declaring the wound of the mind. Love provides the words, but they sound harsh, for the tongue, the mistress of the voice, had lost the skill of speaking. I saw him dying, whom my soul loved, and my soul was completely dissolved by the anguish of sorrow.

"With gentle countenance he gazed at me, his weeping mother, and wished to console me with a few words, and could not do it at all. I wept while speaking, and I spoke while weeping: 'My son! Woe unto me! Woe unto me! Who will only grant that I might die for you? What shall I do? My son is dying. Why can this most sorrowful mother not die with him? My son, my son! My only love, sweetest son, do not leave me behind! Take me to yourself, that I might die with you. It is wrong for you to die alone. Let your own mother die with you. O wretched death, do not spare me: you alone are pleasing to me above all things. Increase your strength: slaughter the mother, kill the mother together with the son. O son, sole delight, singular joy, life of my soul and my entire solace, make me die now, who bore you for death. O son, recognize that I am weak, and hear

dulcissime, noli me derelinquere post te! Trahe me ad teipsum,[19] vt moriar tecum. Male solus moreris. Tecum moriatur ista tua genitrix. O mors misera, noli michi parcere: tu sola michi places pre cunctis. Exaggera vires: trucida matrem, matrem cum filio perime simul. Fili dulcor vnice, singulare gaudium, vita anime mee et omne solacium, fac vt ego ipsa nunc moriar, que te ad mortem genui. O fili, recognosce teneram et exaudi precem meam. Decet enim filium exaudire matrem desolatam. Exaudi me, obsecro! In tuo me suscipe patibulo, vt qui vna carne viuunt et vno amore se diligunt, vna morte pereant. O Iudei impii, O Iudei miseri, nolite michi parcere! Ex quo natum meum vnicum crucifigitis, matrem crucifigite, aut alia quacumque morte seua me perimite, dummodo cum meo simul moriar filio: male solus moritur. Orbas orbem radio; me, Iudea, filio, gaudio, dulcore. Vita mea moritur, et salus perimitur, ac de terra tollitur omnis spes mea. Cur ergo viuit post filium mater in dolore? Tollite, suspendite matrem cum suo pignore! Non parcis proli, non parcas et michi. Tu michi sola mors esto seua. Tunc summe gauderem, si mori possem simul cum filio Christo. Dulce est mori misere, sed mors optata recedit. Ve michi! Infelix tibi Iesu, precipitata venit. Morte michi melius est mori quam vitam ducere mortis. Sed fugit a me misera, et me infelicem relinquit, cum nunc multum mors optata esset. O fili care, o nate benigne, miserere matris, suscipe preces. Desine matri nunc esse durus, qui cunctis semper fuisti benignus. Suscipe matrem tecum in cruce, vt viuam tecum post mortem semper. (fol. 199r) Nil vero dulcius est michi quam te amplexo in cruce tecum mori. Et nil certe amarius quam viuere post mortem tuam. O vere dei nate, tu michi pater, tu michi mater, tu michi sponsus, tu michi filius, tu michi omnia eras. Nunc orbor patre, viduor sponso, desolor prole, omnia perdo. O fili mi, vltra quid faciam? Ve michi, ve michi: fili, nescio quid faciam. Quo vadam, bone, vbi me uertam, dulcissime? Quis michi de cetero subsidium et consilium prestabit? Fili dulcissime, omnia possibilia sunt tibi. Sed si non vis vt moriar tecum, michi relinque aliquod benigne consilium.

Tunc dominus, iam anxius in cruce, oculis et vultu annuens, de Iohanne ait: 'Mulier, ecce filius tuus.'[20] Erat et ipse Iohannes presens vultu tristis. Corde mestissimus, lacrimis semper plorans, ac si dominus diceret: 'O mater dulcissima, mollis ad flendum, mollis ad dolendum, tu scis quia ad hoc veni, ad hoc de te carnem assumpsi, vt per crucis patibulum saluarem genus humanum. Quomodo implebuntur scripture? Scis enim quod oportet me pati pro salute generis humani. Die namque

19. Trahe me ad teipsum: cf Ct 1:3.
20. Mulier, ecce filius tuus: Io 19:26.

my prayer. It is fitting for a son to hear his desolate mother. Hear me, I beg you. Take me up onto your cross, that those who live as one flesh and love each other with one love might perish in one death. O wicked Jews! O wretched Jews, do not spare me! Since you crucify my only child, crucify the mother, or kill me with some other kind of cruel death, so long as I might die together with my son. It is wrong for him to die alone. You deprive the world of its ray; you, Judea, deprive me of my son, my joy, my delight. My life dies, my salvation perishes, and all my hope is taken from the world. Why, therefore, does the mother live on in sorrow after the son? Away, hang the mother with her child! You did not spare the offspring, do not spare me. Death alone be cruel to me. Then I would rejoice greatly if I could die together with Christ my son. It is sweet to die wretchedly, but longed-for death recedes. Woe unto me! Unhappy Jesus, it comes suddenly for you. It is better for me to die by death than to lead a life of death. But it flees from me and leaves me wretched and unhappy, although now death would be greatly desired. O dear son, o kind child, have mercy on your mother; hear her prayers. Be no longer harsh to your mother, you who were always kind to everyone. Take up your mother with you on the cross, so I might live with you always after death. Nothing, indeed, is sweeter to me than to embrace you and die with you on the cross. And nothing, certainly, is more bitter than to live on after your death. O true child of God, you were my father, you were my mother, you were my bridegroom, you were my son, you were my everything. Now I am deprived of a father, bereft of a bridegroom, forsaken by a son. I have lost everything. O my son, what more shall I do? Woe unto me, woe unto me: son, I do not know what I will do. Where will I go, my kind one, where will I turn, my sweetest? Who will henceforth give me aid and counsel? Sweetest son, all things are possible with you. But if you do not wish me to die with you, kindly leave me some advice.'

"Then the lord, who was now troubled on the cross, made signs with his eyes and face, and said concerning John: 'Woman, behold your son.' John himself was present with a sad face. Sad in heart and ever weeping, it was as if the lord said: 'O sweetest mother, mild in weeping, mild in sorrowing, you know that I have come for this; for this I have assumed flesh from you, that through the gallows of the cross I might redeem mankind. How shall the Scriptures be fulfilled? You know that it is indeed necessary for me to suffer for the salvation of mankind. I will rise again on the third day, appearing openly to you and my disciples. Leave off sorrowing,

tercia resurgam, tibi et discipulis meis patenter apparens. Desine dolere, dolorem depone, quia ad patrem vado,[21] ad gloriam paterne maiestatis ascendo. Immo congratulare michi, quia nunc inueni ouem que errauerat.[22] Moriatur vnus, vt inde totus mundus reuiuiscat. Vnius ob meritum ceteri perire minores.[23] Omnes saluantur vnius ob meritum. Quod placet patri, quomodo displicet tibi, o dulcissima mater? Calicem quem dedit michi pater,[24] non vis vt bibam illum? Noli flere, mulier; noli plangere, speciosissima mater. Non te desero. Non te derelinquo. Tecum sum, et tecum ero, omni tempore seculi. Sed secundum carnem subiaceo imperio mortis; per diuinitatem sum, et ero semper, immortalis et impassibilis. Bene scis vnde processi et ueni. Quare igitur tristaris, si ascendo vnde descendi? Tempus est vt reuertar ad eum qui me misit; et quo ego vado, non potes venire modo. Venies autem (fol. 199v) postea.[25] Interim Iohannes, qui est nepos meus, tibi reputabitur filius. Curam habebit tui et solacium fidelissimum erit tibi.

Inde Iohannem intuitus dominus ait: "Ecce mater tua,[26] ei seruias, eam tibi commendo. Suscipe matrem tuam, immo magis suscipe meam." Ipse ad hec pauca dixit. Illi duo dilecti semper lacrimas fundere non cessabant. Tacebant isti martires ambo, et pre dolore immo loqui non poterant. Isti virgines duo Christum audiebant voce rauca, et semiuiua loquentem, et ipsum videbant paulatim morientem. Nec ei poterant respondere verbum, quia illum iam videbant quasi mortuum. Illi enim duo erant quasi mortui, vnde spiritus eorum non poterant exalare. Defecerant spiritus eorum et virtutem loquendi amiserant; audiebant et tacebant, quia pre angustia loqui non poterant. Solus illis dolor luctusque remansit amicus. Amabant flere, et flebant amare; amare flebant, quia amare dolebant. Nam gladius Christi animas utriusque transibat.[27] Transibat seuus, seue perimebat utrumque. Que magis amabat, seuior seuiebat in matre. Mater senciebat, et sentit Christi dolores. Que virgo peperit, gladium est passa doloris. Christi morientis vulnera matris erant; Christi dolores seui fuere tortores in anima matris. Mater erat laniata pignoris morte. Mente mater

21. quia ad patrem vado: Io 14:12.
22. inueni ouem que errauerat: cf Lc 15:6.
23. Vnius . . . minores: Mushacke's edition has "Vnius ob demeritum cuncti periere homines," which is clearer.
24. Calicem quem dedit michi pater: Io 18:11.
25. Tempus est . . . postea: cf Io 13:36.
26. Ecce mater tua: Io 19:26.
27. gladius Christi animas utriusque transibat: see Lc 2:35.

put away grief, for I go to the father, I ascend to the glory of the father's majesty. Rather wish me joy, for now I have found the sheep which went astray. Let one die that henceforth the whole world may be restored to life. Because of the (de)merit of one, the lesser who remain must perish: all are saved through the merit of one. How can what pleases the father be displeasing to you, o sweetest mother? The cup which the father gave me, do you not wish me to drink? Do not weep, woman; do not lament, most beautiful mother. I will not desert you. I will not abandon you. I am with you and I will be with you throughout all time. But, according to the flesh, I submit to the dominion of death; yet by divinity I am and always will be immortal and impassible. You know very well whence I have proceeded and where I have come from. Why, therefore, are you saddened if I ascend to the place whence I descended? It is time that I return to him who sent me, and where I go, you can by no means come. You will come there, however, afterwards [Jn 13:36]. In the mean time, John, my nephew, will be thought of as your son and will take care of you, and will be a most faithful comfort to you.' "

Then the lord looked at John and said: "Behold your mother: keep her; I commend her to you. Receive your mother, or rather, receive my mother." He said few more words. Those two beloved ones did not stop pouring out tears. Those two martyrs were silent, and could not even speak for sorrow. Those two virgins heard Christ speaking in a hoarse and half-dead voice, and they saw him dying little by little. Nor could they answer a word to him, for they saw him now nearly dead. Indeed the two of them were as though dead, hence their spirits could not breathe out. Their spirits grew weak and they lost the power of speaking. They listened and were silent because they could not speak for anguish. Pain and struggle alone remained their companions. They loved to weep, and they wept bitterly. They wept bitterly because they were bitterly grief-stricken, for the sword of Christ had pierced the souls of both of them. The cruel sword had pierced: it killed both of them cruelly. It raged more cruelly in the soul of the mother, whose love was greater. The mother felt and feels the pains of Christ. That virgin who gave birth suffered the sword of sorrow. The wounds of the dying Christ were the wounds of the mother; the pains of Christ were cruel torturers in the soul of the mother. The mother was torn to pieces by the death of her loved one. The mother was struck down in her mind with the point of a weapon with which the wicked slaves had pierced the limbs of Christ. She was one whom great sorrow held. Great sorrows grew in her mind; raging cruelly within, they could not be poured out-

erat percussa cuspide teli quo membra Christi serui foderunt iniqui. Ipsa enim erat, quam dolor magnus tenebat. In mente eius creuerant magni dolores, nec poterant extra refundi, intus atrociter seuientes. Dolor nati matris animam gladiabat. In carne Christi soluebat debitum mortis, quod grauius erat quam mori anime matris.

Interim Christus, commendata matre Iohanni, dixit: "Scicio."[28] Et dederunt ei, qui crucifixerunt eum, acetum cum felle mixtum, quod cum gustasset noluit bibere,[29] sed dixit: "Consummatum est,"[30] et exclamauit voce magna dicens: "Hely, hely, lamazabatani," hoc est, deus meus, deus meus quare me dereliquisti?[31] Et sic dicens, expirauit.[32] Tunc tremuit terra, tunc sol sua lumina clausit. Merebantque poli, me- (fol. 200r) rebant sydera cuncta. Omne suum iubar amisit luna dolendo, recessitque omnis ab alto ethere fulgor. Scinduntur duri lapides, scinduntur fastigia templi. Surrexerunt multi fatentes Christum voce publica deum.[33] Cogitare libet quantus dolor tunc infuit matri, cum sic dolebant que insensibilia erant. Non lingua loqui, non mens cogitare valebit, quanto dolore afficebantur pia viscera Marie.

Nunc soluis, virgo, cum vsura quod in partu mutuasti a natura. Dolorem pariendo filium non sensisti; milies replicatum, filio moriente, passa fuisti. Iuxta Christi crucem stabat emortua mater.[34] Et que sancto <spiritu> conceperat, vox illi non erat. Dolor enim vires abstulit. O verum eloquium iusti Symeonis! Quem provisit gladium senciebat doloris.[35] Ista stabat, hic pendebat. Immo ista strata iacens pallebat anima viuens. Viuebat moriens, et viuens moriebatur. Nec potuit mori, que viuens mortua fuit; hec etenim stabat vulnerata seuo dolore, expectans Christi corpus deponi de cruce.

Plorabat dicens: "O me, O me! Reddite nunc misere corpus vel exanime. Complestis vota, extinctum deponite, matri reddite; vel, si libet,[36] non magis moriente, illi adiungite, vt cum suis pereant et mei dolores. Deponite, queso, illum. Reddite michi liuidum corpus, vt sit michi solamen, vel saltem defunctus."

28. Scicio: Io 19:28.
29. Et dederunt . . . noluit bibere: Mt 27:34.
30. Consummatum est: Io 19:30.
31. Hely, hely . . .me dereliquisti: Mt 27:46.
32. Et sic dicens, expirauit: Lc 23:46.
33. Tunc tremuit terra . . .voce publica deum: cf Mt 27:50–54.
34. Iuxta Christi crucem stabat emortua mater: cf Io 19:25.
35. Quem provisit gladium senciebat doloris: see Lc 2:25–35.
36. silibet: similibus *MS*.

side. The sorrow of the offspring put to the sword the soul of the mother. In the flesh of Christ she paid the debt of death, which was heavier for the soul of the mother than to die herself.

In the meantime, after he had commended his mother to John, Christ said: "I thirst." And those who crucified him gave him vinegar mixed with gall, which, when he had tasted it, he did not wish to drink, but said: "It is finished," and cried out in a loud voice saying: "Ely, ely, lama sabachthani," that is, "my God, my God, why have you forsaken me?" [Mt 27:46] And saying this, he died. Then the earth trembled, then the sun shut off its light. And the heavens grieved, and all the stars mourned. The moon in sorrow lost all its light, and all brightness withdrew from the upper heavens. The hard stones were split apart; the pediments of the temple were broken. Many arose, confessing publicly that Christ was God. It is agreeable to imagine how great was the mother's sorrow, when insensible things sorrowed in such a way. The tongue cannot speak, nor the mind conceive, the extent of the sorrow which affected the pious innards of Mary.

Now, Virgin, you repay with interest what you borrowed from nature in giving birth. You did not feel pain in bearing your son; you suffered a thousand times more in the dying of your son. The dead mother stood near the cross of Christ. And she who had conceived by the holy spirit had no voice. Sorrow truly had carried off her strength. O true utterance of the just Simeon! She felt the sword of sorrow which he had foreseen. She stood there; he hung on the cross. Rather, her living soul grew pale as she lay prostrate. Dying, she lived; and living, she died. Nor could she die, who was a living dead person; in fact she stood wounded with cruel pain, waiting for the body of Christ to be taken down from the cross. She lamented, saying:

"O me! o me! Now return his lifeless body to me his wretched mother. Fulfill your vows, take down the dead one, return him to the mother. He is dying no longer; join me to him, if you please, that my sorrows may perish with his. Take him down, I ask. Return to me the livid body that he might be a comfort to me, even though dead."

Iuxta crucem stabat Maria[37] intuens vultu benigno pendentem in patibulo pedibusque nitens. In altum manus leuabat, crucem amplectens, in osculatum ruens ex qua parte sanguis vnda crucem rigabat. Illuc se vertit anxia, circuibat vt Christum valeret amplecti, quem dudum viuido vbere lactabat. Ex quo non poterat, manus erigere volebat. Sperat amor multa que raro uel nunquam ad effectum possunt deduci. Sibi cuncta cedere amor impaciens credit. Volebat amplecti Christum in alto pendentem, sed manus in frustra tense, in se complexe redibant; se eleuat a terra tangere dilectum, vt sic saltem doloris sui aliquatenus demulceat aculeum. Et quia tangere nequibat, membra virginea ad terram (fol. 200v) collisa iaciuntur. Ibi prostrata iacebat, immensitate doloris depressa. Sed eam compellebat erigere uis magni doloris intensa. In impetu amoris surgit attrectare cupiens[38] filium: sed dolore sauciata, martirioque defossa, terram relisa petebat. O graue martirium! O frequens suspirium! O sanguens pectus virgineum! Liquefacta est anima,[39] facies pallet rosea, sed precioso filii sui rubet cruore respersa. Cadentes guttas sanguinis ore sacro tangebat, terram deosculans quam cruoris vnda rigabat.

Interim vir nobilis Ioseph corpus Christi arridum a Pilato impetrat, Nichodemum secum assumens, venit ad mortuum, et ad fere mortuam; quos, ut mater vidit, volentes eum deponere. Languoris et infirmitatis sue oblita, consurgit; spiritus alquantulum[40] reuiuiscit. Et quantum potuit, illis adiutorium ministrabat. Vnus clauos e manibus traxit, alius ne corpus caderet sustinuit. Maria brachia leuans, vulnera contemplans, manus perforatas intuens, sacroque sanguine respersas, se vix sustinere potuit. Namque manus, caput, brachia, supra triste pectus habebat vel trahebat, dumque eum tangere potuit parumper, in osculis et amplexibus ruens, quia suo dilecto saciari non potuit. Virgo compaciens pie considerat, et tanti candoris, tantive splendoris et pulcritudinis iam erat corpus Iesu, quod nec lingua fari nec litera sufficit ostendere. Erat enim candidius niue, splendidius sole, super balsami odorem redolens, sed dum de cruce

---

37. Iuxta crucem stabat Maria: cf Io 19:25.
38. attrectare cupiens *PL 182: 1138*: visa auctoritate *MS*
39. Liquefacta est anima: cf Ct 5:6.
40. alquantulum = aliquantulum.

Near the cross Mary stood gazing with a gentle face on him hanging on the cross, pressing against his feet. She raised her hands on high, embracing the cross, pouring out kisses where blood had moistened the cross in a stream. There she turned and anxiously went around so she could embrace Christ, whom not long ago she had suckled with her living breast. Since she could not, she wished to raise her hands. Love hopes for many things which can never or rarely be brought about. Impatient love believes that all things yield to it. She wished to embrace Christ hanging on high on the cross, but her hands stretched out in vain and returned enfolding themselves. She raised herself from the ground to touch her beloved, so that she might in this way soften the sting of her sorrow, at least to some extent. And because she could not touch, the virgin limbs were thrown down to the ground and dashed together. There she lay prostrate, weighed down by immense sorrow. But the constraining power of great sorrow forced her to rise. In an impulse of love she arose, desiring to touch her son; but wounded by sorrow, and overwhelmed by martyrdom, she was forced back and fell to the ground.

O heavy martyrdom! O repeated sighing! O bloody virgin breast! Her soul has dissolved, her rosy face grows pale, but grows red sprinkled with the precious gore of her son. She touched the falling drops of blood with her sacred mouth, kissing the ground which the stream of blood watered.

In the meantime, the noble Joseph obtained the withered body of Christ from Pilate, and taking Nichodemus with him, he came to the dead Christ and the nearly dead Mary. The mother saw that they wanted to take him down. Overburdened with her weakness and infirmity, she stood up and her spirit revived a little. And as much as she could, she offered to help them. One drew the nails from his hands, the other supported the corpse so it would not fall. Mary lifted up her arms, contemplated his wounds, and gazed at his hands pierced and sprinkled with sacred blood; she could scarcely hold herself up. Indeed, she held or drew over her sad breast his hands, head, and arms, and as long as she could touch him a little while, she fell down in kisses and embraces, for she could not be sated with her beloved. The suffering virgin piously gazed, and the body of Christ was now of such brilliance, of such splendor and beauty, that neither speech nor writing sufficed to show it. It was indeed whiter than snow, brighter than the sun, giving out an odor beyond the balsam, but when it was taken down from the cross, she fell over it out of uncontrolled grief and immensity of love. Afterwards she stood as though dead and seemed to

depositum fuit, supra ipsum ruens prae incontinencia doloris, et immensitate amoris. Post mortua stetit, et transire uisa est [*MS:* lusa]. Stabat apud caput extincti filii, lacrimis faciem eius rigans, et per diuersa torquebatur suspiria, quaciens caput, et amarissime plangens:

"Quid fecisti, carissime fili? Quare te Iudei crucifixerunt? Que causa mortis tue? Comisistine scelus, vt tali morte deputareris? Non, fili, non; sed sic tuos redimere dignatus es, vt sic posteris exempla relinquas. In gremio meo te mortuum teneo. (fol. 201r) Heu michi tristissima! Vbi est gaudium illud quod in natiuitate tua indescribabile habui? Ve michi, in quantam tristiciam et dolorem versum est gaudium meum. Succurre michi, fili, et spiritum sanctum michi iterum infunde, quia iam gaudium illius, quod in obumbracione concepi et angelica salutacione fere pre dolore immemor deficio."

Interim frontem et genas, os simul et oculos, osculari lassata non desinit. Illius facta et obprobria ad mentem redeunt: quis vel qualis fuerit quem ipsa concepit virgo illeso pudore, et peperit sine dolore, qui erat ei omne, dum viuebat deus et dominus, et vnicus filius? Vnde dicebat: "Dic, fili karissime, dic, amor vnice, vita mee anime, amor meus, singulare gaudium, vnicum solacium, quare sic me dolere permittis? Cur tam longe factus es a me? Deus meus, consolare animam meam, et miserere et respice in me."

Dicat qui dicere audet, virginis dolorem plene posse enarrari non credo, cum rectum erat amoris et meroris continens modum. Non desperabat, sed pie et iuste dolebat, sperans tamenque fortiter, firmiterque credens, ipsum secundum promissum tercio die, morte deuicta, resurgere. In hac enim sola, in triduo, fides ecclesie stabat. Hecque fide concepit fidem, quam semel a deo suscepit nunquam perdidit. Speque certissima domini expectauit graciam resurgentis.

Erant et angeli cum ipsa, simul dolentes, si tamen dolere poterant. Dolebant quidem pro iusto amore Iesu Christi. Compaciebantur Christo in morte dolendo, gaudentes tamen quod genus humanum redimebatur. Flebant, ut arbitror, amarissime, mente turbati, quod matrem Christi tanto videbant dolore teneri. O quis angelorum vel archangelorum, etiam contra naturam illic non flesset, vbi contra naturam auctor nature, deus immortalis, homo mortuus iacebat? Videbant Christum sic male tractatum ab impiis, sic laceratum iacere, et Mariam totam suo cruentatam cruore. Il-

be transformed. She stood at the head of her dead son, watering his face with tears, and was racked by many sobs, shaking her head and bitterly lamenting:

"What have you done, dearest son? Why did the Jews crucify you? What is the cause of your death? Did you commit a crime that you should be considered worthy of such a death? None, my son, none: but in this way you deigned to redeem your own, that you might leave an example for your posterity. I hold you dead in my bosom. Alas for me, most sad! Where is that indescribable joy that I had had at your birth? Woe to me, my joy has changed into such great sadness and pain. Help me, son, and pour out the holy spirit on me again, for now I lack its joy, which I conceived in the overshadowing and the angelic salutation; I have almost forgotten these things because of grief."

Meanwhile, she did not grow tired of kissing his brow and cheeks, his mouth and also his eyes. His deeds and his shame returned to her mind: who or what will he be whom the virgin conceived with her modesty intact and bore without pain, who was everything to her while he lived as God and lord, and her only son? Hence she said:

"Say, dearest son, say, my only love, life of my soul, my love, my singular joy, my only solace, why do you allow me to sorrow so? Why are you so distant from me? My God, comfort my soul, have mercy on me and look on me."

Let him say who dares, but I do not believe that the sorrow of the virgin can be fully told, although it was proper, keeping due limits of love and sorrow. She did not despair, but piously and rightfully sorrowed, hoping bravely and firmly believing that he would rise on the third day according to his promise, when he had conquered death. In her alone, during the three days, the faith of the church rested. And she through faith engendered faith, which once she received from God, she never lost. In this most certain hope she awaited the grace of the risen lord.

There were angels with her, sorrowing with her, if, however, they were able to sorrow. Indeed they did sorrow for the righteous love of Jesus Christ. They had pity on Christ suffering in death, yet they rejoiced that the human race was redeemed. They wept bitterly, I think, troubled in mind that they saw the mother of Christ bound with such sorrow. O what angel or archangel would not weep here, even contrary to nature, where contrary to nature, the author of nature, the immortal God, lies dead as a man? They saw Christ so badly treated by the wicked lying wounded, and Mary com-

lamque piam, sanctam, totam bonam, totam pulcram, totam delectabilem, totam dulcem Mariam, suam beatissimam matrem, tantis cruciari singultibus, tam amaris repleri (fol. 201v) doloribus, tam amarissime flere, quod nullo modo poterat suas lacrimas refrenare. Fiebat luctus et meror ab angelis presentibus qualis decebat spiritus almos. Immo mirarem si angeli cuncti non flessent, etiam in illa beatitudine, ubi impossibile est flere. Credo propter quod et loquor qui dolebant, si dolere valebant. Sicut enim possibile fuit deum per assumptum hominem mori, ita possibile fuit angelos beatos in morte domini sui dolere. Inter hec pia lamenta, et Ioseph et Nichodemus corpus dominicum sepulture dederunt. Tunc illius exequias et victoriam milia milium decantabant angelorum. Illi cantabant, sed Maria gemitus dabat. Illi gloriam deo dabant vel canebant; hec iuxta sepulti sepulcrum amare flebat. Volebat mesta mater sepeliri cum filio; et innitens super filium, amplectens illum, et omni amoris dulcedine deosculans dicebat: "Miseremini mei, miseremini mei, saltim vos amici mei.[41] Illum adhuc paululum michi relinquite, vt faciem subtracto velamine semel valeam contemplari. Nolite, queso, eum tam cito tradere sepulture. Date illum michi, vt michi saltem defunctus; aut si filium in sepulcro deponitis, matrem, iam non matrem, cum illo sepelite: vt quid viuam post illum?"

Illi tumulare volebant. Hec ad se trahebat, hec retinere studet; illi sepelire conantur. Sicque vertitur inter eos pia lis et miseranda contencio. Omnes tamen virgineo compacientes dolori, pro desiderio coacti, flebant eam iam omni solacio destitutam. Sepulto domino, sepulcrum mater amplectitur, et qua poterat voce filium vocans ingemit. O singularis virgo et mater, iam dicere potes: "Anima mea liquefacta est,"[42] vt dilectus locutus est in cruce, scilicet, "Mulier, ecce filius tuus."[43] Nunc potes dicere: "Quesiui, et non inueni illum. Vocaui, et non respondit michi,"[44] et cetera. Ad sepulcrum sedens iuxta illum, extendebat manus cuius animam pertransiuit gladius. Et iterum atque iterum, anxios, lassata dabat singultus. Accessit Iohannes lugens, lugentem erigit. Nam cruciata gemitibus, fatigata doloribus, afflicta ploratibus, pedibus stare nequibat. Tamen, sicut potuit, mulieribus sanctis (fol. 202r) adiuta, cunctis plorantibus, simul Ierusalem ingreditur. Videntes autem eam inconsolabiliter plorantem, miro conpaciuntur affectu. Sic ducitur ad domum Iohannis, quia super propriam ei fideliter et deuote ministrans, omni corde dilexit. Denique resurgente

---

41. Miseremini mei, miseremini mei, saltim vos amici mei: Iob 19:21.
42. Anima mea liquefacta est: Ct 5:6.
43. Mulier, ecce filius tuus: Io 19:26.
44. Quesiui, et non inueni illum. Vocaui, et non respondit michi: Ct 5:6.

pletely bloodied with his gore. And they saw that pious, holy, completely good, entirely beautiful, entirely delightful, entirely sweet Mary, his most blessed mother, tortured with such great sobs, filled with such bitter pains, weeping so bitterly, that she could by no means restrain her tears. Lamentation and grief were made by the angels who were present, of such kind as was fitting for propitious spirits. Indeed, I would be surprised if all the angels did not weep, even in that blessedness where it is impossible to weep. Therefore I believe and I say that they sorrowed if they were able to sorrow. Just as it was possible for God to die in the assumed form of a man, so it was possible for blessed angels to sorrow at the death of their lord.

During these pious laments, Joseph and Nichodemus buried the lord's body. Then thousands of angels sung his funeral rites and the victory. They sung, but Mary sighed. They sung or gave glory to God; she wept bitterly at the tomb of the one they had buried. The grief-stricken mother wished to be buried with her son, and leaning over her son and embracing him, and kissing him with all the tenderness of love, she said:

"Have mercy on me, have mercy on me, at least you, my friends. Leave him for me here yet a little while, so I might at least be able to contemplate his face with the veil drawn back. Do not, I beg, commit him so quickly to the grave. Give him to me; to me, even though he is dead; or if you wish to place the son in the grave, bury the mother, now not a mother, with him, for why should I live after him?"

They wished to bury him. She drew him to herself and sought to keep him; they attempted to bury him. And so a pious dispute and a pitiful struggle broke out among them. Yet all had compassion for the virgin's sorrow; driven by longing, they wept for her now deprived of all solace. When the lord was buried, the mother embraced the tomb and crying out with what voice she could, she mourned for her son. O singular virgin and mother, now can you say: "My soul has fainted," as when your beloved spoke on the cross, namely, "Woman, behold your son." Now you can

filio, pre nimia debilitate membrorum deficiens, ad sepulcrum ire nequibat. Tunc currentibus aliis, et viuum filium cernentibus, dicere virgo potest: "Filie Ierusalem, nunciate dilecto quia amore langueo."[45] O felix et beatus Iohannes: dominus tibi tante prerogatiue commisit thesaurum. Reddet tibi dominus mercedem amoris, mercedem dileccionis quam erga matrem eius tibi commendatam semper habuisti. Benedictus tu a Christo, et benedictus a matre ipsius, quam puro corde dilexisti. Benedicti sint <omnes> ab ea qui diligunt eam. Et super omnia benedictus sit filius eius dominus noster, qui cum patre et spiritu sancto vivit et regnat in secula seculorum. Amen.

45. nunciate dilecto quia amore langueo: cf Ct 5:8.

say, "I have sought him and not found him. I have called: and he has not answered me," etc. [Ct 5:2]. Sitting at the grave near him, she whose soul the sword had pierced extended her hands. And, wearied, she repeatedly gave out troubled sobs. John came mourning, and raised up the one who mourned. For she was tortured with sobbing, worn out by pain, pained by weeping and was not able to stand on her feet. Yet, as she was able, she went toward Jerusalem helped by holy women, all of them weeping. Those who saw her weeping inconsolably had compassion for her in marvelous sympathy. Thus is she led to the house of John, for he loved her beyond his own mother with all his heart, caring for her faithfully and devotedly. Finally, when her son arose, she was unable to go to the tomb, enfeebled by great weakness in her limbs. Then could the Virgin say to the others who were running who had seen the living son: "Daughters of Jerusalem, tell my beloved that I am sick for love" [Ct 5:8]

O happy and blessed John: the lord has committed to you a treasure of great privilege. The lord will repay to you a reward for love, a reward for the affection which you always had toward his mother who was commended to you. You are blessed by Christ, and blessed by his mother whom you loved with a pure heart. May all who love her be blessed by her. And above all, blessed be her son, our lord, who with the father and the holy spirit, lives and reigns for ever and ever. Amen.

Appendix 2: Preliminary Catalogue of Medieval Latin Passion Narratives

The following catalogue includes prose narratives of the Passion mainly from the Latin devotional tradition, 1100–1500. It is preliminary and provisional, designed as a bibliographical introduction or the basis for further research, and should not be considered complete. This caution applies with special force to the section on the fifteenth century. All works of this type referred to in the main text of the book are given here, as well as some others. Coverage extends to meditations and treatises on the Passion. Not included are sermons, homilies, and biblical commentaries; nor such major repositories of ideas on the Passion as the *Glossa ordinaria*, the *Historia scholastica* of Peter Comestor (d. 1179), or the *Legenda aurea* of Jacobus de Voragine (d. 1298); nor visionary literature on the Passion, such as the *Revelations* of Bridget of Sweden (d. 1373).

Entries are divided into centuries and organized chronologically as much as it is possible to do so. Works are listed by author (if known), otherwise by the most common title or pseudonymous author. Each entry gives date, provenance, and the incipit. This is followed by comment on the manuscripts (if the work exists in a single manuscript, this is named). If there is an edition, this is given; editions given by short title are cited in full in the Bibliography to this book. Notes on the contents and other matters conclude each entry. Works marked with an asterisk are not discussed in the main text.

BEFORE 1100

1. The Book of Nunnaminster. Southern England. 8/9 C.
inc: Tu es Christus filius dei.
MS: London, British Library, Harley 2965 (8/9 C).
Ed. Birch (1889).
Extracts from the Passion gospels, followed by prayers, several on events of the Passion.

2. *Regularis concordia*. Southern England; ? Winchester. 10C.
inc: Gloriosus etenim Eadgar.
MSS: London, British Library, Cotton Faustina B.iii (10C); London, British Library, Cotton Tiberius A.iii (11C).
Ed. Symons et al. (1984).
Three Good Friday prayers to Christ recited before the cross.

3. *Aelfwine Prayerbook. Southern England. 11C.
inc: Ælce sunnandæg bebeod (D.xxvi)
MS: London, British Library, Cotton Titus D.xxvi–xxvii (11C).
Ed. Günzel (1993).
Passion according to John and a series of prayers to the cross.

4. pseudo-Augustine [John of Fécamp (d. 1078)?], *Meditationes*. France, Normandy? 11C.
inc: Domine deus meus da cordi meo.
MSS: numerous; the oldest (11/12C) are from northern France.
Ed. PL 40:901–9; PL 158:877–85, 858–65, 888 (prayers 10, 2, 14); Bestul (1987).
The meditation on the Son deals with the Passion.

5. Anselm of Canterbury (d. 1109), *Orationes sive meditationes*. France, Normandy. ca. 1042–79.
inc: Orationes sive meditationes quae subscriptae sunt.
MSS: numerous; the oldest (11/12C) are from Normandy and southern England.
Ed. Schmitt (1938–61).
The Prayer to Christ (*Or.* 2) emphasizes the Passion.

THE TWELFTH CENTURY

6. *Drogo of Laon (d. 1138)?, *Meditatio in passionem et resurrectionem domini*. Northern France. Before 1138?
inc: Noli timere filia Sion.
MSS: numerous, the oldest from 12C.
Ed. PL 166:1515–46; PL 184:741–68; PL 189:1733–60.
Frequently attributed to Bernard; also to Arnold of Bonneval. The sections on the Passion appear to be late additions.

7. *Arnold of Bonneval (d. ca. 1156), *De cardinalibus operibus Christi*. Northern France. Before 1156.
inc: Solent matres infantulis.
MSS: ? numerous.
Ed. PL 189:1609–78.
Chapter 9 is on the Passion.

8. *Arnold of Bonneval (d. ca. 1156), *De septem verbis domini in cruce*. Northern France. Before 1156.
inc: Ultima Christi verba.

MSS: numerous.

Ed. PL 189:1677–1726.

Closely follows the gospel account; also known as *De sex verbis* . . . .

9. Aelred of Rievaulx (d. 1167), *De institutis inclusarum*. England, Yorkshire. ca.
1160–62.

inc: Iam pluribus annis exigis.

MSS: Numerous.

Ed. Hoste and Talbot (1971).

The work ends with a meditation on Christ's life, including the Passion.

10. Ekbert of Schönau (d. 1184), *Stimulus amoris*. Germany, Rhineland. Before 1184.

inc: Iesum Nazarenum a Iudaeis innocenter.

MSS: numerous; oldest English MS is Lambeth Palace Library 437 (14C).

Ed. PL 158:748–61; PL 184:953–66; Roth (1884).

A meditative life of Christ beginning with the incarnation and ending with the
resurrection. Attributions: Bernard, Anselm, Ambrose, Bonaventure. Titles:
*Stimulus amoris, Stimulus dilectionis, Stimulus de caritate, Sermo de passione,
Meditaciones de passione Christi.*

11. * pseudo-Bernard, *De passione domini*. Western England. late 12C.

inc: Si considero vultum pendentis in cruce.

MS: Hereford, Cathedral Library O.9.v (late 12C), fol. 102.

Ed. none.

Attributed to Bernard in the MS. Fragment of one leaf only.

The Thirteenth Century

12. Ogier of Locedio (d. 1214), *Planctus beatae Mariae*. Northern Italy. Before 1205.

inc: Quis dabit capiti meo aquam.

MSS: especially numerous; most 14 and 15C.

Ed. PL 182:1133–42 (imperfect at beginning); Mushacke (1890); Marx (1994).

The most popular Marian lament has many details on the Passion. Usually attributed to Bernard, less often to Augustine or Anselm; known by many titles.

13. Edmund of Abingdon (d. 1240), *Speculum religiosorum* and *Speculum ecclesie*.
Southern England. Before 1240.

inc: In nomine domini nostri Iesu Christi.

MSS: At least 17.

Ed. Forshaw (1973).

Chapters on contemplating God in his humanity refer to the Passion of Christ.

14. Stephen of Sawley (d. 1252), *De informatione mentis circa Psalmodiam diei et noctis*. England, Yorkshire. Before 1252.

inc: Ad reprimendam vagationem cordis

MS: Berlin, Staatsbibliothek, Theol. lat. qu. 297 (13/14C).

Ed. Mikkers (1972).
Includes a meditation on the life and Passion of Christ.

15. *Bonaventure (d. 1274), *De perfectione vitae ad sorores*. Northern France. ca. 1266–68?
inc: Beatus homo quem tu erudieris.
MSS: numerous.
Ed. Peltier (1874–71); Quaracchi, 1882–1902.
Chapter 6 is on remembering the Passion of Christ.

16. Bonaventure (d. 1274), *Lignum vitae*. Northern France. ca. 1266–68?
inc: Christo confixus sum cruci.
MSS: numerous.
Ed. Peltier (1874–71); Quaracchi, 1882–1902.
Meditation on the life, passion, and resurrection of Christ.

17. *Bonaventure (d. 1274), *Officium de passione domini*. Northern France. ca. 1266–68?
inc: Domine labia mea aperies.
MSS: numerous.
Ed. Peltier (1874–71); Quaracchi, 1882–1902.
Liturgical office probably used in private devotion.

18. Bonaventure (d. 1274), *Vitis mystica*. Northern France. ca. 1266–68?
inc: Ego sum vitis vera.
MSS: numerous.
Ed. Peltier (1874–71); Quaracchi, 1882–1902.
Treatise on the Passion organized by the allegory of the vine.

19. pseudo-Anselm, *Dialogus beatae Mariae et Anselmi de Passione domini*. Germany, Rhineland? 13/14C?
inc: Dic mihi carissima domina.
MSS: at least 10; oldest appears to be Oxford, Bodleian Library, Laud Misc. 190, 13/14C, from Mainz, Charterhouse.
Ed. PL 159:271–90.
Based on the Marian lament of Ogier of Locedio, but much more limited in circulation.

20. James of Milan, *Stimulus amoris*. Italy. 13/14C.
Inc: Ad te domine levavi (prologue); Currite gentes undique (Passion section)
MSS: especially numerous; oldest are 14C.
Ed. Peltier, *Opera omnia Bonaventurae*, vol. 12 (1868); Quaracchi, 1949.
Expanded version of 14C includes meditations on the Passion, which sometimes circulated separately; often attributed to Bonaventure.

21. John de Caulibus?, *Meditationes vitae Christi*. Italy? 13/14C.
inc: Inter alia virtutum et laudum (prologue); Adveniente iam et imminente (Passion section).

MSS: especially numerous.

Ed. Peltier, *Bonaventurae Opera omnia*, vol. 12 (1868).

Usually attributed to Bonaventure, the chapters on the Passion often circulated independently as the *Meditationes de passione Christi*.

THE FOURTEENTH CENTURY

22. * pseudo-Bernard, *Meditatio de compassione Christi*. England? 14C.

inc: Caput meum doleo. Caput meum Christi est.

MS: London, British Library, Cotton Vespasian E.i (14C), fols. 202r-204r.

Ed. none.

Attributed in the MS to Bernard; affective and relatively brief.

23. * *Lamentatio in passionem domini*. Germany? 14C?

inc: O quam vehementi amplexu amplexastis me.

MSS: London, British Library, Add. 18318 (14C; Altenberg), fols. 65v-66v; British Library, Burley 359 (early 15C), pp. 111–18.

Ed. none.

Attributed to Bernard in Add. MS and called a prayer; relatively brief.

24. Ubertino da Casale (d. ca. 1329–41), *Arbor vitae crucifixae Jesu*. Italy. ca. 1305.

inc: Universis Christi Iesu fidelibus

MSS: numerous.

Ed. Davis (1961).

Meditative life of Christ; book 4 is on the Passion, Resurrection, and Ascension.

25. pseudo-Bede, *Meditatio de passione Christi per septem diei horas*. German? early 14C?

inc: Septies in die laudem dixi.

MSS: numerous, none older than 14C.

Ed. PL 94:561–68.

Detailed treatment of the Passion. Sometimes dated as early as 12C. Often attributed to Bernard, Bonaventure, or Augustine and known by various titles.

26. * *Meditationes de passione Christi*. England? early 14C?

inc: Post regulas fidei evangelico dogmate.

MS: Oxford, St. John's College 206 (early 14C), fols. 177r-197r.

Ed. none.

MS also includes "narratio de muliere, cujus filius Jhesu passioni interfuit."

27. Heinrich Suso (d. 1366), *Horologium sapientiae*. Germany, Rhineland. ca. 1334.

inc: Sentite de domino in bonitate.

MSS: Especially numerous

Ed. Künzle (1977).

Among the most popular devotional works of the middle ages; begins with meditation on the Passion; translated and expanded by Suso from his German original.

28. Simone Fidati da Cascia (d. 1348), *De gestis domini salvatoris*. Italy. ca. 1338–47.
inc: Multi multa locuti sunt.
MSS: limited in number.
Ed. Regensburg, 1733–34.
Lengthy harmony of the gospels; book 13 is on the Passion.

29. Ludolphus of Saxony (d. 1377), *Vita Christi*. Germany, Rhineland. ca. 1348–77.
inc: Fundamentum aliud nemo potest ponere
MSS: numerous.
Ed. Rigollot (1870).
Compendious life of Christ, with extensive treatment of the Passion.

30. Whiterig, John (d. 1371; "the Monk of Farne"), *Meditationes*. England, Durham. mid 14C.
inc: Loquar ad dominum meum.
MS: Durham, Cathedral Library, B. IV. 34 (14C).
Ed. Farmer (1957).
Includes a lengthy *Meditatio ad crucifixum*.

31. Jordan of Quedlinburg (d. 1380), *Meditationes de vita et passione Christi*. Germany, Saxony. Before 1380.
inc: Ad laudem omnipotentis dei.
MSS: limited in number; many early printed editions.
Ed. Lübeck, 1492 (Hain 9446).
Includes prayers on the 65 articles of the Passion.

32. Gerard Zerbolt of Zutphen (d. 1398), *De spiritualibus ascensionibus*. Netherlands, before 1398.
inc: Beatus vir cuius est auxilium.
MSS: extremely numerous.
Ed. Mahieu (1941).
Has section on meditating on the Passion; popular in the *Devotio moderna* movement.

33. * *Epistola de vita et passione domini nostri*. Netherlands, late 14C?
inc: Qui perseveraverit usque in finem.
MSS: at least 10.
Ed. Hedlund (1975).
Spiritual exercises on the Passion especially popular in the *Devotio moderna* movement.

34. * *Liber meditationum de vita domini et salvatoris nostri Iesu Christi et venerabilis matris eius virginis Mariae*. England. late 14C.
Inc: O domine sancte pater omnipotens.
MS: London, British Library, Royal 8 C.xv (late 14C), fols. 164v–191r (sections on the Passion).
Ed. none.
Full treatment of the Passion.

35. *pseudo-Bridget, *The Fifteen Oes*. Unknown. 14/15C.
inc: O domine Jesu Christe eterna dulcedo.
MSS: especially numerous, most 15C.
Ed. Wordsworth (1920).
Usually attributed to Bridget of Sweden (d. 1373); extremely popular prayers on
    the Passion.

The Fifteenth Century

36. *Meditationes de passione Christi*. England. 15C.
inc: Inspice et fac secundum exemplar.
MS: Cambridge, Pembroke College 199 (15C), fols. 1r-36v.
Ed. none.
The 65 articles of the Passion each followed by a prayer.

37. Hus, Jan (d. 1415), *Passio domini Christi*. Bohemia. ca. 1415.
inc: Cum consumasset Iesus hos sermones.
MSS: at least 23; little evidence of circulation beyond Bohemia.
Ed. Vidmanová-Schmidtová (1973).
An exposition or concordance of the Passion gospels incorporating many common-
    places from the devotional tradition.

38. Gerson, Jean (d. 1429), *Expositio in dominicam passionem*. Northern France. Be-
    fore 1429.
inc: Ad deum siquidem vadit.
MSS: numerous?
Ed. *Opera omnia*, vol. 3 (Antwerp, 1706).
Details of the Passion drawn from the devotional tradition; originally written in
    French.

39. Thomas à Kempis (d. 1471), *Orationes de passione domini*. Netherlands. Before
    1471.
MSS: numerous; many early printed editions.
inc: Respice clementissime pater.
Ed. Pohl, vol. 3 (1903).

40. Thomas à Kempis (d. 1471), *De passione Christi*. Netherlands. Before 1471.
MSS: numerous; many early printed editions.
inc: Benedico et gratias ago tibi.
Ed. Pohl, vol. 5 (1902).
Meditations on the Passion ("tractatus prioris pars altera") are preceded by medi-
    tations on the life of Christ.

41. *Brugman, Johannes (d. 1473), *Devotus tractatus valde incitativus ad exercitia
    passionis domini*. ca. 1450–71. Netherlands.
inc: Quoniam obliti sunt verba legis.
MS: Einsiedeln, Bibliotheca monasterii, 220 (15C).
Ed. van den Hombergh (1967).
Latin translation of a Netherlandish Passion treatise.

Notes

1. See R. W. Southern, *The Life of St. Anselm by Eadmer* (London: Nelson, 1962), pp. xxv–xxxiv; *The Prayers and Meditations of St. Anselm*, trans. Benedicta Ward (Harmondsworth: Penguin, 1973), p. 20.

2. *Political, Religious, and Love Poems*, ed. F. J. Furnivall, EETS OS 15 (1866; re-edited London: K. Paul, 1903), pp. 180–88.

3. See Rosemary Woolf, *The English Religious Lyric in the Middle Ages* (Oxford: Clarendon Press, 1968), pp. 187–91; Stephen Manning, *Wisdom and Number: Toward a Critical Appraisal of the Middle English Religious Lyric* (Lincoln: University of Nebraska Press, 1962), pp. 59–62; James I. Wimsatt, "The Canticle of Canticles, Two Latin Poems, and 'In a valey of this restles mynde'," *Modern Philology* 75 (1978): 327–45; Thomas D. Hill, "Androgyny and Conversion in the Middle English Lyric 'In the Vaile of Restles Mynd'," *ELH* 53 (1986): 459–70; Mary-Ann Stouck, "'In a valey of this restles mynde': Contexts and Meaning," *Modern Philology* 85 (1987): 1–11. Two studies dealing with the devotional aspects and Passion motifs of other important Middle English lyrics are Thomas C. Moser, Jr., "'And I mon Waxe Wod': The Middle English 'Foweles in the Frith'," *PMLA* 102 (1987): 326–37; Sarah Stanbury, "The Virgin's Gaze: Spectacle and Transgression in Middle English Lyrics of the Passion," *PMLA* 106 (1991): 1083–93.

4. For a general discussion of "background" in terms of literary theory and practice, see Herbert Lindenberger, "Toward a New History in Literary Study," *Profession 84: Selected Articles from the Bulletins of the Association of Departments of English and the Association of Departments of Foreign Languages* (New York: Modern Language Association of America, 1984), pp. 17–18.

5. See Gerald Graff, *Professing Literature: An Institutional History* (Chicago: University of Chicago Press, 1987), pp. 259–62; Lee Patterson, *Negotiating the Past: The Historical Understanding of Medieval Literature* (Madison: University of Wisconsin Press, 1987), pp. 41–74.

6. For the Turin edition (M. E. Maretti, 1929), see the *National Union Catalogue* 26:1161; for the 1610 and later editions of Sommalius, as well as the early printed translations of Augustine's *Meditationes* into vernacular languages, see the *British Museum Catalogue of Printed Books* 8:550ff.

7. Giles Constable, "Twelfth-Century Spirituality and the Late Middle Ages," in *Medieval and Renaissance Studies*, ed. O. B. Hardison (Chapel Hill: University of North Carolina Press, 1971), pp. 27–60; and "The Popularity of Twelfth-Century Spiritual Writers in the Late Middle Ages," in *Renaissance Studies in Honor of Hans Baron*, ed. Anthony Molho and John A. Tedeschi (DeKalb: Northern Illinois University Press, 1971), pp. 3–28.

8. Roger Chartier, *The Cultural Uses of Print in Early Modern France*, trans. Lydia G. Cochrane (Princeton, N. J.: Princeton University Press, 1987), pp. 149–50; and see the valuable essay by Paul Saenger, "Books of Hours and the Reading Habits of the Later Middle Ages," in *The Culture of Print: Power and the Uses of Print in Early Modern Europe*, ed. Roger Chartier (Princeton, N. J.: Princeton University Press, 1989), pp. 141–73.

9. See *Gesamtkatalog der Wiegendrucke*, vol. 2 (Leipzig: Hiersemann, 1926), nos. 2032, 2033, 2044 (Anselm); nos. 3906, 4055–60 (pseudo-Bernard). For the early editions of the lament of the pseudo-Bernard, see Leopold Janauschek, *Bibliographia Bernardina*, Xenia Bernardina, pars 4 (Vienna: Alfred Hölder, 1891), pp. 3–64; there appear to have been 15 separate editions of the work before 1500.

10. For the editions of Stanhope, I have relied on the *Eighteenth-Century Short Title Catalogue*, the *National Union Catalogue*, and the *British Museum Catalogue of Printed Books*, with their various supplements.

11. The best theoretical tools for such an undertaking are provided by Hans Robert Jauss, *Toward an Aesthetic of Reception*, trans. Timothy Bahti (Minneapolis: University of Minnesota Press, 1982), esp. pp. 3–45.

12. For the medieval manuscript tradition, see M. Oberleitner et al., *Die handschriftliche Überlieferung der Werke des Heiligen Augustinus*, Sitzungsberichte der Österreichische Akademie der Wissenschaften, philosophisch-historische Klasse 263, 267, 276, 281, 289, 292 (Vienna: Böhlau, 1969–74); for early library catalogues, see Gustav Becker, *Catalogi bibliothecarum antiqui* (Bonn: Cohen, 1885); and the series *Corpus of British Medieval Library Catalogues*, 4 vols. to date (London: British Library, 1990–).

13. *Religious Lyrics of the XIVth Century*, ed. Carleton Brown (Oxford: Clarendon Press, 1924), p. 241 (on no. 1).

14. The popularity of these works is discussed in chapter 2 (see notes 104, 105, 127).

15. On the incompleteness of historical knowledge, a conviction held by many modern historiographers and theoreticians, see Jauss's critique of the "illusion of completed process" in *Toward an Aesthetic of Reception*, pp. 53–56; and the remarks of Lloyd S. Kramer, "Literature, Criticism, and Historical Imagination: The Literary Challenge of Hayden White and Dominick LaCapra," in *The New Cultural History*, ed. Lynn Hunt (Berkeley: University of California Press, 1989), pp. 118–20.

16. For Aelred, Bonaventure, and Anselm, see chapter 2.

17. André Vauchez, *Les laïcs au moyen âge: pratiques et expériences religieuses* (Paris: Cerf, 1987), p. 130.

18. Franz H. Bäuml, "Varieties and Consequences of Medieval Literacy and Illiteracy," *Speculum* 55 (1980): 239. Also see Jack Goody and Ian Watt, "The Consequences of Literacy," *Comparative Studies in Society and History* 5 (1962–63): 304–45; Erich Auerbach, *Literary Language and Its Public in Late Latin Antiquity and in the Middle Ages*, trans. Ralph Manheim (New York: Pantheon, 1965); for the sixteenth century, Natalie Zemon Davis, "Printing and the People," in her *Society and Culture in Early Modern France* (Stanford, Calif.: Stanford University Press, 1975), pp. 189–226, makes a similar point about partial literacy among popular audiences in the age of print, esp. pp. 192–95.

19. Bäuml, "Varieties and Consequences," p. 254.

20. See *S. Anselmi Cantuariensis archiepiscopi Opera omnia*, ed. F. S. Schmitt, 6 vols. (1938–61; rpt. Stuttgart: Fromann, 1968), 3:3; for the scanty information about what was read by monks in community, see the lists published by Ph. Schmitz, "Les Lectures de table à l'abbaye de Saint-Denis vers la fin du Moyen-Age," *Revue Bénédictine* 42 (1930): 163–67, and Schmitz, "Les Lectures du soir à l'abbaye de Saint-Denis au XIIᵉ siècle," *Revue Bénédictine* 44 (1932): 147–49. Bella Millett has suggested that the saints' lives of the Katherine Group may have written with more than a single kind of readership in mind: they may have been read privately by recluses as well as publicly to a general audience; see "The Audiences of the Saints' Lives of the Katherine Group," *Reading Medieval Studies* 16 (1990): 127–56. See also the general discussion of *lectio divina* in Jean Leclercq, *The Love of Learning and the Desire for God: A Study of Monastic Culture*, trans. Catharine Misrahi, 3rd ed. (1957; rpt. New York: Fordham University Press, 1982), pp. 15–17, 72–73.

21. See Anne Middleton, "The Audience and Public of Piers Plowman," in *Middle English Alliterative Poetry and Its Literary Background: Seven Essays*, ed. David Lawton (Woodbridge, Suffolk: D. S. Brewer, 1982), pp. 102–23; Susan Groag Bell, "Medieval Women Book Owners: Arbiters of Lay Piety and Ambassadors of Culture," in *Women and Power in the Middle Ages*, ed. Mary Erler and Maryanne Kowaleski (Athens: University of Georgia Press, 1988), pp. 149–87; Margaret Deanesly, "Vernacular Books in England in the Fourteenth and Fifteenth Centuries," *Modern Language Review* 15 (1920): 349–58; Vincent Gillespie, "Vernacular Books of Religion," in *Book Production and Publishing in Britain 1375–1475*, ed. Jeremy Griffiths and Derek Pearsall (Cambridge: Cambridge University Press, 1989), pp. 317–44; see also the studies of Chartier and Saenger cited above in n. 8.

22. This point is made emphatically by Elizabeth Robertson, *Early English Devotional Prose and the Female Audience* (Knoxville: University of Tennessee Press, 1990), esp. pp. 1–12, 181–98; Robertson's book has full analyses of the Katherine Group and the *Ancrene Riwle*. The other works mentioned in the paragraph are discussed taken up in chapter 2 of this study.

23. The classic study advancing this model is E. R. Curtius, *European Literature and the Latin Middle Ages*, trans. Willard R. Trask (New York: Pantheon, 1953); for a critique of the privileged position of Latin letters in Anglo-Saxon studies, see Allen J. Frantzen, *Desire for Origins: New Language, Old English, and Teaching the Tradition* (New Brunswick, N. J.: Rutgers University Press, 1990), pp. 79–95.

24. Aron Gurevich, *Medieval Popular Culture: Problems of Belief and Perception*, trans. János M. Bak and Paul A. Hollingsworth (Cambridge: Cambridge University Press, 1988), pp. 1–3, 19–21.

25. See Michel Foucault, *The Archeology of Knowledge and the Discourse on Language*, trans. A. M. Sheridan Smith (New York: Pantheon, 1972), pp. 3–17; 135–40.

26. Chartier, *The Cultural Uses of Print in Early Modern France*, p. 3.

27. Roger Chartier, "Texts, Printing, Readings," in *The New Cultural History*, ed. Hunt, p. 169.

28. On the complex, multiple responses of different social groups to religious images of women in texts and in the visual arts (many of them devotional

images) in late-medieval Italy, see Margaret Miles, *Image as Insight: Visual Understanding in Western Christianity and Secular Culture* (Boston: Beacon Press, 1985), pp. 82–93.

29. Chartier, "Texts, Printing, Readings," p. 174; for intelligent discussion of the relation of popular to elite culture, see also Peter Dinzelbacher, "Volkskultur und Hochkultur im Spätmittelalter," in *Volkskultur des europäischen Spätmittelalters*, ed. Peter Dinzelbacher and Hans-Dieter Mück (Stuttgart: Kroner, 1987), pp. 1–14.

30. Some of the visions of Elizabeth of Schönau were uttered in German and translated into Latin by her brother Ekbert; see Anne L. Clark, *Elisabeth of Schönau: A Twelfth-Century Visionary* (Philadelphia: University of Pennsylvania Press, 1992), p. 52; for the Latin version of the *Ancrene Riwle*, see *The Latin Text of the Ancrene Riwle*, ed. Charlotte D'Evelyn, EETS 216 (London: Oxford University Press, 1944).

31. These works are discussed in chapter 2.

32. See Edmund of Abingdon, *Speculum Religiosorum and Speculum Ecclesie*, ed. Helen P. Forshaw, Auctores Britannici Medii Aevi 3 (London: Oxford University Press, 1973), pp. 1–17.

33. Tim Machan, paper given at Illinois Medieval Association, February 20, 1993. For enlightening commentary on the relation between Latin and the vernacular in late-medieval England, see his "Editing, Orality, and Late Middle English Texts," in *Vox Intertexta: Orality and Textuality in the Middle Ages*, ed. A. N. Doane and Carol Braun Pasternack (Madison: University of Wisconsin Press, 1991), pp. 229–45, and "Language Contact in *Piers Plowman*," *Speculum* 69 (1994): 359–85. The vernacularity of *The Cloud of Unknowing* is a particularly interesting case. Though written in English, it is by no means addressed to a popular audience, but, as the Prologue makes clear, is explicitly directed to a restricted and elite readership. The choice of English may have been made to differentiate the work from the popular Latin devotional tradition; works in this tradition did the most to foster the kind of piety the *Cloud* author finds dubious and offensive, namely excessive reliance on mental images, and a kind of crude literalism (see *The Cloud of Unknowing*, trans. Clifton Wolters [Harmondsworth: Penguin, 1961], pp. 57–58). The Latin translations of the *Cloud* may also have been intended to capture a wider English audience, not just a pan-European public. The *Cloud*'s translation into Latin may have been intended to render it in a familiar format aimed at a conservative audience more comfortable with the use of Latin for devotional texts than with the newfangled vernacular: one of the fifteenth-century Latin translations was made by a Carthusian, Richard Methley. See *The Latin Versions of The Cloud of Unknowing*, ed. John Clark, Analecta Cartusiana 119 (Salzburg: Institut für Anglistik und Amerikanistik, 1989), pp. 1–5.

34. For these works and others mentioned in this paragraph, see chapter 2.

35. For an edition with commentary, see André Wilmart, *Auteurs spirituels et textes dévots du Moyen Age latin* (1932; rpt. Paris: Etudes Augustiniennes, 1971), pp. 521–77.

36. For the different versions of Anselm's prayer, see André Wilmart, "Les propres corrections de S. Anselme dans sa grande prière à la Vierge Marie," *Recherches de Théologie Ancienne et Médiévale* 2 (1930): 189–204.

37. On the *Stimulus* of James of Milan, see Walter Hilton, *The Goad of Love:*

An Unpublished Translation of the Stimulus Amoris formerly attributed to St. Bonaventura, ed. Clare Kirchberger (London: Faber, 1952), pp. 15–20; on the composite nature of the *Meditationes vitae Christi*, see the textual studies of Columban Fischer, "Die 'Meditationes vitae Christi': Ihre handschriftliche Überlieferung und die Verfasserfrage," *Archivum Franciscanum Historicum* 25 (1932): 3–35, 175–209, 305–48, 449–83; Sandro Sticca, *The Planctus Mariae in the Dramatic Tradition of the Middle Ages* (Athens: University of Georgia Press, 1988), p. 196; and Sarah McNamer, "Further Evidence for the Date of the Pseudo-Bonaventuran *Meditationes vitae Christi*," *Franciscan Studies* 50 (1990): 235–61.

38. See *A Book of Showings to the Anchoress Julian of Norwich*, ed. Edmund Colledge and James Walsh, 2 vols., Studies and Texts 35 (Toronto: Pontifical Institute of Mediaeval Studies, 1978).

39. See Giles Constable, "Forgery and Plagiarism in the Middle Ages," *Archiv für Diplomatik, Schriftgeschichte, Siegel- und Wappenkunde* 29 (1983): 1–41; and Alastair J. Minnis, *Medieval Theory of Authorship: Scholastic Literary Attitudes in the Later Middle Ages* (London: Scolar, 1984; rpt. Philadelphia: University of Pennsylvania Press, 1987), pp. 10–12.

40. André Wilmart, "Le recueil des prières de S. Anselme," in *Méditations et prières de Saint Anselme*, trans. A. Castel (Paris: Lethielleux, 1923), pp. i–lxii; Wilmart, "La tradition des prières de Saint Anselme," *Revue Bénédictine* 36 (1924): 52–71.

41. See *Die Visionen der hl. Elisabeth und die Schriften der Aebte Ekbert und Emecho von Schönau*, ed. F. W. E. Roth (Brünn: Verlag der Studien aus dem Benedictiner- und Cistercienser-Orden, 1884), pp. 220–29.

42. *Anselmi Opera omnia*, ed. F. S. Schmitt, 3:1–91; for the contents of the early manuscripts, see Schmitt, 3:1.

43. See Patrick Brantlinger, *Crusoe's Footprints: Cultural Studies in Britain and America*, (New York: Routledge, 1990), pp. 3–21.

44. On Peter Lombard, see Beryl Smalley, *The Study of the Bible in the Middle Ages* (Notre Dame, Ind.: University of Notre Dame Press, 1964), p. 64; on Nicholas of Lyra, see Minnis, *Medieval Theory of Authorship*, pp. 148–49.

45. Quoted in Brantlinger, *Crusoe's Footprints*, p. 14; from Michel Foucault, *Language, Counter-Memory, Practice: Selected Essays and Interviews*, trans. Donald F. Bouchard and Sherry Simon (Ithaca, N.Y.: Cornell University Press, 1977), p. 106.

46. *Bonaventurae Opera omnia*, ed. A. C. Peltier, 15 vols. (Paris: Vives, 1864–71), 12:511; translation from *Meditations on the Life of Christ*, ed. and trans. Isa Ragusa and Rosalie B. Green (Princeton, N. J.: Princeton University Press, 1961), p. 5; a similar defense is found in the prooemium to the *Vita Christi* of Ludolphus of Saxony, ed. L. M. Rigollot, 4 vols. (Paris: Palme, 1870), 1:8–12. Such defenses provide a theoretical foundation for the countless late-medieval literary visions disclosing details of Christ's life not found in the Bible, among which the *Revelations* of Bridget of Sweden and the meditations on the Passion in the *Revelations of Divine Love* of Julian of Norwich are noteworthy examples.

47. See Gordon Leff, *The Dissolution of the Medieval Outlook: An Essay on Intellectual and Spiritual Change in the Fourteenth Century* (New York: Harper, 1976), pp. 135–36, 140–41; Anne Hudson, *The Premature Reformation: Wycliffite Texts and Lollard History* (Oxford: Clarendon, 1988), esp. pp. 228–77. Note also the

selections from Wycliffe and John Purvey on scriptural interpretation in *The Law of Love: English Spirituality in the Age of Wyclif*, trans. and ed. David Lyle Jeffrey (Grand Rapids, Mich.: Eerdmans, 1988), pp. 332–51; in the Prologue to the Wycliffite Bible, Purvey specifically takes issue with the approach advocated by Nicholas of Lyra, Jeffrey, pp. 345–46.

48. For the *Cloud of Unknowing*, see above, note 33; it was traditional to regard visual meditation on the events of Christ's life as a lower stage of contemplation; see Walter Hilton, *The Ladder of Perfection*, trans. Leo Sherley-Price (Harmondsworth: Penguin, 1957), pp. 5–6 (I.5); Jean Gerson, *Selections from A Deo exivit, Contra curiositatem studentium and De mystica theologica speculativa*, ed. and trans. Steven E. Ozment (Leiden: Brill, 1969), pp. 53–59. Gerson's criticism of the dangerous illusionism of the spirituality of Ruysbroeck is well known: see André Combes, *Essai sur la critique de Ruysbroeck par Gerson*, 2 vols., Etudes de théologie et d'histoire de la spiritualité 4 (Paris: J. Vrin, 1945).

49. The license of approval for Nicholas Love's English translation of the *Meditationes* ("for the edification of the faithful and the confutation of heretics and Lollards") issued by Thomas Arundel, Archbishop of Canterbury, in 1410 may be perhaps be seen as an attempt by the official church to control and limit the potential subversiveness of that text. See Elizabeth Salter, *Nicholas Love's "Myrrour of the Blessed Lyf of Jesu Christ"*, Analecta Cartusiana 10 (Salzburg: Institut für Englische Sprache und Literatur, 1974), pp. 29–30; text of the certificate, pp. 1–2.

50. Steven E. Ozment, *Mysticism and Dissent: Religious Ideology and Social Protest in the Sixteenth Century* (New Haven, Conn.: Yale University Press, 1973), pp. 1–13; quotation at p. 8.

51. See Paul Zumthor, *Speaking of the Middle Ages*, trans. Sarah White (Lincoln: University of Nebraska Press, 1986), pp. 14–17.

52. Jauss, *Toward an Aesthetic of Reception*, p. 54; for nineteenth-century organicism, see also pp. 6–9.

53. Foucault, *Archeology of Knowledge*, pp. 3–14.

54. Foucault, *Archeology of Knowledge*, pp. 8, 12, 21–30. In place of traditional history of ideas based on premises of unity, influence, and continuity, Foucault proposes "archeology": see esp. the definitions outlined at pp. 135–48.

55. Zumthor, *Speaking of the Middle Ages*, p. 72.

56. Jean-François Lyotard, *The Post-Modern Condition: A Report on Knowledge*, trans. Geoff Bennington and Brian Massumi (Minneapolis: University of Minnesota Press, 1984), p. 37; see also p. 60 on the new scientific paradigm which "is theorizing its own evolution as discontinuous, catastrophic, nonrectifiable, and paradoxical."

57. Louis Montrose, "Professing the Renaissance: The Poetics and Politics of Culture," in *The New Historicism*, ed. H. Aram Veeser (New York: Routledge, 1989), p. 17.

58. Mikhail M. Bakhtin, *The Dialogic Imagination*, trans. Caryl Emerson and Michael Holquist (Austin: University of Texas Press, 1981), pp. 299–300.

59. Raymond Williams, *Marxism and Literature* (Oxford: Oxford University Press, 1977), p. 19; Williams, *The Sociology of Culture* (New York: Schocken, 1982), p. 12.

60. Williams, *Marxism and Literature*, p. 87; on reciprocal action, p. 81.

61. Zumthor, *Speaking of the Middle Ages*, p. 58; in this study I use ideology in two senses as it is defined by Raymond Williams: the first is that ideology is "the formal and conscious beliefs of a class or other social group"; the second is that ideology is "the characteristic world view or general perspective of a class or other social group, which will include formal and conscious beliefs, but also less conscious, less formulated attitudes, habits and feelings, or even unconscious assumptions, bearings and commitments." See Williams, *Sociology of Culture*, p. 26; for further discussion of ideology, see Williams, *Marxism and Literature*, p. 55.

62. Williams, *Marxism and Literature*, p. 115.

63. Williams, *Sociology of Culture*, p. 187.

64. Graff, *Professing Literature*, p. 256

65. Quoted by Stanley Fish, "Commentary: The Young and the Restless," in Veeser, p. 306.

66. Dominick LaCapra, *History and Criticism* (Ithaca, N. Y.: Cornell University Press, 1985), p. 128; quoted in Lloyd S. Kramer, "Literature, Criticism, and Historical Imagination: The Literary Challenge of Hayden White and Dominick LaCapra," in *The New Cultural History*, p. 115.

67. Jonathan Culler, *Framing the Sign: Criticism and Its Institutions* (Norman: University of Oklahoma Press, 1988), p. xiv; see also pp. 147–48, and his critique of Foucault, pp. 62–68.

68. Quoted in Culler, *Framing the Sign*, p. 62.

69. Dominick LaCapra, *Rethinking Intellectual History: Texts, Contexts, Language* (Ithaca, N. Y.: Cornell University Press, 1983), p. 95; quoted in Lloyd S. Kramer, "Literature, Criticism, and Historical Imagination," p. 114.

70. See Hayden White, "New Historicism: A Comment," in Veeser, pp. 293–302; Fish, "Commentary: The Young and the Restless," in Veeser, pp. 303–16.

71. "Commentary," in Veeser, p. 304.

72. My analysis of Bakhtin owes much to Lloyd S. Kramer, "Literature, Criticism, and Historical Imagination," p. 114. Also pertinent is Foucault's definition of discursive formation, *Archeology of Knowledge*, p. 155: "A discursive formation is not, therefore, and ideal, continuous, smooth text that runs beneath the multiplicity of contradictions, and resolves them in the calm unity of coherent thought; nor is it the surface in which, in a thousand different aspects, a contradiction is reflected that is always in retreat, but everywhere dominant. It is rather a space of multiple dissensions; a set of different oppositions whose levels and roles must be described."

73. Georges Duby, *The Three Orders: Feudal Society Imagined*, trans. Arthur Goldhammer (Chicago: University of Chicago Press, 1980), p. 7.

74. On "the temptation of the universal," see Zumthor, *Speaking of the Middle Ages*, pp. 70–72.

75. Aers notes among the Lollards, for example, a "diminished concern for meditation on the Passion," and a rejection of the accretions made to the gospel narrative that are at the heart of many of the narratives I will examine; see "Christ's Humanity and *Piers Plowman*: Contexts and Political Implications," *Yearbook of Langland Studies* 8 (1994): 107–25, esp. 113–14.

76. Foucault, *Archeology of Knowledge*, pp. 149–151 (quotation at p. 149).

77. See the analysis of Catherine Gallagher, "Marxism and the New Historicism," in Veeser, pp. 43–44; the quoted phrase is Gallagher's, p. 43. Also see Paul Zumthor, *Speaking of the Middle Ages*, p. 83: "to grasp the places of rupture, the points of breakdown" as the historian's task. Foucault's "archeological description" is "much more willing than the history of ideas to speak of discontinuities, ruptures, gaps, entirely new forms of positivity, and of sudden redistributions," *Archeology of Knowledge*, p. 169.

78. Quoted in Aletta Biersack, "Local Knowledge, Local History: Geertz and Beyond," in *The New Cultural History*, ed. Hunt, p. 81.

79. Lloyd Kramer, "Literature, Criticism, and Historical Imagination," p. 118.

80. See the well-known and characteristic expression of this viewpoint by G. G. Coulton, *From St. Francis to Dante* (1906; rpt. Philadelphia: University of Pennsylvania Press, 1972), p. 303; cited and discussed by Denise Despres, *Ghostly Sights: Visual Meditation in Late-Medieval Literature* (Norman, Okla.: Pilgrim, 1989), p. 42.

81. See the discussion of the Annales paradigm in Lynn Hunt, "Introduction: History, Culture, and Text," in *The New Cultural History*, ed. Hunt, pp. 1–7.

82. See the seminal studies of Peter Brown, *The Body and Society: Men, Women and Sexual Renunciation in Early Christianity* (New York: Columbia University Press, 1988); Caroline Bynum, *Holy Feast and Holy Fast: The Religious Significance of Food to Medieval Women* (Berkeley: University of California Press, 1987) and *Fragmentation and Redemption: Essays on Gender and the Human Body in Medieval Religion* (New York: Zone Books, 1991). Some of the new approaches to the body are both defined and exemplified in an essay by Stephen F. Kruger, "The Bodies of Jews in the Late Middle Ages," in *The Idea of Medieval Literature: New Essays on Chaucer and Medieval Culture in Honor of Donald R. Howard*, ed. James M. Dean and Christian K. Zacher (Newark: University of Delaware Press, 1992), pp. 301–23; and see the remarkable essay by Victor I. Scherb, "Violence and the Social Body in the Croxton Play of the Sacrament," in *Violence in Drama*, ed. James Redmond (Cambridge: Cambridge University Press, 1991), pp. 69–78. Recent books emphasizing the importance of the body which I have consulted with profit are Karma Lochrie, *Margery Kempe and Translations of the Flesh* (Philadelphia: University of Pennsylvania Press, 1991) and Sarah Beckwith, *Christ's Body: Identity, Culture and Society in Late Medieval Writings* (London: Routledge, 1993). See also the collection of essays, *Feminist Approaches to the Body in Medieval Literature*, ed. Linda Lomperis and Sarah Stanbury (Philadelphia: University of Pennsylvania Press, 1993).

83. Douglas, *Natural Symbols* (1970; rpt. New York: Pantheon, 1982), pp. vi, 65.

84. Williams, *Sociology of Culture*, p. 207.

Chapter 2

1. See below, chapter 5, note 40. The Latin text of the Bible is quoted from the Vulgate version in *Biblia Sacra Juxta Vulgatam Clementinam* (Rome, 1947); for the English translation, I use the Rheims-Douai-Challoner version, with occasional modifications. Unless otherwise noted, other English translations appearing in the text are my own.

2. See the important discussion in F. P. Pickering, *Literature and Art in the Middle Ages* (London: Macmillan, 1970), pp. 223–307. For the use of the verse in this sense in Bonaventura, see *Vitis mystica*, 12.1; *Bonaventurae Opera omnia*, ed. PP. Collegii S. Bonaventurae, 11 vols. (Quarracchi: Collegium S. Bonaventurae, 1882–1902), 8:178; Bonaventure, *The Works of Bonaventure . . . I: Mystical Opuscula*, trans. José de Vinck (Paterson, N.J.: St. Anthony Guild Press, 1960), p. 182.

3. On this passage see J. A. W. Bennett, *Poetry of the Passion* (Oxford: Clarendon Press, 1982), pp. 75–84.

4. James H. Marrow, *Passion Iconography in Northern European Art of the Late Middle Ages and Early Renaissance: A Study of the Transformation of Sacred Metaphor into Descriptive Narrative*, Ars Neerlandica 1 (Kortrijk: Van Ghemmert, 1979), pp. 76–94.

5. See Bennett, *Poetry of the Passion*, pp. 11, 43–44.

6. On the popularity of the apocryphon, see Zbigniew Izydorczyk, *Manuscripts of the Evangelium Nicodemi: A Census*, Subsidia Mediaevalia 21 (Toronto: Pontifical Institute of Mediaeval Studies, 1993). Most of the Marian additions to the Gospel of Nicodemus are late medieval; see *The Middle English Prose Complaint of Our Lady and Gospel of Nicodemus*, ed. C. William Marx and Jeanne F. Drennan, Middle English Texts 19 (Heidelberg: Carl Winter, 1987), p. 33 n.38.

7. PL 114:345.

8. PL 114:169.

9. PL 114:346.

10. PL 114:174.

11. PL 114:240.

12. PL 114:240.

13. PL 114:343.

14. On the wide popularity of the *Historica scholastica* in Latin and the vernaculars, see Beryl Smalley, *The Study of the Bible in the Middle Ages* (Notre Dame, Ind.: University of Notre Dame Press, 1964), pp. 178–79. For a similar harmonized gospel account, see Zacharias the Chrysopolitan, *Unum ex quattuor*, PL 186:11–620; see André Wilmart, "Le grand poème bonaventurien sur les sept paroles du Christ en croix," *Revue Bénédictine* 47 (1935): 236. See also the unprinted harmony by Clement of Llanthony (d. 1190?), *Unum ex quattuor*. For the latter work, see Elizabeth Salter, *Nicholas Love's "Myrrour of the Blessed Lyf of Jesu Christ"*, Analecta Cartusiana 10 (Salzburg: Institut für Englische Sprache und Literatur, 1974), pp. 60–61. Clement's work was translated into Middle English in the fourteenth century: Salter, pp. 67–69.

15. PL 198:1628.

16. PL 198:1628.

17. PL 198:1628.

18. PL 198:1628.

19. PL 198:1628.

20. PL 198:1628.

21. Bennett, *Poetry of the Passion*, p. 45; pp. 45–47.

22. Hans Robert Jauss, *Toward an Aesthetic of Reception*, trans. Timothy Bahti (Minneapolis: University of Minnesota Press, 1982), pp. 139–48. It is the audience's experience of reading the works that forms the horizon of expectations, not something inherent in the works themselves.

23. See PL 198:1619.

24. See Jacobus de Voragine, *The Golden Legend: Readings on the Saints*, trans. William Granger Ryan, 2 vols. (Princeton, N. J.: Princeton University Press, 1993), 1:203–4. In the modern edition of the Latin text of the *Legenda* the reproach is merely summarized as "popule meus quid feci tibi etc." see *Legenda aurea*, ed. Th. Graesse, 3rd ed. (1890; rpt. Osnabrück: Zeller, 1969), p. 224.

25. *Legenda aurea*, 53; ed. Graesse, p. 224; Ryan, 1:204. See Bonaventure, *De perfectione vitae ad sorores*, 6.5: "Attende adhuc melius, quam acerba mors Christi fuerit. Quanto quid tenerius, tanto patitur gravius; nunquam autem fuit corpus ita tenerum ad sustinendum passiones, sicut corpus Salvatoris. Corpus enim mulieris tenerius est quam corpus viri; caro autem Christi tota virginea fuit, quia de Spiritu sancto concepta et de Virgine nata: igitur passio Christi fuit omnium passionum acerbior, quia omnium virginum tenerior" (*Opera omnia*, 8:121). ["You will see even more clearly how cruel was the death of Christ if you consider that whatever is more sensitive suffers more. In general, the body of a woman is more sensitive than that of a man; but never was there a body that felt pain as keenly as that of the Saviour, since his flesh was entirely virginal, conceived of the Holy Spirit and born of the Virgin. Hence the Passion of Christ was as much more painful as he himself was more tender even than any virgin." de Vinck, p. 242.]

26. *Legenda aurea*, 53; Graesse, p. 226; Ryan, 1:206.

27. The words of Isaiah appear to be an inversion of the description of Absalom's beauty in II Rg 14:25: "Porro sicut Absalom, vir non erat pulcher in omni Israel, et decorus nimis: a vestigio pedis usque ad verticem non erat in eo ulla macula" ["but in all Israel there was not a man so comely, and so exceedingly beautiful as Absalom: from the sole of the foot to the crown of the head there was no blemish in him"].

28. Graesse, p. 226; Ryan, 1:206.

29. Graesse, pp. 226–27; Ryan 1:206.

30. See the Carolingian works, *De psalmorum usu* (PL 101:465–508) and *Officia per ferias* (PL 101:509–612). On the early prayerbooks, see Edmund Bishop, *Liturgica Historica: Papers on the Liturgy and Religious Life of the Western Church* (Oxford: Clarendon Press, 1918), pp. 384–91; Henri Barré, *Prières anciennes de l'occident à la Mère du Sauveur: Des origines à saint Anselme* (Paris: Lethielleux, 1963); Pierre Salmon, "Livrets de prières de l'époque Carolingienne," *Revue Bénédictine* 86 (1976): 218–34; and *Revue Bénédictine* 90 (1980): 147–49; Thomas H. Bestul, "Continental Sources of Anglo-Saxon Devotional Writing," in *Sources of*

Anglo-Saxon Culture, ed. Paul E. Szarmach, Studies in Medieval Culture 20 (Kalamazoo, Mich.: Medieval Institute Publications, 1986), pp. 103–26.

31. Barbara Raw, *Anglo-Saxon Crucifixion Iconography and the Art of the Monastic Revival* (Cambridge: Cambridge University Press, 1990), p. 16.

32. Raw, *Anglo-Saxon Crucifixion Iconography*, pp. 24, 55–56; for rare early affectivity, see the Passion Commentary of Candidus (d. 845), PL 106:1480; discussed in Louis Bouyer, Jean Leclercq, and François Vandenbroucke, *The Spirituality of the Middle Ages*, trans. the Benedictines of Holme Eden Abbey, A History of Christian Spirituality 2 (London: Burns and Oates, 1968), p. 86. On affective language associated with the Passion in the early Middle Ages, see the valuable discussion in Erich Auerbach, *Literary Language and Its Public in Late Latin Antiquity and in the Middle Ages*, trans. Ralph Manheim, Bollingen Series 74 (New York: Pantheon, 1965), pp. 67–81.

33. An edition of the Book of Nunnaminster is *An Ancient Manuscript Belonging to St. Mary's Abbey, or Nunnaminster, Winchester*, ed. Walter de Gray Birch, Hampshire Record Society (London: Simpkin and Marshall, 1889); also of interest is the work in German and Latin referred to in the ninth-century St. Riquier library catalogue; see Gustav Becker, *Catalogi bibliothecarum antiqui* (Bonn: Cohen, 1885), p. 28 (items 206 and 207): "passio domini in Theodisco / et in Latino. qui sunt libri VI." The combination in *Nunnaminster* of the Passion gospels with a collection of prayers is not a common one. The closest parallel is found in the so-called Aelfwine Prayerbook (British Library MS Cotton Titus D.xxvi–xxvii), also from Anglo-Saxon England, in which the Passion according to John is followed by a full page illustration of the crucifixion and a series of prayers to the cross, but nowhere else in the early Middle Ages is there such a lengthy and systematic series of prayers whose subjects are the individual events of the Passion. See Raw, *Anglo-Saxon Crucifixion Iconography*, pp. 56, 217; *Ælfwine's Prayerbook*, ed. Beate Günzel, Henry Bradshaw Society 108 (London: Boydell, 1993).

34. See also the prayer made up of a series of petitions to Christ found in the tenth-century *Regularis concordia*, a prayer which was to be recited before the cross in the public services of Good Friday, but is also included in collections of private prayers, and hence was used devotionally as well as liturgically; *Regularis concordia*, ed. Thomas Symons, Sigrid Spath, Maria Wegener, Kassius Hallinger, Corpus Consuetudinum Monasticarum 7.3 (Siegburg: Schmitt, 1984), p. 117; the prayer is discussed in Raw, *Anglo-Saxon Crucifixion Iconography*, pp. 56–57.

35. See R. W. Southern, *The Making of the Middle Ages* (New Haven, Conn.: Yale University Press, 1953), pp. 232–40; and R. W. Southern, *Saint Anselm: A Portrait in a Landscape* (Cambridge: Cambridge University Press, 1990), pp. 99–106. See also Jean Leclercq, "Sur la dévotion à l'humanité du Christ," *Revue Bénédictine* 63 (1953): 128–30; Colin Morris, *The Discovery of the Individual, 1050–1200* (London: S.P.C.K., 1972), esp. pp. 139–57; Robert Hanning, *The Individual in Twelfth-Century Romance* (New Haven, Conn.: Yale University Press, 1977); John F. Benton, "Consciousness of Self and Perceptions of Individuality," in *Renaissance and Renewal in the Twelfth Century*, ed. Robert L. Benson and Giles Constable (Cambridge, Mass.: Harvard University Press, 1982), pp. 263–95; J. A. W. Bennett, *Poetry of the Passion*, pp. 32–61; and the judiciously skeptical chapter "Did the Twelfth

Century Discover the Individual?" in Caroline Bynum, *Jesus as Mother: Studies in the Spirituality of the High Middle Ages* (Berkeley: University of California Press, 1982), pp. 82–109 .

36. Anselm of Canterbury, *Anselmi Opera omnia*, ed. F. S. Schmitt, 6 vols. (1938–61; rpt. Stuttgart: Fromann, 1968), 3:6–9 (*Oratio* 2); translation in *The Prayers and Meditations of Saint Anselm*, trans. Benedicta Ward (Harmondsworth: Penguin, 1973), pp. 93–99.

37. Schmitt, 3:9.

38. Schmitt, 3:7.

39. Schmitt, 3:8.

40. See Louis L. Martz, *The Poetry of Meditation: A Study in English Religious Literature of the Seventeenth Century*, rev. ed. (New Haven, Conn.: Yale University Press, 1962), pp. 25–70; Pamela Gradon, *Form and Style in Early English Literature* (London: Methuen, 1971), pp. 298–331; Denise L. Despres, *Ghostly Sights: Visual Meditation in Late Medieval Literature* (Norman, Okla.: Pilgrim Books, 1989), pp. 19–54.

41. On the doctrine of *compassio*, see the valuable comments in Marrow, *Passion Iconography*, p. 252 n. 41, with references there given. Mary was an exemplar of *compassio*: "Devotion to the Virgin's compassion led to the creation of the paraliturgical *Officium de compassione beatae Mariae virginis* and to the institution of a full *Festum compassionis beatae Mariae virginis* at Cologne in 1423" (Marrow, p. 252). See Otto von Simson, "Compassio and Co-redemptio in Roger vander Weyden's Descent from the Cross," *Art Bulletin* 35 (1953): 9–16.

42. I quote from the edition of a twelfth-century text in *A Durham Book of Devotions*, ed. Thomas H. Bestul, Toronto Medieval Latin Texts 18 (Toronto: Pontifical Institute of Mediaeval Studies, 1987), p. 35; also in PL 40:906.

43. See *English Writings of Richard Rolle, Hermit of Hampole*, ed. Hope Emily Allen (1931; rpt. Oxford: Clarendon Press, 1963), pp. 42, 68; *Religious Lyrics of the XIVth Century*, ed. Carleton Brown (Oxford: Clarendon Press, 1924), p. 1. The Middle English versions are discussed in relation to the Latin text in Rita Copeland, "The Middle English 'Candet nudatum pectus' and Norms of Early Vernacular Translation Practice," *Leeds Studies in English*, n.s. 15 (1984): 57–81.

44. Cited from Bernard of Clairvaux, *On the Song of Songs II*, trans. Kilian Walsh, Cistercian Fathers Series 7 (Kalamazoo, Mich.: Cistercian Publications, 1983), p. 223; for Sermon 20, see *On the Song of Songs I*, trans. Kilian Walsh, Cistercian Fathers Series 4 (Kalamazoo, Mich.: Cistercian Publications, 1981), pp. 147–55. The standard edition of the Latin is *Sancti Bernardi Opera*, ed. J. Leclercq, C. H. Talbot, H. M. Rochais, 8 vols. (Rome: Editiones Cistercienses, 1957–1977), vols. 1 and 2.

45. PL 183:267.

46. PL 183:264; cf Is 53:2, Ps 21:7. See also Sermon 25; Walsh, *On the Song of Songs II*, pp. 56–57; see Ps 44:5 for beauty associated with righteousness.

47. See Bonaventure, *Lignum vitae*, 29 (de Vinck, p. 127; *Opera omnia*, 8:79); *Meditations on the Life of Christ*, 85, trans. Isa Ragusa, and Rosalie B. Green (Princeton, N.J. Princeton University Press, 1961), p. 355; Ubertino da Casale, *Arbor vitae crucifixae Jesu*, 1.9 (Venice, 1485; rpt. with Introduction and Bibliography by

Charles T. Davis, Turin: Bottega d'Erasmo 1961). In the vernacular, see the Middle English meditation on the Passion in *Yorkshire Writers: Richard Rolle of Hampole, An English Father of the Church and His Followers*, ed. C. Horstman, 2 vols. (London: Swan Sonnenschein, 1895–96), 1:112.

48. *De institutis inclusarum*, 29–33; Latin text in *Aelredi Rievallensis Opera omnia, I: Opera ascetica*, ed. A. Hoste and C. H. Talbot, Corpus Christianorum, Continuatio Medievalis 1 (Turnholt: Brepols, 1971), pp. 662–82 (cited below as *Opera ascetica*); English translation in Aelred of Rievaulx, *Treatises and the Pastoral Prayer*, trans. Theodore Berkeley, Mary Paul Macpherson, R. Penelope Lawson, Cistercian Fathers Series 2 (Kalamazoo, Mich.: Cistercian Publications, 1971), pp. 43–102 (cited below as Macpherson).

49. See, for example, the description of the agony in the garden; *De institutis inclusarum*, 31; *Opera ascetica*, p. 669; Macpherson, pp. 87–88.

50. *De institutis inclusarum*, 31; *Opera ascetica*, p. 671; Macpherson, pp 90–91; see Ct 5:1: "comedi favum cum melle meo; bibi vinum meum cum lacte meo"; Ct 2:14: "columba mea, in foraminbus petrae, in caverna maceriae"; Ps 77:16: "et eduxit aquam de petra, et deduxit tanquam flumina aquas"; Ct 4:3: "sicut vitta coccinea labia tua, et eloquium tuum dulce."

51. See Richard Rolle, *Meditation on the Passion*, in *English Writings*, p. 35; James of Milan, *Stimulus amoris* (see below, n. 151). On entering the wounds of Christ, see Douglas Gray, "The Five Wounds of Our Lord," *Notes and Queries* n.s. 10 (1963): 50–51, 82–89, 127–34, 163–68. Note also the observation of Caroline Bynum: "It was clearly women who created, from suggestions in twelfth-century male writing, the thirteenth-century devotion to the sacred heart and to the wounds of Jesus" (*Jesus as Mother*, p. 18).

52. *De institutis inclusarum*, 31; *Opera ascetica*, p. 672; Macpherson, p. 91.

53. *De institutis inclusarum*, 31, *Opera ascetica*, pp. 671–72; Macpherson, p. 91.

54. Bonaventure, *Lignum vitae*, 9 (de Vinck, p. 110 and note; *Opera omnia*, 8:73). In the Patrologia Latina edition of Anselm, the meditative parts of Aelred's treatise are *Meditations* 15, 16, 17 (PL 158:785–98); see André Wilmart, "Les méditations réunies sous le nom de saint Anselme," in *Auteurs spirituels et textes dévots du Moyen Age latin* (1932; rpt. Paris: Etudes Augustiniennes, 1971), pp. 196–97.

55. Aelred of Rievaulx, *De institutione inclusarum: Two English Versions*, ed. John Ayto and Alexandra Barratt, EETS OS 287 (London: Oxford University Press, 1984).

56. See Anne L. Clark, *Elisabeth of Schönau, A Twelfth-Century Visionary* (Philadelphia: University of Pennsylvania Press, 1992); the works of both Ekbert and Elizabeth are edited in *Die Visionen der hl. Elisabeth und die Schriften der Aebte Ekbert und Emecho von Schönau*, ed. F. W. E. Roth (Brünn: Verlag der Studien aus dem Benedictiner- und Cistercienser-Orden, 1884).

57. Manuscripts of the fourteenth and fifteenth centuries also assign the work to Ambrose, and even to Bonaventure, but attibutions to Anselm or Bernard remain the most common.

58. PL 158:755–56.

59. On the beauty of Christ's body, see Etienne Gilson, "Saint Bonaventure

et l'iconographie de la passion," *Revue d'Histoire Franciscaine* I (1924): 405–24; the idea that Christ's bodily suffering was the sharpest and bitterest of all suffering is a commonplace of many passion meditations, which Gilson finds definitively articulated in Bonaventure; see pp. 410–11.

60. PL 158:756.

61. PL 158:756; Is 53:4; Nm 12:12.

62. PL 158:759.

63. PL 158:758; on the *Arma Christi*, see Rudolf Berliner, "Arma Christi," *Münchner Jahrbuch der Bildenden Kunst* 6 (1955): 35–252; Rosemary Woolf, *The English Religious Lyric in the Middle Ages* (Oxford: Clarendon Press, 1968), pp. 208–10; Douglas Gray, *Themes and Images in the Medieval English Religious Lyric* (London: Routledge, 1972), pp. 51–52, 132–33; Rossell Hope Robbins, "The 'Arma Christi' Rolls," *Modern Language Review* 34 (1939): 415–21; C. Carter, "The *Arma Christi* in Scotland," *Proceedings of the Society of Antiquaries of Scotland* 90 (1956–57): 116–29; John C. Hirsh, "Prayer and Meditation in Late Medieval England: MS Bodley 789," *Medium Aevum* 48 (1979): 55–66.

64. Arnold of Bonneval (d. ca. 1156) wrote two treatises in which the Passion is considered, the *Liber de cardinalibus operibus Christi* (PL 189:1609–78) and the *Tractatus de septem verbis domini in cruce* (PL 189:1677–1726). The latter is a straightforward exposition of Christ's words on the cross, restrained in tone and moderate in style, with little elaboration of the gospel account. Arnold's work contains a commonplace interpretation of "I thirst," which is often repeated in later Passion tracts; Christ's thirst is not so much for physical drink as for the salvation of mankind (PL 189:1699). The *Liber de cardinalibus operibus Christi* has a chapter on the Passion which is notable for an early example of the literal application of the verse on the wine press of the Holy Week lection from Isaiah to Christ's body on the cross, which is described as exuding wine in the form of blood ("de torculari crucis mustum expressit," PL 189:1661).

65. Stephen of Sawley, *Treatises*, trans. Jeremiah F. O'Sullivan, ed. Bede K. Lackner, Cistercian Fathers Series 36 (Kalamazoo, Mich.: Cistercian Publications, 1984), p. 100. Latin in "Un 'Speculum Novitii' inédit d'Etienne de Salley," ed. Edmond Mikkers, *Collectanea Ordinis Cisterciensium Reformatorum* 8 (1946): 17–68, at p. 53.

66. Latin text in Edmond Mikkers, "Un traité inédit d'Etienne de Salley sur la Psalmodie," *Cîteaux: Comentarii Cistercienses* 23 (1972): 245–88, at p. 285; trans. O'Sullivan, p. 177. p. 285

67. Mikkers, "Psalmodie," p. 284; O'Sullivan, p. 176.

68. Edmund of Abingdon, *Speculum Religiosorum and Speculum Ecclesie*, ed. Helen P. Forshaw, Auctores Britannici Medii Aevi 3 (London: Oxford University Press, 1973), p. 22; on the textual history, see pp. 1–17.

69. Forshaw, *Speculum*, p. 89.

70. Forshaw, *Speculum*, p. 93; the quatrain is in *English Lyrics of the XIIIth Century*, ed. Carleton Brown (Oxford: Clarendon Press, 1932), pp. 165–66.

71. See John V. Fleming, *An Introduction to the Franciscan Literature of the Middle Ages* (Chicago: Franciscan Herald Press, 1977), pp. 250–56; Despres, *Ghostly Sights*, pp. 19–54. For the devotion to the passion in the later Middle Ages, see the

important studies of Rosemary Woolf, *English Religious Lyric*, pp. 20–66; Douglas Gray, *Themes and Images*, pp. 18–30, 122–45; J. A. W. Bennett, *Poetry of the Passion*, pp. 32–61; Richard Kieckhefer, *Unquiet Souls: Fourteenth-Century Saints and Their Religious Milieu* (Chicago: University of Chicago Press, 1984), pp. 122–49; see ch. 4, "Devotion to the Passion."

72. *Lignum vitae*, 2; de Vinck, p. 97; *Opera omnia*, 8:67.

73. See, respectively, *Lignum vitae*, 17, 22; *Opera omnia*, 8:75, 76; de Vinck pp. 117, 120.

74. *Lignum vitae*, 26, de Vinck, p. 123; *Opera omnia*, 8:78.

75. Marrow, *Passion Iconography*, pp. 52–54.

76. *Lignum vitae*, 29; *Opera omnia*, 8:79; de Vinck, p. 127.

77. Is 12:3: "Haurietis aquas in gaudio de fontibus salvatoris."

78. *Lignum vitae*, 31; *Opera omnia*, 8:80.

79. *Lignum vitae*, 31; *Opera omnia*, 8:80; de Vinck, p. 129.

80. *Lignum vitae*, 35; *Opera omnia*, 8:81; de Vinck, p. 133.

81. *Lignum vitae*, 28; *Opera omnia*, 8:79; de Vinck, p. 126.

82. *Lignum vitae*, 28; *Opera omnia*, 8:79; de Vinck, p. 126.

83. See the discussion of Ubertino da Casale later in this chapter.

84. *Vitis mystica*, chapters 18–23; *Opera omnia*, 8:183–87; de Vinck, pp. 192–201.

85. *Vitis mystica*, 4.1; *Opera omnia*, 8:166; de Vinck, p. 158.

86. *Vitis mystica*, 5.2; *Opera omnia*, 8:169; de Vinck, p. 163.

87. *Vitis mystica*, 2.3–4; *Opera omnia*, 8:161; de Vinck, pp. 149–50.

88. *Vitis mystica*, 5.1; *Opera omnia*, 8:168–69; de Vinck, p. 163.

89. *Vitis mystica*, 5.6; *Opera omnia*, 8:170; de Vinck, p. 167.

90. Lam 1:12; *Vitis mystica*, 2.3; *Opera omnia*, 8:161; de Vinck, p. 150.

91. *Vitis mystica*, 5.7; *Opera omnia*, 8:171; de Vinck, p. 168; see also the last words of the *Vitis* (24.4): "ut conformati imagini passionis tuae, ad eam quoque, quam peccando amisimus, divinitatis tuae imaginem reformemur" ("conforming to the image of your Passion, which we lost by sinning, we may also be reformed to the image of your divinity"); *Opera omnia*, 8:189; de Vinck, p. 205.

92. *Vitis mystica*, 10.1–2; *Opera omnia*, 8:175–76; de Vinck, p. 177.

93. *Vitis mystica*, 3.6; *Opera omnia*, 8:165; de Vinck, p. 156.

94. For the scourging and crown of thorns, see *Vitis mystica*, 4.2–3; *Opera omnia*, 8:166; de Vinck, p. 158. The buffeting adds the details that the Jews may have torn Christ's face with their fingernails and plucked his beard; *Vitis mystica*, 20.1; *Opera omnia*, 8:184; de Vinck, p. 196. See also *Meditationes vitae Christi*, 82 (Peltier, 12:609; Ragusa, p. 342), where it is stated more emphatically that the fact that Christ's beard was plucked is a fulfillment of Is 50:6. On Christ's hair and beard pulled out, see Marrow, *Passion Iconography*, pp. 68–76.

95. *Vitis mystica*, 4.3; *Opera omnia*, 8:167; de Vinck, p. 160. The idea is even more intensely expressed in Bonaventure's *De perfectione vitae ad sorores*, 6.6: "Tanta enim fuit sanguinis tui effusio, ut totum corpus tuum aspergeretur. . . . cum non gutta, sed sanguinis unda ita largiter per quinque partes corporis tui emanaverit de manibus et pedibus in crucifixione, de capite in coronatione, de toto corpore in flagellatione, de ipso corde in lateris apertione; mirum videtur, si quid sanguinis

remansit in te" ["Your blood was shed so abundantly that your whole body was soaked with it. Not just a drop, . . . but a welling stream of blood sprang from five parts of your body: the hands and feet in the crucifixion, the head in the crowning of thorns, the whole body in the flagellation, and the heart in the opening of your side. Not an ounce of blood could have remained in your veins"]. *Opera omnia*, 8:122; de Vinck, p. 243.

96. *Vitis mystica*, 5.1; *Opera omnia*, 8:169; de Vinck, p. 163.

97. *Vitis mystica*, 5.3; *Opera omnia*, 8:169; de Vinck, p. 164.

98. *Vitis mystica*, 5.4; *Opera omnia*, 8:169; de Vinck, p. 164.

99. *Vitis mystica*, 5.4–5; *Opera omnia*, 8:170; de Vinck, p. 165.

100. *Vitis mystica*, 6.2; *Opera omnia*, 8:172; de Vinck, p. 169.

101. *Vitis mystica*, 6.2; *Opera omnia*, 8:172; de Vinck, p. 169.

102. *Vitis mystica*, 7.1; *Opera omnia*, 8:172; de Vinck, p. 171. See Pickering, *Literature and Art*, pp. 285–307; for the drum-head, p. 292; the source seems to have been Augustine, commenting on the tympanum of Psalm 149:3.

103. *Vitis mystica*, 24.2–3; *Opera omnia*, 8:188; de Vinck, pp. 203–4. See also *De perfectione vitae ad sorores*, 6.2: "non solum mitte manum tuam in latus eius, sed totaliter per ostium lateris ingredere usque ad cor ipsius Iesu" ("not only put your hand into his side, but enter with your whole being through the door of his side into Jesus' heart itself") *Opera omnia*, 8:120; de Vinck, p. 239.

104. On the *Meditationes*, see *Meditaciones de passione Christi olim Sancto Bonaventurae attributae*, ed. M. Jordan Stallings, Studies in Medieval and Renaissance Latin Language and Literature 25 (Washington, D.C.: Catholic University of America Press, 1965); Columban Fischer, "Die 'Meditationes vitae Christi': Ihre handschriftliche Überlieferung und die Verfasserfrage," *Archivum Franciscanum Historicum* 25 (1932), 3–35, 175–209, 305–48, 449–83; John Fleming, *Franciscan Literature*, pp. 245–52; and Sarah McNamer, "Further Evidence for the Date of the pseudo-Bonaventuran *Meditationes vitae Christi*," *Franciscan Studies* 50 (1990): 235–61.

105. For a discussion of authorship, see Elizabeth Salter, *Nicholas Love*, pp. 39–41; the modern scholar is Fischer, as cited in the previous note.

106. Latin text of the *Meditationes* in *Bonaventurae Opera omnia*, ed. A. C. Peltier, 15 vols. (Paris: Vives, 1864–71), 12:510–630 (hereafter cited as Peltier); translation in Ragusa and Green (see above, note 47).

107. See, for example, *Meditationes*, 74; Peltier, 12:600; Ragusa, p. 320; and *Meditationes*, 78; Peltier, 12:605; Ragusa, p. 333.

108. *Meditationes*, 71; Peltier, 12:594; Ragusa p. 306; and *Meditationes*, 79; Peltier, 12:607; Ragusa, p. 336. See Bonaventure, *Vitis mystica*, 11.2; *Opera omnia*, 8:177; de Vinck, p. 179; and Arnold of Bonneval above, note 64.

109. *Meditationes*, 76; Peltier, 12:604; Ragusa, p. 329.

110. *Meditationes*, 77; Peltier, 12:604; Ragusa, p. 331; and *Meditationes*, 82; Peltier, 12:610; Ragusa, p. 345. See *Historia scholastica*, PL 198:634.

111. Is 1:6; *Meditationes*, 79; Peltier, 12:607; Ragusa, p. 338.

112. *Meditationes*, 76; Peltier, 12:604; Ragusa, p. 329.

113. *Meditationes*, 76; Peltier, 12:603–04; Ragusa, pp. 328–29.

114. *Meditationes*, 74; Peltier, 12:600; Ragusa, p. 320.

115. *Meditationes*, 78; Peltier, 12:605–06; Ragusa, p. 334.

116. *Meditationes*, 78; Peltier, 12:606; Ragusa, p. 334. See Chaucer's *Parson's Tale* (X.271), for instance.

117. *Meditationes*, 78; Peltier, 12:605; Ragusa, p. 333.

118. See Rolle, *Meditation on the Passion*, in Horstman, *Yorkshire Writers*, 1:84–85.

119. *Meditationes*, 80; Peltier, 12:608; Ragusa, pp. 338–40.

120. *Meditationes*, 81; Peltier, 12:608; Ragusa, pp. 341–42. This account offered much in the way of objective information to inspire medieval artists who sought to illustrate the deposition from the cross; for an attempt to draw the connections between the *Meditationes* and the painting of Giotto, see Michael Thomas, "Zur Rolle der 'Meditationes Vitae Christi' innerhalb der Europäischen Bild-Entwicklung der Giotto-Zeit," *Miscellanea codicologica F. Masai dicata*, ed. Pierre Cockshaw, Monique-Cécile Garand, and Pierre Jodogne, 2 vols. (Ghent: E. Story-Scientia S.P.R.L., 1979), 1:319–60.

121. *Meditationes*, 82; Peltier, 12:609; Ragusa, p. 342.

122. *Meditationes*, 82; Peltier, 12:610; Ragusa, p. 344.

123. Editions of these works will be cited as each is discussed. Another treatise that might have been included here is the *Meditatio de passione et resurrectione domini*, beginning "Noli timere filia Sion," attributed to Drogo of Laon, Archbishop of Ostia (d. 1138), printed in PL 166:1515–46. As Jean Leclercq has pointed out, what is printed in Migne is not found in the early manuscripts; and in particular, as Hereford, Cathedral Library, MS. O.i.ii, and other early MSS show, the parts that are added in Migne are what transforms this early twelfth-century treatise on the cross and calvary into a Passion meditation. We cannot be sure when the additions were made, but since there is no manuscript evidence for the text in Migne, it seems unwise to include it in this discussion. It seems likely that the treatise of Drogo was brought into conformity with late medieval taste by adding materials on the Passion of Christ to an earlier core. See Lili Gjerløw, "A Twelfth-Century Victorine or Cistercian Manuscript in the Library of Elverum," *Revue Bénédictine* 82 (1972): 313–38, at p. 317; the reference to Leclercq is cited there: it is from "Drogon et saint Bernard," *Revue Bénédictine* 63 (1953): 117–28.

124. For the date, see Salter, *Nicholas Love*, p. 155, quoting Wilmart, "Le grand poème bonaventurien," p. 269 and n. 5; Marrow, *Passion Iconography*, pp. 11–12; Felix Vernet in *Dictionnaire de Spiritualité*, 1:1325 ("n'est pas antérieure au XIIe siècle"). Recently Jeffrey Hamburger has accepted a twelfth-century date: "A Liber Precum in Sélestat and the Development of the Illustrated Prayer Book in Germany," *Art Bulletin* 83 (1991): 227 n. 88.

125. See Stallings, above, note 104.

126. An early example is the multiple recensions of the prayer to the Virgin of Anselm of Canterbury (Or. 7, ed. Schmitt); see André Wilmart, "Les propres corrections de S. Anselme dans sa grande prière à la Vierge Marie," *Recherches de Théologie Ancienne et Médiévale* 2 (1930), 189–204. One may also note the several versions of Edmund's *Speculum Religiosorum*, discussed above; the several versions of the *Ancrene Riwle*; and the two versions of the *Revelations* of Julian of Norwich (see above, chapter 1, note 38). On textual communities, see Brian Stock, *The Im-*

plications of Literacy: Written Language and Models of Interpretation in the Eleventh and Twelfth Centuries (Princeton, N.J.: Princeton University Press, 1983); Anne Bartlett uses the term textual community in connection with devotional works in "Miraculous Literacy and Textual Communities in Hildegard of Bingen's *Scivias*," *Mystics Quarterly* 18 (1992): 43–55; and see Julia Bolton Holloway, "Bride, Margery, Julian, and Alice: Bridget of Sweden's Textual Community in Medieval England," in *Margery Kempe: A Book of Essays*, ed. Sandra J. McEntire (New York: Garland, 1992), pp. 203–22.

127. On authorship and popularity, see Henri Barré, "Le 'Planctus Mariae' attribué à saint Bernard," *Revue d'Ascétique et de Mystique* 28 (1952): 243–66. A new edition has recently appeared: C. W. Marx, "The *Quis dabit* of Oglerius de Tridino, Monk and Abbot of Locedio," *Journal of Medieval Latin* 4 (1994): 118–29. Marx edits the version in the thirteenth-century manuscript, Turin, Biblioteca Nazionale, MS E.V.4. The older editions are as follows: PL 182:1133–42 (imperfect at the beginning); Augustine, *Sermones inediti*, ed. A. B. Caillau (Paris: Mellier, 1842), pp. 238–41 (partial text); G. Kribel, "Studien zur Richard Rolle de Hampole, II, Lamentatio St. Bernardi de compassione Mariae," *Englische Studien* 8 (1884): 85–114 (based on a seventeenth-century printed edition); W. Mushacke, *Altprovenzalische Marienklage des XIII Jahrhunderts*, Romanische Bibliothek 3 (Halle: Niemeyer, 1890), pp. 41–50 (based on early printed editions; cited below). I supply an edition and translation based on a fourteenth-century English manuscript in an Appendix. I have counted some 35 Latin manuscripts of the thirteenth through the fifteenth centuries in English libraries. An indication of its popularity to the end of the Middle Ages and beyond is the 29 printed editions appearing between 1467–1568; see Leopold Janauschek, *Bibliographia Bernardina*, *Xenia Bernardina*, vol. 4 (Vienna: Hölder, 1891), pp. viii (n. 51) and 499.

128. See esp. André Wilmart, *Auteurs spirituels*, pp. 505–36 ("Prières de compassion"); also *The Middle English Prose Complaint of Our Lady and Gospel of Nicodemus*, ed. C. William Marx and Jeanne F. Drennan, pp. 26–37, and, especially, Sandro Sticca, *The Planctus Mariae in the Dramatic Tradition of the Middle Ages* (Athens: University of Georgia Press, 1988).

129. Mushacke, *Altprovenzalische Marienklage*, pp. 42–43.

130. The title is from the Migne edition, PL 159:271–90, which is cited subsequently; for its influence on later spiritual writers see Fidèle de Ros, "Le planctus Mariae du pseudo-Anselme à Suso et à Louis de Grenade," *Revue d'Ascétique et de Mystique* 25 (1949): 270–83. For its possible influence on the ME *Complaint of Our Lady*, see Marx and Drennan, pp. 33–37.

131. See *Dialogus*, PL 159:271: "quia glorificata sum, flere non possum: ideo tibi passionem mei filii per ordinem explicabo" and Mushacke, p. 42: "sed quia iam glorificata sum, flere non possum, Tu cum lacrimis scribe que cum magnis doloribus ipsa persensi"; *Dialogus*, PL 159:275, use of "Quis dabit capiti meo aquam" in reference to Mary's sorrows; *Dialogus*, PL 159:275, "commota sunt omnia viscera ejus" and Mushacke, p. 43 [Gn 43:30]; *Dialogus*, PL 159:286, "Quis mihi det ut ego moriar pro te" and Mushacke, p. 44 [II Rg 18:33].

132. See *Dialogus*, PL 159:276 and Ekbert, *Stimulus amoris*, PL 158:749, for common use of the verse Gn 6:6: "tactus dolore cordis intrinsecus"; cf. *Dialo-*

gus, PL 159:276: "illam desiderabilem faciem sputis Judaeorum maculatam" with *Stimulus amoris*, PL 158:754.

133. For example, the column of the flagellation was so thick that two hand spans could not surround it; the crown of thorns was made of marine rushes (*juncis marinis*) and the King of France owns it now; the cross is fifteen feet in length; see PL 159:279–81.

134. PL 159:282.

135. When the cross is lifted up, Christ is suspended so high that Mary cannot even touch his feet. Now for the first time blood pours out of the nail wounds, which have been pulled open by the weight of his body; see PL 159:283. On the latter detail, see the meditation by the pseudo-Bernard in London, British Library, MS. Cotton Vespasian E.i, fol. 202v–203r; and Bridget of Sweden, *Revelationes*, 7.15.26; in *Birgitta of Sweden: Life and Selected Revelations*, trans. Albert Ryle Kezel (New York: Paulist Press, 1990), p. 190.

136. PL 159:288.

137. Wilmart, "Le grand poème," p. 269.

138. Wilmart, "Le grand poème," p. 270: "Il semble bien en effet que l'auteur ait été Cistercien."

139. PL 94:567.

140. PL 94:561–62.

141. See, for example, PL 94:563.

142. PL 94:564.

143. See above, note 94.

144. PL 94:565; but see Marrow, *Passion Iconography*, pp. 99–104, for some plausible biblical sources (for the rough and stony way, Dt 21:4; for the fact that Christ was barefoot, II Rg 15:30, David as a type of Christ); the motif was conventional in later Passion tracts.

145. PL 94:566.

146. PL 94:566.

147. PL 94:564; see the recension of the treatise in the fourteenth-century manuscript, Cambridge, Trinity College MS. O. 8. 26 [1401], fol. 62v, for a much expanded version of these events.

148. PL 94:564.

149. PL 94:565–66.

150. PL 94:567–68.

151. See Walter Hilton, *The Goad of Love*, trans. Clare Kirchberger (London: Faber, 1952), pp. 16–18; James of Milan, *Stimulus amoris Jacobi mediolanensis*, 2nd ed., Bibliotheca Franciscana ascetica medii aevi 4 (Quaracchi: Collegium S. Bonaventurae, 1949).

152. Peltier, 12:639.

153. Peltier, 12:634; see also 12:650.

154. *Arbor vitae crucifixae Jesu*, p. 308 (see above, note 47). For important commentary on the work with notes on its diffusion, see the Introduction and Bibliography by Charles T. Davis prefixed to the reprint edition .

155. *Arbor vitae*, p. 312.

156. *Arbor vitae*, p. 312.

157. *Arbor vitae*, p. 316.

158. *Arbor vitae*, p. 317.

159. *Arbor vitae*, p. 336.

160. *Arbor vitae*, p. 335.

161. *Arbor vitae*, pp. 322–25; see Sticca, *Planctus Mariae*, pp. 109–111.

162. For these and other examples, see Richard Kieckhefer, "Recent Work on Pseudo-Bonaventure and Nicholas Love," *Mystics Quarterly* 21 (1995):44–45.

163. Mary Immaculate Bodenstedt, *The Vita Christi of Ludolphus the Carthusian*, Studies in Medieval and Renaissance Latin Language and Literature 16 (Washington, D. C.: Catholic University of America Press, 1944), p. 16.

164. Bodenstedt, p. 16; for the Passion in Ludolphus, see Charles Abbot Conway, Jr., *The Vita Christi of Ludolphus of Saxony and Late Medieval Devotion Centered on the Incarnation*, Analecta Cartusiana 14 (Salzburg: Institut für Englische Sprache und Literatur, 1976), and Walter Baier, *Untersuchungen zu den Passionsbetrachtungen in der "Vita Christi" des Ludolf von Sachsen: Ein quellenkritischer Beitrag zu Leben und Werk Ludolfs und zur Geschichte der Passionstheologie*, 3 vols., Analecta Cartusiana 44 (Salzburg: Institut für Englische Sprache und Literatur, 1977).

165. See Elizabeth Salter, "Ludolphus of Saxony and his English Translators," *Medium Aevum* 33 (1964): 26–35.

166. Ludolphus of Saxony, *Vita Christi*, ed. L.-M. Rigollot, 4 vols. (Paris: Palme, 1870), 1:8–10.

167. The story that the number was marvelously revealed to an aged female recluse was widely circulated, being prefixed to several manuscripts of the devotion known as the *Fifteen Oes*, which was often falsely attributed to Bridget of Sweden in the manuscript tradition. For a text, see *Horae Eboracenses*, ed. Christopher Wordsworth, Surtees Society 132 (Durham: Andrews, 1920), pp. 76–80. See also Charity Meier-Ewert, "A Middle English Version of the *Fifteen Oes*," *Modern Philology* 68 (1971): 355–61; John C. Hirsh, "A Middle English Version of *The Fifteen Oes* from Bodleian Library MS. Add. B. 66," *Neuphilologische Mitteilungen* 75 (1974): 98–114.

168. Rigollot, 2:491, 504–07, 537–43.

169. Rigollot, 2:565–66.

170. PL 159:283.

171. Rigollot, 2:568; PL 159:283.

172. Rigollot, 2:591, 623–35.

173. *De perfectione vitae ad sorores*, 6.5–6; *Opera omnia*, 8:121–22; deVinck, pp. 241–43; see Rigollot, 2:617, 621,623.

174. Rigollot, 2:617.

175. See *Heinrich Seuses Horologium sapientiae*, ed. Pius Künzle, Spicilegium Friburgense 23 (Freiburg, Switzerland: Universitätsverlag, 1977), esp. pp. 514–16. The *Horologium* is an expanded and rearranged version of Suso's *Little Book of Eternal Wisdom*, written in German. For a modern English translation of the latter, as well as discussion of the *Horologium*, see *Henry Suso: The Exemplar, with Two German Sermons*, trans. Frank Tobin (New York: Paulist Press, 1989).

176. See *Gerardi a Zutphania, De spiritualibus ascensionibus*, ed. J. Mahieu (Bruges: Beyaert, 1941). Gerard's work was early translated into Dutch and especially popular among the adherents of the *Devotio moderna*; also associated with

this movement are the spiritual exercises on the Passion in the *Epistola de vita et passione domini nostri*, probably written in the late fourteenth century, which draws on Bonaventure and the *Meditationes vitae Christi*. See *Epistola de vita et passione domini nostri: Der lateinische Text mit Einleitung und Kommentar*, ed. Monica Hedlund (Leiden: Brill, 1975). These works are translated and discussed in *Devotio Moderna: Basic Writings*, trans. John Van Engen (New York: Paulist Press, 1988).

177. *The Meditations of the Monk of Farne*, ed. Hugh Farmer, Studia Anselmiana 41 (Rome: Pontificium Institutum S. Anselmi, 1957), p. 167; see also W. A. Pantin, "The Monk-Solitary of Farne: A Fourteenth-Century English Mystic," *English Historical Review* 59 (1944): 162–86; and the English translation in *The Monk of Farne: The Meditations of a Fourteenth-Century Monk*, ed. Hugh Farmer, trans. a Benedictine of Stanbrook (London: Darton, 1961).

178. See Farmer, Studia Anselmiana, p. 175.

179. See Marrow, *Passion Iconography*, p. 22; for the editions, see Hain 9446, Copinger 3372–77. Subsequent references are to the numbered articles in the 1492 Lübeck edition (Hain 9446). There is a similar Latin text including 65 articles of Christ's Passion in the fifteenth-century English manuscript, Cambridge, Pembroke College MS. 199, fols. 1r-36v; and a Middle Scots version of the 65 articles printed in *Devotional Pieces in Verse and Prose from MS. Arundel 285 and MS. Harleian 6919*, ed. J. A. W. Bennett, Scottish Text Society, 3rd ser. 23 (Edinburgh: William Blackwood, 1955), pp. 213–37.

180. As the prologue states, the aim is "to instruct the interior man in doctrine and in the Christian life, and to adjust the exterior man to Christian actions;" quoted in Mary Germaine McNeil, *Simone Fidati and his De Gestis Domini Salvatoris*, Studies in Medieval and Renaissance Latin Language and Literature 21 (Washington, D. C.: Catholic University of America, 1950), p. 96; see also p. 69 on the purpose of the work.

181. Simone Fidati da Cascia, *Gesta Salvatoris Dominis Nostri Jesu Christi seu Commentaria super IV Evangelia*, 2 vols. (Regensburg, H. Lenzius: 1733–34).

182. Book 13, Regensburg ed., 2:297–436.

183. Regensburg ed., 2:345.

184. For the last work, see Marrow, *Passion Iconography*, note 435.

185. Jan Hus, *Passio Domini Jesu Christi*, in *Magistri Iohannis Hus Opera omnia*, vol. 8, ed. Anezka Vidmanová-Schmidtová (Prague: Academia Scientiarum, 1973).

186. Hus, *Opera omnia*, 8:142.

187. Hus, *Opera omnia*, 8:136

188. Hus, *Opera omnia*, 8:196.

189. Hus, *Opera omnia*, 8:195.

190. Jean Gerson, *In dominicam passionem expositio e gallico in latinum versa*, in *Opera omnia*, vol. 3 (Antwerp: Sumptibus Societatis, 1706), col. 1185; the whole work is found at cols. 1153–1203.

191. Gerson, *Opera omnia*, col. 1190.

192. *Thomae Hemerken a Kempis Opera omnia*, ed. Michael Joseph Pohl, 6 vols. (Freiburg-im-Breisgau: Herder, 1902–18), 5:91–92.

193. Thomas, *Opera omnia*, 5:114.

194. Thomas, *Opera omnia*, 5:121.

195. Thomas, *Opera omnia*, 5:197; see above, notes 77, 153. Thomas also wrote a number of lengthy prayers on the Passion; see *Opera omnia*, 3:333–55.

196. *Vita beatae Virginis Mariae et Salvatoris rhythmica*, ed. A. Vögtlin, Bibliothek des Literarischen Vereins in Stuttgart 180 (Tübingen: Literarischer Verein in Stuttgart, 1888).

197. *Philomena*, 49.7–8; in *Analecta Hymnica* 50:606.

198. *John Hovedens Nachtigallenlied*, ed. Clemens Blume, Hymnologische Beiträge 4 (Leipzig: O. R. Reisland, 1930), p. viii.

199. Strophe 109; Blume, *Nachtigallenlied*, p. 13.

200. The Passion is also treated in Hoveden's meditative poem known as the *Quinquaginta cantica*. See *The Poems of John of Hoveden*, ed. F. J. E. Raby, Surtees Society 154 (Durham: Andrews, 1939), pp. 17–24.

201. See *The Mirour of Mans Saluacioun: A Middle English Translation of Speculum humanae salvationis*, ed. Avril Henry (Philadelphia: University of Pennsylvania Press, 1987).

202. *Speculum humanae salvationis*, ed. J. Lutz and P. Perdrizet, 2 vols. (Mulhouse: Meininger, 1907), 1:89 (lines 95–96).

203. *Speculum*, 1:90 (line 148).

204. *Speculum*, 1:91 (line 165).

205. *Le Livre de la Passion: poème narratif du xive siècle*, ed. Grace Frank (Paris: Champion, 1930).

206. See Charity Cannon Willard, "The Franco-Italian Professional Writer: Christine de Pizan," in *Medieval Women Writers*, ed. Katharina M. Wilson (Athens: University of Georgia Press, 1984), p. 339.

207. *Christi Leiden in einer Vision Geschaut*, ed. F. P. Pickering (Manchester: Manchester University Press, 1952); *Der Passionstraktat des Heinrich von St. Gallen*, ed. Kurt Ruh (Thayngen: Augustin, 1940).

208. See Marrow, *Passion Iconography*, esp. pp. 95–170.

209. See Kurt Ruh, *Bonaventura deutsch*, Bibliotheca Germanica 7 (Bern: Francke, 1956), pp. 159–72; 183–86.

210. Ruh, *Bonaventura deutsch*, pp 269–78.

211. London, British Library, MS Add. 15690, fols 1–23 (unprinted).

212. The poem is in *Cantari religiosi senesi del trecento: Neri Pagliaresi, Fra Felice Tancredi da Massa, Niccolò Cicerchia*, ed. Giorgio Varanini, Scrittori d'Italia 230 (Bari: Laterza, 1965), pp. 309–79.

213. Jacopone da Todi, *Laude*, ed. Franco Mancini, Scrittori d'Italia 257 (Bari: Laterza, 1974); see John Fleming, *Franciscan Literature*, pp. 183–86.

214. "Il 'Planctus B. Mariae' operetta falsamente attribuita a San Bernardo," ed. A. Chiari, *Rivista storica benedettina* 17 (1926): 56–111.

215. For Woolf and Gray, see above, note 63; for Bennett, see note 3. See also David L. Jeffrey, *The Early English Lyric and Franciscan Spirituality* (Lincoln: University of Nebraska Press, 1975).

216. *Cursor Mundi*, ed. Richard Morris, EETS OS 57, 59, 62, 66, 68, 99, 101 (1874–93; rpt. London: Oxford University Press, 1961–66), lines 23945–24730 (vol. 5 [EETS OS 68], pp. 1368–1416). For a newer edition, see *The Southern Version of*

Cursor Mundi, ed. Sarah M. Horrall, Roger Fowler, Peter H. J. Mous, and Henry J. Stauffenberg, Ottawa Medieval Texts and Studies 5, 13, 14, 16 (Ottawa: University of Ottawa Press, 1978–).

217. *The Southern Passion*, ed. Beatrice Daw Brown, EETS OS 169 (London: Oxford University Press, 1927), pp. liii–xcii; there is also the possibility of the influence of Bonaventure's *Lignum vitae*; for a summary of ME verse narratives of the Passion, see Brown, p. xiii.

218. *The Northern Passion*, ed. Frances A. Foster, EETS OS 145, 147 (London: Kegan Paul, 1913–16); *Supplement*, ed. William Heuser and Frances A. Foster, EETS OS 183 (London: Oxford University Press, 1930); for these details, see, respectively, *Supplement*, pp. 79, 95, 121.

219. *A Stanzaic Life of Christ*, ed. Frances A. Foster, EETS OS 166 (London: Oxford University Press, 1926), p. xx.

220. The poem is found in *Religious Pieces in Prose and Verse*, ed. George G. Perry, revised ed., EETS OS 26 (London: Kegan Paul, 1914), pp. 63–75; and in Horstman, *Yorkshire Writers*, 2:334–39; the commonplaces include the clothing sticking to the body (Perry, lines 217–20); stretching to fit the cross (Perry, lines 235–48); the cross dropped violently into a mortise (Perry, lines 242–43).

221. Texts of both poems in Bennett, *Devotional Pieces in Verse and Prose*: Kennedy, pp. 7–63 ("Lendulphus," line 196); Dunbar, pp. 266–69. Bennett's anthology has much material on the Passion. We may also mention the thirteenth-century verse Passion of Our Lord in *An Old English Miscellany*, ed. Richard Morris, EETS OS 49 (London, Trübner, 1872), pp. 37–57 and the 400-line fifteenth-century meditation on the Passion in *Three Middle English Religious Poems*, ed. R. H. Bowers, University of Florida Monographs: Humanities 12 (Gainesville: University of Florida Press, 1963), pp. 33–43. The fourteenth-century metrical paraphrase of the gospel known as the *Evangelie* has several elaborations of the Passion account, including stretching the body of Christ with ropes: see "The Middle English *Evangelie*," ed. Gertrude H. Campbell, *PMLA* 30 (1915): 529–613, at p. 601.

222. See *Old English Homilies and Homiletic Treatises*, ed. Richard Morris, EETS OS 29, 34 (London: Trübner, 1868), p. 282.

223. See, respectively, Rolle, *English Writings*, pp. 67–69, 19–27, 27–36. Fuller and more recent texts of the meditations are in *Richard Rolle: Prose and Verse*, ed. S. J. Ogilvie-Thomson, EETS 293 (Oxford: Oxford University Press, 1988), pp. 64–83. For a valuable general study, see Vincent Gillespie, "Strange Images of Death: The Passion in Later Medieval English Devotional and Mystical Writing," *Analecta Cartusiana* 117 (1987): 111–59.

224. See *Yorkshire Writers*, 1:112–21; 2:377–80; 2:440–41. See also William F. Pollard, "Mystical Elements in a Fifteenth-Century Prayer Sequence: 'The Festis and the Passion of Oure Lord Ihesu Crist'," in *The Medieval Mystical Tradition in England: Exeter Symposium IV*, ed. Marion Glasscoe (Woodbridge: Boydell and Brewer, 1987), pp. 47–61. Among much that remains unprinted mention should be made of the fifteenth-century Middle English prose meditation on the Passion in Cambridge, Trinity College, MS. O. 1. 74, fols. 106v–126r.

225. *A Talkyng of þe Loue of God*, ed. M. Salvina Westra (The Hague: M. Nijhoff, 1950), pp. 46–54, esp. p. 50.

226. See *The Middle English Prose Complaint of Our Lady and Gospel of Nicodemus*, ed. C. William Marx and Jeanne F. Drennan, pp. 26–37 (see note 6, above). The Middle English prose account of the Passion in *The Pepysian Gospel Harmony*, ed. Margery Goates, EETS OS 157 (London: Oxford University Press, 1922), is unelaborated.

227. See *The Tretyse of Love*, ed. John H. Fisher, EETS OS 223 (London: Oxford University Press, 1951), esp. pp. 56–63, 69–74.

228. *Meditations on the Supper of Our Lord, and the Hours of the Passion*, ed. J. Meadows Cowper, EETS OS 60 (London: Trübner, 1875); *Meditations on the Life and Passion of Christ*, ed. Charlotte D'Evelyn, EETS OS 158 (London: Oxford University Press, 1921).

229. For an example of the former, see the pseudo-Bonaventuran *The Privity of the Passion*, in Horstman, *Yorkshire Writers*, 1:198–212; for Love, see Salter, *Nicholas Love* (cited above, note 14), and *Nicholas Love's Mirror of the Blessed Life of Jesus Christ: A Critical Edition Based on Cambridge University Library Additional MSS 6578 and 6686*, ed. Michael G. Sargent, Garland Medieval Texts 18 (New York: Garland, 1992). Sargent has a thorough discussion of the various English versions of the *Meditationes*, pp. xv–xx; among the most important is the Carthusian *Speculum devotorum* of the fifteenth century; see *The Speculum devotorum of an Anonymous Carthusian of Sheen*, ed. James Hogg (Salzburg: Institut für Anglistik und Amerikanistik, 1973).

230. *The Prickynge of Love*, ed. Harold Kane, 2 vols., Salzburg Studies in English Literature 92:10 (Salzburg: Institut für Anglistik und Amerikanistik, 1983); Walter Hilton, *The Goad of Love*, trans. Clare Kirchberger (London: Faber, 1952); see also note 233.

231. See Horstman, *Yorkshire Writers*, 2:274–82; *The Minor Poems of the Vernon Manuscript*, ed. Carl Horstmann, EETS OS 98 (London: Kegan Paul, 1892), pp. 298–328. See also F. J. Tanquerey, *Plaintes de la Vierge en Anglo-Français, xiiie et xive siècles* (Paris: Champion, 1921), and C. W. Marx, "The Middle English Verse 'Lamentation of Mary to Saint Bernard' and the 'Quis dabit,'" in *Studies in the Vernon Manuscript*, ed. Derek Pearsall (Cambridge: D. S. Brewer, 1990), pp. 137–57. The Marian lament by Lydgate, beginning "Who shal yeve vn-to myn hed a welle" is only generally influenced by the Latin lament: see *The Minor Poems of John Lydgate*, ed. Henry MacCracken, EETS OS 192 (London: Oxford University Press, 1934), 1:324–29.

232. "*Orologium sapientiae*, or *The Sevene Poyntes of Trewe Wisdom*, aus MS Douce 114," ed. Carl Horstmann, *Anglia* 10 (1888): 323–89.

233. For a translation of Anselm's *Meditatio* 1, see Horstman, *Yorkshire Writers*, 2:443–45; there are unpublished fifteenth-century Middle English translations of *Meditationes* 1–3 and *Oratio* 2 in London, British Library, MS. Harley 535, fol. 121r-142r (attributed to Ambrose).

234. See above, note 55.

235. See Perry, *Religious Pieces*, pp. 16–50. On the popularity of earlier devotional writings in the later Middle Ages, see the two studies of Giles Constable cited in chapter 1, note 7. On late Middle English versions of Ludolphus, see Elizabeth Salter, "Ludolphus of Saxony and His English Translators," pp. 26–35; and

for Thomas à Kempis, see Roger Lovatt, "The Imitation of Christ in Late Medieval England," *Transactions of the Royal Historical Society* 5th ser. 18 (1968): 97–121.

236. Susan Groag Bell, "Medieval Women Book Owners: Arbiters of Lay Piety and Ambassadors of Culture," in *Women and Power in the Middle Ages*, ed. Mary Erler and Maryanne Kowaleski (Athens: University of Georgia Press, 1988), pp. 149–87; Carol M. Meale, "'. . . Alle the bokes that I haue of latyn, englisch, and frensch': Laywomen and Their Books in Late Medieval England," in *Women and Literature in Britain, 1150–1500*, ed. Carol M. Meale (Cambridge: Cambridge University Press, 1993), pp. 128–58; Felicity Riddy, "'Women Talking About the Things of God': A Late Medieval Sub-culture," in Meale, *Women and Literature*, pp. 104–27; Anne Clark Bartlett, *Male Authors, Female Readers: Representation and Subjectivity in Middle English Devotional Literature* (Ithaca, N. Y.: Cornell University Press, 1995), pp. 1–33; and see above, chapter 1, note 21.

237. Michael G. Sargent, "The Transmission by the English Carthusians of Some Late Medieval Spiritual Writings," *Journal of Ecclesiastical History* 27 (1976): 225–40.

238. See Susan Bell, "Medieval Women Book Owners," p. 165, and the references cited there.

Chapter 3

1. See George Keiser's review of Sandro Sticca, *The Planctus Mariae in the Dramatic Tradition of the Middle Ages*, *Studies in the Age of Chaucer* 12 (1990): 325–27.

2. Some of the important studies are Solomon Grayzel, *The Church and the Jews in the XIIIth Century: A Study of Their Relations during the Years 1198–1254*, 2nd ed. (1933; rpt. New York: Hermon, 1966); *The Church and the Jews in the XIIIth Century*, Vol. 2 (1254–1314), ed. Kenneth R. Stow (New York: Jewish Theological Seminary, 1989); Léon Poliakov, *The History of Anti-Semitism: Volume One: From the Time of Christ to the Court Jews* (London: Elek Books, 1965); Jeremy Cohen, *The Friars and the Jews: The Evolution of Medieval Anti-Judaism* (Ithaca, N.Y.: Cornell University Press, 1982); Shlomo Simonsohn, *The Apostolic See and the Jews*, Studies and Texts 94, 95, 99, 104 (Toronto: Pontifical Institute of Mediaeval Studies, 1988–91); Joshua Trachtenberg, *The Devil and the Jews: The Medieval Conception of the Jew and its Relation to Modern Antisemitism* (Philadelphia: Jewish Publication Society, 1983); Kenneth R. Stow, *Alienated Minority: The Jews of Medieval Latin Europe* (Cambridge, Mass.: Harvard University Press, 1992).

3. Bernhard Blumenkranz, *Le juif médiéval au miroir de l'art chrétien* (Paris: Etudes Augustiniennes, 1966), pp. 96–98; and the texts cited passim in his *Les auteurs chrétiens latins du moyen âge sur les juifs et le judaïsme* (Paris: Mouton, 1963), esp. pp. 86, 134–35; see also Trachtenberg, *The Devil and the Jews*, p. 20; and Jeremy Cohen, "The Jews as the Killers of Christ in the Latin Tradition from Augustine to Jerome," *Traditio* 39 (1983): 1–27.

4. "ab impiis crudeliter dissecari," Anselm of Canterbury, *Anselmi opera omnia*, ed. F. S. Schmitt, 6 vols. (1938–61; rpt. Stuttgart: Fromann, 1968), 3:8;

translation in Benedicta Ward, *The Prayers and Meditations of St. Anselm* (Harmondsworth: Penguin, 1973), p. 96.

5. See the Gospel of Nicodemus, in *The Apocryphal New Testament*, trans. Montague Rhodes James (Oxford: Clarendon Press, 1924), pp. 103–7.

6. See *Historia scholastica*, PL 198:1614–38; *Glossa ordinaria*, PL 114:167–77.

7. See Thomas H. Bestul, "The *Meditationes* of Alexander of Ashby: An Edition," *Mediaeval Studies* 52 (1990): 62; Ekbert, MS. Oxford, Univ. Coll. 30, p. 14; cf. PL 184:953 (my translation).

8. Blumenkranz, *Le juif médiéval*, pp. 91–104.

9. The portrait of the late Middle Ages painted by J. Huizinga in *The Waning of the Middle Ages*, first published in 1919, has been especially influential in establishing this point of view; note, for example, the following observation (*The Waning* [Garden City, N.Y.: Doubleday, 1954], p. 190): "Ever since the gentle mysticism of Saint Bernard, in the twelfth century, had started the strain of pathetic tenderness about the Passion of Christ, the religious sensibility of the medieval soul had been increasing. The mind was saturated with the concepts of Christ and the cross." See also David Knowles, *The Religious Orders in England*, vol. 2 (Cambridge: Cambridge University Press, 1979), pp. 222–23; and Louis Bouyer, Jean Leclercq, and François Vandenbroucke, *The Spirituality of the Middle Ages*, trans. Benedictines of Holme Eden Abbey, A History of Christian Spirituality 2 (London: Burns and Oates, 1968), pp. 481–99: for a critique of these views, see Gail M. Gibson, *The Theater of Devotion* (Berkeley: University of California Press, 1989), pp. 3–5, where the passage cited from Knowles above is quoted.

10. This is a topic that has been intensely studied: see Pamela Gradon, *Form and Style in Early English Literature* (London: Methuen, 1971), pp. 298–314; Douglas Gray, *Themes and Images in the Medieval English Religious Lyric* (London: Routledge, 1972), pp. 18–30; Rosemary Woolf, *The English Religious Lyric in the Middle Ages* (Oxford: Clarendon, 1968), pp. 20–66. See also Margaret R. Miles, *Image as Insight: Visual Understanding in Western Christianity and Secular Culture* (Boston: Beacon Press, 1985), esp. ch. 4, "Images of Women in Fourteenth-Century Tuscan Painting," pp. 63–93; Denise Despres, *Ghostly Sights: Visual Meditation in Late Medieval Literature* (Norman, Okla.: Pilgrim, 1989), pp. 19–54; S. Ringbom, "Devotional Images and Imaginative Devotions: Notes on the Place of Art in Late Medieval Private Piety," *Gazette des Beaux Arts*, ser. 6, 73 (1969): 159–70; David Freedberg, *The Power of Images: Studies in the History and Theory of Response* (Chicago: University of Chicago Press, 1989), pp. 162–71; Hans Belting, *The Image and Its Public in the Middle Ages: Form and Function of Early Paintings of the Passion*, trans. Mark Bartusis and Raymond Meyer (New Rochelle, N.Y.: Caratzas, 1990). For the representation of the Jews in the visual arts, see, in addition to the basic work of Blumenkranz, cited above, Ruth Mellinkoff, *The Horned Moses in Medieval Art and Thought* (Berkeley: University of California Press, 1970); the important chapter in Michael Camille, *The Gothic Idol: Ideology and Image-making in Medieval Art* (Cambridge: Cambridge University Press, 1989), pp. 165–94; and Ruth Mellinkoff, *Outcasts: Signs of Otherness in Northern European Art of the Late Middle Ages*, 2 vols. (Berkeley: University of California Press, 1993).

11. On Franciscan realism, see especially Despres, *Ghostly Sights*, pp. 19–54;

and Despres, "Franciscan Spirituality: Margery Kempe and Visual Meditation," *Mystics Quarterly* 11 (1985): 12–18.

12. On the crusades as a manifestation of interest in the humanity of Jesus, see Gavin Langmuir, *History, Religion and Antisemitism* (Berkeley: University of California Press, 1990), pp. 289–90; on Anselm's theology, see the classic summary in R. W. Southern, *The Making of the Middle Ages* (New Haven, Conn.: Yale University Press, 1953), pp. 226–40; on the cultural significance of the doctrine of transubstantiation, see Miri Rubin, *Corpus Christi: the Eucharist in Late Medieval Culture* (Cambridge: Cambridge University Press, 1991), pp. 12–82.

13. I have found useful Lee Patterson's Introduction, "Critical Historicism and Medieval Studies," to the collection of essays, *Literary Practice and Social Change in Britain, 1380-1530*, ed. Lee Patterson (Berkeley: University of California Press, 1990), pp. 1–14; see Raymond Williams, *Marxism and Literature* (Oxford: Oxford University Press, 1977), pp. 128–135, 145–50.

14. See R. I. Moore, *The Formation of a Persecuting Society: Power and Deviance in Western Europe, 950-1250* (Oxford: Basil Blackwell, 1987). The Third Lateran Council of 1179 was the first general council of the church to prescribe penalties for sodomy, an action which signaled the beginning of an era of growing persecution of male homosexuality, which, by the year 1300 was a capital offense in most of western Europe; Moore, p. 93; see also John Boswell, *Christianity, Social Tolerance, and Homosexuality: Gay People in Western Europe from the Beginning of the Christian Era to the Fourteenth Century* (Chicago: University of Chicago Press, 1980), pp. 269–302. The same council also repeated that lepers should be rigidly segregated from the rest of society and provided rituals of exclusion for this purpose; eventually, they were deprived of legal rights, including the right to dispose of property; Moore, *Persecuting Society*, pp. 11, 58.

15. Moore, *Persecuting Society*, pp. 7–8.

16. See Grayzel, *The Church and the Jews*, 1:306–13.

17. Camille, *Gothic Idol*, p. 180.

18. See Stow, *Alienated Minority*; Stow emphasizes the reiteration of earlier conciliar decrees in the edicts of Lateran IV, pp. 246–48. I have also relied on the account of Jewish status in Lester K. Little, *Religious Poverty and the Profit Economy in Medieval Europe* (Ithaca, N.Y.: Cornell University Press, 1978), pp. 42–57 ("The Jews in Christian Europe"); on the process of marginalization, see Moore, *Persecuting Society*, p. 99.

19. Little, *Religious Poverty*, p. 4; also John Hine Mundy, *Europe in the High Middle Ages 1150-1309* (New York: Basic Books, 1973), pp. 81–85.

20. Mundy, *Europe in the High Middle Ages*, p. 81; for the so-called "golden age" of European Jewry, see also Trachtenberg, *The Devil and the Jews*, pp. 159–60.

21. Poliakov, *History of Anti-Semitism*, p. 43.

22. Poliakov, *History of Anti-Semitism*, pp. 42–45. Speyer, Worms, and Mainz were recalled in Jewish memory as the "cities of blood"; Poliakov, p. 83.

23. Little, *Religious Poverty*, pp. 48–49; Moore, *Persecuting Society*, p. 31; Poliakov, *History of Anti-Semitism*, pp. 48–49. Bernard reflects the older, more tolerant, Augustinian view of the Jewish role in a Christian society.

24. Little, *Religious Poverty*, p. 49; Moore, *Persecuting Society*, p. 31.

25. Moore, *Persecuting Society*, pp. 36–37; Little, *Religious Poverty*, pp. 51–53; Gavin Langmuir, "Thomas Monmouth, Detector of Ritual Murder," *Speculum* 59 (1984): 820–46; R. Po-Chia Hsia, *The Myth of Ritual Murder: Jews and Magic in Reformation Germany* (New Haven, Conn.: Yale University Press, 1988), esp. pp. 1–13.

26. Poliakov, *The History of Anti-Semitism*, p. 60.

27. Poliakov, *The History of Anti-Semitism*, p. 59; Trachtenberg, *The Devil and the Jews*, pp. 109–23.

28. Moore, *Persecuting Society*, pp. 34–36; Langmuir, *History, Religion and Anti-Semitism*, pp. 298–300; and the important discussion of Trachtenberg, *The Devil and the Jews*, pp. 124–39.

29. R. W. Hunt, "The Disputation of Peter of Cornwall Against Symon the Jew," in *Studies in Medieval History Presented to F. M. Powicke*, ed. R. W. Hunt, W. A. Pantin, and R. W. Southern (Oxford: Clarendon Press, 1948), pp. 146–47.

30. The work is discussed by Cohen, *The Friars and the Jews*, pp. 24–25, 28.

31. Is 1:3; Sermon 60.4–5; in *Bernard of Clairvaux: On the Song of Songs*, vol. 3, trans. Kilian Walsh and Irene M. Edmonds, Cistercian Fathers Series 31 (Kalamazoo, Mich.: Cistercian Publications, 1979), pp. 132–33.

32. These portrayals are analyzed in James Marrow, *Passion Iconography in Northern European Art of the Late Middle Ages and Early Renaissance: A Study of the Transformation of Sacred Metaphor into Descriptive Narrative*, Ars Neerlandica 1 (Kortrijk: Van Ghemmert, 1979), pp. 34–43, although Marrow does not explicitly connect the animal portrayals with the Jews.

33. "Quid justius cum ut his, quae fraudulenter lucrati sunt, destituantur?" PL 189:367; *Ep.* 4.36; see Grayzel, *The Church and the Jews*, 1:29.

34. PL 189:367.

35. *De civ. dei*, 18.46; for a summary of Augustine's views concerning the Jews, see Stow, *Alienated Minority*, pp. 17–20.

36. Grayzel, *The Church and the Jews*, 1:10; for the letter, see Grayzel, *The Church and the Jews*, 1:127 (quoted by Langmuir, *History, Religion and Antisemitism*, p. 295).

37. See Moore, *Persecuting Society*, pp. 39–42; the general point remains, but Langmuir has convincingly demonstrated that there was considerable variation in the practical political and legal application of the theory; see his chapter " 'Tanquam Servi': The Change in Jewish Status in French Law About 1200," in *Toward a Definition of Antisemitism* (Berkeley: University of California Press, 1990), pp. 167–94.

38. See Langmuir, *History, Religion, and Antisemitism*, p. 294; Rubin, *Corpus Christi*, pp. 53–55; an important study of the process of demetaphorization of Biblical metaphor in respect to the medieval Jew is Ruth Mellinkoff, *The Horned Moses in Medieval Art and Thought*, passim.

39. Grayzel, *The Church and the Jews*, 1:30–31; Cohen, *The Friars and the Jews*, pp. 51–73; Little, *Religious Poverty*, pp. 51–52.

40. The official recognition of the feast of Corpus Christi took place in 1264; see Little, *Religious Poverty*, p. 52; and especially Rubin, *Corpus Christi*, pp. 164–212.

41. Little, *Religious Poverty*, p. 52. See also Langmuir, *History, Religion and Antisemitism*, pp. 300–301; Bernard Hamilton, *Religion in the Medieval West* (Lon-

don: Edward Arnold, 1986), p. 191; the Cathars, for example, rejected the doctrine: see Ekbert, *Sermo 11 contra Catharos* (PL 195:84–94).

42. See Denise Despres, "Cultic Anti-Judaism and Chaucer's Little Clergeon," *Modern Philology* 91 (1994): 413–27.

43. On Elizabeth, see Anne L. Clark, *Elisabeth of Schönau: A Twelfth-Century Visionary* (Philadelphia: University of Pennsylvania Press, 1992).

44. Clark, *Elisabeth*, pp. 11–12.

45. The details of his life are summarized in the article on him in the *New Catholic Encyclopedia*; and in Clark, *Elisabeth*, pp. 50–67. The main source of information is the biography by Emecho, his successor as Abbot of Schönau: see *Die Visionen der hl. Elisabeth und die Schriften der Aebte Ekbert und Emecho von Schönau*, ed. F. W. E. Roth (Brünn: Verlag der Studien aus dem Benedictiner- und Cistercienser-Orden, 1884), pp. 196–208, 348–53.

46. Moore, *Persecuting Society*, p. 22 (on ecclesiastical structure). On the Cathars, see R. I. Moore, *The Origins of European Dissent*, 2nd ed. (Oxford: Blackwell, 1985), pp. 168–96; for other references, see Hamilton, *Religion*, p. 211.

47. Moore, *Persecuting Society*, p. 148.

48. F. W. E. Roth, *Die Visionen*, p. 203; for a good analysis of Ekbert's anti-Cathar activities, see Moore, *European Dissent*, pp. 175–82.

49. Roth, *Die Visionen*, p. 352. Even Ekbert's saintly sister Elizabeth was troubled by the Cathar menace; she wrote a letter to Hildegard of Bingen complaining of threat to the church from the secret activities of the Cathar heretics, whom she calls "venenosos serpentes" (Roth, *Die Visionen*, p. 74); see also Clark, *Elisabeth*, pp. 22–24.

50. See Moore, *Persecuting Society*, p. 123.

51. Ekbert's biographer tells us, perhaps significantly, that he was especially missed by the those who were worthy (precipue illi, qui digni fuerunt) who had grown accustomed to being informed by his teaching (Roth, *Die Visionen*, p. 348). The treatise against the Jews does not survive.

52. Roth, *Die Visionen*, p. 352.

53. Camille, *Gothic Idol*, p. 298; for these ideas, see Langmuir, *History, Religion and Antisemitism*, p. 303; Moore, *Persecuting Society*, pp. 100–101, 139.

54. Moore, *Persecuting Society*, p. 4.

55. Moore, *Persecuting Society*, p. 5.

56. Moore, *Persecuting Society*, p. 151.

57. Jacques Le Goff, *The Medieval Imagination*, trans. Arthur Goldhammer (Chicago: University of Chicago Press, 1988), p. 102.

58. PL 158:751–52.

59. PL 158:753; see II Cor 6:15–16.

60. M. D. Chenu, *Nature, Man, and Society in the Twelfth Century*, ed. J. Taylor and L. Little (Chicago: University of Chicago Press, 1957), p. 65; the passage is cited by Paul Strohm in his acutely delineated account of changing social relations in the later Middle Ages, *Social Chaucer* (Cambridge, Mass.: Harvard University Press, 1989), pp. 13–21 (quotation at p. 13).

61. Aelred of Rievaulx, *Sermones inediti*, ed. C. H. Talbot, Series Scriptorum S. Ordinis Cisterciensis, vol. 1 (Rome: Curia Generalis Sacri Ordinis Cister-

ciensis, 1952), p. 44. On the kiss of peace in the mass, see John Bossy, "The Mass as a Social Institution, 1200–1700," *Past and Present* 100 (1983): 52–58.

62. On the kiss as symbol, see Nicholas J. Perella, *The Kiss Sacred and Profane: An Interpretive History of Kiss Symbolism and Related Religio-Erotic Themes* (Berkeley: University of California Press, 1969); and see Glenn Burger, "Kissing the Pardoner," *PMLA* 107 (1992): 1143–56.

63. Jacques Le Goff, *Time, Work and Culture in the Middle Ages*, trans. Arthur Goldhammer (Chicago: University of Chicago Press, 1980), pp. 242–43.

64. Le Goff, *Time*, pp. 242–43.

65. Le Goff, *Time*, pp. 255, 261.

66. *Roman de la Rose*, vv. 1931–40; as quoted, with translation, in Le Goff, *Time*, pp. 262–63. The text in the Langlois edition is as follows; see *Le Roman de la Rose*, ed. Ernest Langlois, Société des Anciens Textes Français, vol. 2 (Paris: Firmin-Didot, 1920), pp. 100–101 (vv. 1933–40):

> Que je veuil, por ton avantage,
> Qu'orendroit me faces omage;
> Si me baiseras en la bouche,
> A cui nus vilains on ne touche.
> Je n'i laisse mie touchier
> Chascun vilain, chascun bouchier,
> Ainz doit estre cortois e frans
> Cil que j'ensi a ome prens.

67. Lee Patterson, "'No Man His Reson Herde': Peasant Consciousness, Chaucer's Miller, and the Structure of the *Canterbury Tales*," in *Literary Practice and Social Change in Britain*, p. 135, n. 55.

68. PL 158:754.

69. Bernard of Clairvaux, *Sermons on the Song of Songs*, 60.5; trans. Walsh and Edmonds, 3:134.

70. Grayzel, *The Church and the Jews*, 1:126–27.

71. For the statute, see Langmuir, *Toward a Definition of Antisemitism*, pp. 167–94.

72. PL 94:563: "et eum sine honore etc."; also many instances in Ludolphus.

73. Quoted in Poliakov, *The History of Anti-Semitism*, p. 48 (I have corrected the Latin transcription).

74. Le Goff, *Time, Work and Culture*, p. 244; on the importance of the body in medieval culture, see the studies cited in chapter 1, note 82.

75. Mary Douglas, *Purity and Danger* (New York: Praeger, 1966), p. 121; quoted in Julia Kristeva, *Powers of Horror: An Essay on Abjection*, trans. Leon S. Roudiez (New York: Columbia University Press, 1982), p. 69.

76. See the popular Marian lament beginning "Quis dabit capiti meo aquam," printed in W. Mushacke, *Altprovenzalische Marienklage des XIII Jahrhunderts* (Halle: Niemeyer, 1890), p. 43; and see the forthcoming study of Martha Bayless on excrement in the Middle Ages.

77. *Sermones inediti*, ed. C. H. Talbot, p. 44; see also Bernard of Clairvaux, *Sermons on the Song of Songs*, 2.2–3; in *On the Song of Songs, I*, trans. Kilian Walsh, Cistercian Fathers Series 4 (Kalamazoo, Mich.: Cistercian Publications, 1981), pp. 8–10; and note the legend of Judas's death: when he hanged himself, his guts burst and his soul departed from his belly (instead of the usual way, through the mouth), so that the mouth that kissed Christ would not be further defiled by the exit of his soul. The story is a medieval commonplace and is found, for example, in the *Legenda aurea*; see *The Golden Legend: Readings on the Saints*, trans. William Granger Ryan, 2 vols. (Princeton, N.J.: Princeton University Press, 1993), 1:168; in the *Vita Christi* of Ludolphus of Saxony, ed. L. M. Rigollot, 4 vols. (Paris: Palme, 1870), 2:516; and in *Le Livre de la Passion*, ed. Grace Frank, Les Classiques Français du Moyen Age (Paris: Champion, 1930), p. 33.

78. Le Goff, *Time, Work and Culture*, p. 252.

79. Caroline Bynum, *Fragmentation and Redemption: Essays on Gender and the Human Body in Medieval Religion* (New York: Zone Books, 1991), p. 184

80. See Poliakov, *The History of Anti-Semitism*, pp. 49, 58–60; Moore, *Persecuting Society*, p. 38; Rubin, *Corpus Christi*, p. 126.

81. Some of those sentiments are recorded in Poliakov, *The History of Anti-Semitism*, pp. 48–49.

82. John H. Mundy, *Europe in the High Middle Ages*, p. 89; Langmuir, *Toward a Definition of Antisemitism*, pp. 167–94.

83. See Poliakov, *The History of Anti-Semitism*, pp. 115–17.

84. Cohen, *The Friars and the Jews*, p. 13.

85. See the *New Catholic Encyclopedia*, s.v. Bonaventure; Bonaventure spent time in the small friary of Mantes-sur-Seine, near Paris, in 1266–68. The author of the article suggests that "some of his ascetical writings date from this period."

86. Cohen, *The Friars and the Jews*, pp. 51–76.

87. Poliakov, *The History of Anti-Semitism*, pp. 69–71; Cohen, *The Friars and the Jews*, p. 62.

88. Cohen, *The Friars and the Jews*, p. 63.

89. Poliakov, *The History of Anti-Semitism*, p. 71.

90. Poliakov, *The History of Anti-Semitism*, p. 72.

91. Strohm, *Hochown's Arrow: The Social Imagination of Fourteenth-Century Texts* (Princeton, N. J.: Princeton University Press, 1992), p. 70; see also pp. 58, 66 for further elaboration of Strohm's helpful concept of textual environment.

92. Bonaventure, *De perfectione vitae ad sorores*, 6.4; in *Bonaventurae Opera omnia*, ed. pp. Collegii S. Bonaventurae, 11 vols. (Quaracchi: Collegium S. Bonaventurae, 1882–1902), 8:121; trans. in *The Works of Bonaventure . . . I: Mystical Opuscula*, trans. José de Vinck (Paterson, N.J.: St. Anthony Guild Press, 1960), p. 241.

93. *Vitis mystica*, 4.3; *Opera omnia*, 8:167; trans. de Vinck, p. 160.

94. Georges Duby, *The Three Orders: Feudal Society Imagined*, trans. Arthur Goldhammer (Chicago: University of Chicago Press, 1980), pp. 187, 190, 317, 340–42.

95. *Vitis mystica*, 20.1; *Opera omnia*, 8:184–85; de Vinck, p. 196.

96. In the Latin dictionary of Lewis and Short, brood or swarm is a possible

translation of *gens*, especially in reference to animals. To take *gens* as race or people, of course universalizes Bonaventure's condemnation, extending it beyond the narrow circle of those Jews who actually participated in the torments of Christ.

97. Jacobus de Voragine (c. 1230–1298); on the date of the *Legenda*, see Sherry Reames, *The Legenda aurea: A Reexamination of its Paradoxical History* (Madison: University of Wisconsin Press, 1985).

98. *Lignum vitae*, 17; *Opera omnia*, 8:75; de Vinck, p. 116–117.

99. *Lignum vitae*, 22; *Opera omnia*, 8:76; de Vinck, p. 120.

100. *Lignum vitae*, 31; *Opera omnia*, 8:80; de Vinck, p. 129. In place of "yielding to the cries of an adulterous mob," Ekbert has "yield to an adulterous voice" ("adulterinae voci acquiescere," PL 184:961).

101. *Lignum vitae*, 23–24; *Opera omnia*, 8:77; de Vinck, p. 121; cf. Ekbert of Schönau, PL 184:959.

102. de Vinck's translation mitigates the anti-Judaism, by confining the impiety to the mob, whereas Bonaventure's Latin is totalizing in application.

103. Quoted in Duby, *Three Orders*, p. 320.

104. See John Gower, *Vox Clamantis*, in *The Major Latin Works of John Gower*, trans. Eric Stockton (Seattle: University of Washington Press, 1962), p. 210; the first sentence is quoted by David Aers, *Community, Gender, and Individual Identity: English Writing 1360–1430* (London: Routledge, 1988), p. 32.

105. See Patterson, *Literary Practice and Social Change in Britain*, p. 135.

106. For these prohibitions, see Stow, *Alienated Minority*, pp. 235–37; Poliakov, *The History of Anti-Semitism*, pp. 105–6, 149–50; Mundy, *Europe in the High Middle Ages*, p. 101. For the relevant papal bulls, see Grayzel, *The Church and the Jews*, 1:114–17, 127, 167, 204–6, 252–53, 297, 307–9; 2:64–65, 110–11, 241, 257–58, 261–62; 2:69 and note: "The prohibition against resorting to Jewish physicians is rooted in those canons which forbid social mingling with infidels, especially Gratian, *Decretum*, C.28, q.l, c.13, *nullus*, which prohibits the use of Jewish physicians, bathing with Jews, and the eating of Passover *matzot*."

107. Mundy, *Europe in the High Middle Ages*, p. 101; for the text, see Grayzel, *The Church and the Jews*, 2:272–73.

108. Mundy, *Europe in the High Middle Ages*, p. 101. The same restriction had earlier been made by the Council of Arles in 1275; see Grayzel, *The Church and the Jews*, 2:272–73.

109. Camille, *Gothic Idol*, p. 171. The episode is treated in Trachtenberg, *The Devil and the Jews*, p. 187; see also Stow, *Alienated Minority*, p. 235.

110. Robert's wedding occurred in 1274; see Stow, *Alienated Minority*, p. 289; and Decima Douie, *Archbishop Pecham* (Oxford: Clarendon Press, 1952), p. 326. Consider also the case of Obadiah the Norman at the end of the eleventh century: see S. D. Goitein, "Obadyah, a Norman Proselyte," *Journal of Jewish Studies* 4 (1953): 74–84; Norman Golb, "Obadiah the Proselyte: Scribe of a Unique Twelfth-Century Hebrew Manuscript Containing Lombardic Neumes," *Journal of Religion* 45 (1965): 153–56; and Joshua Prawer, "The Autobiography of Obadyah the Norman, a Convert to Judaism in the First Crusade," in *Studies in Medieval Jewish History and Literature*, ed. Isidore Twersky (Cambridge, Mass.: Harvard Univer-

sity Press, 1979), pp. 110–134. On other medieval conversions to Judaism, see Stow, *Alienated Minority*, pp. 58–59.

111. Text in Grayzel, *The Church and the Jews*, 2:103; see also Grayzel, 2:247–48.

112. See Moore, *Persecuting Society*, pp. 33, 45.

113. Grayzel, *The Church and the Jews*, 2:186–87.

114. For the prohibition against intermingling, see Grayzel, *The Church and the Jews*, 2:162; for the wedding, see Grayzel, 2:161–62; Douie, *Archbishop Pecham*, p. 327.

115. Grayzel, *The Church and the Jews*, 2:190; on the tension and psychological stress resulting from these policies, see Langmuir, *History, Religion and Anti-Semitism*, p. 260.

116. For his early life, see Douie, *Archbishop Pecham*, pp. 3–10.

117. Douie, *Archbishop Pecham*, p. 326.

118. Douie, *Archbishop Pecham*, p. 43.

119. Grayzel, *The Church and the Jews*, 2:161.

120. Grayzel, *The Church and the Jews*, 2.191; Douie, *Archbishop Pecham*, pp. 52, 328.

121. For both instances, see Douie, *Archbishop Pecham*, p. 324.

122. Douie, *Archbishop Pecham*, p. 325.

123. Douie, *Archbishop Pecham*, p. 326.

124. Grayzel, *The Church and the Jews*, 2:257–58.

125. "periculosus morbus"; Douie, *Archbishop Pecham*, p. 160; Grayzel, *The Church and the Jews*, 2:158–160.

126. Douie, *Archbishop Pecham*, pp. 327–29.

127. Douie, *Archbishop Pecham*, p. 12.

128. *Philomena, Proemium*, stanza 15; text in *Analecta hymnica*, 50:602–10.

129. See G. G. Willis, *Further Essays in Early Roman Liturgy*, Alcuin Club Collections 50 (London: SPCK, 1968), p. 82; for an example, see *Missale Gallicanum Vetus*, ed. Leo C. Mohlberg, Rerum Ecclesiasticarum Documenta, Series Maior, Fontes 3 (Rome: Herder, 1958), p. 29: "oremus et pro perfidis Iudaeis, ut deus . . ."

130. PL 207:870; Grayzel, *The Church and the Jews*, 1:92.

131. Grayzel, *The Church and the Jews*, 1:250.

132. Grayzel, *The Church and the Jews*, 2:99.

133. Grayzel, 2:158, 161.

134. On the meaning of perfidy in papal bulls, and in Middle Ages generally, see Grayzel, *The Church and the Jews*, 1:92

135. Poliakov, *The History of Anti-Semitism*, pp. 99–100; Stow, *Alienated Minority*, pp. 233–34.

136. Poliakov, *The History of Anti-Semitism*, p. 115. On the expulsions from France, see Stow, pp. 295–97, and William C. Jordan, *The French Monarchy and the Jews: From Philip Augustus to the Last Capetians* (Philadelphia: University of Pennsylvania Press, 1989).

137. Poliakov, *The History of Anti-Semitism*, pp. 102–4.

138. Poliakov, *The History of Anti-Semitism*, pp. 100, 107. For the alleged alli-

ance of Jews and lepers, see Stow, *Alienated Minority*, p. 296; Jeffrey Richards, *Sex, Dissidence, and Damnation: Minority Groups in the Middle Ages* (London: Routledge, 1991), pp. 20–21.

139. Knowles, *Christian Monasticism* (New York: McGraw Hill, 1969), p. 123.

140. See Mary Immaculate Bodenstedt, *The Vita Christi of Ludolphus the Carthusian*, Studies in Medieval and Renaissance Latin Language and Literature 16 (Washington, D. C.: Catholic University of America Press, 1944), pp. 3–4.

141. Bodenstedt, *The Vita Christi*, pp. 1–3; on his involvement in controversy, see Francis Rapp, *Réformes et réformation à Strasbourg: Eglise et société dans la diocèse de Strasbourg 1450–1525* (Paris: Ophrys, [1974]), p. 113; L. Pfleger, "Ludolf von Sachsen über die kirchlichen Zustände im 14. Jht.," *Historisches Jahrbuch* (1908): 96–99.

142. Poliakov, *The History of Anti-Semitism*, pp. 114–15; p. 107.

143. Poliakov, *The History of Anti-Semitism*, pp. 109–13 (quotation at p. 111); see also Trachtenberg, *The Devil and the Jews*, pp. 101–04.

144. On the connection between the body of Christ and the plague, see Stow, *Alienated Majority*, p. 239; and see above, n. 25.

145. Bodenstedt, *The Vita Christi*, pp. 5–8.

146. Bodenstedt, *The Vita Christi*, p. 17.

147. Ludolphus of Saxony, *Vita Christi*, ed. L. M. Rigollot, 1:522.

148. Rigollot, *Vita Christi*, 2:483; Ludolphus, however, does not neglect the general tropological application of this and other passages: e.g. those who receive the sacrament unworthily are like Judas (Rigollot, 2:483); according to Bede, all false Christians colaphize Christ (Rigollot, 2:504); according to Jerome, they spit in the face of Christ who pollute their conscience with foul thoughts and deeds (Rigollot, 2:502).

149. Rigollot, *Vita Christi*, 2:506.

150. Rigollot, *Vita Christi*, 2:506–7.

151. Rigollot, *Vita Christi*, 2:502.

152. For the alliance of Jews and lepers in a plot to poison wells, see Stow, *Alienated Minority*, p. 296.

153. Rigollot, *Vita Christi*, 2:502.

154. The story is not found in Exodus 32; for the history of the typology, see Marrow, *Passion Iconography*, pp. 132–34. Marrow points out that the typological association with Christ dates only from the fourteenth century.

155. See Peter Comestor, *Historia scholastica* (PL 198:1189–90), who reports the episode without typological elaboration; no trace of the legend is found in Bede, *Commentarii in Pentateuchum* (PL 91:130), or the *Glossa ordinaria* (PL 113: 286–88).

156. See *The Mirour of Mans Saluacioun: A Middle English Translation of Speculum Humanae Salvationis*, ed. Avril Henry (Philadelphia: University of Pennsylvania Press, 1987), pp. 114, 117; *Der Passionstraktat des Heinrich von St. Gallen*, ed. Kurt Ruh (Thayngen: Augustin, 1940), p. 57; and see Marrow, *Passion Iconography*, pp. 307–9.

157. See Marrow, *Passion Iconography*, pp. 132–34; also seemingly indebted to this typology is the spitting contest in the late medieval Arras Passion play: the contestants strive to see who can cover Christ with the most and foulest excretions;

see Rainer Warning, "On the Alterity of Medieval Religious Drama," *New Literary History* 10 (1979): 278–80 (I owe this reference to Lawrence Clopper).

158. Poliakov, *The History of Anti-Semitism*, pp. 105–6; on the fear of poisoning by Jewish physicians, see Trachtenberg, *The Devil and the Jews*, pp. 97–101; also related to the fear of poisoning is the increased late-medieval fear of the Jew as sorcerer; see Trachtenberg, pp. 196–206.

159. Poliakov, *The History of Anti-Semitism*, p. 105.

160. Poliakov, *The History of Anti-Semitism*, p. 105; Ruh, *Passionstraktat*, p. 57.

161. In the visual arts, the most violent and graphic late medieval portrayals of the Passion seem also to come from Germanic areas. For a contrasting, and more positive, interpretation of the preoccupation with physicality, see Caroline Bynum's analysis of somatic piety in *Holy Feast and Holy Fast*, pp. 244–76.

162. For these examples, see Poliakov, *The History of Anti-Semitism*, pp. 121, 135.

163. The crudeness of the semiology, but without the malevolence, was sometimes applied to Christ as well; F. P. Pickering cites Dürer's use of Lam 3:16, "he has broken my teeth one by one," as the basis for his gruesome depiction of Christ's teeth being broken out before the crucifixion; *Literature and Art in the Middle Ages* (London: Macmillan, 1970), p. 282.

164. Langmuir, *History, Religion and Antisemitism*, p. 368.

Chapter 4

1. See Sandro Sticca, *The Planctus Mariae in the Dramatic Tradition of the Middle Ages* (Athens: University of Georgia Press, 1988), pp. 19–30; Marina Warner, *Alone of All Her Sex: The Myth and Cult of the Virgin Mary* (London: Weidenfeld and Nicolson, 1976), pp. 206–23.

2. See Victor Saxer, *La culte de la Marie Madeleine en Occident: des origines à la fin du moyen âge* (Auxerre: Publications de la Société des Fouilles Archéologiques et des Monuments Historiques de l'Yonne, 1959); Benedicta Ward, *Harlots of the Desert: A Study of Repentance in Early Monastic Sources*, Cistercian Studies 106 (Kalamazoo, Mich.: Cistercian Publications, 1987), pp. 12–25 (for the visit to Marseilles, see p. 17).

3. The classic statement of this view is in Abelard, Letter 6, available in *Woman Defamed and Woman Defended: An Anthology of Medieval Texts*, ed. Alcuin Blamires (Oxford: Clarendon Press, 1992), pp. 233–34; there were other traditions, however: for Ambrose's negative assessment of her role in announcing the Passion, see Blamires, pp. 61–63; and for Magdalene as the type of the penitent whore, see Warner, pp. 224–35.

4. Sticca, *Planctus*, p. 33.

5. Sticca, *Planctus*, p. 20; and see the discussion of the stoic Virgin in Karma Lochrie, *Margery Kempe and Translations of the Flesh* (Philadelphia: University of Pennsylvania Press, 1991), p. 178–79.

6. Sticca, *Planctus*, p. 20 (on Richard and Alan); Stephen of Sawley, *Trea-*

tises, Cistercian Fathers Series 36, ed. Bede K. Lackner, trans. Jeremiah O'Sullivan (Kalamazoo, Mich.: Cistercian Publications, 1984), pp. 48–50.

7. Sticca, *Planctus*, pp. 31–40.

8. Sticca, *Planctus*, pp. 118–69 (for the dramatic tradition); Erwin Panofsky, "Imago Pietatis," in *Festschrift für Max J. Friedlander zum 60. Geburtstage* (Leipzig: Seeman, 1927), pp. 262–308; F. O. Büttner, *Imitatio pietatis: Motive der christlichen Ikonographie als Modelle zur Verähnlichung* (Berlin: Mann, 1983); Hans Belting, *The Image and Its Public in the Middle Ages: Form and Function of Early Paintings of the Passion*, trans. Mark Bartusis and Raymond Meyer (New Rochelle, N.Y.: Caratzas, 1990).

9. Sticca, *Planctus*, pp. 19–30; Warner, *Alone of All Her Sex*, pp. 220–21.

10. See Warner, *Alone of All Her Sex*, pp. 134–74; Etienne Gilson denies any connection between love of women and Cistercian longing; see Colin Morris, *The Discovery of the Individual, 1050-1200* (London: SPCK, 1972), p. 119.

11. The eroticism of the Marian laments is pointed out by Charles Witke in his review of Sticca, *The Planctus Mariae*, in *Medievalia et Humanistica* n.s. 17 (1991): 169; see also Michael Camille, *The Gothic Idol: Ideology and Image-Making in Medieval Art* (Cambridge: Cambridge University Press, 1989), pp. 220–41.

12. R. Howard Bloch, *Medieval Misogyny and the Invention of Western Romantic Love* (Chicago: University of Chicago Press, 1991), pp. 165–97; Penny Schine Gold, *The Lady and the Virgin: Image, Attitude, and Experience in Twelfth-Century France* (Chicago: University of Chicago Press, 1985), pp. 116–44.

13. The classic summary of this outlook (without, to be sure, any sign of naive optimism or faith in progress) is found in R. W. Southern, *The Making of the Middle Ages* (New Haven, Conn.: Yale University Press, 1953), pp. 222–28.

14. Caroline Bynum, *Fragmentation and Redemption: Essays on Gender and the Human Body in Medieval Religion* (New York: Zone Books, 1991), p. 151.

15. See Bloch, *Medieval Misogyny*, pp. 3–8, 89–90; quotation at p. 90. Michael Camille has made a similar argument about the idealization of women in the visual arts. The procedure of "placing woman on a pedestal" in the courtly tradition has the effect of turning woman into an idol, marginalizing her, and thereby isolating her from an active role in society. See *The Gothic Idol*, pp. 308–37.

16. Warner, *Alone of All Her Sex*, p. 153.

17. Warner, *Alone of All Her Sex*, p. 191.

18. Elizabeth Robertson, *Early English Devotional Prose and the Female Audience*, (Knoxville: University of Tennessee Press, 1990), pp. 3, 44, 74.

19. Robertson, *Early English Devotional Prose*, p. 3; and esp. p. 148.

20. Karma Lochrie, "The Language of Transgression: Body, Flesh, and Word in Mystical Discourse," in *Speaking Two Languages: Traditional Disciplines and Contemporary Theory in Medieval Studies*, ed. Allen J. Frantzen (Albany: State University of New York Press, 1991), pp. 115–40.

21. Theresa Coletti, "Purity and Danger: The Paradox of Mary's Body and the En-gendering of the Infancy Narrative in the English Mystery Cycles," in *Feminist Approaches to the Body in Medieval Literature*, ed. Linda Lomperis and Sarah Stanbury (Philadelphia: University of Pennsylvania Press, 1993), pp. 65–95; quotation at p. 66.

22. Anne Clark Bartlett, *Male Authors, Female Readers: Representation and*

Subjectivity in Middle English Devotional Literature (Ithaca, N.Y.: Cornell University Press, 1995), esp. pp. 2–3.

23. Hans Robert Jauss, *Toward an Aesthetic of Reception*, trans. Timothy Bahti (Minneapolis: University of Minnesota Press, 1982), pp. 14–15.

24. Jauss, *Toward an Aesthetic of Reception*, pp. 74–75.

25. Jauss, *Toward an Aesthetic of Reception*, pp. 3–45.

26. Margaret Miles, *Image as Insight: Visual Understanding in Western Christianity and Secular Culture* (Boston: Beacon Press, 1985), p. 93.

27. For a discussion of the useful concepts of "immasculation" and of "regendering," see Carolyn Dinshaw, *Chaucer's Sexual Poetics* (Madison: University of Wisconsin Press, 1989), pp. 54, 64–67; Bartlett, *Male Authors, Female Readers*, p. 2 n. 4.

28. Jauss's theorizing of the horizon of expectations is the best refutation of such notions; see *Toward an Aesthetic of Reception*, pp. 22–32.

29. Derek Pearsall, *The Canterbury Tales* (London: Allen and Unwin, 1985), p. 43.

30. Jauss, *Toward an Aesthetic of Reception*, p. 147.

31. Caroline Bynum, *Jesus as Mother: Studies in the Spirituality of the High Middle Ages* (Berkeley: University of California Press, 1982), pp. 140–41.

32. Bynum, *Jesus as Mother*, p. 162.

33. The terms are from the title and chapter headings of Colin Morris's influential study, *The Discovery of the Individual, 1050–1200*; see chapter 4, "The Search for Self." On individuality, see above, chapter 2, note 35 and the references given there.

34. Lee Patterson, *Chaucer and the Subject of History* (Madison: University of Wisconsin Press, 1991), pp. 1–12. The male interest in female psychology, of course, extends beyond devotional literature, and may be seen, for example, in the romances of Chrétien de Troyes and Gottfried von Strassburg and in the writings of Chaucer, notably his Wife of Bath.

35. Elaine Tuttle Hansen, "The Powers of Silence: The Case of the Clerk's Griselda," in *Women and Power in the Middle Ages*, ed. Mary Erler and Maryanne Kowaleski (Athens: University of Georgia Press, 1988), pp. 230–49, esp. p. 245.

36. Dinshaw, *Chaucer's Sexual Poetics*, pp. 193, 2. She has in mind Donald Howard's assessment of Chaucer as having an "androgynous personality" that allowed him to see the world from women's point of view; see Howard, *Chaucer: His Life, His Works, His World* (New York: Dutton, 1987), p. 97.

37. Dinshaw, *Chaucer's Sexual Poetics*, p. 193.

38. Anselm, *Oratio 2*; *Anselmi Opera omnia*, ed. F. S. Schmitt, 6 vols. (1938–61; rpt. Stuttgart: Friedrich Fromann, 1968), 3:8; *The Prayers and Meditations of Saint Anselm*, trans. Benedicta Ward (Harmondsworth: Penguin, 1973), p. 96.

39. Bonaventure, *Lignum vitae*, 28; *Bonaventurae Opera omnia*, ed. PP. Collegii S. Bonaventurae, 11 vols. (Quaracchi: Collegium S. Bonaventurae, 1882–1902), 8:78; *The Works of Bonaventure I: Mystical Opuscula*, trans. José de Vinck (Paterson, N. J.: St. Anthony Guild Press, 1960), p. 125.

40. Hans Belting, *The Image and Its Public in the Middle Ages: Form and Function of Early Paintings of the Passion*, p. 165 (basing his remarks on Theo Meier's opinion of the revelations of Bridget of Sweden).

41. *Bonaventurae Opera Omnia*, ed. A. C. Peltier, 15 vols. (Paris: Vives, 1864–

71), 12:606; *Meditations on the Life of Christ: An Illustrated Manuscript of the Four-teenth Century*, trans. Isa Ragusa and Rosalie B. Green (Princeton, N.J.: Princeton University Press, 1961), p. 335.

42. Julia Kristeva, *Powers of Horror: An Essay on Abjection*, trans. Leon S. Roudiez (New York: Columbia University Press, 1982), p. 46; her discussion of voyeurism is complex and should be consulted; it lies behind my understanding of the peculiar way that the suffering of Mary is constituted in the Passion narratives.

43. Kristeva, *Powers of Horror*, p. 22.

44. For a full and indispensable discussion of these matters, see A. C. Spear-ing, *The Medieval Poet as Voyeur: Looking and Listening in Medieval Love Narratives* (Cambridge: Cambridge University Press, 1993); and Sarah Stanbury, "The Voyeur and Private Life in *Troilus and Criseyde*," *Studies in the Age of Chaucer* 13 (1991): 141–58; Stanbury cites the work of Lacan on the gaze, the scholarship on the male gaze in modern cinema studies, and refers to Georges Duby on the power implications of the loss of privacy attendant on voyeurism. She also alludes to the anthropologi-cal function of "the stare" as a means of control or aggression in certain cultures; see Michel Foucault, *Discipline and Punish: The Birth of the Prison*, trans. Alan Sheri-dan (New York: Vintage, 1979), pp. 170–228.

45. Peltier, 12:605; trans. Ragusa and Green, p. 332.

46. Peltier, 12:605; trans. Ragusa and Green, p. 333.

47. Peltier, 12:608; trans. Ragusa and Green, p. 339.

48. These characteristics are shared by other male representations of victim-ized women, including many saints' lives; cf. Margaret Miles's claim that in some fourteenth-century iconographical and narrative representations, "The Virgin is not merely the passive, receptive, visible woman. She is also a powerful woman." *Image and Insight*, p. 89.

49. I quote the text in *The Oxford Book of Medieval Latin Verse*, ed. F. J. E. Raby (Oxford: Clarendon Press, 1959), p. 435.

50. Bonaventure, *Lignum vitae*, 28; *Opera omnia*, 8:79; de Vinck, p. 126.

51. On the feminized body of Christ see Caroline Bynum, *Holy Feast and Holy Fast: The Religious Significance of Food to Medieval Women* (Berkeley: University of California Press, 1987), pp. 260–69; and Bynum, *Fragmentation and Redemption*, pp. 79–117, 151–79.

52. Peltier, 12:607; trans. Ragusa and Green, p. 337.

53. *The Book of the City of Ladies*, trans. Earl Jeffrey Richards (New York: Persea Books, 1982), p. 28 (1.10.5). Chaucer's Tale of Melibee also asserts that Christ's appearance to Magdalene was a sign of his esteem for women: *Canterbury Tales*, VII.1075. On women's speech, see the useful discussion in Patricia Parker, *Literary Fat Ladies: Rhetoric, Gender, Property* (London: Methuen, 1987), pp. 8–35.

54. PL 94:568.

55. PL 159:271–90; see col. 280 for an example of this technique.

56. PL 159:287.

57. Belting, *The Image and Its Public*, pp. 157–58.

58. See Bloch, *Medieval Misogyny*, pp. 143–64; Peter Dronke, *Women Writers of the Middle Ages* (Cambridge: Cambridge University Press, 1984), pp. 84–106.

59. London, British Library, MS. Cotton Vespasian E.i, fol. 196v; see also

fol. 197r: "Currite filie, currite virgines sacre, currite matres Christo castitatem vouentes" ("Run, daughters; run, holy virgins; run, you mothers pledged in chastity to Christ"). Since the editions of the "Quis dabit" lament are incomplete or difficult to access and based upon late manuscript traditions, I quote from a fuller version of the text in the fourteenth-century English MS. cited above, which is edited and translated in Appendix 1 of this book. But see now the edition of C. W. Marx, "The *Quis dabit* of Oglerius de Tridino, Monk and Abbott of Locedio," *Journal of Medieval Latin* 4 (1994): 118–29. The Vespasian version has additions which heighten the emotionalism of the narrative edited by Marx from an earlier manuscript.

60. Cotton Vespasian E.i, fol. 197v.

61. Cotton Vespasian E.i, fols. 198v–199r.

62. Bonaventure, *De perfectione vitae*, 6.2; *Opera omnia*, 8:120; trans. de Vinck, pp. 239–40.

63. On the transgressive behavior of medieval holy women, see Bynum, *Holy Feast and Holy Fast*, pp. 113–86; and Richard Kieckhefer, *Unquiet Souls: Fourteenth-Century Saints and Their Religious Milieu* (Chicago: University of Chicago Press, 1984), pp. 21–33. My understanding of Mary's disorderly behavior and its social significance has been influenced by the classic essay of Natalie Zemon Davis, "The Reasons of Misrule," which builds on Bakhtin's notions of carnival, in her *Society and Culture in Early Modern France: Eight Essays* (Stanford, Calif.: Stanford University Press, 1975), pp. 97–123; also relevant is the essay, "Women on Top," pp. 124–51.

64. Cotton Vespasian E.i, fol. 199v.

65. Cotton Vespasian E.i, fol. 200r.

66. Cotton Vespasian E.i, fol. 200r-200v.

67. Cotton Vespasian E.i, fol. 201v.

68. Cotton Vespasian E.i, fol. 201v.

69. Davis, *Society and Culture*, pp. 142–43, 151. For the possibility of diverse responses to representations of the Virgin, see also the points made by Margaret Miles, cited above, notes 26 and 48.

70. On Bakhtin, see Davis, *Society and Culture*, p. 103.

71. Luce Irigaray has analyzed the erotic and sexual elements of the crucifixion scene, emphasizing the transsexual union between the woman and her son, "that most female of men," whom she enters by way of "that glorious slit," the wound in his side, bathing in the blood "that flows over her, hot and purifying." Irigaray, *Speculum of the Other Woman*, trans. Gillian C. Gill (Ithaca, N.Y.: Cornell University Press, 1985), pp. 199–200.

72. Cotton Vespasian E.i, fol. 198v.

73. Cotton Vespasian E.i, fol. 199r.

74. Cotton Vespasian E.i, fol. 199v.

75. Cotton Vespasian E.i, fol. 200r.

76. Cotton Vespasian E.i, fol. 200v.

77. Cotton Vespasian E.i, fol. 200v.

78. *Medieval Women's Visionary Literature*, ed. Elizabeth Petroff (New York: Oxford University Press, 1986), p. 182.

79. Petroff, *Medieval Women's Visionary Literature*, p. 196.

80. Petroff, *Medieval Women's Visionary Literature*, p. 225.

81. Petroff, *Medieval Women's Visionary Literature*, p. 257.

82. *The Book of Margery Kempe*, ed. Sanford Meech and Hope Emily Allen, EETS OS 212 (London: Oxford University Press, 1940), p. 208 (ch. 85); trans. B. A. Windeatt (Harmondsworth: Penguin, 1985), p. 249.

83. On the infantilization of Christ's body in the *Book of Margery Kempe*, see David Aers, *Community, Gender, and Individual Identity: English Writing 1360–1430* (London: Routledge, 1988), pp. 104–08; see also Leah Sinanoglou, "The Christ Child as Sacrifice: A Medieval Tradition and the Corpus Christi Plays," *Speculum* 48 (1973): 491–509.

84. Bynum, *Jesus as Mother*, pp. 247–62; the quoted phrases are at p. 262.

85. See Bloch, *Medieval Misogyny*, pp. 165–97; Gold, *The Lady and the Virgin*, pp. 116–44; Brigitte Bedos Rezak, "Women, Seals, and Power in Medieval France, 1150–1350," in *Women and Power in the Middle Ages*, pp. 61–82, esp. pp. 73–75.

86. Christine de Pisan, *The Treasure of the City of Ladies*, trans. Sarah Lawson (Harmondsworth: Penguin, 1985), p. 82.

87. Christine, *Treasure*, pp. 156–57.

88. Christine, *Treasure*, Introduction, p. 18.

89. *Dialogus beatae Mariae et Anselmi de Passione Christi*, PL 159:286–88; *Meditationes vitae Christi*, chs. 82–83, in Bonaventura, *Opera omnia*, ed. A. C. Peltier (Paris: Vives, 1864–71), 12:609–10; trans. Ragusa and Green, pp. 342–45; Ludolphus, *Vita Christi*, 2.65, ed. L. M. Rigollot (Paris, 1870), 2:621–23.

90. See F. J. Tanquerey, *Plaintes de la Vierge en Anglo-Français (xiiie et xive siècles)* (Paris: Champion, 1921); A. Chiari, "Il 'Planctus B. Mariae' operetta falsamente attribuita a San Bernardo," *Rivista Storica Benedettina* 17 (1926): 56–111; Rosemary Woolf, *The English Religious Lyric in the Middle Ages* (Oxford: Clarendon Press, 1968), pp. 247–48; for the numerous early printed editions, see above, chapter 2, note 127.

91. See *The Book of Margery Kempe*, ed. Meech and Allen, pp. 187–97 (ch. 79–81); trans. Windeatt, pp. 228–35.

92. *The Book of Margery Kempe*, ed. Meech and Allen, p. 194 (ch. 80); trans. Windeatt, pp. 234–35.

93. *The Book of Margery Kempe*, Meech and Allen, p. 194; trans. Windeatt, p. 235. Compare the language of the *Meditationes vitae Christi*, 82 [Peltier, 12:609]: "Ad hanc vocem tanquam grata et discreta, cogitans quod ipsi Joanni commissa est per filium, noluit amplius contendere, et benedicens eum, permisit aptari et involvi" ("At these words, as she was grateful and discreet, and remembering that she was committed to John by the Son, she resisted no longer, but blessed Him and permitted Him to be prepared and shrouded," trans. Ragusa and Green, p. 343).

94. PL 94:568; the passage is quoted above, note 66.

95. PL 94:568.

96. PL 94:562.

97. PL 94:568.

98. Ludolphus, *Vita Christi*, 2.65; Rigollat, 2:623.

99. Marguerite Porete, *The Mirror of Simple Souls*, trans. Gwendolyn Bryant,

in *Medieval Women Writers*, ed. Katharina M. Wilson (Athens: University of Georgia Press, 1984), p. 223.

100. But see Karma Lochrie's analysis of the male valorization of the emotional language of devotion in her account of the fifteenth-century Carthusian Richard Methley, *Margery Kempe*, pp. 212–20.

Chapter 5

1. *Christi Leiden in einer Vision Geschaut*, ed. F. P. Pickering (Manchester: Manchester University Press, 1952), pp. 74–75:

Ouwe, do gienck it an die noit. Sy namen dat krutze vnd wurffen it van syme rucke vnd zoegen dem got vereynigen menschen sin gewant vss, Vnd namen in mit dem haire vnd wurffen in vff dat cruce, he mochte aller zo sprungen hauen, Vnd zoegen eme synen verwonten vnd zurmurtin rucke ouer die knorren des cruces, dat die stumpe van dem hultze die wunden van eyn ander ryssen. Sy sprungen auch mit wilder doeunder vnzuchte mit iren vnreynen voissen vff den doit versierden lyff Christi, sy kneden eme vff syne bruste vnd zo dienden eme syne armen van eyn ander so sy allermeiste mochten. Sy namen eme die rechte hant vnd zoegen sy eme zo dem loche des astes vnd sloegen eme eynen nagel dar durch. Der nagel was stumpetich vnd drieckig, Vnd die ecken waren scharpe als eyn messer, vnd vurten eme die huyt in der hant vnd etzwie vil des vleissches durch dat loch des cruces, vnd sloegen den naile so vaste, dat der knouff des nagils in der hant geflecht stunt, Vnd vulte die wonde so vol, dat eyn bloitz troppe neit dar vs in mochte. Do namen sy do die ander hant vnd zoegen sy eme ouer des cruces aste. Do was die hant so verre van dem loche, dat sy is neit in mochten erlangen. Do namen sy seil vnd daden eme eynen strick an die hant vnd zoegen in so vaste, dat die aderen vnd geleder vss eyn ander giengen, dat die hant gereichte dat loch. Vnd sloegen auch dar durch eynen nagel als vur, dat eyn eynich troppen bloitz neit dar vss in mochte gaen. Vnd giengen do vff eme hyn zo den voissen vnd streckten eme die voisse vff dem boume des cruces. Do gebrach in dat syne voisse neit in mochten gelangen zo dem loche etzwie manche spanne eyns mans.

Do namen sy seile vnd machten eme stricke an beyde syne voisse, Vnd zoegen in so vaste vnd dienden in so sere , dat nye keyne seite so sere ader so veste vff eyn breit wart gedenet, bis dat sy gereichten dat loch. Vnd traden eme do vff die beyne vnd satten eme do die voisse vff eyn ander. Vnd ee dat der vnder vois durch slagen wurde, do was der ouerste vois van eyn ander gesplissen, vnd sloegen auch den nail so vaste, dat der knouff in dem voisse gevloicht stunt. Sy duchten synre noit neit genoich, Vnd namen eynen anderen nagel, der was groisser vnd langer dan der andere eyniger: den satzten sy eme vff dat geruste des vois, vff die dickte by dem beyne, vnd sloegen so grymmelichen vff den nagel mit alle ire crafte, dat dem nagel wurden zwey vnd XXX starcker hamer slege, Vnd wurden die wunden des nagels also grois, dat eyn eynich troppe bloitz dar vss neit in mochte. Vnd hüeuen do dat cruce vff vnd staichen it in eynen steyn, den hatten sy dar zo gehoilt. Der steyn was hohe van der erden vil na eyme manne bis an synen gurtel.

For assistance with the English translation, I am greatly indebted to my colleague, James A. Schultz.

2. James H. Marrow, *Passion Iconography in Northern European Art of the Late Middle Ages and Early Renaissance: A Study of the Transformation of Sacred Metaphor into Descriptive Narrative*, Ars Neerlandica 1 (Kortrijk: Van Ghemmert, 1979), esp. pp. 207–22.

3. Text from *Yorkshire Writers: Richard Rolle of Hampole, An English Father of the Church and His Followers*, ed. C. Horstman, 2 vols. (London: Swan Sonnenschein, 1895–96) 1:100.

4. Elaine Scarry, *The Body in Pain: The Making and Unmaking of the World* (New York: Oxford University Press, 1985), p. 3.

5. Scarry, *The Body in Pain*, p. 4.

6. Scarry, *The Body in Pain*, p. 4.

7. Scarry, *The Body in Pain*, p. 5.

8. Scarry, *The Body in Pain*, p. 6.

9. F. P. Pickering, *Literature and Art in the Middle Ages* (London: Macmillan, 1970); Pickering's work has been built upon by James Marrow; see *Passion Iconography*, passim.

10. Bernard, *Sermon on the Song of Songs* 43; in *Bernard of Clairvaux: On the Song of Songs II*, trans. Kilian Walsh (Kalamazoo, Mich.: Cistercian Publications, 1976), pp. 220–24.

11. Pickering, *Literature and Art*, p. 282 (the verse is the basis for Dürer's woodcut of the subject).

12. Owst is quoted by Mary Felicitas Madigan, *The Passio Domini Theme in the Works of Richard Rolle: His Personal Contribution in its Religious, Cultural, and Literary Context*, Elizabethan and Renaissance Studies 79 (Salzburg: Institut für Englische Sprache und Literatur, 1978), p. 45.

13. J. A. W. Bennett, *Poetry of the Passion* (Oxford: Clarendon Press, 1982), pp. 57, 59, 60.

14. Scarry, *The Body in Pain*, pp. 4–6.

15. For newer approaches emphasizing the importance of the body in medieval culture, see the works cited in chapter 1, note 82.

16. The Passion is treated in Anselm's Prayer to Christ (*Oratio* 2); the prayer was certainly written by 1104. See *The Prayers and Meditations of St. Anselm*, trans. Benedicta Ward (Harmondsworth: Penguin, 1973), pp. 60, 93–99.

17. Eusebius, *The History of the Church*, 14.8–15.9; trans. G. A. Williamson (Harmondsworth: Penguin, 1967), pp. 168–69.

18. Caroline Bynum, following earlier scholars, calls attention to the "archaizing" tendencies of late medieval collections of saints' lives, including the *Legenda aurea*, and remarks on the late medieval interest in the details of torture and mutilation; see *The Resurrection of the Body in Western Christianity, 200–1336* (New York: Columbia University Press, 1995), pp. 309, 327–28.

19. Peter Brown, *The Body and Society: Men, Women and Sexual Renunciation in Early Christianity* (New York: Columbia University Press, 1988), p. 441.

20. Bynum, *The Resurrection of the Body*, p. 309.

21. PL 40:906.

22. *Lignum vitae*, 2.26; in *Bonaventurae Opera omnia*, ed. PP. Collegii S. Bonaventurae (Quaracchi: Collegium S. Bonaventurae, 1882–1902), 8:78; *The Works of Bonaventure . . . I Mystical Opuscula*, trans. José de Vinck (Paterson, N.J.: St. Anthony Guild Press, 1960), p. 123.

23. *Lignum vitae*, 2.29; *Opera omnia*, 8:79; de Vinck, p. 127.

24. *Vitis mystica*, 5.7 *Opera omnia*, 8:171; de Vinck, pp. 167–68.

25. See Bynum, *The Resurrection of the Body*, pp. 229–78.

26. A notable example is in Bridget of Sweden, *Revelations*, 7.15.18–23:

"Then too, his fine and lovely eyes appeared half dead; his mouth was open and bloody; his face was pale and sunken, all livid and stained with blood; and his whole body was as if black and blue and pale and very weak from the constant downward flow of blood. Indeed, his skin and the virginal flesh of his most holy body were so delicate and tender that, after the infliction of a slight blow, a black and blue mark appeared on the surface. At times however, he tried to make stretching motions on the cross because of the exceeding bitterness of the intense and most acute pain that he felt. For at times the pain from his pierced limbs and veins ascended to his heart and battered him cruelly with an intense martyrdom; and thus his death was prolonged and delayed amidst grave torment and great bitterness. Then, therefore, in distress from the exceeding anguish of his pain and already near to death, he cried to the Father in a loud and tearful voice, saying: 'O Father, why have you forsaken me?' He then had pale lips, a bloody tongue, and a sunken abdomen that adhered to his back as if he had no viscera within." (translation from *Birgitta of Sweden: Life and Selected Revelations*, trans. Albert Ryle Kezel, Classics of Western Spirituality [New York: Paulist Press, 1990], p. 189)

27. Bynum, *The Resurrection of the Body*, p. 314 n. 129.

28. Bonaventure, *Vitis mystica*, 24.3–4 (de Vinck, pp. 204–5).

29. Bennett, *Poetry of the Passion*, p. 60.

30. Bennett, *Poetry of the Passion*, p. 61.

31. Caroline Bynum, *Holy Feast and Holy Fast: The Religious Significance of Food to Medieval Women* (Berkeley: University of California Press, 1987), p. 246.

32. Douglas Gray, *Themes and Images in the Medieval English Religious Lyric* (London: Routledge, 1972), p. 28.

33. John H. Langbein, *Torture and the Law of Proof: Europe and England in the Ancien Régime* (Chicago: University of Chicago Press, 1977), pp. 4–8 (quotation at p. 6). For a succinct general account, see Stephan Kuttner, "The Revival of Jurisprudence" in *Renaissance and Renewal in the Twelfth Century*, ed. Robert L. Benson and Giles Constable (Cambridge, Mass.: Harvard University Press, 1982), pp. 299–323.

34. Edward Peters, *Torture* (New York: Basil Blackwell, 1985, rpt. Philadel-

phia: University of Pennsylvania Press, 1996), pp. 48–52. For an excellent guide to earlier scholarship on judicial torture, see the bibliographical essay in Peters, *Torture*, pp. 188–99.

35. Peters, *Torture*, p. 52.

36. Peters, *Torture*, p. 45.

37. Peters, *Torture*, p. 65.

38. Peters, *Torture*, p. 60.

39. Peters, *Torture*, pp. 55, 58.

40. Peters, *Torture*, p. 68. For the commonplace, see Thomas H. Bestul, "Chaucer's Parson's Tale and the Late-Medieval Tradition of Religious Meditation," *Speculum* 64 (1989): 600–619.

41. See Bestul, "Chaucer's Parson's Tale," pp. 608–9, and references cited there; cf Bonaventure, *Lignum vitae*, 2.31; *Opera omnia*, 8:80; de Vinck, p. 129; and *Vitis mystica*, 2.4; *Opera omnia*, 8:161; de Vinck, p. 150.

42. Peters, *Torture*, p. 68.

43. *Meditationes vitae Christi*, 75; in *Bonaventurae Opera omnia*, ed. A. C. Peltier (Paris: Vives, 1864–71), 12:602; *Meditations on the Life of Christ: An Illustrated Manuscript of the Fourteenth Century*, trans. Isa Ragusa and Rosalie B. Green (Princeton, N.J.: Princeton University Press, 1961), p. 326; see also *Christi Leiden in einer Vision Geschaut*, p. 67; Ludolphus of Saxony, *Vita Christi*, 2.60; ed. L. M. Rigollot (Paris: Palme, 1870), 2:512; Richard Rolle, "Meditation B," in *Richard Rolle: Prose and Verse*, ed. S. J. Ogilvie-Thomson, EETS 293 (Oxford: Oxford University Press, 1988), p. 77.

44. *Lignum vitae*, 2.25; *Opera omnia*, 8:78; de Vinck, pp. 122–23; for a later example, see Ludolphus of Saxony, *Vita Christi*, 2.60; ed. Rigollot, 2:502.

45. R. I. Moore, *The Formation of a Persecuting Society: Power and Deviance in Western Europe, 950–1250* (Oxford: Basil Blackwell, 1987), p. 11.

46. Moore, *Persecuting Society*, pp. 47–62.

47. Michel Foucault, *Discipline and Punish: The Birth of the Prison*, trans. Alan Sheridan (New York: Vintage, 1979), pp. 7–31.

48. Bynum, *Holy Feast and Holy Fast*, pp. 144–45; Moore, *Persecuting Society*, p. 61.

49. Girard, *The Scapegoat*, trans. Yvonne Freccero (Baltimore: Johns Hopkins University Press, 1989), pp. 101–3 (quotation at p. 103).

50. Girard, *The Scapegoat*, p. 9.

51. Girard, *The Scapegoat*, p. 204.

52. Bloomfield, "The Man of Law's Tale: A Tragedy of Victimization and a Christian Comedy," *PMLA* 87 (1972): 384–90.

53. The terminology is from Bruce Lincoln, "Festivals and Massacres: Reflections on St. Bartholomew's Day," in *Discourse and the Construction of Society: Comparative Studies of Myth, Ritual, and Classification* (New York: Oxford University Press, 1989), pp. 89–102 (I owe this reference to Denise Despres); and see Natalie Zemon Davis, "The Rites of Violence," in *Society and Culture in Early Modern France: Eight Essays* (Stanford, Calif.: Stanford University Press, 1975), pp. 152–87.

54. Peters, *Torture*, p. 46.

55. See Bernard, *Sermon on the Song of Songs* 43, trans. Kilian Walsh, pp. 220–24 (see above, note 10).

56. Michel de Certeau, *Heterologies: Discourse on the Other*, trans. Brian Massumi (Minneapolis: University of Minnesota Press, 1986), pp. 35–46; quotation at p. 40.

57. Scarry, *The Body in Pain*, p. 207.

58. Julia Kristeva, *Powers of Horror: An Essay on Abjection*, trans. Leon S. Roudiez (New York: Columbia University Press, 1982), p. 3.

59. Namely *Christi Leiden in einer Vision Geschaut*; but also *Der Passionstraktat des Heinrich von St. Gallen*, ed. Kurt Ruh (Thayngen: Karl Augustin, 1940); the Passion was also treated in an exceptionally graphic manner in the visual arts of that part of Europe; see Marrow, *Passion Iconography*, passim.

60. Scarry, *The Body in Pain*, p. 215.

61. Scarry, *The Body in Pain*, p. 216.

62. Girard, *The Scapegoat*, p. 173; Kristeva, "Holbein's Dead Christ," in *Fragments for a History of the Human Body, Part One*, ed. Ramona Naddaff, Michel Feher, and Nadia Tazi (New York: Zone, 1989), pp. 243–45.

63. Kristeva, "Holbein's Dead Christ," p. 245. Gaudenio Ferrari's starkly unidealized, highly illusionistic terracotta figures of the Passion in the *Sacro Monte* of Varallo of about 1500 provide a contemporary analogue to Holbein's painting. The purpose of the figures was to popularize Franciscan Passion spirituality by promoting solitary, affective meditation; see William Hood, "The *Sacro Monte* of Varallo: Renaissance Art and Popular Religion," in *Monasticism and the Arts*, ed. Timothy Gregory Verdon (Syracuse, N.Y.: Syracuse University Press, 1984), pp. 291–311. Hood says that "the *Sacro Monte* stands in the most forward advance of sixteenth-century illusionism" (p. 305). The Passion scenes of the *Sacro Monte*, however, unlike Holbein's picture, are crowded with humanity. For illuminating commentary on the *Sacro Monte*, see also David Freedberg, *The Power of Images: Studies in the History and Theory of Response* (Chicago: University of Chicago Press, 1989), chapter 9, "Verisimilitude and Resemblance: From Sacred Mountain to Waxworks" (pp. 192–245).

64. Eamon Duffy, *The Stripping of the Altars: Traditional Religion in England c. 1400–c. 1580* (New Haven, Conn.: Yale University Press, 1992), passim.

65. Kristeva, "Holbein's Dead Christ," p. 249.

Bibliography

PRIMARY SOURCES

Aelred of Rievaulx. *Aelred of Rievaulx, De institutione inclusarum: Two English Versions*. Ed. John Ayto and Alexandra Barratt. EETS OS 287. London: Oxford University Press, 1984.

———. *Aelredi Rievallensis Opera omnia 1: Opera ascetica*. Ed. A. Hoste and C. H. Talbot. CCCM 1. Turnholt: Brepols, 1971.

———. *Sermones inediti*. Ed. C. H. Talbot. Series Scriptorum S. Ordinis Cisterciensis 1. Rome: Curia Generalis Sacri Ordinis Cisterciensis, 1952.

———. *Treatises and the Pastoral Prayer*. Trans. Theodore Berkeley, Mary Paul Macpherson, and R. Penelope Lawson. Cistercian Fathers Series 2. Kalamazoo, Mich.: Cistercian Publications, 1971.

Alexander of Ashby. *See* Bestul.

Anselm of Canterbury. *Anselmi opera omnia*. Ed. F. S. Schmitt. 6 vols. 1938–61; rpt. Stuttgart: Friedrich Fromann, 1968.

———. *The Prayers and Meditations of St. Anselm*. Trans. Benedicta Ward. Harmondsworth: Penguin, 1973.

Augustine, pseudo-. *Sermones inediti*. Ed. A. B. Caillau. Paris: Mellier, 1842.

Augustine, pseudo-; Anselm; pseudo-Bernard. *Diui Aurelii Augustini Meditationes, Soliloquia et Manuale, Meditationes B. Anselmi cum tractatu de humani generis redemptione, D. Bernardi, Idiotae, viri docti, de amore Diuino*. Ed. Henri Sommalius. Lyon: P. Rigaud, 1610.

———. *D. Aurelii Augustini Meditationes, Soliloquia et Manuale; accedunt Meditationes B. Anselmi, D. Bernardi, et Idiotae Contemplationes*. Turin: Maretti, 1929.

Becker, Gustav. *Catalogi bibliothecarum antiqui*. Bonn: Cohen, 1885.

Bennett, J. A. W. *Devotional Pieces in Verse and Prose from MS. Arundel 285 and MS. Harleian 6919*. Scottish Text Society Third Series 23. Edinburgh: William Blackwood, 1955.

Bernard of Clairvaux. *On the Song of Songs*. Trans. Kilian Walsh and Irene M. Edmonds. Cistercian Fathers Series 4, 7, 31, 40. Kalamazoo, Mich.: Cistercian Publications, 1971–1980.

———. *Sancti Bernardi Opera*. Ed. J. Leclercq, C. H. Talbot, and H. M. Rochais. 8 vols. Rome: Editiones Cistercienses, 1957–77.

Bestul, Thomas H., ed. *A Durham Book of Devotions Edited from London, Society of Antiquaries, MS. 7*. Toronto Medieval Latin Texts 18. Toronto: Pontifical Institute of Mediaeval Studies, 1987.

———. "The *Meditationes* of Alexander of Ashby: An Edition." *Mediaeval Studies* 52 (1990): 24–81.

Birch, Walter de Gray, ed. *An Ancient Manuscript Belonging to St. Mary's Abbey, or Nunnaminster, Winchester*. Hampshire Record Society. London: Simpkin and Marshall, 1889.

Blamires, Alcuin, ed. *Woman Defamed and Woman Defended: An Anthology of Medieval Texts*. Oxford: Clarendon Press, 1992.

Bonaventure. *Bonaventurae Opera omnia*. Ed. A. C. Peltier. 15 vols. Paris: Vives, 1864–71.

———. *Bonaventurae Opera omnia*. Ed. PP. Collegii S. Bonaventurae. 11 vols. Quaracchi: Collegium S. Bonaventurae, 1882–1902.

———. *The Works of Bonaventure . . . I Mystical Opuscula*. Vol. I. Trans. José de Vinck. Paterson, N.J.: St. Anthony Guild Press, 1960.

Bowers, R. H., ed. *Three Middle English Religious Poems*. University of Florida Monographs: Humanities 12. Gainesville: University of Florida Press, 1963.

Bridget of Sweden. *Birgitta of Sweden: Life and Selected Revelations*. Trans. Albert Ryle Kezel. Classics of Western Spirituality. New York: Paulist Press, 1990.

Brown, Beatrice Daw, ed. *The Southern Passion*. EETS 169. London: Oxford University Press, 1927.

Brown, Carleton, ed. *English Lyrics of the XIIIth Century*. Oxford: Clarendon Press, 1932.

———, ed. *Religious Lyrics of the XIVth Century*. Oxford: Clarendon Press, 1924.

Brugman, Johannes. *Leven en Werk van Jan Brugman O.F.M.*, ed. Frederik A. H. van den Hombergh. Groningen: Wolters, 1967.

Campbell, Gertrude H. "The Middle English *Evangelie*." *PMLA* 30 (1915): 529–613.

Chiari, A. "Il 'Planctus B. Mariae' operetta falsamente attribuita a San Bernardo." *Rivista Storica Benedettina* 17 (1926): 56–111.

Christine de Pisan. *The Book of the City of Ladies*. Trans. Earl Jeffrey Richards. New York: Persea Books, 1982.

———. *The Treasure of the City of Ladies*. Trans. Sarah Lawson. Harmondsworth: Penguin, 1985.

Clark, John, ed. *The Latin Versions of The Cloud of Unknowing*. Analecta Cartusiana 119. Salzburg: Institut für Anglistik und Amerikanistik, 1989.

The Cloud of Unknowing. Trans. Clifton Wolters. Harmondsworth: Penguin, 1961.

Corpus of British Medieval Library Catalogues. 4 vols. London: British Library, 1990–.

Cowper, J. Meadows, ed. *Meditations on the Supper of our Lord, and the Hours of the Passion*. EETS OS 60. London: Trübner, 1875.

D'Evelyn, Charlotte, ed. *Meditations on the Life and Passion of Christ*. EETS OS 158. London: Oxford University Press, 1921.

———, ed. *The Latin Text of the Ancrene Riwle*. EETS 216. London: Oxford University Press, 1944.

Edmund of Abingdon. *Speculum Religiosorum and Speculum Ecclesie*. Ed. Helen P. Forshaw. Auctores Britannici Medii Aevi 3. London: Oxford University Press, 1973.

Ekbert of Schönau. *Die Visionen der hl. Elisabeth und die Schriften der Aebte Ekbert und Emecho von Schönau*. Ed. F. W. E. Roth. Brünn: Verlag der Studien aus dem Benedictiner- und Cistercienser-Orden, 1884.

Eusebius. *The History of the Church*. Trans. G. A. Williamson. Harmondsworth: Penguin, 1967.

Farmer, Hugh, ed. *The Monk of Farne: The Meditations of a Fourteenth-Century Monk*. Trans. a Benedictine of Stanbrook. London: Darton, 1961.

——. "The Meditations of the Monk of Farne." *Studia Anselmiana* 41 (1957): 141–245.

Fisher, John H., ed. *The Tretyse of Love*. EETS OS 223. London: Oxford University Press, 1951.

Foster, Frances A., ed. *A Stanzaic Life of Christ*. EETS OS 166. London: Oxford University Press, 1926.

——, ed. *The Northern Passion*. EETS OS 145, 147. London: Kegan Paul, 1913–16.

Frank, Grace, ed. *Le Livre de la Passion: poème narratif du xive siècle*. Les Classiques Français du Moyen Age 64. Paris: Champion, 1930.

Furnivall, F. J., ed. *Political, Religious, and Love Poems*. EETS OS 15. London: K. Paul, 1866; re-edited 1903.

Gerson, Jean. *Opera omnia*. Vol. 3. Antwerp: Sumptibus Societatis, 1706.

——. *Selections from A Deo exivit, Contra curiositatem studentium and De mystica theologica speculativa*. Ed. Steven E. Ozment. Leiden: Brill, 1969.

Goates, Margery, ed. *The Pepysian Gospel Harmony*. EETS OS 157. London: Oxford University Press, 1922.

Gower, John. *The Major Latin Works of John Gower*. Trans. Eric Stockton. Seattle: University of Washington Press, 1962.

Guillaume de Lorris and Jean de Meun. *Le Roman de la Rose*. Ed. Ernest Langlois. 5 vols. Société des Anciens Textes Français. Paris: Firmin-Didot; Champion, 1914–24.

Günzel, Beate, ed. *Ælfwine's Prayerbook*. Henry Bradshaw Society 108. London: Boydell, 1993.

Hedlund, Monica, ed. *Epistola de vita et passione domini nostri: der lateinische Text mit Einleitung und Kommentar*. Leiden: Brill, 1975.

Henry of St. Gall. *Der Passionstraktat des Heinrich von St. Gallen*. Ed. Kurt Ruh. Thayngen: Karl Augustin, 1940.

Henry, Avril, ed. *The Mirour of Mans Saluacioun: A Middle English Translation of Speculum humanae salvationis*. Philadelphia: University of Pennsylvania Press, 1987.

Heuser, William and Frances A. Foster, eds. *The Northern Passion: Supplement*. EETS OS 183. London: Oxford University Press, 1930.

Hilton, Walter. *The Goad of Love: An Unpublished Translation of the Stimulus Amoris formerly Attributed to St. Bonaventura*. Ed. Clare Kirchberger. London: Faber, 1952.

——. *The Ladder of Perfection*. Trans. Leo Sherley-Price. Harmondsworth: Penguin, 1957.

Hirsh, John C. "A Middle English Version of *The Fifteen Oes* from Bodleian Library MS. Add. B. 66." *Neuphilologische Mitteilungen* 75 (1974): 98–114.

Hogg, James, ed. *The Speculum devotorum of an Anonymous Carthusian of Sheen*. Analecta Cartusiana 12. Salzburg: Institut für Anglistik und Amerikanistik, 1973.

Horrall, Sarah M., Roger R. Fowler, Peter H. J. Mous, and Henry J. Stauffenberg, eds. *The Southern Version of Cursor Mundi*. 4 vols. Ottawa Medieval Texts and Studies 5, 13, 14, 16. Ottawa: University of Ottawa Press, 1978–.

Horstman, C., ed. *Yorkshire Writers: Richard Rolle of Hampole, An English Father of the Church and His Followers*. 2 vols. London: Swan Sonnenschein, 1895–96.

Horstmann, Carl, ed. "*Orologium sapientiae*, or *The Sevene Poyntes of Trewe Wisdom*, aus MS Douce 114." *Anglia* 10 (1888): 323–89.

——, ed. *The Minor Poems of the Vernon Manuscript*. EETS OS 98. London: Kegan Paul, 1892.

Hus, Jan. *Magistri Iohannis Hus Opera omnia*. Vol. 8. Ed. Anezka Vidmanová-Schmidtová. Prague: Academia Scientiarum, 1973.

Jacobus de Voragine. *Legenda Aurea*. Ed. Th. Graesse. 3rd ed. 1890; rpt. Osnabrück: Zeller, 1969.

——. *The Golden Legend: Readings on the Saints*. Trans. William Granger Ryan. 2 vols. Princeton, N.J.: Princeton University Press, 1993.

Jacopone da Todi. *Laude*. Ed. Franco Mancini. Scrittori d'Italia 257. Bari: Laterza, 1974.

James of Milan. *Stimulus amoris Jacobi mediolanensis*. 2nd ed. Bibliotheca Franciscana Ascetica Medii Aevi 4. Quaracchi: Collegium S. Bonaventurae, 1949.

James, Montague Rhodes, ed. *The Apocryphal New Testament*. Oxford: Clarendon Press, 1924.

Jeffrey, David Lyle, ed. *The Law of Love: English Spirituality in the Age of Wyclif*. Grand Rapids, Mich.: Eerdmans, 1988.

John of Hoveden. *John Hovedens Nachtigallenlied*. Ed. Clemens Blume. Hymnologische Beiträge: Quellen und Forschungen zur Geschichte der Lateinischen Hymnendichtung im Anschluss an die Analecta Hymnica 4. Leipzig: O. R. Reisland, 1930.

——. *The Poems of John of Hoveden*. Ed. F. J. E. Raby. Surtees Society 154. Durham: Andrews, 1939.

Jordan of Quedlinburg. *Meditationes de passione Christi*. Lübeck, 1492.

Julian of Norwich. *A Book of Showings to the Anchoress Julian of Norwich*. Ed. Edmund Colledge and James Walsh. 2 vols. Studies and Texts 35. Toronto: Pontifical Institute of Mediaeval Studies, 1978.

——. *Revelations of Divine Love*. Trans. Clifton Wolters. Harmondsworth: Penguin, 1966.

Kane, Harold, ed. *The Prickynge of Love*. Salzburg Studies in English Literature 92:10. Salzburg: Institut für Anglistik und Amerikanistik, 1983.

Kempe, Margery. *The Book of Margery Kempe*. Ed. Sanford Meech and Hope Emily Allen. EETS OS 212. London: Oxford University Press, 1940.

——. *The Book of Margery Kempe*. Trans. B. A. Windeatt. Harmondsworth: Penguin, 1985.

Kribel, G. "Studien zur Richard Rolle de Hampole, II, *Lamentatio St. Bernardi de compassione Mariae*." *Englische Studien* 8 (1884): 85–114.

Love, Nicholas. *Nicholas Love's Mirror of the Blessed Life of Jesus Christ: A Critical Edition Based on Cambridge University Library Additional MSS 6578 and 6686*. Ed. Michael G. Sargent. Garland Medieval Texts 18. New York: Garland, 1992.

Ludolphus of Saxony. *Vita Christi*. Ed. L. M. Rigollot. 4 vols. Paris: Palme, 1870.

Lutz, J. and Paul Perdrizet, eds. *Speculum humanae salvationis*. 2 vols. Mulhouse: Meininger, 1907.

Lydgate, John. *The Minor Poems of John Lydgate*. Ed. Henry MacCracken. EETS OS 192. London: Oxford University Press, 1934.

Marx, C. William and Jeanne F. Drennan, eds. *The Middle English Prose Complaint of Our Lady and Gospel of Nicodemus*. Middle English Texts 19. Heidelberg: Carl Winter, 1987.

Marx, C. W. "The *Quis dabit* of Oglerius de Tridino, Monk and Abbot of Locedio." *Journal of Medieval Latin* 4 (1994): 118–29.

Meier-Ewert, Charity. "A Middle English Version of the *Fifteen Oes*." *Modern Philology* 68 (1971): 355–61.

Mikkers, Edmond. "Un 'Speculm Novitii' inédit d'Etienne de Salley." *Collectanea Ordinis Cisterciensium Reformatorum* 8 (1946): 17–68.

———. "Un traité inédit d'Etienne de Salley sur la Psalmodie." *Cîteaux: Comentarii Cistercienses* 23 (1972): 245–88.

Mohlberg, Leo C., ed. *Missale Gallicanum Vetus*. Rerum Ecclesiasticarum Documenta Series Maior, Fontes 3. Rome: Herder, 1958.

Morris, Richard, ed. *An Old English Miscellany*. EETS OS 49. London: Trübner, 1872.

———, ed. *Cursor Mundi*. EETS OS 57, 59, 62, 66, 68, 99, 101. 1874–93; rpt. London: Oxford University Press, 1961–66.

———, ed. *Old English Homilies and Homiletic Treatises*. EETS OS 29. London: Trübner, 1868.

Mushacke, W., ed. *Altprovenzalische Marienklage des XIII. Jahrhunderts*. Romanische Bibliothek 3. Halle: Niemeyer, 1890; rpt. Geneva: Slatkine, 1975.

Perry, George G., ed. *Religious Pieces in Prose and Verse*. Rev. ed. EETS OS 26. London: Kegan Paul, 1914.

Petroff, Elizabeth, ed. *Medieval Women's Visionary Literature*. New York: Oxford University Press, 1986.

Pickering, F. P., ed. *Christi Leiden in einer Vision Geschaut*. Manchester: Manchester University Press, 1952.

Raby, F. J. E., ed. *The Oxford Book of Medieval Latin Verse*. Oxford: Clarendon Press, 1959.

Ragusa, Isa and Rosalie B. Green, trans. *Meditations on the Life of Christ: An Illustrated Manuscript of the Fourteenth Century*. Princeton, N.J.: Princeton University Press, 1961.

Rolle, Richard. *English Writings of Richard Rolle, Hermit of Hampole*. Ed. Hope Emily Allen. 1931; rpt. Oxford: Clarendon Press, 1963.

———. *Richard Rolle: Prose and Verse*. Ed. S. J. Ogilvie-Thomson. EETS 293. Oxford: Oxford University Press, 1988.

Ruh, Kurt, ed. *Bonaventura deutsch*. Bibliotheca Germanica 7. Bern: Francke, 1956.

Simone Fidati da Cascia. *Gesta salvatoris domini nostri Jesu Christi, seu, Commentaria super IV Evangelia in XV libros in duobos tomis distributa*. 5th ed. 2 vols. Regensburg: H. Lenzius, 1733–34.

Southern, R. W. *The Life of St. Anselm by Eadmer*. London: Nelson, 1962.

Stallings, M. Jordan, ed. *Meditaciones de passione Christi olim Sancto Bonaventurae attributae*. Studies in Medieval and Renaissance Latin Language and Literature 25. Washington, D.C.: Catholic University of America Press, 1965.

Stanhope, George, trans. *Pious Breathings: Being the Meditations of St. Augustine, His Treatise of the Love of God, Soliloquies, and Manual, To Which Are Added Select Contemplations from St. Anselm and St. Bernard*. London: S. Sprint, 1701.

Stephen of Sawley. *Treatises*. Trans. Jeremiah F. O'Sullivan, ed. Bede K. Lackner. Cistercian Fathers Series 36. Kalamazoo, Mich.: Cistercian Publications, 1984.

———. *See* Mikkers.

Suso, Henry. *Heinrich Seuses Horologium sapientiae*. Ed. Pius Künzle. Spicilegium Friburgense 23. Freiburg, Switzerland: Universitätsverlag, 1977.

———. *Henry Suso: The Exemplar, with Two German Sermons*. Trans. Frank Tobin. New York: Paulist Press, 1989.

Symons, Thomas, Sigrid Spath, Maria Wegener, and Kassius Hallinger, eds. *Regularis concordia*. Corpus Consuetudinum Monasticarum 7.3. Siegburg: Schmitt, 1984.

Tanquerey, F. J. *Plaintes de la Vierge en Anglo-Français (xiiie et xive siècles)*. Paris: Champion, 1921.

Thomas à Kempis. *Thomae Hemerken a Kempis Opera omnia*. Ed. Michael Joseph Pohl. 6 vols. Freiburg-im-Breisgau: Herder, 1902–18.

Ubertino da Casale. *Arbor vitae crucifixae Jesu*. 1485; rpt. Turin: Bottega d'Erasmo, 1961, with Introduction and Bibliography by Charles T. Davis.

Van Engen, John, trans. *Devotio Moderna: Basic Writings*. Classics of Western Spirituality. New York: Paulist Press, 1988.

Varanini, Giorgio, ed. *Cantari religiosi senesi del trecento: Neri Pagliaresi, Fra Felice Tancredi da Massa, Niccolò Cicerchia*. Scrittori d'Italia 230. Bari: Laterza, 1965.

Vögtlin, A., ed. *Vita beatae Virginis Mariae et Salvatoris rhythmica*. Bibliothek des literarischen Vereins in Stuttgart 180. Tübingen: Literarischer Verein in Stuttgart, 1888.

Westra, M. Salvina, ed. *A Talkyng of þe Loue of God*. The Hague: M. Nijhoff, 1950.

Wilson, Katharina M., ed. *Medieval Women Writers*. Athens: University of Georgia Press, 1984.

Wordsworth, Christopher, ed. *Horae Eboracenses*. Surtees Society 132. Durham: Andrews, 1920.

Zerbolt, Gerard, of Zutphen. *Gerardi a Zutphania, De spiritualibus ascensionibus*. Ed. J. Mahieu. Bruges: Beyaert, 1941.

SECONDARY SOURCES

Aers, David. *Community, Gender, and Individual Identity: English Writing 1360–1430*. London: Routledge, 1988.

———. "Christ's Humanity and *Piers Plowman*: Contexts and Political Implications." *Yearbook of Langland Studies* 8 (1994): 107–25.

Auerbach, Erich. *Literary Language and Its Public in Late Latin Antiquity and in the Middle Ages*. Trans. Ralph Manheim. Bollingen Series 74. New York: Pantheon, 1965.

Baier, Walter. *Untersuchungen zu den Passionsbetrachtungen in der "Vita Christi" des Ludolf von Sachsen. Ein quellenkritischer Beitrag zu Leben und Werk Ludolfs und zur Geschichte der Passionstheologie.* Analecta Carthusiana 44. Salzburg: Institut für Englische Sprache und Literatur, 1977.

Bakhtin, Mikhail M. *The Dialogic Imagination.* Trans. Caryl Emerson and Michael Holquist. Austin: University of Texas Press, 1981.

Barré, Henri. "Le 'Planctus Mariae' attribué à saint Bernard." *Revue d'Ascétique et de Mystique* 28 (1952): 243–66.

———. *Prières anciennes de l'occident à la Mère du Sauveur: des origines à saint Anselme.* Paris: Lethielleux, 1963.

Bartlett, Anne Clark. "Miraculous Literacy and Textual Communities in Hildegard of Bingen's *Scivias.*" *Mystics Quarterly* 18 (1992): 43–55.

———. *Male Authors, Female Readers: Representation and Subjectivity in Middle English Devotional Literature.* Ithaca, N.Y.: Cornell University Press, 1995.

Bäuml, Franz H. "Varieties and Consequences of Medieval Literacy and Illiteracy." *Speculum* 55 (1980): 237–75.

Beckwith, Sarah. *Christ's Body: Identity, Culture and Society in Late Medieval Writings.* London: Routledge, 1993.

Bell, Susan Groag. "Medieval Women Book Owners: Arbiters of Lay Piety and Ambassadors of Culture." In *Women and Power in the Middle Ages*, ed. Mary Erler and Maryanne Kowaleski. 149–87. Athens: University of Georgia Press, 1988.

Belting, Hans. *The Image and Its Public in the Middle Ages: Form and Function of Early Paintings of the Passion.* Trans. Mark Bartusis and Raymond Meyer. New Rochelle, N.Y.: Caratzas, 1990.

Bennett, J. A. W. *Poetry of the Passion.* Oxford: Clarendon Press, 1982.

Benson, Robert L. and Giles Constable, ed. *Renaissance and Renewal in the Twelfth Century.* Cambridge, Mass.: Harvard University Press, 1982.

Benton, John F. "Consciousness of Self and Perceptions of Individuality." In *Renaissance and Renewal in the Twelfth Century*, ed. Robert L. Benson and Giles Constable. 263–95. Cambridge, Mass.: Harvard University Press, 1982.

Berliner, Rudolf. "Arma Christi." *Münchner Jahrbuch der Bildenden Kunst* 6 (1955): 35–252.

Bestul, Thomas H. "Chaucer's Parson's Tale and the Late-Medieval Tradition of Religious Meditation." *Speculum* 64 (1989): 600–19.

———. "Continental Sources of Anglo-Saxon Devotional Writing." In *Sources of Anglo-Saxon Culture*, ed. Paul E. Szarmach. 103–26. Studies in Medieval Culture 20. Kalamazoo, Mich.: Medieval Institute Publications, 1986.

Biersack, Aletta. "Local Knowledge, Local History: Geertz and Beyond." In *The New Cultural History*, ed. Lynn Hunt. 72–96. Berkeley: University of California Press, 1989.

Bishop, Edmund. *Liturgica Historica: Papers on the Liturgy and Religious Life of the Western Church.* Oxford: Clarendon Press, 1918.

Bloch, R. Howard. *Medieval Misogyny and the Invention of Western Romantic Love.* Chicago: University of Chicago Press, 1991.

Bloomfield, Morton. "The Man of Law's Tale: A Tragedy of Victimization and a Christian Comedy." *PMLA* 87 (1972): 384–90.

Blumenkranz, Bernhard. *Le juif médiéval au miroir de l'art chrétien*. Etudes Augus-
    tiniennes. Paris: Études Augustiniennes, 1966.
———. *Les auteurs chrétiens latins du moyen âge sur les juifs et le judaïsme*. Paris:
    Mouton, 1963.
Bodenstedt, Mary Immaculate. *The Vita Christi of Ludolphus the Carthusian*. Studies
    in Medieval and Renaissance Latin Language and Literature 16. Washington,
    D.C.: Catholic University of America Press, 1944.
Bossy, John. "The Mass as a Social Institution, 1200–1700." *Past and Present* 100
    (1983): 29–61.
Boswell, John. *Christianity, Social Tolerance, and Homosexuality: Gay People in West-
    ern Europe from the Beginning of the Christian Era to the Fourteenth Century*.
    Chicago: University of Chicago Press, 1980.
Bouyer, Louis, Jean Leclercq, and François Vandenbroucke. *The Spirituality of the
    Middle Ages*. Trans. Benedictines of Holme Eden Abbey. London: Burns and
    Oates, 1968.
Brantlinger, Patrick. *Crusoe's Footprints: Cultural Studies in Britain and America*.
    New York: Routledge, 1990.
Brown, Peter. *The Body and Society: Men, Women and Sexual Renunciation in Early
    Christianity*. New York: Columbia University Press, 1988.
Burger, Glenn. "Kissing the Pardoner." *PMLA* 107 (1992): 1143–56.
Büttner, F. O. *Imitatio pietatis: Motive der christlichen Ikonographie als Modelle zur
    Verähnlichung*. Berlin: Mann, 1983.
Bynum, Caroline Walker. *Jesus as Mother: Studies in the Spirituality of the High
    Middle Ages*. Berkeley: University of California Press, 1982.
———. *Holy Feast and Holy Fast: The Religious Significance of Food to Medieval
    Women*. Berkeley: University of California Press, 1987.
———. *Fragmentation and Redemption: Essays on Gender and the Human Body in
    Medieval Religion*. New York: Zone Books, 1991.
———. *The Resurrection of the Body in Western Christianity, 200–1336*. New York:
    Columbia University Press, 1995.
Camille, Michael. *The Gothic Idol: Ideology and Image-making in Medieval Art*. Cam-
    bridge: Cambridge University Press, 1989.
Carter, C. "The *Arma Christi* in Scotland." *Proceedings of the Society of Antiquaries
    of Scotland* 90 (1956–57): 116–29.
Chartier, Roger. *The Cultural Uses of Print in Early Modern France*. Trans. Lydia G.
    Cochrane. Princeton, N.J.: Princeton University Press, 1987.
———, ed. *The Culture of Print: Power and the Uses of Print in Early Modern Europe*.
    Trans. Lydia G. Cochrane. Princeton, N.J.: Princeton University Press, 1989.
———. "Texts, Printings, Readings." In *The New Cultural History*, ed. Lynn Hunt.
    154–75. Berkeley: University of California Press, 1989.
Chenu, M. D. *Nature, Man, and Society in the Twelfth Century*. Ed. J. Taylor and
    L. Little. Chicago: University of Chicago Press, 1957.
Clark, Anne L. *Elisabeth of Schönau: A Twelfth-Century Visionary*. Philadelphia: Uni-
    versity of Pennsylvania Press, 1992.
Cohen, Jeremy. *The Friars and the Jews: The Evolution of Medieval Anti-Judaism*.
    Ithaca, N.Y.: Cornell University Press, 1982.

————. "The Jews as the Killers of Christ in the Latin Tradition from Augustine to Jerome." *Traditio* 39 (1983): 1–27.

Coletti, Theresa. "Purity and Danger: The Paradox of Mary's Body and the Engendering of the Infancy Narrative in the English Mystery Cycles." In *Feminist Approaches to the Body in Medieval Literature*, ed. Linda Lomperis and Sarah Stanbury. 65–95. Philadelphia: University of Pennsylvania Press, 1993.

Combes, André. *Essai sur la critique de Ruisbroeck par Gerson*. Etudes de Théologie et d'Histoire de la Spiritualité 4. Paris: J. Vrin, 1945.

Constable, Giles. "The Popularity of Twelfth-Century Spiritual Writers in the Late Middle Ages." In *Renaissance Studies in Honor of Hans Baron*, ed. Anthony Molho and John A. Tedeschi. 3–38. DeKalb: Northern Illinois University Press, 1971.

————. "Twelfth-Century Spirituality and the Late Middle Ages." In *Medieval and Renaissance Studies*, ed. O. B. Hardison. 27–60. Chapel Hill: University of North Carolina Press, 1971.

————. "Forgery and Plagiarism in the Middle Ages." *Archiv für Diplomatik, Schriftgeschichte, Siegel- und Wappenkunde* 29 (1983): 1–41.

Conway, Charles Abbott, Jr. *The Vita Christi of Ludolphus of Saxony and Late Medieval Devotion Centered on the Incarnation*. Analecta Cartusiana 14. Salzburg: Institut für Englische Sprache und Literatur, 1976.

Copeland, Rita. "The Middle English 'Candet nudatum pectus' and Norms of Early Vernacular Translation Practice." *Leeds Studies in English* n.s. 15 (1984): 57–81.

Coulton, G. G. *From St. Francis to Dante*. 1906; rpt. Philadelphia: University of Pennsylvania Press, 1972.

Culler, Jonathan. *Framing the Sign: Criticism and Its Institutions*. Norman: University of Oklahoma Press, 1988.

Curtius, E. R. *European Literature and the Latin Middle Ages*. Trans. Willard R. Trask. New York: Pantheon, 1953.

Davis, Natalie Zemon. *Society and Culture in Early Modern France: Eight Essays*. Stanford, Calif.: Stanford University Press, 1975.

de Certeau, Michel. *Heterologies: Discourse on the Other*. Trans. Brian Massumi. Minneapolis: University of Minnesota Press, 1986.

de Ros, Fidèle. "Le planctus Mariae du pseudo-Anselme à Suso et à Louis de Grenade." *Revue d'Ascétique et de Mystique* 25 (1949): 270–83.

Deanesly, Margaret. "Vernacular Books in England in the Fourteenth and Fifteenth Centuries." *Modern Language Review* 15 (1920): 349–58.

Despres, Denise L. "Franciscan Spirituality: Margery Kempe and Visual Meditation." *Mystics Quarterly* 11 (1985): 12–18.

————. *Ghostly Sights: Visual Meditation in Late Medieval Literature*. Norman, Okla.: Pilgrim Books, 1989.

————. "Cultic Anti-Judaism and Chaucer's Little Clergeon." *Modern Philology* 91 (1994): 413–27.

Dinshaw, Carolyn. *Chaucer's Sexual Poetics*. Madison: University of Wisconsin Press, 1989.

Dinzelbacher, Peter. "Volkskultur und Hochkultur im Spätmittelalter." In *Volkskultur des europäischen Spätmittelalters*, ed. Peter Dinzelbacher and Hans-Dieter Mück. 1–14. Stuttgart: Kroner, 1987.

Doane, A. N. and Carol Braun Pasternack, eds. *Vox Intertexta: Orality and Textuality in the Middle Ages*. Madison: University of Wisconsin Press, 1991.

Douglas, Mary. *Purity and Danger*. New York: Praeger, 1966.

———. *Natural Symbols: Explorations in Cosmology*. 1970; rpt. New York: Pantheon, 1982.

Douie, Decima L. *Archbishop Pecham*. Oxford: Clarendon Press, 1952.

Dronke, Peter. *Women Writers of the Middle Ages*. Cambridge: Cambridge University Press, 1984.

Duby, Georges. *The Three Orders: Feudal Society Imagined*. Trans. Arthur Goldhammer. Chicago: University of Chicago Press, 1980.

Duffy, Eamon. *The Stripping of the Altars: Traditional Religion in England c. 1400-c. 1580*. New Haven, Conn.: Yale University Press, 1992.

Erler, Mary and Maryanne Kowaleski, eds. *Women and Power in the Middle Ages*. Athens: University of Georgia Press, 1988.

Fischer, Columban. "Die 'Meditationes vitae Christi': ihre handschriftliche Überlieferung und die Verfasserfrage." *Archivum Franciscanum Historicum* 25 (1932): 3–35, 175–209, 305–48, 449–83.

Fish, Stanley. "Commentary: The Young and the Restless." In *The New Historicism*, ed. H. Aram Veeser. 303–16. New York: Routledge, 1989.

Fleming, John V. *An Introduction to the Franciscan Literature of the Middle Ages*. Chicago: Franciscan Herald Press, 1977.

Foucault, Michel. *The Archeology of Knowledge and the Discourse on Language*. Trans. A. M. Sheridan Smith. New York: Pantheon, 1972.

———. *Discipline and Punish: The Birth of the Prison*. Trans. Alan Sheridan. New York: Pantheon, 1977.

———. *Language, Counter-Memory, Practice: Selected Essays and Interviews*. Trans. Donald F. Bouchard and Sherry Simon. Ithaca, N.Y.: Cornell University Press, 1977.

Frantzen, Allen J. *Desire for Origins: New Language, Old English, and Teaching the Tradition*. New Brunswick, N.J.: Rutgers University Press, 1990.

———, ed. *Speaking Two Languages: Traditional Disciplines and Contemporary Theory in Medieval Studies*. Albany: State University of New York Press, 1991.

Freedberg, David. *The Power of Images: Studies in the History and Theory of Response*. Chicago: University of Chicago Press, 1989.

Gallagher, Catherine. "Marxism and the New Historicism." In *The New Historicism*, ed. H. Aram Veeser. 37–48. New York: Routledge, 1989.

Gibson, Gail M. *The Theater of Devotion*. Berkeley: University of California Press, 1989.

Gillespie, Vincent. "Strange Images of Death: The Passion in Later Medieval English Devotional and Mystical Writing." *Analecta Cartusiana* 117 (1987): 111–59.

———. "Vernacular Books of Religion." In *Book Production and Publishing in Brit-*

ain 1375–1475, ed. Jeremy Griffiths and Derek Pearsall. 317–44. Cambridge: Cambridge University Press, 1989.

Gilson, Etienne. "Saint Bonaventure et l'iconographie de la passion." *Revue d'Histoire Franciscaine* 1 (1924): 405–24.

Girard, René. *The Scapegoat*. Trans. Yvonne Freccero. Baltimore: Johns Hopkins University Press, 1989.

Gjerløw, Lili. "A Twelfth-Century Victorine or Cistercian Manuscript in the Library of Elverum." *Revue Bénédictine* 82 (1972): 313–38.

Goitein, S. D. "Obadyah, a Norman Proselyte." *Journal of Jewish Studies* 4 (1953): 74–84.

Golb, Norman. "Obadiah the Proselyte: Scribe of a Unique Twelfth-Century Hebrew Manuscript Containing Lombardic Neumes." *Journal of Religion* 45 (1965): 153–56.

Gold, Penny Schine. *The Lady and the Virgin: Image, Attitude, and Experience in Twelfth-Century France*. Chicago: University of Chicago Press, 1985.

Goody, Jack, and Ian Watt. "The Consequences of Literacy." *Comparative Studies in Society and History* 5 (1962–63): 304–45.

Gradon, Pamela. *Form and Style in Early English Literature*. London: Methuen, 1971.

Graff, Gerald. *Professing Literature: An Institutional History*. Chicago: University of Chicago Press, 1987.

Gray, Douglas. "The Five Wounds of Our Lord." *Notes and Queries* n.s 10 (1963): 50–51, 82–89, 127–34, 163–68.

———. *Themes and Images in the Medieval English Religious Lyric*. London: Routledge, 1972.

Grayzel, Solomon. *The Church and the Jews in the XIIIth Century: A Study of Their Relations During the Years 1198–1254*. 2d ed. 1933; rpt. New York: Hermon, 1966.

———. *The Church and the Jews in the XIIIth Century, Volume 2 (1254–1314)*, ed. Kenneth R. Stow. New York: Jewish Theological Seminary, 1989.

Griffiths, Jeremy and Derek Pearsall, eds. *Book Production and Publishing in Britain 1375–1475*. Cambridge: Cambridge University Press, 1989.

Gurevich, Aron. *Medieval Popular Culture: Problems of Belief and Perception*. Trans. János M. Bak and Paul A. Hollingsworth. Cambridge: Cambridge University Press, 1988.

Hamburger, Jeffrey F. "A Liber Precum in Sélestat and the Development of the Illustrated Prayer Book in Germany." *Art Bulletin* 83 (1991): 209–36.

Hamilton, Bernard. *Religion in the Medieval West*. London: Edward Arnold, 1986.

Hanning, Robert. *The Individual in Twelfth-Century Romance*. New Haven, Conn.: Yale University Press, 1977.

Hansen, Elaine Tuttle. "The Powers of Silence: The Case of the Clerk's Griselda." In *Women and Power in the Middle Ages*, ed. Mary Erler and Maryanne Kowaleski. 230–49. Athens: University of Georgia Press, 1988.

Hill, Thomas D. "Androgyny and Conversion in the Middle English Lyric 'In the Vaile of Restles Mynd'." *ELH* 53 (1986): 459–70.

Hirsh, John C. "Prayer and Meditation in Late Medieval England: MS Bodley 789." *Medium Aevum* 48 (1979): 55–66.

Holloway, Julia Bolton. "Bride, Margery, Julian, and Alice: Bridget of Sweden's Textual Community in Medieval England." In *Margery Kempe: A Book of Essays*, ed. Sandra J. McEntire. 203–22. New York: Garland, 1992.

Hood, William. "The *Sacro Monte* of Varallo: Renaissance Art and Popular Religion." In *Monasticism and the Arts*, ed. Timothy Gregory Verdon. 291–311. Syracuse, N.Y.: Syracuse University Press, 1984.

Howard, Donald. *Chaucer: His Life, His Works, His World*. New York: Dutton, 1987.

Hsia, R. Po-Chia. *The Myth of Ritual Murder: Jews and Magic in Reformation Germany*. New Haven, Conn.: Yale University Press, 1988.

Hudson, Anne. *The Premature Reformation: Wycliffite Texts and Lollard History*. Oxford: Clarendon Press, 1988.

Huizinga, J. *The Waning of the Middle Ages*. 1924; rpt. Garden City, N. Y.: Doubleday, 1954.

Hunt, Lynn, ed. *The New Cultural History*. Berkeley: University of California Press, 1989.

———. "Introduction: History, Culture, and Text." In *The New Cultural History*, ed. Lynn Hunt. 1–22. Berkeley: University of California Press, 1989.

Hunt, R. W. "The Disputation of Peter of Cornwall Against Symon the Jew." In *Studies in Medieval History Presented to F. M. Powicke*, ed. R. W. Hunt, W. A. Pantin, and R. W. Southern. 143–56. Oxford: Clarendon Press, 1948.

Irigaray, Luce. *Speculum of the Other Woman*. Trans. Gillian C. Gill. Ithaca, N.Y.: Cornell University Press, 1985.

Izydorczyk, Zbigniew. *Manuscripts of the Evangelium Nicodemi: A Census*. Subsidia Mediaevalia 21. Toronto: Pontifical Institute of Mediaeval Studies, 1993.

Janauschek, Leopold. *Bibliographia Bernardina*. Xenia Bernardina, pars 4. Vienna: Hölder, 1891.

Jauss, Hans Robert. *Toward an Aesthetic of Reception*. Trans. Timothy Bahti, intro. Paul de Man. Minneapolis: University of Minnesota Press, 1982.

Jeffrey, David L. *The Early English Lyric and Franciscan Spirituality*. Lincoln: University of Nebraska Press, 1975.

Jordan, William C. *The French Monarchy and the Jews: From Philip Augustus to the Last Capetians*. Philadelphia: University of Pennsylvania Press, 1989.

Keiser, George. "Sandro Sticca, *The Planctus Mariae in the Dramatic Tradition of the Middle Ages*" (review). *Studies in the Age of Chaucer* 12 (1990): 325–27.

Kieckhefer, Richard. *Unquiet Souls: Fourteenth-Century Saints and Their Religious Milieu*. Chicago: University of Chicago Press, 1984.

———. "Recent Work on Pseudo-Bonaventure and Nicholas Love." *Mystics Quarterly* 21 (1995): 41–50.

Knowles, David. *The Religious Orders in England*. 1948; rpt. Cambridge: Cambridge University Press, 1979.

———. *Christian Monasticism*. New York: McGraw Hill, 1969.

Kramer, Lloyd S. "Literature, Criticism, and Historical Imagination: The Literary Challenge of Hayden White and Dominick LaCapra." In *The New Cultural*

History, ed. Lynn Hunt. 97–128. Berkeley: University of California Press, 1989.

Kristeva, Julia. *Powers of Horror: An Essay on Abjection*. Trans. Leon S. Roudiez. New York: Columbia University Press, 1982.

———. "Holbein's Dead Christ." In *Fragments for a History of the Human Body, Part One*, ed. Ramona Naddaff, Michel Feher, Nadia Tazi. 238–69. New York: Zone, 1989.

Kruger, Steven F. "The Bodies of Jews in the Late Middle Ages." In *The Idea of Medieval Literature: New Essays on Chaucer and Medieval Culture in Honor of Donald R. Howard*, ed. James M. Dean and Christian K. Zacher. 301–23. Newark: University of Delaware Press, 1992.

Kuttner, Stephan. "The Revival of Jurisprudence." In *Renaissance and Renewal in the Twelfth Century*, ed. Robert L. Benson and Giles Constable. 299–323. Cambridge, Mass.: Harvard University Press, 1982.

LaCapra, Dominick. *Rethinking Intellectual History: Texts, Contexts, Language*. Ithaca, N.Y.: Cornell University Press, 1983.

———. *History and Criticism*. Ithaca, N.Y.: Cornell University Press, 1985.

Langbein, John H. *Torture and the Law of Proof: Europe and England in the Ancien Régime*. Chicago: University of Chicago Press, 1977.

Langmuir, Gavin. "Thomas Monmouth: Detector of Ritual Murder." *Speculum* 59 (1984): 820–46.

———. *History, Religion, and Antisemitism*. Berkeley: University of California Press, 1990.

———. *Toward a Definition of Antisemitism*. Berkeley: University of California Press, 1990.

Le Goff, Jacques. *Time, Work and Culture in the Middle Ages*. Trans. Arthur Goldhammer. Chicago: University of Chicago Press, 1980.

———. *The Medieval Imagination*. Trans. Arthur Goldhammer. Chicago: University of Chicago Press, 1988.

Leclercq, Jean. "Drogon et saint Bernard." *Revue Bénédictine* 63 (1953): 117–28.

———. "Sur la dévotion à l'humanité du Christ." *Revue Bénédictine* 63 (1953): 128–30.

———. *The Love of Learning and the Desire for God: A Study of Monastic Culture*. 3rd ed. Trans. Catharine Misrahi. 1957; rpt. New York: Fordham University Press, 1982.

Leff, Gordon. *The Dissolution of the Medieval Outlook: An Essay on Intellectual and Spiritual Change in the Fourteenth Century*. New York: Harper, 1976.

Lincoln, Bruce. *Discourse and the Construction of Society: Comparative Studies of Myth, Ritual, and Classification*. New York: Oxford University Press, 1989.

Lindenberger, Herbert. "Toward a New History in Literary Study." In *Profession 84: Selected Articles from the Bulletins of the Association of Departments of English and the Association of Departments of Foreign Languages*, 16–23. New York: Modern Language Association of America, 1984.

Little, Lester K. *Religious Poverty and the Profit Economy in Medieval Europe*. Ithaca, N.Y.: Cornell University Press, 1978.

Lochrie, Karma. "The Language of Transgression: Body, Flesh, and Word in Mystical Discourse." In *Speaking Two Languages: Traditional Disciplines and Contemporary Theory in Medieval Studies*, ed. Allen J. Frantzen. 115–40. Albany: State University of New York Press, 1991.

———. *Margery Kempe and Translations of the Flesh*. Philadelphia: University of Pennsylvania Press, 1991.

Lomperis, Linda and Sarah Stanbury, eds. *Feminist Approaches to the Body in Medieval Literature*. Philadelphia: University of Pennsylvania Press, 1993.

Lovatt, Roger. "The Imitation of Christ in Late Medieval England." *Transactions of the Royal Historical Society* 5th ser. 18 (1968): 97–121.

Lyotard, Jean-François. *The Post-Modern Condition: A Report on Knowledge*. Trans. Geoff Bennington and Brian Massumi. Minneapolis: University of Minnesota Press, 1984.

Machan, Tim. "Editing, Orality, and Late Middle English Texts." In *Vox Intertexta: Orality and Textuality in the Middle Ages*, ed. A. N. Doane and Carol Braun Pasternack. 229–45. Madison: University of Wisconsin Press, 1991.

———. "Language Contact in *Piers Plowman*." *Speculum* 69 (1994): 359–85.

Madigan, Mary Felicitas. *The Passio Domini Theme in the Works of Richard Rolle: His Personal Contribution in its Religious, Cultural, and Literary Context*. Elizabethan and Renaissance Studies 79. Salzburg: Institut für Englische Sprache und Literatur, 1978.

Manning, Stephen. *Wisdom and Number: Toward a Critical Appraisal of the Middle English Religious Lyric*. Lincoln: University of Nebraska Press, 1962.

Marrow, James H. *Passion Iconography in Northern European Art of the Late Middle Ages and Early Renaissance: A Study of the Transformation of Sacred Metaphor into Descriptive Narrative*. Ars Neerlandica 1. Kortrijk: Van Ghemmert, 1979.

Martz, Louis L. *The Poetry of Meditation: A Study in English Religious Literature of the Seventeenth Century*. rev. ed. New Haven, Conn.: Yale University Press, 1962.

Marx, C. William. "The Middle English Verse 'Lamentation of Mary to Saint Bernard' and the 'Quis dabit'." In *Studies in the Vernon Manuscript*, ed. Derek Pearsall. 137–57. Cambridge: D. S. Brewer, 1990.

McNamer, Sarah. "Further Evidence for the Date of the Pseudo-Bonaventuran *Meditationes vitae Christi*." *Franciscan Studies* 50 (1990): 235–61.

McNeil, Mary Germaine. *Simone Fidati and His De Gestis Domini Salvatoris*. Studies in Medieval and Renaissance Latin Language and Literature 21. Washington, D.C.: Catholic University of America Press, 1950.

Meale, Carol M. "'. . . Alle the bokes that I haue of latyn, englisch, and frensch': Laywomen and Their Books in Late Medieval England." In *Women and Literature in Britain, 1150–1500*, ed. Carol M. Meale. 128–58. Cambridge: Cambridge University Press, 1993.

Meale, Carol M., ed. *Women and Literature in Britain, 1150–1500*. Cambridge: Cambridge University Press, 1993.

Mellinkoff, Ruth. *The Horned Moses in Medieval Art and Thought*. Berkeley: University of California Press, 1970.

————. *Outcasts: Signs of Otherness in Northern European Art of the Late Middle Ages*. Berkeley: University of California Press, 1993.

Middleton, Anne. "The Audience and Public of Piers Plowman." In *Middle English Alliterative Poetry and Its Literary Background*, ed. David Lawton. 102–23. Woodbridge, Suffolk: D. S. Brewer, 1982.

Miles, Margaret R. *Image as Insight: Visual Understanding in Western Christianity and Secular Culture*. Boston: Beacon Press, 1985.

Millett, Bella. "The Audiences of the Saints' Lives of the Katherine Group." *Reading Medieval Studies* 16 (1990): 127–56.

Minnis, Alastair J. *Medieval Theory of Authorship: Scholastic Literary Attitudes in the Later Middle Ages*. London: Scolar, 1984, rpt. Philadelphia: University of Pennsylvania Press, 1988.

Montrose, Louis. "Professing the Renaissance: The Poetics and Politics of Culture." In *The New Historicism*, ed. H. Aram Veeser. 15–36. New York: Routledge, 1989.

Moore, R. I. *The Origins of European Dissent*. 2nd ed. Oxford: Blackwell, 1985.

————. *The Formation of a Persecuting Society: Power and Deviance in Western Europe, 950–1250*. Oxford: Blackwell, 1987.

Morris, Colin. *The Discovery of the Individual 1050–1200*. London: SPCK, 1972.

Moser, Thomas C., Jr. " 'And I Mon Waxe Wod': The Middle English 'Foweles in the Frith'." *PMLA* 102 (1987): 326–37.

Mundy, John H. *Europe in the High Middle Ages 1150–1309*. New York: Basic Books, 1973.

Oberleitner, M. et al. *Die handschriftliche Überlieferung der Werke des Heiligen Augustinus*. Sitzungsberichte der Österreichische Akademie der Wissenschaften, philosophisch-historische Klasse 263, 267, 276, 281. Vienna: Böhlau, 1969–74.

Ozment, Steven E. *Mysticism and Dissent*. New Haven, Conn.: Yale University Press, 1973.

Panofsky, Erwin. "Imago Pietatis." In *Festschrift für Max J. Friedländer zum 60. Geburtstage*. 261–308. Leipzig: Seeman, 1927.

Pantin, W. A. "The Monk-Solitary of Farne: A Fourteenth-Century English Mystic." *English Historical Review* 59 (1944): 162–86.

Parker, Patricia. *Literary Fat Ladies: Rhetoric, Gender, Property*. London: Methuen, 1987.

Patterson, Lee, ed. *Literary Practice and Social Change in Britain, 1380–1530*. Berkeley: University of California Press, 1990.

————. " 'No Man His Reson Herde': Peasant Consciousness, Chaucer's Miller, and the Structure of the *Canterbury Tales*." In *Literary Practice and Social Change in Britain, 1380–1530*, ed. Lee Patterson. 113–55. Berkeley: University of California Press, 1990.

————. *Chaucer and the Subject of History*. Madison: University of Wisconsin Press, 1991.

————. *Negotiating the Past: The Historical Understanding of Medieval Literature*. Madison: University of Wisconsin Press, 1987.

Pearsall, Derek. *The Canterbury Tales*. London: Allen and Unwin, 1985.

————, ed. *Studies in the Vernon Manuscript*. Cambridge: D. S. Brewer, 1990.

Perella, Nicholas James. *The Kiss Sacred and Profane: An Interpretive History of Kiss Symbolism and Related Religio-Erotic Themes*. Berkeley: University of California Press, 1969.

Peters, Edward. *Torture*. New York: Basil Blackwell, 1985, rpt. Philadelphia: University of Pennsylvania Press, 1996.

————. *Inquisition*. New York: Free Press, 1988.

Pfleger, L. "Ludolf von Sachsen über die kirchlichen Zustände im 14. Jht." *Historisches Jahrbuch* (1908): 96–99.

Pickering, F. P. *Literature and Art in the Middle Ages*. London: Macmillan, 1970.

Poliakov, Léon. *The History of Anti-Semitism: Volume One: From the Time of Christ to the Court Jews*. Trans. Richard Howard. London: Elek Books, 1965.

Pollard, William F. "Mystical Elements in a Fifteenth-Century Prayer Sequence: 'The Festis and the Passion of Oure Lord Ihesu Crist'." In *The Medieval Mystical Tradition in England: Exeter Symposium IV*, ed. Marion Glasscoe. 47–61. Woodbridge: Boydell and Brewer, 1987.

Prawer, Joshua. "The Autobiography of Obadyah the Norman, a Convert to Judaism in the First Crusade." In *Studies in Medieval Jewish History and Literature*, ed. Isidore Twersky. 110–34. Cambridge, Mass.: Harvard University Press, 1979.

Rapp, F. [Francis]. *Réformes et réformation à Strasbourg: Église et société dans le diocèse de Strasbourg (1450–1525)*. Association des Publications près les Universités de Strasbourg: Collection de l'Institut des Hautes Études Alsaciennes 23. Paris: Ophrys, n.d. [1974?].

Raw, Barbara. *Anglo-Saxon Crucifixion Iconography and the Art of the Monastic Revival*. Cambridge: Cambridge University Press, 1990.

Reames, Sherry. *The Legenda Aurea: A Reexamination of Its Paradoxical History*. Madison: University of Wisconsin Press, 1985.

Rezak, Brigitte Bedos. "Women, Seals, and Power in Medieval France, 1150–1350." In *Women and Power in the Middle Ages*, ed. Mary Erler and Maryanne Kowaleski. 61–82. Athens: University of Georgia Press, 1988.

Richards, Jeffrey. *Sex, Dissidence, and Damnation: Minority Groups in the Middle Ages*. London: Routledge, 1991.

Riddy, Felicity. " 'Women talking about the things of God': A Late Medieval Sub-Culture." In *Women and Literature in Britain, 1150–1500*, ed. Carol M. Meale. 104–27. Cambridge: Cambridge University Press, 1993.

Ringbom, S. "Devotional Images and Imaginative Devotions: Notes on the Place of Art in Late Medieval Private Piety." *Gazette des Beaux Arts* ser. 6, 73 (1969): 159–70.

Robbins, Rossell Hope. "The 'Arma Christi' Rolls." *Modern Language Review* 34 (1939): 415–21.

Robertson, Elizabeth. *Early English Devotional Prose and the Female Audience*. Knoxville: University of Tennessee Press, 1990.

Rubin, Miri. *Corpus Christi: The Eucharist in Late Medieval Culture*. Cambridge: Cambridge University Press, 1991.

Saenger, Paul. "Books of Hours and the Reading Habits of the Later Middle Ages."

In *The Culture of Print*, ed. Roger Chartier. 141–73. Princeton, N.J.: Princeton University Press, 1989.

Salmon, Pierre. "Livrets de prières de l'époque carolingienne." *Revue Bénédictine* 86 (1976): 218–34; 90 (1980): 147–49.

Salter, Elizabeth. "Ludolphus of Saxony and His English Translators." *Medium Aevum* 33 (1964): 26–35.

———. *Nicholas Love's "Myrrour of the Blessed Lyf of Jesu Christ"*. Analecta Cartusiana 10. Salzburg: Institut für Englische Sprache und Literatur, 1974.

Sargent, Michael G. "The Transmission by the English Carthusians of Some Late Medieval Spiritual Writings." *Journal of Ecclesiastical History* 27 (1976): 225–40.

Saxer, Victor. *La culte de la Marie Madeleine en Occident: des origines à la fin du moyen âge*. Auxerre: Publications de la Societé des Fouilles Archéologiques et des Monuments Historiques de l'Yonne, 1959.

Scarry, Elaine. *The Body in Pain: The Making and Unmaking of the World*. New York: Oxford University Press, 1985.

Scherb, Victor. "Violence and the Social Body in the Croxton Play of the Sacrament." In *Violence in Drama*, ed. James Redmond. 69–78. Cambridge: Cambridge University Press, 1991.

Schmitz, Ph. "Les lectures de table à l'abbaye de Saint-Denis vers la fin du Moyen-Age." *Revue Bénédictine* 42 (1930): 163–67.

———. "Les lectures du soir à l'abbaye de Saint-Denis au XIIᵉ siècle." *Revue Bénédictine* 44 (1932): 147–49.

Simonsohn, Shlomo. *The Apostolic See and the Jews*. 4 vols. Studies and Texts 94, 95, 99, 104. Toronto: Pontifical Institute of Mediaeval Studies, 1988–91.

Sinanoglou, Leah. "The Christ Child as Sacrifice: A Medieval Tradition and the Corpus Christi Plays." *Speculum* 48 (1973): 491–509.

Smalley, Beryl. *The Study of the Bible in the Middle Ages*. Notre Dame, Ind.: University of Notre Dame Press, 1964.

Southern, R. W. *The Making of the Middle Ages*. New Haven, Conn.: Yale University Press, 1953.

———. *Saint Anselm: A Portrait in a Landscape*. Cambridge: Cambridge University Press, 1990.

Spearing, A. C. *The Medieval Poet as Voyeur: Looking and Listening in Medieval Love Narratives*. Cambridge: Cambridge University Press, 1993.

Stanbury, Sarah. "The Virgin's Gaze: Spectacle and Transgression in Middle English Lyrics of the Passion." *PMLA* 106 (1991): 1083–93.

———. "The Voyeur and Private Life in *Troilus and Criseyde*." *Studies in the Age of Chaucer* 13 (1991): 141–58.

Sticca, Sandro. *The Planctus Mariae in the Dramatic Tradition of the Middle Ages*. Trans. Joseph R. Berrigan. Athens: University of Georgia Press, 1988.

Stock, Brian. *The Implications of Literacy: Written Language and Models of Interpretation in the Eleventh and Twelfth Centuries*. Princeton, N.J.: Princeton University Press, 1983.

Stouck, Mary-Ann. "'In a valey of this restles mynde': Contexts and Meaning." *Modern Philology* 85 (1987): 1–11.

Stow, Kenneth R. *Alienated Minority: The Jews of Medieval Latin Europe*. Cambridge, Mass.: Harvard University Press, 1992.

Strohm, Paul. *Social Chaucer*. Cambridge, Mass.: Harvard University Press, 1989.

———. *Hochown's Arrow: The Social Imagination of Fourteenth-Century Texts*. Princeton, N.J.: Princeton University Press, 1992.

Thomas, Michael. "Zur Rolle der 'Meditationes Vitae Christi' innerhalb der Europäischen Bild-Entwicklung der Giotto-Zeit." In *Miscellanea codicologica F. Masai dicata*, ed. Pierre Cockshaw, Monique-Cécile Garand, and Pierre Jodogne. 1:319–60. 2 vols. Ghent: E. Story-Scientia S.P.R.L., 1979.

Trachtenberg, Joshua. *The Devil and the Jews: The Medieval Conception of the Jew and its Relation to Modern Antisemitism*. Philadelphia: Jewish Publication Society of America, 1983.

Vauchez, André. *Les laïcs au moyen âge: pratiques et expériences religieuses*. Paris: Cerf, 1987.

Veeser, H. Aram, ed. *The New Historicism*. New York: Routledge, 1989.

von Simson, Otto. "Compassio and Co-redemptio in Roger vander Weyden's Descent from the Cross." *Art Bulletin* 35 (1953): 9–16.

Ward, Benedicta. *Harlots of the Desert: A Study of Repentance in Early Monastic Sources*. Cistercian Studies 106. Kalamazoo, Mich.: Cistercian Publications, 1987.

Warner, Marina. *Alone of All Her Sex: The Myth and Cult of the Virgin Mary*. London: Weidenfeld and Nicolson, 1976.

Warning, Rainer. "On the Alterity of Medieval Religious Drama." *New Literary History* 10 (1979): 265–92.

Willard, Charity Cannon. "The Franco-Italian Professional Writer: Christine de Pisan." In *Medieval Women Writers*, ed. Katharina M. Wilson. 333–63. Athens: University of Georgia Press, 1984.

Williams, Raymond. *Marxism and Literature*. Oxford: Oxford University Press, 1977.

———. *The Sociology of Culture*. New York: Schocken, 1982.

Willis, G. G. *Further Essays in Early Roman Liturgy*. Alcuin Club Collections 50. London: SPCK, 1968.

Wilmart, André. "Le recueil des prières de S. Anselme." In *Méditations et prières de Saint Anselme*, ed. A. Castel. i-lxii. Paris: Lethielleux, 1923.

Wilmart, André. "La tradition des prières de S. Anselme." *Revue Bénédictine* 36 (1924): 52–71.

———. "Les propres corrections de S. Anselme dans sa grande prière à la Vierge Marie." *Recherches de Théologie Ancienne et Médiévale* 2 (1930): 189–204.

———. *Auteurs spirituels et textes dévots du Moyen Age latin*. 1932: rpt. Paris: Etudes Augustiniennes, 1971.

———. "Le grand poème bonaventurien sur les sept paroles du Christ en croix." *Revue Bénédictine* 47 (1935): 235–78.

Wimsatt, James I. "The Canticle of Canticles, Two Latin Poems, and 'In a valey of this restles mynde'." *Modern Philology* 75 (1978): 327–45.

Witke, Charles. "Sandro Sticca, *The Planctus Mariae in the Dramatic Tradition of the Middle Ages*" (review). *Medievalia et Humanistica* n.s. 17 (1991): 167–70.

Woolf, Rosemary. *The English Religious Lyric in the Middle Ages*. Oxford: Clarendon Press, 1968.

Zumthor, Paul. *Speaking of the Middle Ages*. Trans. Sarah White. Lincoln: University of Nebraska Press, 1986.

Index